*Potter and Patron
in Classical Athens*

by the same author

FROM MYCENAE TO HOMER
GREEK ART AND LITERATURE 700–530 B.C.
HELLENISTIC POETRY AND ART
HELLENISTIC ART
THE TRAGEDIES OF EURIPIDES
AN INTRODUCTION TO SOPHOCLES
GREEK THEATRE PRODUCTION
THE GREEK CHORUS

Potter and Patron in Classical Athens

T. B. L. WEBSTER

METHUEN & CO LTD
LONDON

First published in 1972
by Methuen & Co Ltd
11 New Fetter Lane, London EC4P 4EE
© *1972 by T. B. L. Webster*
Printed in Great Britain
by Richard Clay (The Chaucer Press) Ltd
Bungay, Suffolk

SBN 416 75630 1

Distributed in the USA by
HARPER & ROW PUBLISHERS, INC.
BARNES & NOBLE IMPORT DIVISION

Contents

v

Contents

Contents

List of Illustrations

ix

List of Illustrations

Abbreviations

(excluding journals, which are quoted by the abbreviations used in
L'Année philologique)

ABL	C. H. E. Haspels, *Attic Black-Figured Lekythoi.* Paris, 1936.
ABV	J. D. Beazley, *Attic Black-Figure Vase-Painters.* Oxford, 1956.
ARV²	J. D. Beazley, *Attic Red-Figure Vase-Painters.* Oxford, 1963.
Caskey–Beazley	L. D. Caskey and J. D. Beazley, *Attic Vase-Paintings in the Museum of Fine Arts, Boston.* Oxford, 1931–63.
CV	*Corpus Vasorum Antiquorum.*
DBF	J. D. Beazley, *The Development of Attic Black-Figure.* Berkeley, 1951.
Dedications	A. E. Raubitschek and L. H. Jeffery, *Dedications from the Athenian Akropolis.* Cambridge, Mass., 1949.
Enc. Phot.	*Encyclopédie photographique de l'art: Musée du Louvre.* Paris, 1937.
FAS	H. Bloesch, *Formen attischer Schalen.* Berne, 1940.
Graef–Langlotz	B. Graef and E. Langlotz, *Die antiken Vasen von der Akropolis zu Athen.* Berlin, 1925–33.
GTP	T. B. L. Webster, *Greek Theatre Production.* London, 1970.

Abbreviations

GVI	W. Peek, *Die griechische Versinschriften.* Berlin, 1955.
Hoffmann	H. Hoffmann, *Attic Red-Figured Rhyta.* Mainz, 1962.
Kretschmer	P. Kretschmer, *Die griechischen Vaseninschriften.* Gütersloh, 1894.
Metr. Stud.	*Metropolitan Museum Studies.* New York.
Metzger, *Imagerie*	H. Metzger, *Recherches sur l'imagerie athénienne.* Paris, 1965.
MTS[2]	T. B. L. Webster, *Monuments Illustrating Tragedy and Satyr Play.* B.I.C.S. Suppl. 20. London, 1967.
Nilsson, *Gesch.*	M. P. Nilsson, *Geschichte der griechischen Religion.* Munich, 1941.
PH[2]	A. D. Trendall, *Phlyax Vases.* B.I.C.S. Suppl. 19. London, 1967.
Philippaki	B. Philippaki, *The Attic Stamnos.* Oxford, 1964.
PMG	D. L. Page, *Poetae Melici Graeci.* Oxford, 1962.
PP	J. D. Beazley, *Potter and Painter in Ancient Athens.* London, 1946.

Foreword

This book originated in two ideas: a growing conviction that some of the best Attic pottery was commissioned for a single symposion and then reached Etruria by the second-hand market, and secondly the feeling that a subject index to attributed Attic vases would be valuable in itself. In *Attic Black-Figure Vase-Painters* (1956) and *Attic Red-Figure Vase-Painters* (second edition 1963) Sir John Beazley attributed well over 30,000 vases to their painters. In addition Professor C. H. E. Haspels in 1936 had attributed a very large number of black-figure lekythoi to their painters, but her lists in *Attic Black-Figured Lekythoi* have been considerably extended later by Beazley. These three works, which are abbreviated in what follows as *ABV*, *ARV²* and *ABL*, are the basis of this book, and I have only occasionally mentioned either unattributed vases or later attributions. I have also restricted myself to the sixth and fifth centuries because it seemed to me that fourth-century vase-painting raised a number of new problems, into the complexities of which I did not want to go here. *ABV* and *ARV²* have an index of mythological subjects but no index of subjects from everyday life. My own index is not complete; it does not include, for instance, fights or warriors leaving home, but I hope that it contains most of the interesting subjects and therefore gives some idea of the range of information which can be obtained from Attic vases.

The index of everyday subjects, like the mythological indexes of *ABV* and *ARV²*, provide a history of the purchaser's taste, and in the special commissions we can reasonably speak of a patron's taste. So the book naturally fell into three parts, first the potters and painters, then the subjects, in which the painter meets the purchaser's taste, and finally the market, patrons in Athens, ordinary purchasers in Athens and traders who purchased for the export trade.

In the first chapter I have tried to give the evidence for the status of the potter and the size of his workshop. *ABV* and *ARV²* are primarily concerned with isolating the style of individual painters and to a lesser extent individual potters. Most of the evidence for the combination of painters and potters in larger units is indeed to be found there, but it needed assembling. The picture that emerges is of a dozen or so family workshops surviving through several generations, employing at any one time ten or more craftsmen, who were often both potters and painters, and producing painted pottery, black-glaze pottery and lamps, moulded vases and coarse pottery. I have put all the evidence together in a kind of summary history of Attic workshops at the end of the first chapter, which serves at the same time as a guide through *ABV*, *ARV²* and *ABL*. The picture is by no means tidy, but I suspect that the Kerameikos was an untidy place, and that pots and painters moved from one workshop to another to meet rush orders.

The next four chapters deal with special commissions, which can be detected either because the scene depicted is unique or very rare, or because the names attached to the participants in a stock scene make it an individual occasion. From this point on the chapters are concerned each with its own type of stock scene, and each contains one or more sections of the subject index. In Chapters 6 to 8 the relation of shape to subject is of particular interest, and the question is raised how far fountain scenes are confined to water pots, wedding scenes to wedding vases, symposion and komos scenes to pots used in the symposion. The connection between certain types of dance and the komos is so close that dances naturally became the subject of the next chapter. Dances in their turn led on to cult scenes. Then three chapters deal with victories in the games, victories in musical performances and Nike in her other manifestations. In all these chapters and in the succeeding chapters on horsemen and chariots, athletics, men and women, women, and various subjects special commissions become rarer (partly because some in all these categories have been discussed in the earlier chapters) and more and more of the vases are stock vases. The last chapter of this section uses the mythological indexes of *ABV* and *ARV²* to find what myths were particularly popular at different times. Only a selection of myths are treated in the attempt to show the different factors that may have influenced the purchaser's choice, factors such as the relevance of the myth to his particular situation (a factor that was predictable by the vase-painter) or, less predictably, his personal taste or the external stimulus of some new interpretation of myth by a poet of choral lyric or tragedy.

The final chapter gives a selection of the evidence for purchase. Inscriptions on the bottom of the vase tell us a little about traders, the size of consignments and prices. Findspots show what vases were dedicated in shrines, what were bought for private houses and what were given to the dead. We can also distinguish what was found in Attica, what was found in Greek cities all over the world and what was found in Etruria. My impression from all this is that there were comparatively few 'special lines'. We can name Panathenaic amphorai, special kinds of wedding vases and funeral vases and a very few shapes made for the western trade, but the vast majority of Attic vases were equally acceptable for use in the home, bestowal on the dead, dedication in a shrine or export. Their shapes were both beautiful and practical for containing wine, water, olive-oil or perfume; but who determined their decoration? As the finds show pretty clearly that the ordinary man had only a few decorated vases and a much larger proportion of black-glaze, we can assume that the lead was given by the large consumers who ordered a new set of pots for each of their symposia. These large consumers in the second half of the sixth century and the first half of the the fifth were the leading men of Athens and their sons; they were the patrons, with whom the great potters and painters seem to have associated on more or less equal terms.

Much of this book consists of lists, and many vases are only given their references in *ABV*, *ABL* and *ARV*[2]. In any given section the references are in chronological order, and the *ABL* references are inserted in their place in the *ABV* sequence. Vases in the addenda of *ABV* and *ARV*[2] are also inserted in their correct chronological place, but the addenda page only is given when the vase has no number. The reader should be warned that some pages of *ABV* and *ARV*[2] contain several painters, so that, for example, four different vases have the reference 1216/1, but this should not cause confusion as their subjects are different. When listing several vases by the same painter I have usually referred to the first page or an early page for the painter and have not repeated the page number for every vase.

Foreword

In these lists where I have known that a vase has changed its location or where I have known a recent and useful publication I have often added it. But I could not have given full references for every vase without enormously increasing the size of the book, and indeed in many cases there was no further reference to give. Where, however, I have discussed a vase at greater length, I have usually given the museum number and a reference to some accessible publication, very often the *Corpus Vasorum*.

I am extremely grateful to Dr J. R. Green for reading through my manuscript, and I have profited much from his comments. The errors which remain are mine.

Acknowledgements for illustrations are due to the authorities of the Ashmolean Museum, the British Museum, the Louvre, the Museum of Fine Arts, Boston, the Metropolitan Museum, New York, the Agora Museum, Athens, the Staatliche Museen in Berlin, the Antiken Sammlungen in Munich, and the Museo Archeologico at Ferrara.

T. B. L. WEBSTER

Stanford 1970

1

Potters

My title intentionally recalls Sir John Beazley's famous lecture of 1942,[1] 'Potter and Painter in Ancient Athens', partly because without it this book could not have been written, partly because I want to ask some questions about a third, necessary person, the purchaser of the pot. Beazley's lecture was a call to study potters as distinct from painters. The call has partly been answered by Beazley himself in *ABV* and *ARV*[2], by Bloesch in various articles (but his great work is still to come), by Barbara Philippaki in *The Attic Stamnos*; and studies are promised of the neck-amphora, of oinochoai, shapes 1–3[2] and of red-figure lekythoi. But we are still a long way from knowing anything like as much about potters as we know about painters.

It is difficult to form any idea of the scale of the industry as a whole or of the size of individual workshops within the industry. A rough attempt can be made to estimate the number of potters and painters whom we can identify. Beazley in *ABV* introduced the important terminological distinction between group and class: group of London B 250 means London B 250 and other vases like it in style of painting; class of London B 352 means London B 352 and other vases like it in style of potting. Thus we have painters and groups, potters and classes. The two new terms have each their own imprecision. A group of vases is alike in style of painting but not so alike that it can be regarded as the work of a single artist. A class of vases probably is the work of a single potter, but it is not often possible to say what other classes of vases he made. The following figures are an attempt to estimate the known potters and painters for each quarter of a century from 600 B.C., when

---

[1] Published in *PBA* 30 (1944); abbreviated below as *PP*.
[2] J. R. Green in *BSA* 66 (1971), 189.

the black-figure style was well established, to the end of the fifth century.

600–575	8 painters, 5 groups.	
575–550	29 painters, 14 groups.	4 potters.
550–525	59 painters, 65 groups.	43 potters, 18 classes.
525–500	91 painters, 47 groups.	23 potters, 39 classes.
500–475	112 painters, 67 groups.	8 potters, 38 classes.
475–450	167 painters, 81 groups.	3 potters, 15 classes.
450–425	168 painters, 69 groups.	1 potter, 9 classes.
425–400	73 painters, 35 groups.	4 potters, 3 classes.

These figures certainly show a growth of personnel in the Kerameikos, notably from the middle of the sixth century onwards, and then a contraction in the late fifth century. This is probably a true impression. But there are various reservations which must be made. Two have already been stated: our knowledge of anonymous potters is far less advanced than our knowledge of anonymous painters; therefore, whereas the figure for painters is a figure for known stylistic personalities (including those who sign their names), the figure for potters depends almost entirely on signatures. The high figure for potters between 550 and 525 is largely due to the fact that on Little Master cups the signature is part of the decoration, and therefore very often present. The second difficulty is the impossibility of equating groups with painters and classes with potters; the number of groups[1] is smaller by an unknown amount than the number of painters who painted the vases included in them, and the number of classes may be greater than the number of potters because one potter may make more than one class. The problem is different: a group of pots is connected by style, but it is called a group because normally they cannot be ascribed to one hand. A class properly so called is the work of a single potter, but we seldom know what other class or classes can be attributed to him.[2]

---

[1] For these figures I have included with Beazley's groups also vases designated as 'manner of', 'akin to', 'related to', 'near', etc., because in each case the vases were painted by some other painter or painters. Beazley does sometimes suggest that a group is by one hand (e.g. *ARV*² 1316) or that manner may include the painter himself (e.g. *ARV*² 1315).

[2] Note however that (*a*) *ABV* 422, 429, the Altenburg class of oinochoai shape I corresponds to class of Vatican G 47 of shape II; (*b*) *ABV* 428, 593, the Collar-of-esses class of oinochoai come from the same workshop as the Light-make class of small neck-amphorai. Cf. also Bloesch's classes in *JHS* 71 (1951), 29 ff.

Thirdly, the chronological lines cannot be drawn so precisely as these figures suggest: Lydos, Exekias and the Amasis painter, to quote the most obvious examples, were all working before 550 B.C. but have only been included in the numbers for 550–525 B.C., and in the last quarter of the fifth century the old classical painters and the young fourth-century painters are both excluded.

With all these reservations it looks as if in the great period of the late sixth and early fifth century there were something like 200 painters and 50 potters working on fine pottery in the Kerameikos.[1] It is difficult to form any notion of their productivity. The total number of attributed vases in *ABV* and *ARV*[2] is something over 30,000, covering the period from the late seventh century to the late fourth. The relation of attributed vases to preserved and published vases seems to be somewhere between three-quarters and two-thirds. But what is the relation of published vases to lost vases? Here there is only one kind of vase for which we can suggest production figures and that is the prize amphorai given at the Panathenaic games. The evidence is fairly good that 1,300 of them were given as prizes every fourth year from 566 B.C. until late in the Hellenistic age.[2] The number surviving over this long period is something over 300. But they may have had rather less chance of survival than other kinds of painted pottery. In the first place they contained oil, and therefore many of them were probably just thrown away when the oil had been used – whether the oil was used in Athens or elsewhere. Secondly, their subjects – the warrior Athena and an athletic event – were of little interest in themselves except to the victor; they were likely to be less attractive on the second-hand market than vases painted with scenes of mythology and everyday life, and they were not obviously useful in the way that cups, hydriai, wine jars and mixing-bowls were useful. Moreover, after the late sixth century the black-figure technique became a curiosity. A rough estimate for the last eight festivals of the sixth century suggests that rather over 30 have survived out of 10,400, or about 0·3 per cent.[3] If all the Euphiletos painter's 10

---

[1] This is a rough total from the figures given above. How many were working in any one year is impossible to say. On our evidence the work span of a painter varied from less than five to more than forty years. For other estimates cf. R. M. Cook, *JDAI* 74 (1959), 119; Kluwe, *Wiss. Ztschr. Rostock* 16 (1967), 471.

[2] Cf. most recently D. A. Amyx in *Hesperia* 27 (1958), 181 ff.

[3] R. M. Cook, loc. cit., arrives at the same figure for the fifth century. It may be relevant that a considerable number were dedicated (over 200 fragments were found on the

Panathenaic prize amphorai were made for a single festival 0·8 per cent have survived. Very tentatively we might guess that something over 1 per cent of good black- and red-figure vases have survived, but this may be very wrong.

If we cannot use the prize amphorai to get a ratio for the number of vases produced, they have great interest. For our immediate purpose the interesting point is that here was a large contract given every four years to a pottery by the state, and the pottery knew that it had to produce 1,300 prize amphorai in that period.

Another indication of the scale of a workshop is given by the dedications made by potters which are described as tithes or first-fruits. Dedications may be divided into small dedications of pottery and large dedications which have left inscribed stone bases on the Acropolis. The former class do not tell us much: a black-figure plate with the two Boreads by Lydos dedicated by a potter,[1] a plate made and painted by Epiktetos (see below, p. 12), a plaque with a picture of potters,[2] a red-figure plaque[3] dedicated by Kallis to Athena Hygieia – probably not a prayer or thanksgiving for his health but for the health of his pots (cf. L.S.J.), a black-figure hydria[4] by the painter of Acropolis 601 dedicated by potter or vase-painter as 'the first-fruits of his works'. These were presumably offerings for minor successes, and only the last uses the word 'first-fruits', which occurs in the large dedications. (Other examples are: Graef–Langlotz I, 2134, kantharos with Gigantomachy dedicated to Athena by its maker (about 560 B.C.); 2556, b.f. plaque with Apollo dedicated by Skythes, probably the vase-painter, *ABV* 352; Graef II, 238, foot of cup dedicated by Smikros, perhaps the vase-painter, Bloesch, *FAS* 124, no. 3; 762, volute-krater with man holding myrtle boughs before Athena: on neck in white 'Oreibelos made. Sacred to Athena', *ARV²* 499 (Deepdene painter); 806, column-krater 'Myson painted and made', A. youth with myrtle boughs before seated Athena, B. male before altar with standing Athena, *ARV²* 237; 1078, cup with oil and sprigs of olive, perhaps dedicated by Sosimos as 'first-

Acropolis; cf. also dedication to Zeus at Labraunda, *Act. Inst. Ath.* V, ii, 1, P. Hellström) but the vast majority of preserved vases come from tombs (cf. E. Langlotz, *Wiss. Ztschr.* Rostock 16 (1967), 474).

[1] *ABV* 112/54; Immerwahr, *James Sprunt Studies* 46 (1964), 16.
[2] *PP* 7; *ABV* 353.   [3] *ARV²* 1556.   [4] *ABV* 80; Beazley, *JHS* 47 (1927), 224 ff.

fruits', *ABV* 350. Sosimos also dedicated a phiale at Eleusis as 'first-fruits to Demeter', ibid. (Perhaps also, from Eleusis, *ABV* 85, Kleimachos.)

The large dedications were studied by A. E. Raubitschek in various articles from 1939 to 1942, reviewed by Beazley in *Potter and Painter* (21 ff.), and republished by Raubitschek in *Dedications from the Athenian Acropolis*. Without the description *kerameus* it is difficult to be certain whether the dedicator is a potter or not.[1] The words *ergon* or *techne* do not necessarily indicate a potter; they are applicable to any craft, including textiles.[2] However, five dedications are certain (nos. 44, 70, 178, 197, 225), six probable (nos. 30, 42, 48, 92, 209, 220) and three doubtful (nos. 53, 184, 291).[3] Some are dedications with nothing more specified, some are 'first-fruits', some are 'tithes'. Presumably the difference is that 'first-fruits' are payment for an unexpected gain and are not necessarily on the scale of a tenth.

The dedications are arranged here, as far as possible, in descending scale of value:

Nos. 178 Bronze statue. Andokides and Mnesiades. 525/500 B.C. No specification.

220 ?Bronze statue. Kriton son of Skythes. About 500 B.C. No specification.

30 Statue. Phrynos and Aristogeiton. 490/480 B.C. No specification.

197 Large Kore (prob. Acr. 681). Nearchos. 520/510 B.C. 'First-fruits'.

44 Small seated statue. Peikon. 500/480 B.C. 'Tithe'.

48 Statue. Aischines. 520/500 B.C. 'Tithe'.

225 Statue. Euphronios. 480 B.C. 'Tithe'.

53 Statue. Smikros and *paides*. 500/490 B.C. 'Memory of flourishing works'.

---

[1] Probably no. 217 Onesimos, and those that go with it should be excluded on these grounds.

[2] Therefore nos. 155, 210, 224, 234, 244 are too doubtful to be accepted.

[3] No. 150 is an artist's signature and does not strictly concern us, but it seems to give a potter making a bronze statue. Did he provide the model which was cast? Metrically Euthymides (suggested by Raubitschek) is impossible. No. 32, if rightly ascribed to the sons of Nearchos, is also a signature, not a dedication, but they may have signed their own dedication.

Nos. 291 Statue. X and *paides*. 500/490 B.C. 'First-fruits'.

70 Relief. . . . aios. 510/500 B.C. 'Tithe'.

42 Vase. Xenokles. 510/500 B.C. No specification.

209 Vase. Iatroklees and Kephalos. 500 B.C. ?'Tithe'.

184 Bronze relief. Archeneides. 510/500 B.C. 'Tithe of works and money'.

92 Unknown. Brygos. No date. 'First-fruits'.

Notes

No. 220. Skythes is a red-figure painter of the late sixth century. Kriton is known as a potter about 550/540 B.C.; he may have been a grandfather of this Kriton. (Lauffer, *MDAI(A)/62* (1937), 108, dates 530.)

No. 30. Phrynos may be the grandson of the black-figure painter Phrynos, whose son dedicated a clay cup, Acr. 1300.

No. 197. According as to whether 'first-fruits' are interpreted as a gift on retirement or a gift on receiving an inheritance, Nearchos may be the early black-figure painter-potter or his grandson.

No. 225. Another inscription on the same stone recording the dedication of first-fruits and mentioning 'health' (again the health of the pots?) seems incompatible with the Euphronios dedication, and the stone of an earlier potter dedication may have been reused.

Nos. 53 and 291 seem to go together. Raubitschek interprets 53 as Smikros (the red-figure vase-painter) and his pupils (note that Beazley doubts the restoration 'works'), and 291 as a potter and his pupils, who include the known potter Charinos. If this is right, 291 gives a workshop of six men.

No. 70. Raubitschek says that there is room for twelve letters before -*aios*, and takes -*aios* as the end of a demotic. Note that Payne dated the relief 530–520 B.C. The cups which the potter holds were identified by Bloesch with Acrocups but Beazley notes that the pronounced fillet is absent.[1] Perhaps we should think rather of cups type B with offset lip, as made by Euergides.[2]

Nos. 42, 209. As the dedication is a vase, the dedicant is perhaps a potter. Note that Xenokles and Archeneides (184) are the names of potters of Little Master cups (cf. above on Nearchos, Phrynos). Kephalos may have been the ancestor of Aristophanes' Kephalos (*Eccl.* 253).

---

[1] *FAS* 144; *PP* 22.   [2] *FAS* 51, pl. 15, 1.

These dedications clearly differ in scale, but all of them were sufficiently important to be set up on a marble base on the Acropolis. It is worth making a rough guess at the price of the larger ones. An epigram of Simonides (114D) mentions the price of 200 drachmai for a statue of Artemis in Paros which was presumably roughly contemporary with these works. In the late fifth century 60 drachmai was the price for a 60 cm figure on the Erechtheion frieze.[1] By that time the drachma was already worth less than in the sixth century, and thus prices are not necessarily out of step with Simonides. In the Hellenistic age, when the drachma had fallen further, a life-size bronze-portrait statue cost 3,000 drachmai. If we think of our bronze statues as costing in the neighbourhood of 500 drachmai and our marble statues as costing in the neighbourhood of 200 drachmai we shall perhaps not be far from the mark. If again we suppose that the tenth of the tithe is not far astray from the figures on which the unspecified dedications and the first-fruits were based we get a figure of 5,000 drachmai for the 'capital' on which Andokides calculated his dedication and 2,000 drachmai for the 'capital' of Nearchos and Euphronios.

In the case of Andokides, who, as we shall see, seems to have taken over the workshop of Exekias and negotiated the transition from black-figure to red-figure, a workshop largely but not exclusively concerned with large vases, it is possible that the dedication celebrated the winning of a single large contract such as the making of prize Panathenaic amphorai rather than the general prosperity of the business. The other two, Nearchos and Euphronios, appear to us primarily as makers of small vases. As noted above, we cannot tell whether Nearchos is the old Nearchos, who started painting about 560 B.C., celebrating his retirement, or a homonymous grandson taking over the business, which survived into the red-figure period, since Tleson, a son of the old Nearchos or a younger relation, made a cup (type A) decorated by Oltos. It is tempting to connect the 'first-fruits' with a prosperous new line, red-figure cups (type A), which had succeeded the Little Master cups made very successfully by Tleson, the son of Nearchos; but Nearchos may have been more important than this (see below, pp. 9 f.). Euphronios, as we shall see, ran one of the four successful cup-workshops of the early fifth century.

[1] *IG*² 374; J. J. Pollitt, *The Art of Greece* (Englewood Cliffs, 1965), 121.

From the little that is known about prices[1] an average price of two drachmai for predominantly large vases and one drachma for cups and small vases would seem possible, nor would it seem impossible that Euphronios, with his assistant potters and the ten painters that Beazley gives him, should turn out 2,000 vases in a good year. In fact we know about 600 vases surviving for the period 500–475 from the Euphronios shop, which would be about 1·2 per cent of the total production. Similarly it seems possible that Andokides' shop turned out 2,500 large vases in a good year; if he got the contract to produce Panathenaic prize amphorai and, as was apparently the later practice,[2] produced them over three years this would cut down his normal production to a little over 2,000 vases in those years. These figures are, of course, guesswork and are only suggested to give some idea of the scale of large and prosperous potteries in Athens. More important and quite certain is the evidence of the large dedications that at those moments at any rate the successful potters took their place beside athletic and musical victors and high Athenian officials. As Raubitschek[3] concludes, 'the artisans who profited from this trade and produced these accurate illustrations of Greek civilization played an important part as individuals in the life of the city'.

Pictures of potters' shops on vases do not take us very far because they can only use the restricted space which the vase provides (Pl. 1). They do, however, tell us a little. The shop is divided into a covered area, where the potters and painters work, and an open area where the kiln is, and coarse pottery is made in the same shop as fine pottery. The fullest picture is on the shoulder of a black-figure hydria[4] of the Leagros group where the long narrow shoulder gives room for the painter to show a boy handing a fine amphora to a seated youth, a potter fashion-

[1] See Amyx, *Hesperia* 27 (1958), 277, and below, pp. 273 ff.

[2] Beazley, *AJA* 47 (1943), 461, notes that of the amphorai dated by the archon's name none were made in a Panathenaic year, 4 in the following year, 19 in the year after that and 10 in the year after that.

[3] *Dedications* 458.

[4] *ABV* 362/36; *PP* 6, pl. 2, 1; J. V. Noble, *Techniques of Painted Attic Pottery* (London 1966), figs. 73, 78, 230; Munich 1717. The other pictures are all discussed in *PP* 1 ff. J. R. Green has shown (*JHS* 81 (1961), 74) that the Caputi hydria (*PP* 11) is a metal-worker's shop rather than a pottery. I suspect that it takes with it at least the Euergides painter's cup (*PP* 8, pl. 1, 2–3). D. Metzler, *AA* (1969), 138, publishes a lip-cup in Carlsruhe with A. potter making a lip-cup, B. patron giving instructions when ordering a lip-cup. A red-figure cup with a potter is published *Arch. Esp. de Arqueologia* 31 (1958).

ing a rough pithos on the wheel, which is spun by a boy, a youth carrying a similar rough pithos out of the building, and outside the old master of the pottery watching a porter carrying fuel to the furnace, which a stoker is raking out. Eight figures are shown, and we may think of this as a minimum. We may also suppose that the rough pottery had a steady demand and was sold at 'the pots'[1] in the Agora, while the demand for fine pottery fluctuated. There must also have been a steady demand for lamps, which seem to have been made by potters.[2] Fine pottery includes also black-glaze and moulded vases.

To go further we have to see how painters, whether known from signatures or from style alone, and potters, both those who sign and those whom we can infer from the identification of classes, fit together. First there are three rather special cases: potter families, painters who are also potters, and thirdly cases of two potters or two painters collaborating to make a single vase.

There are several interesting potter families:[3] Ergotimos,[4] who about 570 B.C. made the volute-krater known now as the François vase (Florence 4209, *ABV* 76/1) for Kleitias to paint, had a son Eucheiros and he in his turn had a son. Ergotimos also made two sorts of cup and a standlet. His son Eucheiros made cups, and his type, the lip-cup, is an obvious development from the 'Gordion' cup made by Ergotimos. One of them was signed by the good painter Sakonides. The son of Eucheiros also made a lip-cup. This does not take us very far, but it does give us father, son and grandson making cups.[5]

Nearchos[6] belongs also to our second class because he signs as painter as well as signing as potter, both in the second quarter of the sixth century. He had two sons Tleson and Ergoteles. The name Ergoteles is so like Ergotimos that Nearchos probably married Ergotimos' sister or daughter. Tleson signed lip-cups and band-cups in the third quarter of

---

[1] R. E. Wycherley, *Athenian Agora* III, *Testimonia* (Princeton, 1957), nos. 656, 684. B. Sparkes and L. Talcott, *Pots and Pans of Classical Athens* (Princeton, 1958), figs. 12 and 13, show that fine pottery and rough pottery were sold together.

[2] Howland, *Athenian Agora* IV, *Greek Lamps* (Princeton, 1958), 14, 16, 26, 35.

[3] See also above, p. 6, on Phrynos, Xenokles, Archeneides and Kephalos.

[4] *ABV* 79, 162–3.

[5] See below on a younger Eucheiros who made or painted an alabastron near the Dutuit and Diosphos painters in style (*ARV²* 306): this may indicate that the Diosphos workshop was a later manifestation of the Ergotimos family. The young Tlempolemos on Phintias' hydria (*ARV²* 23/7) may be a descendant of the maker of Little Master cups.

[6] *ABV* 82, 162, 178; *ARV²* 66.

the sixth century. It is possible that he also painted them, but in default of a painter signature we call the artist rather the Tleson painter. And about 515 B.C. he (or perhaps, more likely, a younger relative) made a type-A cup which was painted in red-figure by Oltos. Ergoteles made lip-cups. This must have been a prosperous workshop since, as we have seen, the father Nearchos (unless it was rather a homonymous grandson) dedicated a large kore in 510 B.C. or a little earlier, by which time the workshop had successfully made the transition from Little Master cups to cups type A and from black-figure to red-figure. (Probably both the Ergotimos shop and the Nearchos shop employed several of the Little Master potters known to us, but we have no means of knowing which.)

The third family is father and son. Amasis[1] was a very distinctive and successful potter, whose work runs from about 560 B.C. into the red-figure period. He may also have been the equally distinctive painter who decorated most of these vases, but again no painter signature clinches this. Two of his preserved amphorai were painted by a contemporary painter called Lydos (see below, p. 14). Olpai from his workshop were painted by the Kriton group and three other potters, Kriton,[2] Lysias and Priapos, were associated in making them. A quite late class of black-figure cups (type C), the class of Providence 22.214, seems to have come from Amasis' shop, and an early red-figure group is called the AMA group because Amasis seems to have made their cups. Finally a red-figure potter, Kleophrades, signs once in a form which is most easily restored as Kleophrades son of Amasis. His two signed cups were painted by two early fifth-century red-figure painters, Douris and the Kleophrades painter. (The Kleophrades painter takes his name from this cup, but his name was in fact Epiktetos, so that he may have been son or nephew of the late sixth-century cup-painter, which would give us a painter family.) Kleophrades' hand may be traceable in a number of larger vases (see below, p. 28).

Two later cases must be mentioned. A potter-signature of Phintias occurs on a late fifth-century Meidian vase (*ARV*[2] 1317/1; *CV* Frankfurt, pl. 81). If it is genuine, he is presumably a descendant of the potter-

---

[1] *ABV* 150, 446, 631; *ARV*[2] 160, 191, 1555.
[2] This potter Kriton may have been the father of the vase-painter Skythes (see above), who may therefore have worked in Amasis' shop.

painter Phintias of the late sixth century.[1] A certain and very interesting potter-family is the family of Bakchios and Kittos in the fourth century. It takes us beyond our period but is the one instance where we can see something of a workshop which concentrated on Panathenaic amphorai and black-glaze. Two inscriptions refer to Bakchios. In his epitaph (*IG* ii/iii, 6320; Peek, *GVI*, no. 897) about 330 he claims to have won all the competitions instituted by the city of Athens, and as he and his family made Panathenaic amphorai for the Panathenaia of 374 (*ABV* 413/2), this strongly suggests that the Panathenaic contract was awarded by competition. More of the family is given by a decree welcoming Bakchios' sons, Bakchios and Kittos, to Ephesos before 321.[2] The name Kittos occurs earlier as a maker of Panathenaics for the festival of 366; he was therefore the brother of the elder Bakchios and a member of the family firm.[3] If there is any truth in the elder Bakchios' claim, we must suppose that the family firm was also responsible for the Asteios group made for the festival of 370 (*ABV* 412), for the Charikleides group made for the festival of 362 (*ABV* 414; P. Themelis, *Analecta Archaeologica* 2 (1969), 413) and the Kallimedes group made for the festival of 358 (P. Themelis, loc. cit.). How much longer the workshop goes on we cannot say. For us the big Nikomachos series (*ABV* 414) starts with the festival of 338 and goes on till at least the festival of 318, which is after the departure of Bakchios' sons to Ephesos. We can say that the potting of the Asteios group, the Charikleides group and the Kittos group is very much alike, and they may have been made in the same shop but decorated by different painters.

The second special case, potter-painters, may be more common than we know. We can only quote the cases that are certain or probable. Nearchos certainly, Tleson and Amasis possibly, painted as well as potting. Nearchos' style cannot be traced after about 550 B.C. so that if it was he who dedicated the kore he presumably gave up painting for potting. The Amasis painter's style can be traced as long as the Amasis potter's style – from 560 to the late sixth century. The other

---

[1] Cf. also Kephalos, above, p. 6.

[2] Preuner, *JDAI* 35 (1920), 70. They undertake 'to make black-glaze ware for the city and the hydria for the goddess'.

[3] One of his amphorai is standard in size and decoration but omits the inscription. It may have been a piece which he put in for the competition. Such pieces are called below 'competition pieces'. Cf. *DBF* 97.

potter-painters are Exekias, Epiktetos, Pasiades, Phintias, Euphronios and Douris. The most interesting of these from our point of view are Exekias, Euphronios and Douris. Epiktetos[1] signed a single plate as potter as well as painter; it was found on the Acropolis and has a picture of Athena; probably he dedicated it to Athena. He was primarily a painter, and he painted vases made by six different potters. (He also collaborated with the Euergides painter.) Pasiades[2] we only know as a potter of red-figure alabastra and the painter of a white-ground lekythos. Phintias made cups and cockle-shell aryballoi, and his cups were painted by the Berlin painter and the Salting painter.[3] He himself painted very early a cup made by Deiniades, who stands near Nikosthenes.[4] He also painted amphorai and a hydria; these are attributed to four potters, who supplied other painters of the Pioneer group (Pezzino group and Hypsis).[5]

Exekias,[6] one of the greatest painters of the mid-sixth-century, signed usually as potter but twice as painter and potter. Two of the vases with potter-signature are painted in the same style as the two signed as painter. Five of the signed vases are too slightly decorated for it to be certain whether he also painted them. One, the amphora with Herakles and Geryon in the Louvre, is ascribed to group E.[7] So we have a superb painter (descended from Nearchos and passing his art on to the Lysippides painter and the Andokides painter), who was also a superb potter and invented two shapes with a great future, the kalyx-krater and the eye-cup (type A), if not also the amphora type A. He was the star of the workshop in which the painters of group E painted. Two other potters signed vases painted by members of group E, Antidoros and Andokides. Antidoros[8] signed a cup and this may perhaps be a case of the potter going outside his normal workshop, since the workshop was primarily but not exclusively concerned with large vases. Andokides[9] made an early amphora for a member of group E and carried on the Exekias potting tradition into the red-figure period. He may have also painted, but if he did we do not know whether he was the Lysippides painter, who painted black-figure vases and the black-figure sides of

[1] *ARV²* 78. [2] *ARV²* 102.
[3] *FAS* 61; *ARV²* 25, 178; M. Robertson, *AJA* 62 (1958), 62.
[4] *FAS* 32, n. 35. [5] Bloesch, *JHS* 71 (1951), 29.
[6] *ABV* 143, *ARV²* 1699. [7] *ABV* 133. [8] *ABV* 159.
[9] See in addition to *ABV* 253, *ARV²* 1, Bloesch, *FAS* 12, *JHS* 71 (1951), 30, 35.

bilinguals, or the Andokides painter, who probably invented the red-figure style and painted the red-figure sides of bilinguals. At any rate Andokides made pots and cups for the Andokides painter, the Lysippides painter and a painter who worked in the manner of the Lysippides painter. He also made a kalyx-krater for Epiktetos to paint. Andokides' amphorai for Psiax and the Antimenes painter and his hydria for the Antimenes painter were perhaps rather special commissions made for another workshop. With Mnesiades he dedicated a bronze statue on the Acropolis between 525 and 500 B.C.

Euphronios[1] was one of the great painters of the Pioneer group about 515 with Phintias and Euthymides. He painted a cup made by Euxitheos, who also made a cup for the Pezzino group (again within the Pioneer group). He also painted a cup for Kachrylion, who potted for at least nine other painters *not* in the Pioneer group. He painted a stamnos for a potter[2] who also made stamnoi for Smikros (within the Pioneer group). He painted other large vases including a prize Panathenaic amphora. Then at the beginning of the sixth century he set up as a potter, and made cups and other small vases which were painted by Onesimos, the Antiphon painter, the Colmar painter, the Foundry painter, the Pistoxenos painter, Douris, a painter near the Triptolemos painter, and a painter near Makron, and a couple of other artists who have not been identified. The steadies of this workshop seem to have been Onesimos, the Antiphon painter and the Colmar painter. The Pistoxenos painter was younger and went on into the workshop of the Early Classical Three-Edge potter,[3] whose chief painter was the Penthesileia painter. Douris painted cups by Euphronios before he set up on his own, and the painters near the Triptolemos painter and Makron should also be regarded as roving artists. In style the Foundry painter is close to the Brygos painter, who painted for one of the other great cup-shops run by Brygos;[4] but although the Foundry painter did paint for Brygos, he painted chiefly for Euphronios, so that it is again clear that the divisions between shops were not watertight. Euphronios shifted from being a successful painter chiefly of large vases to being a potter

[1] *ABV* 403; *ARV²* 13, 313, 426; Bloesch, *FAS* 70.
[2] Philippaki, 4 ff.
[3] Bloesch, *FAS* 103; *PP* 29.
[4] Brygos the potter may have been identical with the Brygos painter, cf. A. Cambitoglou, *The Brygos Painter* (Canberra, 1968), 11.

chiefly of small vases. His dedication on the Acropolis of a statue as a 'tithe' was made about 480 B.C. when the workshop was well established.

Douris[1] signed a kantharos as potter and painter and an aryballos, which he also painted, as potter only. But we know him primarily as a painter of cups and small vases. His chief association is with the potter Python. But in his early period he also painted for Kleophrades and Euphronios (as we have seen) and for Brygos[2] and in his middle period for Kalliades. Python was presumably well established when Douris joined him since he made a chalcidizing cup for Epiktetos about 515 B.C. or earlier. The other painters in the workshops were the Triptolemos painter, all that goes as the manner of Douris, and later the Oedipus painter and the Cartellino painter.

The third special case mentioned above was the collaboration of two potters or two painters in making a vase.[3] Two potters only sign twice, on Little Master cups; it may merely mean that an older master is allowing a younger potter to sign with him. Collaboration of painters we have already noticed – Lysippides painter and Andokides painter in bilinguals, Epiktetos and Euergides painter in a cup.[4]

Collaboration necessitates working in the same workshop. This has a bearing on our view of the black-figure painter Lydos.[5] His career runs from about 560 to about 530 B.C. He painted two amphorai for Amasis, an amphora and a band-cup for Nikosthenes and a special trick oinochoe for Kolchos; and a lip-cup potted by Epitimos is very close to him in style. At first sight he looks like a roving painter. But these are only a few of the total of 85 vases and plaques painted by him which survive, and among the rest the ovoid amphorai and shouldered hydriai are distinctive shapes, which recur in vases in the manner of Lydos, in the vases related to Lydos, in the works of the painters of Vatican 309, Louvre F 6 and the Ready painter. This suggests a considerable workshop, and the suggestion is reinforced by the evidence of collaboration.

---

[1] *ARV*[2] 425. He signs 38 times as painter.
[2] Bloesch, *FAS* 83; *ARV*[2] 442.
[3] *PP* 26 ff.
[4] P. Mingazzini, *Annuario* 45–6 (1967–8), 337, argues that Smikros painted the komasts on the neck of Euphronios' volute-krater with Herakles and Amazons, *ARV*[2] 15/6. The inscription under the Herakles appears to be a compliment to Smikros, *not* a description of Herakles.
[5] *ABV* 107, 114, 120, 123. Add K. Friis-Johansen, *Act. Arch.* 31 (1963), 130.

In the works of the painter of Vatican 309 and Louvre F 6, the styles of
the human figures differ from each other and differ from Lydos, but the
animals are described as 'purely Lydan' or 'barely distinguishable from
Lydos'; it looks as if a single painter was responsible for the animals on
the vases of all three. Lydos was then the leading painter in a workshop
which employed more than six other painters and has left us well over
300 vases. But he also occasionally painted pots made by others.

So far we have noted two different kinds of collaboration: in one the
two painters paint the figure scenes on different parts of the pot, in the
other one painter paints the major scene and the other the minor
decoration. (Further possibilities which show a workshop connection
between painters will be considered below.) Other archaic collaborations of the first kind are Skythes and another (*ARV*² 86), Thalia painter
and Oltos (112/1), Flying Angel painter and Triptolemos painter
(280/18), Kleophrades painter and another (*ABV* 405/3). The largest-
scale collaboration is in the workshop of the Penthesilea painter, which
runs from the early classical into the classical period: some twenty
hands can be detected, and more than twelve of them collaborate
(*ARV*² 877). These are cups with the outside painted by one painter and
the inside by another. Pelikai with reverses indistinguishable from the
Sabouroff painter have obverses by the painter of Munich 2363, the
Trophy painter, the painter of Altenburg 273 and another (853–4).
Single instances of collaboration are Hermonax and Zannoni painter
(486/43), Achilles painter and Westreenen painter (990/47), Chrysis
painter and Manner of Dinos painter (1159, ii and iii), Calliope painter
and Eretria painter (1254/86), Marlay painter and Lid painter (1277/23).

Some of these associations are confirmed by collaborations of the
second kind where one painter does the main and another the subsidiary decoration. This is a long list and must be given in detail.

*ARV*² 195. Neck-amphora, shape and ornament as Kleophrades
painter but no connection in drawing.
219. Nolan amphorai, etc., decorated only with floral ornament which recurs on vases by the Berlin painter but also
on vases by the Dutuit painter.
225/1–2. Cups by painter of London E 2, with black-figure
ships in style of Leagros group.

ARV^2 234/11 and 1. Column-kraters by Göttingen painter with silhouette figures on the neck, linking to Leagros group.

254. Class of Cab. Med. 390, large pelikai alike in shape, handle-palmettes, and sometimes ornament, decorated by Syleus painter, Siren painter and perhaps Argos painter. The same painters with the Geras painter decorated a class of stamnoi (Philippaki 97 ff.).

283. The painter of Louvre G 238 (near the Flying Angel painter) is linked by his maeander pattern to the Geras painter and the Argos painter.

633/1. Bell-krater by Methyse painter linked by shape and pattern to 485/23, Hermonax.

633/8. Stamnos by Methyse painter linked by shape and ornament to 620/30, Villa Giulia painter (Philippaki).

823/6. Cup by Orléans painter. Palmettes are by the same hand as on a cup by the Aischines painter (718/42) and a cup near the Calliope painter (1263/1).

835. Bordeaux painter. Same maeander as Lyandros painter.

841/112. Loutrophoros. Neck and small zone under main picture by Sabouroff painter, main picture by Achilles painter.

987/20. Neck-amphora by Achilles painter, pattern bands by another.

1003/25. White lekythos. Manner of Achilles painter, palmettes by another.

1676. Class of Achilles painter's pelikai, alike in shape and patterns with figure-scenes by Achilles painter, Westreenen painter, Dwarf painter, Clio painter, Trophy painter, painter of Munich 2335, Phiale painter.

1002/8. Nolan amphora, shape and pattern Achillean, figure-work not.

1007. Red-figure lekythoi, shape and pattern Achillean, drawing by Phiale painter, Sabouroff painter and five other small groups.

1009. White-line class of squat lekythoi by Achilles painter, related to Achilles painter, by Phiale painter and others.

ARV² 1031/39. Pelike by Polygnotos with floral decoration by same
hand as 1045/2, Lykaon painter, and 1146/44, Kleophon
painter.

1062/166. Cup, group of Polygnotos, with pattern-work recalling latest cups of Euaion painter.

1062. Hydria, shape and pattern-work with Coghill painter,
1042/2, drawing not Polygnotan.

1072, 1562. Volute-krater, Kensington class, drawing Polygnotan.

1178. Pelike which recalls Aison is of same model as pelike by
Shuvalov painter, 1209/57.

1211, 1697; J. R. Green, *Hesperia* 31 (1962), 89 f. Class of Agora
P 15840, special oinochoai, linked by neck, mouth and
florals to the workshop of the Shuvalov painter and by
drawing to the Jena painter.

1243. The painter of Berlin 2464 uses the same maeander as the
Reed painter.

1262/65–75. Pelikai by Calliope painter of same class as Disney
painter, 1265/4–10.

1264/2, 1267/13–4. Collaboration between Disney painter and
painter of Naples hydriskai on neck-amphorai by a single
potter.

1272/46. Cup-skyphos by Codrus painter of same shape as cup-
skyphos by Polion, 1172/21.

1278/33, 35, 48–52 bis, 67, cups, etc., with figures by Marlay
painter and 1282/3–4, 10–13, 20, cups, etc., by Lid painter
connected by lozengy patterns, which may be by either of
these or a third painter.

1397, 1398. Palmettes connect cups by painter of Bonn 1645
with cups by painter of Ferrara T 715.

Beazley has noted a certain number of cases where an Attic red-
figure painter copies or imitates the work of another. Here too it is
natural to suppose that the second painter was in the same workshop as
the first.

ARV² 69. Mastoid. Close imitation of Oltos, apparently by a be-
ginner.

*ARV*² 1635. Two oinochoai, said to have been found together, are careful copies of two vases by the Berlin painter, probably by the Harrow painter, with whom the pattern band connects them.

1570/30. Free replica of 443/225 by Douris in a style related to him.

1034. Group of Bologna PU 289. Two imitations by one hand of Polygnotos and the Hector painter.

1256. Two cups, imitations of the Eretria painter.

1263–4. Oinochoe, imitation of the Calliope painter.

1273/10. Stemless cup, stiff imitation of the Codrus painter.

1273/iii. Cup, copy of particular cup by the Codrus painter.

1315. Painter of the Carlsruhe Paris, laboured copies of pictures by the Meidias painter.

Two special kinds of ware help further in establishing the workshop connections of painters, red-figure cups with incised or impressed decoration inside, and moulded vases with red-figure decoration. We have, of course, many black-glaze cups with incised or impressed decoration inside. The small number with red-figure decoration outside have been discussed by Mrs Ure (*JHS* 56, 1936, 205). The red-figure painters of her first group are the Carlsruhe painter (*ARV*² 737/ 129–30), Sotades painter (764/5), Manner of Sotades painter (768/34, 38), Imitator of Sotades painter (769/1–2), Hippacontist painter (769/ 1–4), related to Sotades painter (770/1, 4–5), later (770, bottom), Amphitrite painter (832/28). This first group seems to me to be linked by a very late cup decorated outside by the Euaion painter (797/141) to a later group decorated outside by the painter of Ruvo 325 (1400/1–3) and the painter of Ruvo 1346 (1401/1–3). The useful point here is the workshop connection between the Carlsruhe painter, the Amphitrite painter and the Sotades painter and his companions.

The moulded vases are of two main types: head-vases, which serve as aryballoi, oinochoai or kantharoi; and drinking horns (rhyta), which end in an animal or bird head. The head-vases have been classified by Beazley in *ARV*² 1529 ff. and the rhyta by H. Hoffmann in *Attic Red-Figured Rhyta* (Mainz, 1962). Our concern is to show the workshop connections which can be established when vases from the same moulds are decorated by different painters. In Etruria and elsewhere in Italy moulds were sometimes taken from older vases to produce copies; but in Athens itself, when a mould is reused after a lapse of time, it is more likely to have been one that remained in the workshop than one borrowed from another workshop. A few signatures on moulded vases which coincide with signatures on ordinary vases show that the moulded vases were made in the same shops and did not come from professional coroplasts: Phintias signed two moulded cockle-shell aryballoi (*ARV*² 25), Syriskos a moulded astragalos (264/67) and Sotades signed rhyta (772).

Here I list the links between moulded vases and painters in roughly chronological order:

(i) *ARV*² 1531. Class C, signed by Charinos, who may appear on an Acropolis dedication (cf. above, p. 6). The chequer pattern on the bowl of nos. 1 and 2 connects with a mastoid like Psiax (9), a plate signed by Euthymides (28/18) and a plate possibly early work by him (30).

(ii) *ARV*² 1533. Class G. No. 8 decorated by the Brygos painter, no. 13 recalls Epeleios painter, no. 16 decorated by the Syriskos painter.

1537. Class K. Nos. 2 and 5 decorated by the Syriskos painter.

1538. Class M. Nos. 1, 2, 6, 7 decorated by the Syriskos painter, no. 5 by the Eretria painter.

1545. Class P. No. 1, Syriskos painter.

1546. Class R. (Satyr head later version of class K and might be by the modeller of class M.) Nos. 2–3, Carlsruhe painter, no. 7 Eretria painter (same vase as M 5).

Hoffmann, 10. Brygan class: nine rhyta decorated by the Brygos painter, one by the Syriskos painter, one by the Bordeaux painter, one in the manner of the Eretria painter, possibly also one by the Sabouroff painter. Hoffmann's Brygan class of rhyta seems to have a workshop connection with the head-vases of the classes listed above. There is no signature but both Brygos and Syriskos were potters. In the head-vases class G seems to stand rather apart from the rest; perhaps Brygos made its moulds and the moulds for the heads of Brygos painter 382/183, which Beazley notes as akin to class L (itself related to class M) but much better. The rest may be Syriskos.

(iii) Hoffmann 13. Dourian class, decorated by Douris, the Villa Giulia painter, and the painter of London E 798 (imitating the Villa Giulia painter).

(iv) Hoffmann 19. Sotadean class. Seven rhyta decorated by the Sotades painter, twenty in his manner, two by the Carlsruhe painter, one near him, one by the Marlay painter, one by the Lid painter, three by the group of class W.

The Carlsruhe painter links the Brygan class to the Sotadean class, but the Sotadean class goes on longer; Sotades may have been a younger man who came into the pottery of Brygos and Syriskos. (A weak copy of the Sotadean sphinx was decorated by the Tarquinia painter (870/89).)

(v) Hoffmann 29. Dresden class. Decoration of four is near the Phiale painter, of one by the Orléans painter and of one by the Calliope painter.

(vi) Hoffmann 31. New York–Paris class. The decoration is attributed to the Villa Giulia painter, the painter of London E 100 and the Group of Two Cow-heads.

(vii) Hoffmann 33. Penthesilean class, decorated by painters of Bologna 417, Brussels R 330, London E 777, and undetermined Penthesileans.

(viii) Hoffmann 36. Spetia class made by same potter as head-vases, class V (ARV^2 1549). The Eretria painter painted two of the rhyta and one of the head-kantharoi, the Orléans painter painted one of the rhyta and Aison one of the head-kantharoi.

(ix) Hoffmann 41. Persian class made by same potter as head-vases, class W (ARV^2 1550). All are decorated by the Sub-Meidian group of class W except one rhyton by the Nikias painter, which according to Hoffmann differs from the class.

If we look at these groups, we see that (i) connects with the Pioneer group, (iii) and (vi) belong to Douris and his successors, (vii) belongs to the Penthesilean group. Much the most interesting is the sequence of (ii), (iv), (v), (viii), (ix), where we seem to be able to follow a single workshop from the archaic period through to late in the fifth century with Brygos and Syriskos as the early potters joined rather later by

Sotades and continuing anonymously with the Dresden class of rhyta and classes V and W. This brings together a succession of painters, notably the Brygos painter, the Carlsruhe painter, the Sotades painter, the Bordeaux painter, the Orléans painter, the Eretria painter, the Marlay painter, the Meidias painter and their associates, and these connections are supported by and in their turn support the connections already established by studying collaboration and the cups with incised design.

Before trying to put this evidence together with the stylistic affinities of potters and painters, one other criterion for detecting workshops is worth testing. Names of historical individuals with the word *kalos* attached to them were painted on many vases before firing. We shall have to return to this subject again and again when we discuss commissioned vases. For the moment it does not matter whether the individual was the purchaser or the recipient of the vase, if these were different. In either case he was in some sense the patron of the potter. The immediate question is whether the occurrence of the same *kalos* name on vases by different painters may sometimes be evidence that these painters worked in the same workshop.

The following *kalos* names may be significant. (References can be found in *ABV* 664 ff., *ARV*² 1559 ff.) First, some *kalos* names which are exclusively black-figure:

Aristomenes: neck-amphora near group E, hydria by Mnesiades (potter-colleague of Andokides).

Automenes: two hydriai in manner of Lysippides painter, perhaps red-figure cup by Oltos.

Euphiletos: two vases and a plaque by the Euphiletos painter, one hydria by the Antimenes painter and an olpe unattributed.

Hippokrates: one vase Manner of Lysippides painter, one recalls Lysippides painter, one by Psiax (who painted for Andokides), one possibly by Psiax.

Lysippides: one vase by Lysippides painter, one related to him, one by another painter but inscribed by the same hand as the last and therefore painted in the same shop.

Onetorides: four by Exekias, one near Exekias, two related to the Lysippides painter, one from the Three-Line group (drawing recalls the Lysippides painter), one by the Princeton painter.

Stesias: three vases of group E.

Timotheos: one by the Antimenes painter, one by the Long Nose painter (who may be a later stage of the Euphiletos painter).

All these except Euphiletos and Timotheos patronized the shop which passed from Exekias to Andokides. Euphiletos and Timotheos both join the Antimenes painter to the Euphiletos (Long Nose) painter, which may mean that they were in the same workshop.

Leagros and his son Glaukon deserve special treatment. The black-figure vases with Leagros *kalos* are five hydriai of the Leagros group and one unattributed lekythos. Fourteen of the red-figure vases are attributed to the Pioneer group, the red-figure painters of the same workshop. An early cup by Myson may well have been made when Myson was associated with the Pioneer Phintias. Two of the cups painted by Euphronios were made by Kachrylion, who also made two other cups for Leagros painted by the Thalia painter and another. Rather later, when Euphronios became a potter, fourteen cups with Leagros *kalos* were painted by painters who worked for Euphronios and five more are said to be akin to two of these painters. Thus 36 of the 51 red-figure vases with Leagros *kalos* can be associated with the Pioneer workshop and its successor Euphronios' cup-shop.

Leagros' son Glaukon is *kalos* on five cups by the Pistoxenos painter, a lekythos in his manner, and a chous and a cup by his two associates, the Tarquinia painter and the Cat and Dog painter. The Pistoxenos painter's early cups were made by Euphronios, so that father and son appear on symposion vases from closely allied potters and painters over a period of something like thirty-five years. The lekythoi with Glaukon *kalos* present a rather more complicated problem, but I think a case can be made for thinking that they too were made in a closely allied workshop.

Let us, however, first consider a number of other *kalos* names which show a strong association with a particular workshop:

(*a*) The cups painted for Euphronios have a number of *kalos* names strongly associated with them: Antias (starts with the Pioneer group), Aristarchos, Erothemis, Laches, Lykos (starts with Pioneer group and continues to the Tarquinia painter; a hydria comes from the workshop of the Berlin painter, who himself issues from the Pioneer group), Lysis (continues to Pistoxenos painter), Panaitios (also uses Douris and the Magnoncourt painter; the Douris cup was made by Kleophrades, a Pioneer potter).

(b) A number of painters are named after *kalos* names which are exclusive to them or at any rate predominant on their vases: Elpinikos painter, Epidromos painter (but Epidromos *kalos* has a wider range), Epeleios painter (Isarchos is also restricted to him), Oionokles painter, Pedieus painter.

(c) A number of *kalos* names are connected with only one workshop. Epilykos is *kalos* for Skythes, the Pedieus painter (who is close to him), on a cup near the Carpenter painter which was probably made in the same workshop, and on a moulded aryballos linked by its palmettes to Skythes. Memnon is *kalos* for Oltos. Sokrates is *kalos* for the Berlin painter. Hipparchos is *kalos* for Epiktetos and the Euergides painter, and we know that they collaborate. Dromippos, Hygiainon and Axiopeithes are *kalos* for the Achilles painter. Diphilos II is *kalos* on fourteen white lekythoi by the Achilles painter and two by the earlier painter of Athens 12789.

If, as appears from what we have seen so far, patrons did tend to patronize single workshops, identity of *kalos* names on vases by different painters may suggest that those painters belonged to the same workshop. A good case is Dion, whose name connects the Sabouroff painter, a painter near the Sabouroff painter, and the Dwarf painter, who is a follower of the Achilles painter; the Sabouroff painter we already know as collaborating with the Achilles painter so that Dion confirms that evidence. It is in this context that we have to consider the lekythoi with Glaukon *kalos*. He is tabulated here with eight other men whose *kalos* inscriptions have a remarkably similar range:

> *Glaukon:* Providence painter, painter of Yale lekythos, Timokrates painter, Nikon painter, Pistoxenos painter and associates.
> *Charmides:* Providence painter, painter of Yale lekythos, Nikon painter, Charmides painter, Dresden painter, following of Douris, Cat and Dog painter.
> *Hippon II:* Providence painter, Charmides painter, Dresden painter, near the Pan painter.

Kallikles: Providence painter, Nikon painter, Dresden painter.

Nikon II: Providence painter, Nikon painter, Villa Giulia painter, near the Alkimachos painter.

Timonides: Providence painter, Nikon painter.

Akestorides: Oionokles painter (follower of Providence painter), Timokrates painter.

Kallias I: Oionokles painter, Nikon painter, Charmides painter.

Timoxenos: Charmides painter, Dresden painter.

The hard core of this list comprises the Providence painter, the Oionokles painter, the painter of the Yale lekythos, the Timokrates painter, the Nikon painter, the Charmides painter and the Dresden painter, and I suggest that they worked in the same workshop, which was patronized by these nine young men.

Five further *kalos* names allow us to extend the list a little further:

Alkimaches I: Timokrates painter, Vouni painter (near the Timokrates painter), Alkimachos painter (cf. Nikon II above), early manner of Achilles painter.

Timokrates: Timokrates painter, Alkimachos painter.

Lichas: Timokrates painter, Alkimachos painter, Achilles painter, Makron shop.

Kleinias: Alkimachos painter, Achilles painter.

Euaion: Providence painter, Achilles painter, Phiale painter (pupil of Achilles painter), Euaion painter, Lykaon painter.

These names suggest that the Vouni painter, the Alkimachos painter, the Achilles painter and the Phiale painter should be added to the list. The Providence painter at the beginning and the Achilles painter at the end are both pupils of the Berlin painter so that it looks as if these painters belong to the continuation of his workshop through the early classical and classical periods. The Berlin painter himself 'issued from the group of Euthymides and Phintias', the colleagues of Euphronios when he was still painting, so that his workshop ran parallel to Euphronios' cup-shop, where Leagros and later his son Glaukon bought their cups.

Even from these lists it is clear that patrons were not always faithful to a single workshop. The Pan painter, the Villa Giulia painter,

Makron, the Euaion painter and the Lykaon painter have nothing to do with the workshops of Euphronios and the Berlin painter. Other *kalos* names such as Antimachos, Diogenes, Hiketas, Hippodamas, Krates and Nikostratos produce lists of painters in which no choice can be detected. This is what we should expect, the roving patron as well as the steady patron. But it is legitimate to use as evidence the forty or so *kalos* names which do seem to indicate steady patrons.

It is now necessary to put all these different kinds of evidence with the evidence of style in potting and painting to try and form a general picture of the main workshops in their development from 600 to 400 B.C. What follows is essentially a summary of *ABV* and *ARV²*, and this is part of its purpose. It is, however, much simplified by leaving out many of the less important painters and potters. It is an attempt to show briefly the larger units in the Kerameikos and the connections between them. Even so simplified the picture is complex, and though it is possible to establish a number of nuclei which do presumably represent workshops, it is clear that, whether to meet a sudden demand or for some other reason a painter might move from one potter to another or alternatively one shop might obtain vases from another for its painter to decorate.

I EARLIEST BLACK-FIGURE. 600 B.C.
ABV 1 ff.
Nettos painter, etc.

II EARLY BLACK-FIGURE. From 600 B.C.
(a) *ABV* 8–14, 37 ff.
Gorgon painter, etc. Tradition carried on by Sophilos. Lekythoi and olpai continued later by Amasis painter and others. Coarsely painted ware: Polos painter.
(b) *ABV* 20, 23 ff.
Komast group workshop. Perhaps derives from Ceramicus painter, who is an older contemporary of the Gorgon painter. Strong Corinthian influence. Corinthian-shaped cups, but Siana cups probably invented in this workshop.
(c) *ABV* 51–62, 161.
C painter workshop. Potters: Cheiron and Psoleas. Predominantly Siana cups, but Cheiron may also have made Little Master cups.

(*d*)   *ABV* 63 ff.
Heidelberg painter. Younger colleague of C painter and probably teacher of Amasis painter.

(*e*)   *ABV* 76 ff., 162 f.; *ARV*² 306.
Ergotimos potter. Kleitias painter. Volute-krater, Gordion cups, etc. Eucheiros, son of Ergotimos, made lip-cups. His son was working towards the end of the sixth century. A younger Eucheiros seems to be connected with the Sappho-Diosphos painters' workshop in the early fifth century.

(*f*)   *ABV* 62 ff., 162, 178; *ARV*² 66; *FAS* 39; *ARV*² 174/24, 1611.
Nearchos, potter and painter. He had two sons, Tleson and Ergoteles. The latter name suggests that he married Ergotimos' sister, and the two workshops may have been one. He or a younger Nearchos dedicated a kore about 510. Tleson, or the younger Tleson who is *kalos* for the Ambrosios painter, made a cup painted by Oltos, which belongs in shape near Hischylos cups.

(*g*)   *ABV* 95 ff.
Tyrrhenian workshop. Chiefly ovoid neck-amphorai and round-bodied and shouldered hydriai, which were very successful on the Etruscan market.

III   MIDDLE BLACK-FIGURE. From 560 B.C.

(*a*)   *ABV* 162, 171; *FAS* 39; *ARV*² 66/127.
Sons of Nearchos and Ergotimos. Sakonides painted for Eucheiros. His other signatures may bring in Kaulos and Tlempolemos as potters; he also painted for Hischylos, who is linked with Tleson.

(*b*)   *ABV* 133–49, 297, 253, 314, 159.
Exekias, potter and painter. Style derives from Nearchos, and he probably worked in the Nearchos–Ergotimos workshop. Other painters, group E, and near group E, perhaps also Princeton painter.[1] Other potters: Andokides (see below), Mnesiades and Antidoros, who also made Droop cups.

(*c*)   *ABV* 106–32.
Lydos. Collaborated with painter of Louvre F 6 and painter of Vatican 309. Other painters: Camel painter, Ready painter,

---

[1] If this is correct (cf. above, p. 21), probably also the Swing painter and the painter of Munich 1410. *ABV* 300/16 may associate Mnesiades with the Princeton painter, cf. p. 198.

North Slope group, Snake and Spots group. Kolchos and Epitimos may have made pots for this workshop, but Lydos himself went outside the workshop to paint for Amasis and Nikosthenes.

(*d*)   *ABV* 150 ff., 446, 457, 631; *ARV* 160, 192, 1555.

Amasis. Father of Kleophrades, potter. Other potters: Kriton (probably father of the painter Skythes, who had a son, the potter Kriton), Lysias, Priapos. Chief painter: Amasis painter, who may be identical with the potter and probably learnt from the Heidelberg painter. Lydos painted occasionally. Links to Dolphin group of lekythoi and to the Mannerist shop.

(*e*)   *ABV* 238: Von Bothmer, *RA* (1969), 3.

Mannerist shop. Painters: the Affecter and Elbows Out. Very successful in the Etruscan market. Potting connection with lekythoi of Amasis painter.

(*f*)   *ABV* 159, 217 ff.; *FAS* 23.

Nikosthenes. Also very successful with the Etruscan market. Begins near the end of the period and continues nearly to the end of the century. Collaborated early with Anakles and probably trained Pamphaios (see below). Painters in this period: BMN painter, Centaur painter, painter of London B 620, painter of Louvre F 117, N painter, group of Louvre F 110. Lydos occasionally.

IV   LATE BLACK-FIGURE AND EARLY RED-FIGURE. 530–500 B.C.

(*a*)   *ARV*² 122 ff., 160; *FAS* 9.

Nikosthenes (put first because he does not continue into fifth century). Red-figure painters: Oltos, Epiktetos, Nikosthenes painter, group of Louvre F 125, painter of Boulogne horse.

(*b*)   *ABV* 235, 205; *ARV*² 11, 1618, 127 ff., 137, 173; *FAS* 62 ff.

Pamphaios, younger companion of Nikosthenes: black-figure painters, Euphiletos painter, group of Walters 48.42, painters of class of Cab. Med. 218; red-figure painters, Oltos, Epiktetos, Nikosthenes painter, Ambrosios painter, Aktorione painter, Pythokles painter.

(*c*)   Cf. above III(*a*).

Nearchos–Ergotimos succession: son of Eucheiros potting. Dedication of kore by Nearchos. Association of Tleson with Hischylos. Note possibility that Andokides and his circle belong here.

(*d*)   *ABV* 166, 172; *ARV*² 161, 109, 87, 110, 102, 166, 168, 170, 124/3;
        FAS 31 ff.

   Hischylos. Associated with Tleson, Chelis, Antimachos class,
   probably also Euergides, Hermaios, Pasiades, Paidikos. Painters:
   (1) for Hischylos, Sakonides (black-figure), Hischylos painter,
   Oltos, Epiktetos, Pheidippos, (2) for Antimachos class and near,
   Oltos, painter of Bowdoin eye-cup, painter of Scheeurleer eye-
   cup, Winchester painter, Nikosthenes painter, (3) for Tleson,
   Oltos, (4) for Chelis, Oltos, Thalia painter, Chelis painter, (5) for
   Euergides, Euergides painter once collaborating with Epiktetos,
   (6) for Hermaios, Oltos and Hermaios painter, (7) for Pasiades
   and Paidikos, Pasiades painter and Euergides painter. This workshop rather than the Nikosthenes workshop seems to be the
   firmer and possibly later home of Oltos and Epiktetos. Several
   indications suggest connections with Andokides and forward to
   the Pioneer workshop: Epiktetos also paints for Andokides,
   Oltos paints for Pioneer potters, Tlempolemos (possibly descended from the Little Master potter) is *kalos* for the Euergides
   painter (*ARV*² 1625) and is painted with Euthymides by Phintias
   (*ARV*² 23/7).

(*e*)   *ABV* 253, 265, 266/120–1, 320; *ARV*² 1 ff.

   Andokides. Associated with the potter Mnesiades by the Acropolis
   dedication. Painters: black-figure, the Lysippides painter and his
   following, group E, Nikesippos group, Psiax, Antimenes painter;
   red-figure, Andokides painter, Psiax, Epiktetos.

(*f*)   *ABV* 631; *ARV*² 160; *ABV* 388, 343; *ARV*² 82–6, 1530.

   Amasis. Latest vases of Amasis painter. Black-figure cups, class of
   Providence 21.24; red-figure cups painted by AMA group. If
   Amasis' son Kleophrades is the KL of the graffito on a stamnos of
   Miniature class C,[1] he potted for the Leagran group of Louvre
   F 314 and for the Perizoma group. Kriton, who made olpai for
   Amasis, had a son Skythes, who painted in the late sixth century
   and worked with the Pedieus painter; the shop also made head-
   vases of the Epilykos class (class B).

(*g*)   *ABV* 266–95; *ARV*² 6 ff., 9 with 28/18, 30, 1531/1–2; *ABV* 423,
        697; Philippaki 8, 11.

[1] Cf. below, p. 280, and Philippaki, 18, n. 2.

Psiax may have been the pupil of the Amasis painter, and the Antimenes painter is the 'brother' of Psiax. Possibly the majority of their large vases were made in Amasis' workshop. Both also painted for Andokides, and Psiax for Menon and Hilinos as well. The circle comprises more than twelve painters and groups; the Euphiletos painter may be connected. Late on there are contacts with the Leagros–Pioneer workshop: Psiax is linked by a chequer pattern with Euthymides and with the head vases of Charinos, who also made oinochoai of a class decorated by Leagran painters; and two classes of stamnoi were painted by both Antimenean and Leagran painters.

(*h*) *ABV* 355–97; *ARV²* 13–36. (1) *ARV²* 13 f., 32; *FAS* 44; *ARV²* 107; *FAS* 45, 119; *ARV²* 22, 21, 25; *FAS* 61; Robertson, *AJA* 62 (1958), 62 f. (2) Philippaki 8, 11, 16, 4. (3)–(5) Bloesch, *JHS* 71 (1951), 31 ff.; *ABV* 340, 321, 335.

Black-figure Leagros group and red-figure Pioneer group. Stylistically these painters represent a new violent style which continues from the last quarter of the sixth century into the fifth. The black-figure painters are perhaps nearer to the Lysippides painter than to anyone else, and the red-figure painters derive from the Andokides painter. Among the black-figure painters are painter A, painter S, the Antiope group, the Acheloos painter and the Red-Line painter; the Nikoxenos painter and the Eucharides painter, who both also painted in red-figure, and the Edinburgh painter all belong to the fifth century. The chief red-figure painters are Euphronios, Smikros, Phintias and Euthymides, who lead on to the Berlin painter and the Kleophrades painter in the fifth century. Some of the vases made in the workshops were decorated by outsiders. The main workshop was probably a successor of the Andokides workshop. Representative potters and classes:

(1) Cups, red-figure and bilingual: Euxitheos (for Oltos, Euphronios, Pezzino group), Kachrylion (for Oltos, Thalia painter, painter of Louvre G 36, Hermaios painter, Euphronios), Deiniades (for Phintias very early), Sosias (for Sosias painter), Phintias (for Salting painter, Berlin painter very early).

(2) Stamnoi. Two classes shared with Antimenean painters (see

above); miniature class C (see above); Euphronios–Smikros stamnoi.

(3) Amphorai A: Eukleo A (Euthymides, Dikaios painter), Eukleo B (Phintias), Eukleo C (Leagros group, Euthymides), Eukleo D (Leagros group, Kleophrades painter).

(4) Neck-amphorai: Lea class (Leagros group), Club-foot potter (Leagros group, Nikoxenos painter), Canoe potter (Nikoxenos painter).

(5) Hydriai: Lea class (Leagros group), Ring-Foot potter (Phintias, Pezzino group), potter of Hypsis hydria (Hypsis, Phintias and a black-figure painter), Club-Foot potter (Leagros group).

The Canoe potter also made neck-amphorai for the group of London B 250 and for the painter of London B 252; the Club-Foot potter also made for the Euphiletos painter and the Rycroft painter (who is related to Psiax).

(i) (1) *ABV* 481. (2) *ABV* 593–600, 428. (3) *ABV* 483. (4) *ABV* 422–3. (5) *ABV* 425. (6) *ABV* 428. (7) *ABV* 433. (8) *ABV* 439. (9) *ABV* 526. (10) *ABV* 487–506, *ABL* 221–5. (11) *ABV* 476, *ABL* 215.

Classes of smaller black-figure vases decorated by Leagros group and other painters. Many of them run into or start in the fifth century. Some and perhaps all of them were made in independent workshops.

(1) Doubleens: Red-Line painter, Edinburgh painter, Diosphos painter.

(2) Light-make class (small neck-amphorai): Red-Line painter, Pescia painter, Manner of Haimon painter, others. Collar of Esses class of oinochoai were made in the same workshop.

(3) Dot-band class (small neck-amphorai): Leagros group, Edinburgh painter, Perizoma group, various.

(4) Altenburg class (oinochoai I): Leagros group and others. Shape like Charinos oinochoe.

(5) Keyside class (oinochoai I): Red-Line painter, other Leagrans, painter of class of Athens 581.

(6) Class of London B 495 (oinochoai I): Leagran painters, various, Manner of Haimon painter.

(7) Class of Cambridge G 162 (oinochoai II): Leagros group, Acheloos painter, one recalls late Psiax, Theseus painter.

(8) Class of Vatican G 50 (oinochoai): one in manner of Red-Line painter.

(9) Oinochoai I from Theseus–Athena painters' workshop: Leagran painters, Athena painter.

(10) Lekythoi, class of Athens 581: Leagran painters, Pescia painter, Marathon painter, various. Links back to Cock group and forwards to Haimon group.

(11) Lekythoi from Edinburgh painter's shop: Edinburgh painter, Theseus painter, Athena painter.

(*j*) *ABV* 518–37; A. D. Ure, *JHS* 75 (1955), 90 ff.

Theseus–Athena workshop. The Theseus painter painted with Leagran painters (cf. above). He started about 520 perhaps with Pamphaios, as his earliest cups and skyphoi are close to the group of Walters 48.42, for whom Pamphaios made a cup; so also his kyathoi may have been made in the Nikosthenes workshop. Then he set up a shop on his own with the Athena painter which produced cups, skyphoi, oinochoai and lekythoi on into the fifth century.

V LATE ARCHAIC RED-FIGURE AND LATEST BLACK-FIGURE. 500–475 B.C.

(*a*) *ARV²* 1555, 181–95; Philippaki 48 ff., 52 ff.; *ARV²* 296, 297, 412, 657; Philippaki 36, 53.

Kleophrades, son of Amasis, made a cup for Douris and a cup for the Kleophrades painter. If the KL graffito is his, he also made a psykter and pelike for the Kleophrades painter, whose real name was Epiktetos, possibly son or nephew of the cup-painter Epiktetos. The Kleophrades painter was the pupil of Euthymides and carries on his strong style. Among other vases, mostly large, he painted stamnoi of two classes, the class of the Louvre Kaineus and a speira-footed class which is related to miniature class C (possibly made by Kleophrades). The Troilos painter, Hephaisteion painter and Dokimasia painter decorated both classes, the painter of the Yale lekythos only the second. Here we see cross-links to independent or semi-independent workshops; the painter of the Yale lekythos and the Dokimasia painter also painted stamnoi of the Berlin painter's late class, the Troilos painter painted stamnoi of the Copenhagen painter's late class (see below). The Kleophrades shop and the Berlin painter's shop are both descended from the Leagros–Pioneer shop.

(b) ARV^2 196–219; 1635; 1596. (1) ARV^2 1634. (2) Philippaki 32. (3) Philippaki 34. (4) Philippaki 36. (5) ABV 481, ARV^2 200. (6) ARV^2 218, 307, 300 ff., 306, 675, 709. (7) ARV^2 280/18. (8) ABV 538–587; ABL 130, 137, 165, 170; ARV^2 750.

The Berlin painter issues from the group of Euthymides and Phintias. Two of his very early cups are signed by Phintias and Gorgos as makers: possibly Gorgos was his own name. In this period works of his were copied by the Harrow painter and the Flying Angel painter. He goes on into the early classical period when a number of his pupils can be detected. Some workshop connections can be established:

(1) Hydria no. 166 with Copenhagen painter no. 26 and black-figure hydria in Frankfurt.

(2) Early stamnoi with Copenhagen painter, Harrow painter.

(3) Transitional stamnoi with Providence painter (pupil), Aegisthus painter (pupil of Copenhagen painter), Tyszkiewicsz painter.

(4) Late stamnoi with Providence painter (pupil), Hermonax (pupil), group of London E 445, painter of Yale lekythos, Dokimasia painter.

(5) Doubleens of the same class as the Edinburgh painter.

(6) Floral Nolan amphorai connected with the Berlin painter are also connected by their ornament with the Dutuit painter. The Dutuit painter is related to the circle of the Diosphos painter, who with the Sappho painter presides over a flourishing black-figure lekythos workshop deriving from the Edinburgh painter and the Leagros group; the younger Eucheiros probably belongs to it. The Dutuit painter and a number of others, including the painter of the Yale lekythos, paint red-figure PL lekythoi, one of the shapes developed from the DL lekythoi of the Diosphos workshop.

(7) The Flying Angel painter, who apparently belonged to the

1 Potter's shop. Bell-krater, Komaris painter.
Oxford 526. (See p. 8)

2 Aeschylus, Toxotides. Bell-krater, Lykaon painter.
Boston 00.346. (See p. 47)

Berlin painter's workshop, collaborated in a pelike with the Triptolemos painter (see below). He paints red-figure ATL lekythoi, which were also developed from DL lekythoi.

(8) The very numerous Haimon group of lekythoi and other small vases, particularly skyphoi, also starts with the DL lekythos and continues into the next period with the chimney lekythoi and the BEL lekythoi of the Pholos painter, the Emporion painter and the Beldam painter.

(c)   *ARV*² 256 ff.; Philippaki 32, 63 ff.; *ARV*² 1534, 1537, 1539; Hoffmann, no. 7; *ARV*² 398–417; *FAS* 81; *ARV*² 837; Hoffmann, no. 17.

Syriskos and Brygos. The Copenhagen painter, who is the 'brother' of the Syriskos painter, besides painting stamnoi from the Berlin painter's workshop, painted a class of his own, also decorated by the Harrow painter, the Tyszkiewicsz painter, the Troilos painter and the Triptolemos painter.

The Syriskos painter decorated small vases as well as large, including an astragalos made by Syriskos (who gives him his name), two skyphoi made by Pistoxenos, head-vases of classes G, K, M and P, and a moulded rhyton of the Brygan class.

Brygos probably worked in the same shop as Syriskos, and brings in the cups decorated by the Brygos painter (who may be the same man as the potter), Foundry painter, Briseis painter, painter of the Paris Gigantomachy, Dokimasia painter, Schifanoia group, and exceptionally by Douris, the Triptolemos painter, the Eucharides painter and the Sabouroff painter, who also painted a rhyton of the Brygan class.

(d)   *ARV*² 244–55, 285–9; Philippaki 59, 95, 98.

The Syleus sequence of four painters may in fact be one man. The class of the Siren painter's stamnoi and the class of Cab. Med. 390 (pelikai) link the Syleus painter to the Argos painter, the Siren painter and the Geras painter. These are still in the neighbourhood of the Berlin painter, because (i) Geras and Argos painters use the same maeander as the Berlin painter, (ii) the painter of the Munich amphora in the Syleus sequence paints a stamnos of the class of the Tyszkiewicsz painter, (iii) an early classic class of stamnoi links the Syleus painter to the Aegisthus painter, who painted for the transitional class of the Berlin painter's stamnoi.

(*e*)   *ARV*² 220–32; *FAS* 85.

Nikoxenos painter and Eucharides painter. Their red-figure work falls in this period. Two cups by the painter of London E 2 and two column-kraters by the Göttingen painter have minor black-figure decoration in Leagran style.

(*f*)   *ARV*² 13, 313–58; *FAS* 70, 137; *ARV*² 859, 1554.

Euphronios, the painter of the Pioneer group, set up as a potter, and made cups, which were painted primarily by Onesimos, the Antiphon painter, and the Colmar painter, and in the next period by the Pistoxenos painter, but also occasionally by Douris, the Triptolemos painter, Makron and the Foundry painter. The Pistoxenos painter is named after two skyphoi made by Pistoxenos, who also made skyphoi decorated by Epiktetos and the Syriskos painter.

(*g*)   *ARV*² 237.

Myson, potter and painter, as a pupil of Phintias, derives from the Pioneer group and is the 'father' of the earlier Mannerists, who belong to the next period.

(*h*)   *ARV*² 425–56; Hoffmann 13.

Douris, potter and painter, painted cups made by Kleophrades, Euphronios, Kalliades and Brygos, but the firm association in his own shop is with Python, who probably originally belonged to the Pioneer workshop as one of his cups was decorated by Epiktetos. The Triptolemos painter worked with Douris, and Douris had a number of imitators and followers in the next period. The class of rhyta called after him was decorated by him, the Villa Giulia painter, and an imitator of the Villa Giulia painter.

(*i*)   *ARV*² 458–81; *FAS* 91, 127.

Hieron was the potter for the painter Makron, who had a large following in the next period. Hieron may have started in Pamphaios' workshop, as the Ambrosios painter painted both for Pamphaios and for Hieron. The Apollodoros class of cups, painted by the Ambrosios painter, Epidromos painter and Apollodoros, was probably produced in Hieron's shop.

(*j*)   *ABV* 518–37; *ARV*² 677.

The Theseus–Athena workshop runs right through the period and the black-figure Athena painter has been identified with the red-figure Bowdoin painter.

VI   EARLY CLASSICAL PERIOD. 475–450 B.C.

(a)   *ARV*² 821.

The Kleophrades painter. The cups of the Boot painter may be his late works.

(b)   *ARV*² 483–95; Philippaki 46, 103; *ARV*² 672, 1665; 633.

Berlin painter. His transitional and late works belong to this period. His pupil Hermonax, who has various followers, painted two classes of stamnoi besides the Berlin painter's late class, the class of Hermonax signed stamnoi and the class of the Louvre Philoktetes, which he shared with his follower the painter of Munich 2413 and the Persephone painter (the Persephone painter belongs to the next period and is said to be akin to the Achilles painter in spirit; the Achilles painter was himself a pupil of the Berlin painter). The reverse of a pelike by Hermonax was painted by the Zannoni painter, who may draw in the painter of London E 342 and his fellows. Two bell-kraters, one by Hermonax and one by the Methyse painter, were made by the same potter; a close connection between the Berlin painter's workshop and the Villa Giulia painter's workshop, to which the Methyse painter belongs, is probable.

(c)   *ARV*² 635–63, 743–4, 529; 674, 696–708, 844; 709–29, 753–62, 846.

The Providence painter was a pupil of the Berlin painter and painted his transitional and late stamnoi. He was also a painter of lekythoi, and a group of painters, chiefly of lekythoi, are linked to him partly by style, partly by *kalos* names, and lead on to the Achilles painter: they are the Timokrates painter, the Vouni painter, the Nikon painter, the Charmides painter, the Oionokles painter, the Dresden painter, the Alkimachos painter and the painter of the Yale lekythos. Of these the Providence painter, Oionokles painter, Charmides painter, but also the painter of Munich 2660 (a follower of Douris) and the Briseis painter (who paints cups for Brygos) paint Nolan amphorai with reels and triple handles made by a single potter (Caskey–Beazley II, 40).

The painter of the Yale lekythos painted the secondary PL lekythos (noted above as derived from the Diosphos painter's DL lekythos); in the same shop also were probably the Icarus–Seireniske group and the Sabouroff painter. (But the Carlsruhe painter and the Bowdoin painter, who also paint PLs, belong elsewhere.)

The other derivative of the DL, the ATL, is painted at this time by the Aeschines painter and painters related to him, by the Tymbos group and by the Sabouroff painter.

(d)   *ARV*² 677–95; 706.
The red-figure Bowdoin painter, who is the black-figure Athena painter, has his own BL lekythos, which is also painted by a number of his minor companions, but also paints PL, ATL, CL, so that the boundaries between the shops are not firm.

(e)   *ARV*² 1547, 730–42; 750–3, *ABV* 584–6; *ABL* 263–6; Hoffmann, nos. 33, 52; *ARV*² 763–72; Hoffmann, nos. 26 ff.; A. D. Ure, *JHS* 56 (1936), 205; *ARV*² 737, 764, 768, 769, 770, 797, 832; Hoffmann, no. 17; *ARV*² 837, 835, Hoffmann, nos. 68, 99 bis; *ARV*² 824, 718, 1263.
The Brygos–Syriskos workshop can be traced on by the head-vases and rhyta. Class R is painted by the Carlsruhe painter, a very productive painter of lekythoi; his own shape is CL, but he also painted PL and BEL.

He also painted rhyta of the Sotadean class, and Sotades was probably a young potter in this shop, with which we can then associate the Sotades painter and vases in his manner. Another link are the cups with incised decoration, which are also painted by the Euaion painter and the Amphitrite painter.

Rhyta of the Brygan class are painted by the Bordeaux painter and the Sabouroff painter. The Dresden class are painted by the Orléans painter. The Orléans painter, the late Calliope painter and the Aischines painter paint cups by a single potter.

(f)   Philippaki 56 ff., 73 ff.; *ARV*² 589–617, 574, 925, 1071 f., 1562; 536.
The early classic class of stamnoi noted above as painted by the Syleus painter, the Aegisthus painter and his followers, connects a number of other painters, notably the Oreithyia painter, the Syracuse painter (who is a follower of Makron) and the Altamura

painter, who is the oldest painter in the important group of at least eight painters round the Niobid painter. The Altamura painter's own class of stamnoi is painted by him, the Blenheim painter, and in the manner of the Niobid painter; outside the group three variations are painted by the Mannerist Agrigento painter, the painter of Brussels R 330 (who is a follower of the Penthesilea painter) and by the Kensington painter. The last variation (which in fact belongs to the next period) is called the Kensington class: two of the painters recall Polygnotos, which is interesting since Polygnotos himself came from the school of the Niobid painter. There is also a potting connection between the Niobid painter's group and the Boreas–Florence group (see below, p. 87).

(*g*) Philippaki 120, 110; *ARV*² 618–34; 1012, 1014, 1027; Hoffmann, nos. 72–6; *ARV*² 777, 834; 781–800.

The Villa Giulia painter is connected with the Berlin painter and with Douris. The class of his stamnoi were decorated by himself, and by the Menelaos painter and Danae painter, who are connected with his group. The class of the Chicago painter's stamnoi (he is a follower of the Villa Giulia painter and leads over into the next period) are decorated by the Villa Giulia painter, the Chicago painter and the Methyse painter, but also by the Persephone painter and the Phiale painter of the Achilles painter's group, by Polygnotos, and by others. The Villa Giulia painter also decorates rhyta of the New York–Paris class, which brings in the painter of London E 100 and the group of Two Cow Heads. Nine cup-painters, who are followers of Douris, also belong here; of these the Euaion painter painted one of the cups with impressed decoration, and his late cups go closely with Polygnotos.

(*h*) *ARV*² 562–84, 550–60.

Myson's workshop employs seven early Mannerists and more undetermined; the Pan painter is near but much better.

(*i*) *ARV*² 806–20.

Makron has seven identified followers; Hieron is still the potter for the Clinic painter and the Telephos painter, and made a cup for the Amphitrite painter.

(*j*)   *ARV*² 859–76; *FAS* 103; *ARV*² 877–930; Hoffmann, nos. 77 ff.
Euphronios still makes cups for the Pistoxenos painter, who with
his group of eight associates mainly works here, although the
Tarquinia painter also decorated a Sotadean rhyton. The new
potter of the group is the Three-Edge potter, and he brings in the
large group of the Penthesilea painter and his nineteen or so
associates, who carry the shop on to the end of the classical
period and have their own class of moulded rhyta.

VII   THE CLASSICAL PERIOD. 450–425 B.C.

(*a*)   *ARV*² 1072–7.
The Eupolis painter is related to the Villa Giulia painter. The
Danae and Menelaos painters, mentioned above, also belong
here. The class of London E 195 (hydriai) connects the Barclay
painter with the Danae painter.

(*b*)   *ARV*² 1027–63, 1143–59; Philippaki 123 ff.; *ARV*² 1083, 1062.
Polygnotos, who derives from the Niobid painter, is the centre of
a large group containing sixteen painters and much undetermined. It continues with the Kleophon painter, Dinos painter
and Chrysis painter. The Polygnotan class of stamnoi links many
of the Polygnotan painters with the Kleophon and the Dinos
painters, but also with some outsiders, the Danae and Menelaos
painters, and the Cassel painter from the Achilles painter's group.
The London Andromeda hydria (E 169) is by the same potter as
a Polygnotan hydria but the style is different.

(*c*)   *ARV*² 1247–74; 1538, 1547, 1549, 1174; Hoffmann, nos. 34, 43;
*ARV*² 1278, 1284; Hoffmann, no. 69; *ARV*² 1126–42; 1206–11;
J. R. Green, *Hesperia* 31 (1962), 89 ff.; *BSA* 66 (1971), 189.
The Brygos–Syriskos workshop has new painters to decorate the
head-vases and rhyta which attest its continuation. Epigenes signs
once as potter for the Eretria painter. Head-vases of classes M and
R are decorated by the Eretria painter and class V by the Eretria
painter and Aison. Sotadean rhyta are decorated by the Marlay
painter and the Lid painter, who collaborate on other vases. The
Dresden class of rhyta is decorated by the Calliope painter, who
collaborates on other vases with the Eretria painter. These two
have also several assistants. The Calliope painter links back to the

Orléans painter in cups and rhyta. He also paints pelikai of the same class as the Disney painter, who is tied to the painter of the Naples hydriskai by his neck-amphorai.

Aison paints pelikai of the same make as the Washing painter and one of the same make as one by the Shuvalov painter, who is linked by the potting of his neck-amphorai to the special Acropolis oinochoai and by his choes to the Eretria painter and the Meidias painter with a cross-connection also to the Kraipale painter, Persephone painter and Marlay painter. Five cups are said to be between Aison and the slightly earlier Codrus painter, and the Codrus painter paints a cup-skyphos made by a potter also used by Polion.

(d) *ARV²* 986–1084; 837–57, 1194; 1676; 1161–70; 1231–6; 1371–6; 1007; 1009.

The Achilles painter, who was a pupil of the Berlin painter, was the centre of a considerable workshop, producing among many other vases excellent white lekythoi. He collaborated in a loutrophoros with the Sabouroff painter and in a pelike with the Westreenen painter. The Sabouroff painter, who started in the early classical period, collaborated in pelikai with the painter of Munich 2363, the Trophy painter and the painter of Altenburg 273. These and six other painters close to the Sabouroff painter should be reckoned to this workshop.

Pelikai of the Achilles painter's class are painted by him, the Westreenen painter, the Dwarf painter, the Clio painter, the Trophy painter and the painter of Munich 2335. (The Clio painter is near to the Phiale painter, who is a pupil of the Achilles painter; the painter of Munich 2335, who also painted hydriai of the Achilles painter's type, painted white lekythoi as well as other vases and leads on to the Bird group and later the Woman group.)

Red-figure lekythoi of the Achilles painter's class were painted also by the Sabouroff painter, the Phiale painter, the painter of Athens 13702, the group of Naples Stg. 252 and others.

The White-Line class of squat lekythoi was painted by the Achilles painter, painters related to the Achilles painter, the Phiale painter and others.

(*e*) *ARV*² 1180, 1024/3 bis, 1184–91.

A fragment by the *Phiale painter* and fragments by the Cassel painter, who is remotely related to him, were found in the discards of a potter's shop in Athens, which included works by the painter of the Athens Dinos and fragments in the manner of the Kadmos painter. This may put the Kadmos and Pothos painters' workshop in the neighbourhood of the Achilles painter's workshop but in style they are completely different.

(*f*) *ARV*² 1106–24.

The later Mannerists. (1) The Nausicaa painter, who connects with the Oinanthe painter among the earlier Mannerists, the painter of Tarquinia 707, Orestes painter, Hephaistos painter, Duomo painter, painter of Oxford 529, painter of London E 488. (2) Io painter. (3) Painter of Athens 1183 and Academy painter carry on into the last quarter of the fifth century.

(*g*) *ARV*² 1303.

The Penthesilea workshop continues. The skyphoi of the painter of Athens 17278 may be belated work of the painter of Brussels R 330.

VIII LATE FIFTH CENTURY. 425–400 B.C.

(*a*) *ARV*² 1346–7.

The Kadmos and Pothos painters are continued by the Kekrops and Kiev painters.

(*b*) *ARV*² 1550; 1312–32; 1391–9, 1360, 1351; 1400–1; J. R. Green, *BSA* 66 (1971), 189.

The Meidias painter is tied to the Eretria painter by the choes mentioned above, and class W head-vases link sub-Meidian painters and the Nikias painter back to the Brygos–Syriskos workshop. The Meidias painter and his circle are considerable, including the Meidias painter himself (with potter Meidias), the painter of the Carlsruhe Paris, the painter of the Frankfurt Acorn (with the younger Phintias as potter), the painter of the Athens Wedding, Aristophanes (with potter Erginos) and several others. To these must be added the sub-Meidian cup-group, the pyxides of the painter of Athens 1585, the oinochoai of the painter of Ferrara T 264, and on the evidence of the cups with impressed designs the painters of Ruvo 325 and 1346.

(c)   *ARV²* 1333–40, 1334.

Nikias may, of course, be a stray painter when he decorates class W. His larger vases go rather with the Talos painter, the Pronomos painter and the Suessula painter, but as far as I know no workshop connection has been established.

(d)   *ARV²* 1371–6.

The Woman painter, with the Revelstoke group, the painter of London D 72 and the group of Athens 1810, continues the white lekythoi of the Bird group.

(e)   *ARV²* 1376–83; 1243.

The Reed painter, group R, and the group of the huge lekythoi are interconnected groups of white lekythoi. In the classical period the painter of Berlin 2464 has the same maeander as the Reed painter but it is not clear where his affinities are.

What conclusions can be drawn so far? First, that the normal workshop probably employs something between 10 and 20 potters and painters on fine pottery. Secondly, that the successful potter can make on occasion dedications of the same order as the athletic victor, the successful businessman or the successful official, and belongs therefore to the same social milieu. Thirdly, that all boundaries are fluid. Potter was often painter and painter potter, but we can only be certain of this when we have signatures. On the whole shops seem to have had a steady membership of potters and painters, but there were roving painters, and special arrangements were made for rush orders; painters could be called in from outside and pots could be bought from neighbouring shops for the home painters to decorate. But the existence of rush orders immediately leads to the question of patrons.

2

Special Commissions

We have already noticed a number of vases and plaques which were
dedicated by potters and painters.[1] These were surely specially made for
this purpose. We can add a small number of vases made for other special
purposes of the painter or potter. Beazley[2] quotes four cases from the
Pioneer group (of about 515 B.C.). (1) On a signed stamnos (Brussels
A 717, CV pls. 12–13) Smikros paints a symposion with himself,
Pheidiades and another young man, pairing with Helike, Choro and
Rhode. On the other side a man and youth are filling a mixing-bowl
and the names Antias and Eualkides, both with *kalos*, apply to them.
This was clearly painted for a special party and prompts the question,
did he paint a whole set of drinking vessels for this party? More recently
a fragmentary kalyx-krater by Euphronios[3] has come to light with a
similar symposion, comprising Theodemos, Melas, Suko (flautist),
Smikros and Ekphantides. On the back boys fetch more wine from a
mixing-bowl, as on the stamnos; over the mixing-bowl is Leagros
kalos, which rather suggests that he ordered the vase (see below, p. 49).
(2) On the shoulder of a hydria from Vulci (Munich 2421, CV pl. 223)
Phintias paints two women drinking, one of whom toasts Euthymides.[4]
On the body Euthymides sits with his lyre, ready to accompany the
singing of the boy Tlempolemos, who is being instructed by the
bearded Smikythos and watched by the bearded Demetrios. Again this
is a special vase painted for a colleague to give to a girlfriend or for use

[1] Cf. above, p. 4.
[2] PP 19. ARV² 20/1 (no provenance); 23/7; 33/8 (no provenance); 26/1.
[3] ARV² 1619/3 bis; 1705; Munich 8935; E. T. Vermeule, A.K. 8 (1965), 34. Ekphantides
sings a hymn to Apollo.
[4] The same formula is used by the hetaira Smikra to toast Leagros on Euphronios' psykter
(ARV² 16/15) found in Cervetri.

at a special party, and it can only have come to Etruria by the second-hand market. It raises a question which must be discussed later, whether other school vases were special commissions. Further, Tlempolemos is known as a maker of lip-cups soon after 550 B.C., and it is tempting to suppose that this boy is a young relation. (3) On another hydria (Louvre G 41, *CV* pl. 51) by a contemporary a greeting to Euthymides and a greeting to Sostratos are added, an expression of goodwill, which implies a special vase perhaps for a joint party; the inscription is on the shoulder, which has a chariot and warriors making ready; the body has Dionysos and Ariadne, Poseidon and Amphitrite, and Hermes. Was one of them going on a sea voyage? and the party a *propemptikon*? (4) A signed amphora by Euthymides (Munich 2307, *CV* pls. 165–8) with the departure of Hektor has written on it before firing: 'as never Euphronios'. This good-humoured boast would not have been written unless Euthymides knew the purchaser. The revellers on the back, Komarchos, Teles and Heledemos, presumably joined the party. Later the vase found its way to Vulci.

Further instances can be added where potters greet their friends as *kalos* and their girlfriends as *kale* (the word simply signifies approval and is used of mythological heroes, boys, girls and adults, and even things).[1] The boy Tlempolemos is greeted as *kalos* on two cups contemporary with the Phintias hydria; on one of them he may be himself represented as a dancer, with Hipparchos as a dancer on the other side of the cup;[2] on the second cup[3] 'Tlempolemos *kalos*' is written over a panther. It is simply an indication that the cup has been made for him; it was found in Orvieto and presumably reached there by the second-hand market. A cup made by the Ambrosios painter in the late sixth century has 'Tleson *kalos*' written beside a naked boy at a laver, and this may well be the Tleson who made a cup for Oltos.[4] An alabastron[5] of the early fifth century has on the mouth 'Aphrodisia *kale*', on one side a woman with 'Aphrodisia *kale*. So she seems to Eucheiros' and on the other side a woman with 'Erosanthe O *kale*'. This Eucheiros is probably a younger relative of Eucheiros son of Ergotimos and made

[1] A recent sensible discussion by K. Schauenburg in *Gymnasium* 76 (1969), 42.
[2] *ARV*[2] 1625/52 bis (no provenance).　　[3] *ARV*[2] 1699, Orvieto.
[4] *ARV*[2] 174/24 (no provenance), Brussels R 349, *CV* pl. 4, 2. Cf. above, pp. 10, 26; Langlotz, *Zeitbestimmung* (Leipzig), 47.
[5] *ARV*[2] 306 (no provenance), London E 718.

and/or painted the alabastron. A similar formula appears much earlier on a black-figure hydria[1] with Herakles and Triton: 'Andokides seems *kalos* to Timagoras'. As the potter Andokides was contemporary with Timagoras, there seems no reason to doubt the identification or that the hydria was a present from one potter to another. Immerwahr[2] has suggested that the formula with the ellipse of 'seems' is used the same way on two skyphoi by the Pantoxena painter: 'Pantoxena *kala* to Korinthos'. One has Eos and Tithonos, the other the death of Orpheus. One comes from Vulci, the other from the Peiraeus; but they seem to be a pair made by the vase-painter for his lady-friend. It would be interesting to know why he chose these subjects.

A bell-krater by the Nikias painter, found in Greece, is exceptionally signed by the potter with his father's name and his deme: 'Nikias, son of Hermokles, of Anaphlystos'. Whether Nikias was also the painter we cannot say, but it is a possibility. The picture has two young torchracers on either side of a central group; in the centre Nike crowns the tribal hero Antiochos (the name inscribed on his headband) by an altar, behind which stands an old wreathed man, probably rightly interpreted as Prometheus. The tribe Antiochis, to which Nikias' deme belonged, had evidently won a torch-race at the Prometheia, and the bell-krater was painted for the celebrations. The exceptional signature with patronymic and deme perhaps means that Nikias was himself a member of the winning team or in some way connected with its organization.

Others, besides potters and painters, ordered special vases for dedication. An early instance (second quarter of the sixth century) is a fragmentary cup[4] by the C painter found in Boeotia with a dedication to Apollo painted before firing. Such dedications are naturally found on the Acropolis at Athens. A few examples may be quoted:[5] a red-figure cup, which bears some relation to Epiktetos, with an owl and olivebranch inside and a combat outside and the word 'dedicated' in red, a cup with Athena giving Herakles wine on the inside and an inscription

---

[1] *ABV* 174/7 (no provenance), Louvre F 38, *CV* pl. 63, 1–4.
[2] *ARV²* 1050/1–2; Immerwahr, *James Sprunt Studies* 46 (1964), 21.
[3] *ARV²* 1333/1, London 98.7–16.6. R. Hampe and K. Reinhardt, *Hermes* 85, 125.
[4] *ABV* 51/2, Boston 03.852. Contrast the *incised* dedication to Hera on a lekythos with a picture of Dionysos (*ABL* 199/1).
[5] Graef–Langlotz II, 75 (=*ARV²* 80); 351; 247.

in white, 'I am sacred to Dionysos', and a curious cup with a gilded figure of Artemis in relief and the word 'dedicated' painted on before firing. One more example, a fragmentary cup made by Euphronios and painted in the manner of Onesimos,[1] has not (or has no longer) a dedication, but subject and painted inscriptions show that this was a specially commissioned dedication: inside, Athena with a phiale; outside, A. seated man with a phiale, saying 'Saviour Zeus', B. hand with a kantharos and the words 'I pour a libation to the good daimon'.

Others also, besides potters and painters, gave special vases as presents. A dinos[2] (large mixing-bowl) with a decoration of ships has two inscriptions on the rim: 'Exekias made me' in Attic letters and 'Epainetos gave me to Charops' in Sikyonian letters. The inscriptions were incised after the vase was made, but they are both in the hand of Exekias, as known from his painted inscriptions. Epainetos must have been a Sikyonian who visited Athens; whether Charops was in Athens or not and whether Epainetos presented him with a complete set of symposion vases we do not know. The vase was found in Cervetri. Douris,[3] as we have said, signed an aryballos as potter. He also painted it with two Erotes pursuing a boy, and he added another inscription before firing: 'the lekythos belongs to Asopodoros'. This was evidently a present specially ordered for Asopodoros by a friend, and as it was found in a tomb in Athens, he presumably kept it.

Many of the vases with *kalos* inscriptions are probably special presents, but in some cases it is easier to suppose that the *kalos* name is the name of the purchaser: from our point of view this makes no difference since the *kalos* name was put on before firing. We shall have to return to this problem again and again; here I give a few obvious instances. The lovely cup[4] by Douris with Eos lifting her dead son Memnon has a painted inscription which Beazley has interpreted as 'Hermogenes is *kalos* if he counts me in'. This, then, is a present with a request attached; Hermogenes evidently did not keep it, as it was found in Capua. The hydria[5] with a picture of boys washing at a fountain-house which gave the Antimenes painter his name has '*kalos* Antimenes'

[1] Graef–Langlotz II, 434 = *ARV*[2] 330/5, 1646.
[2] *ABV* 146/20, Villa Giulia 50599.
[3] *ARV*[2] 447/274, Athens 15375.
[4] *ARV*[2] 434/74; *AJA* 64 (1960), 219; Louvre G 115, *Enc. Phot.* iii, 13–15.
[5] *ABV* 267/1, Leyden 1428; *JHS* 47 (1927), 63, pl. 11, from Vulci.

painted in the right section of the fountain-house and outside the left-hand column *Philon se*, which Beazley interprets as 'Philon will . . . you'. This would then be a present with a declaration rather like the Douris cup. A black-figure oinochoe[1] of about 520 B.C. has a conversation worked into the floral ornament: 'Nikolas is *kalos*. Dorotheos seems *kalos* to me too. Yes, and the other boy is *kalos*, Memnon. I too have a *kalos* friend.' Dorotheos and Memnon are known from many other vases. It sounds as if two friends had combined to have a jug made for a party with the three who are named. An alabastron[2] of the second quarter of the fifth century has a picture of mistress, maid and youth with the inscriptions: 'Timodemos *kalos*. The bride is *kale*.' This would seem to be a wedding present from Timodemos; one can guess that his friend is getting married but he does not know the lady's name. This is getting near to saying that 'Timodemos *kalos*' primarily gives the purchaser's name.

This seems to be the case in the many white lekythoi which have *kalos* names. White lekythoi are given as offerings to the dead. The Achilles painter's many white lekythoi[3] with pictures of women would naturally be regarded as offerings to dead women, and one would therefore suppose that, for example, 'Axiopeithes *kalos*, son of Alkimachos' painted on such a lekythos means that he ordered it and offered it at the dead woman's tomb. When they had been placed on the steps of the tomb (as we see them in pictures of tombs), they were presumably cleared away periodically, and so could reach Gela, Suessula, Cyprus and the Troad by the second-hand market.[4]

When the picture on a vase represents a unique event in the history of Athens the vase must have been ordered by a participant to celebrate the event. The Pronomos vase[5] is a volute-krater found in Ruvo with A. Dionysos and the cast of a satyr-play, and B. Dionysos and Ariadne with satyrs and maenads. On A. the flute-player is Pronomos, the poet Demetrios and the lyre-player Charinos, and all the satyr-chorus (but not the actors) are named. It will be remembered that according to Plato (*Symp.* 173a) after his victory at the Dionysia the tragic poet

---

[1] *ABV* 425, Munich 2447. Perhaps cf. *ARV*[2] 89/20, 'Philokomos is loved'.
[2] *ARV*[2] 1610 (no provenance), Cab. Med. 508.   [3] *ARV*[2] 995 ff.
[4] The reverse case is given *ARV*[2] 1687, eleven white lekythoi in a single sarcophagus at Anavysos, Attica.
[5] *ARV*[2] 1336/1; Webster, *MTS*[2] 47, AV 25; Naples 3240.

Agathon had a party with his choreutai (the actors are not mentioned).
The Pronomos vase must have been painted for a party celebrating a
victory with a satyr-play by Demetrios, assisted by the famous Theban
flute-player Pronomos. And it is a reasonable guess that more special
crockery was needed for a party of at least twelve than a single mixing-
bowl.

Sophocles' *Andromeda* inspired five vase-pictures,[1] which certainly
belong to a single decade and may be more nearly contemporary: a
white-ground kalyx-krater by the Phiale painter, a kalyx-krater by the
Kleophon painter, a bell-krater from the circle of Polygnotos, a hydria
which connects in pattern work with Polygnotan vases and a pelike
which connects in pattern work with the Niobid painter. Common to
all of them and unique is the representation of Andromeda in Eastern
dress being fastened to posts. The white-ground kalyx-krater comes
from Agrigento, the bell-krater from Vassallaggi (also in Sicily), the
hydria from Vulci. Against the head of Perseus on the white-ground
kalyx-krater in Agrigento the painter has written 'Euaion *kalos*, son of
Aeschylus'. Euaion is called in the Souda lexikon *tragikos*, which may
mean either poet or actor. As we have no trace of him as a poet, he may
have acted in Sophocles' play. It is possible that we have five scenes
painted for a party in celebration of a production of Sophocles' play.

Euaion's name occurs again on a hydria by the Phiale painter from
Vulci in the Vatican, which shows Sophocles' *Thamyras*; here 'Euaion
kalos' is written against Argiope, Thamyras' mother, and Euaion may
have played that part, as we know that Sophocles played Thamyras.
The Phiale painter painted another hydria with the same scene, which
was found at Nola. A third contemporary hydria (Oxford 530) from
the group of Polygnotos (undetermined) has a later stage of the play,
Thamyras blinded, and was found in Greece. Again we have three vases
celebrating a single production.[2]

Euaion's name without *kalos* is attached to Aktaion on a bell-krater
by the Lykaon painter found in Vico Equense.[3] The version of the
Aktaion story is inspired by Aeschylus' *Toxotides*, and Euaion must have

[1] *ARV*² 1017/53; 1684; 1062; *MTS*² AV 53–6, and p. 147; Webster, *Introduction to
Sophocles*, 2nd ed. (London, 1969), 203 ff.
[2] *ARV*² 1020/92, 93; 1061/152 *MTS*² AV 58–9, and p. 152.
[3] *ARV*² 1045/7, Boston 00.346, here pl. 2; 1046/11, Oxford 289, *CV* pl. 66. Cf. *MTS*²
145 f.

played in a revival of this play. The Lykaon painter painted the same scene again on a kalyx-krater found in Gela.

In each of these cases one of the vases can be tied to a particular name, Euaion, but there are many other theatrical vases without *kalos* names which must nevertheless have been special commissions. It is possible that what we have may be vases painted for the symposia of the thiasos which Sophocles founded in honour of the Muses. Both the white-ground kalyx-krater with Andromeda and the Phiale painter's white-ground kalyx-krater from Vulci[1] in the Vatican with a picture of Sophocles' *Dionysiskos* have Muses on the back, and this may be an allusion to Sophocles' thiasos. On the other hand, a bell-krater from Sorrento by the Lykaon painter with a symposion in which Euainetos, Kallias and another take part, while Euaion plays the flute for a girl dancing the pyrrhic, must have been made for a private party.[2]

A performance of dithyramb is illustrated on a bell-krater (Copenhagen 13817) by the Kleophon painter,[3] perhaps as Friis-Johansen has suggested, dithyramb at the Anthesteria rather than at the City Dionysia. The performers are named: the poet Phrynichos (probably the poet of Old Comedy), the flautist Amphilochos and singers Theomedes, Chremes, Pleistias and Epinikos. Friis-Johansen notes the possibility that this Pleistias was sent as ambassador to Perdikkas in 426/5 B.C. and that this Theomedes appears in an Athenian casualty list of about 413 B.C.: 'Presumably the vase-painter by such allusions to people who were known to all wanted to give his works a realism which would attract the Athenian public.' This is surely much less likely than that the vase was specially ordered by Phrynichos or his choregos for the party which celebrated the performance of the dithyramb.

Another tribal victory (or two victories) is recorded by two contemporary but badly preserved vases, a skyphos from the Acropolis at Athens and a neck-amphora from Nola.[4] In both the victorious tribe is Akamantis, and the prize is a tripod, which suggests dithyramb. On the

---

[1] *ARV*[2] 1017/54; *MTS*[2] AV 57 and p. 148.

[2] *ARV*[2] 1045/9, Naples Stg. 281; *BCH* 92 (1968), 600, fig. 53. See *ARV*[2] 1579 for six other vases with Euaion *kalos*.

[3] *ARV*[2] 1145/35; K. Friis-Johansen, *Med. Dan. Vid. Selsk.* 4, 2 (1959). Polion's bell-krater (*ARV*[2] 1172/8) with men dressed as old satyrs has the unique inscription, 'Singers at the Panathenaia', but does not give their names. Cf. my *Greek Chorus* (London, 1970), 28, 133 and fig. 9.

[4] *ARV*[2] 1581/20, Acropolis 504 and London E 298. On Glaukon *kalos*, cf. above, p. 22.

3 Oligarchs' sacrifice. Bell-krater, Manner of Kleophon painter.
Boston 95.25. (See p. 50)

4 (a) Archenautes' sacrifice. Stamnos, Polygnotos. London E 455.
(See pp. 50 f.)

4 (b) Diomedes' sacrifice. Stamnos, group of Polygnotos. London E 456.
(See pp. 50 f.)

amphora the victory inscription is on the top step of the base supporting the tripod, and the bottom step carries the inscription 'Glaukon *kalos*'. It seems a reasonable conjecture that he was the choregos. On other early classical vases he is identified as Glaukon, son of Leagros, who was later, in 433/2 B.C., strategos. The skyphos was not necessarily made for the same party as the neck-amphora, and too little of it remains to give a *kalos* name if there was one. It does, however, attest the practice of having special cups in which to celebrate a tribal victory, as well as larger vases.[1]

A pelike[2] by the Epimedes painter found in Bulgaria has a unique picture of a man singing to the kithara surrounded by four winged victories (Nikai); one of them has a wreath with which to crown him and one of them a phiale with which to pour a libation. They are labelled 'Victory at the Panathenaia', 'Victory at Nemea', 'At Marathon', 'At the Isthmos'. The platform on which he stands is labelled 'Alkimachos *kalos*'. Alkimachos was therefore a young concert-singer who won four victories at different festivals, and this wine-jar was made for a symposion celebrating it. Afterwards it went on the second-hand market. Alkimachos also appears as a youth in a symposion by the Lykaon painter, which was found in Campania, and a number of vases have 'Alkimachos *kalos*'.[3]

Two other vases have named instrumentalists. On the back of Euphronios' kalyx-krater[4] with Herakles and Antaios a young man named Polykles mounts the platform to play the double-flute: Leagros, Melas and Kephisodoros sit in the audience. It is a natural guess that the subject of the song which he interspersed with flute accompaniment was Herakles' struggle with Antaios. Leagros was the father of Glaukon and himself fell in battle as strategos in 465 B.C. Melas appears again on Euphronios' kalyx-krater in the company of Smikros at the symposion (see above); that vase has 'Leagros *kalos*' on the back, so that Leagros presumably ordered it for the party. The concert vase was found at

---

[1] Graef–Langlotz I, no. 816, pl. 49, is also suggested, but only 'conquered' remains of the inscription.

[2] *ARV*[2] 1044/9.

[3] *ARV*[2] 1045/8. Vases with 'Alkimachos *kalos*', *ARV*[2] 1562.

[4] *ARV* 14/2, Louvre G 103, *Enc. Phot.* iii, 4–5; *CV* pls. 4–5. Beazley takes the 'Melas *kalos*' written on the platform to be the flautist; the difficulty is that the inscription Polykles runs from the head of the flautist and would naturally apply to him.

Cervetri. The other named concert performer is a kithara-singer labelled 'Nikomas *kalos*' on a bell-krater[1] by Polygnotos. He sings before an old man with a stick, a seated man and a youth. Beazley takes the name to be Nikomachos with two letters omitted. Nikomachos[2] is written against a young man in a symposion on a stamnos from Falerii also by Polygnotos. As noted above for Euaion and Alkimachos, we have besides vases which celebrated a victory a special symposion vase on which the victor is named, whether it was painted for the victory symposion or for another occasion.

Four vases show sacrifices in which the participants are named. A bell-krater[3] in the manner of the Kleophon painter from Capua illustrates the sacrifice of a young ram, which is held by Mantitheos, while Kallias plays the flute, a bearded man whose name has been lost stands by the altar, Hippokles holds a tray, Aresias watches. Beazley has identified Aresias as one of the Thirty, Kallias as one of those prosecuted for mutilating the herms and Hippokles as one of the Ten – a nest of very conservative Athenians who might well have celebrated a sacrifice together[4] in the early days of the Peloponnesian War. Kallias is the only one who appears again on vases: we have seen him already in the symposion with Euaion, and he watches girls dancing the pyrrhic on a hydria of the group of Polygnotos.

A tomb in Cervetri yielded two stamnoi,[5] one by Polygnotos and the other near him, with extremely similar pictures of sacrifices. They must have been painted to hold wine at the same celebration in Athens. They differ in the names and in one detail. The bearded man sacrificing on Polygnotos' stamnos is Archenautes (a good Athenian name but no identification is possible), Nikodemos is the boy next to the altar and the other boy is simply *kalos*, and the flute-player is Sosibios; on the other the bearded man alone is named, and he is Diomedes, perhaps the

---

[1] *ARV*² 1029/20 (provenance unknown), New York 21.88.73; G. Richter, *Handbook of Greek Art* (New York, 1930), 240 g.

[2] *ARV*² 1028/15, Villa Giulia 3584, *CV* pl. 11. Philippaki 122 seems to date this 450–440 B.C.

[3] *ARV*² 1149/9, Boston 95.25, here, pl. 3. Other Kallias vases, *ARV*² 1588. Only the Euaion vase has a provenance, Sorrento. But the hydria in Florence and the pelike in Naples are likely to have been found in Italy.

[4] Perhaps to the Pythian Apollo, if *ARV*² 1159, iii, Boston 95.24, was painted for the same occasion (also found in Capua). Then *ARV*² 1143, i, and a bell-krater in Agrigento (*Arch. Class.* 20 (1968), 238), may have belonged to the same set.

[5] *ARV*² 1028/9; 1051/17, London E 455–6, *CV* pls. 24/2 and 3. Here, pl. 4 (*a*) and (*b*).

Diomedes[1] who fell foul of Alkibiades over his share in a chariot-victory at Olympia. The Nike descending over Archenautes' altar holds a scroll, but the Nike over Diomedes' altar holds an oinochoe. Nike with scroll means that Archenautes has won a competition with a piece of literature, probably a song. Since the vases are clearly twins, it was probably a choral song and Diomedes was the choregos of the chorus for which Archenautes wrote. (A third stamnos (ARV^2 1028/10), also from Cervetri, should belong: Diomedes sacrifices to Apollo, who holds a lyre; the Nike is labelled '[Pyth]ia'.)

The fourth vase[2] is a loutrophoros from the Acropolis at Athens. Men holding myrtle boughs are taking a large pig to sacrifice. One would like to know the occasion, perhaps something to do with the Mysteries: the loutrophoros is a marriage-vase and suitable to a goddess like Demeter. But whatever the occasion, this was a special vase made in the late sixth century, by a painter related to Phintias, perhaps Myson at the beginning of his career. The men are named: Lykos, Olympiodoros *kalos* and Proxenides. All of them are known from contemporary vases. This vase is included here because of its subject-matter, but it is not a vase made for a symposion like the other three; it is more likely that it was dedicated to the goddess after the sacrifice of the pig.

Finally from the Athenian Agora came a late fifth-century amphora[3] of Panathenaic shape with a unique scene. The vase is badly damaged: what is preserved gives on one side three wreathed youths moving past an olive-tree; they carry light trays, one has a name beginning Chrys- and one is called Kopreus; on the other side three more wreathed youths moving in the same direction, the third, who is called Eupompos, has a Panathenaic amphora on his shoulder. Professor Corbett has suggested that the occasion depicted might be the transfer by the Athlothetai of the Panathenaic prize amphorai from the Acropolis where the prize oil was stored to the place where the prizes were awarded. This is extremely attractive; in any case the shape of the vase itself, the shape of the vase carried and the olive-tree suggest that this

---

[1] Kirchner, *Prosopographia Attica*, no. 4070. He appears on a chariot with Athena on a fragment by the Achilles painter, ARV^2 992/64.

[2] ARV^2 25/1, 237, 1596; ABV 673; Graef–Langlotz II, no. 636. Compare for the subject the loutrophoros from Eleusis by the Swing painter, ABV 309/97.

[3] P. E. Corbett, *Hesperia* 18 (1949), 306; Agora P 10, 554. Cf. also ABV 369/119, Acr. 842, and below, p. 129.

was a Panathenaic occasion, and the vase must have been specially painted to celebrate the performance of this service by this group of men. The vase was found in a well which seems to have been used as a dump after some major disaster involving more than one household.[1] It was therefore not a dedication but presumably preserved by one of the drinkers after a symposion which celebrated the Panathenaic occasion.

We have looked at twenty-three vases which were specially painted for a unique Athenian occasion: two of them, the Akamantis skyphos and the loutrophoros with the pig were dedicated on the Acropolis; the Panathenaic amphora was apparently preserved by its owner. The hydria with the blinded Thamyras was found in Greece and nothing more can be said. Four have no provenance. The other fifteen were found far away in Bulgaria, Sicily, Apulia, Campania or Etruria. This does show that it was common, after having a special vase painted for a special occasion, to use it for that occasion and then dispose of it. One other point may be made here: in the case of the Andromeda vases, the Thamyras vases, the Aktaion vases and the sacrifice vases of Arche-nautes and Diomedes (and perhaps of Kallias) more than one vase from a special order has survived, so that we should probably reckon with a complete set of vases made and painted for each special occasion.

The vases which we have looked at represented a unique occasion and named at least one of the actors in it. But we included also a few pictures where it was only the names that transformed a scene commonly represented into a special occasion: the two symposion vases with Smikros, the symposion vases with Alkimachos, Euaion, Kallias, Nikomachos, the athlete vase with Kallias. Here we probably cannot hope to say – except perhaps in the case of the symposia with the vase-painter Smikros – whether the vase was specially commissioned or whether the symposion or athlete scene was already being painted when the purchaser came in and told the painter to name the figures after his friends. There are a number of such vases particularly in the ripe archaic period and sometimes the figures are known historical characters. If some of these were already nearing completion, at least they were at that late moment converted into bespoke pieces.

Already about 560 B.C. Ergotimos[2] made a cup with two men danc-

---

[1] It contained 23 red-figure vases, 58 black-glaze vases, 11 lamps and a large amount of coarse pottery.   [2] *ABV* 79, Berlin 3151, Greifenhagen, *Führer* (Berlin, 1968), pl. 48.

ing to a flute-player after a symposion: the men are called Charidemos and Nikaulos and the flute-player is called Empedokrates. This cup was found in Aegina. About 550–540 B.C. an oinochoe[1] by the Taleides painter found in Vulci has a man playing the flute to a fat, ivy-crowned man who sits holding a skyphos inscribed 'Kallias *ka[los]*'. He says 'Hail, and drink well'. The name Dionysios runs down below the skyphos. 'Neokleides *kalos*' runs down the right side. It is impossible to unravel these names, but certainly a compliment was intended to Kallias and Neokleides, and one of the two men was called Dionysios.

A typical symposion vase with names of the early fifth century is a cup[2] by the Brygos painter which was found in Vulci. Inside, a boy reclining on a couch, with a table carrying a skyphos beside him, holds a flute while he watches a girl dancing; he is named Philippos, she Kallisto. Outside, there are two couches on each side, one with a bearded man and one with a boy; on each side the man on the left-hand couch is more interested in the woman by or on the other couch than the woman seated at the foot of his own couch. On each side one woman plays the flutes. The woman standing with the lyre on one side corresponds to the standing boy holding ladle and strainer on the other. The names outside are Philon *kalos* on one side, Diphilos *kalos* and Nikophile *kale* on the other. Beazley calls all three '*tag*-kalos': they are not *kalos* names, but names of the figures depicted, to which *kalos* has been attached. So we have a symposion cup with two named figures inside, and ten figures outside of which three are named. We can suppose that the five decided to have a symposion and one of them ordered cups from the Brygos painter before the rest of the party was decided.

Two living lyric poets are represented on vases. Of the first, Kydias, we know practically nothing.[3] He appears on two vases[4] of about 510 B.C. in the komos which follows the symposion; both of them were found at Vulci; on the Dikaios painter's psykter he is bald and plays the lyre; on the Ambrosios painter's cup (which has Hermes inside and outside a komos on both sides) he is a young flautist, who moves between

---

[1] *ABV* 176/2, Berlin 31131.
[2] *ARV²* 371/24. A. Cambitoglou, *Brygos Painter* (Sydney, 1968), 10, pl. II, 1, 3 and 4.
[3] See A. W. Pickard-Cambridge, *Dithyramb Tragedy and Comedy*, 2nd rev. ed. (Oxford, 1962), 30; *PMG* 714–15.
[4] *ARV²* 31/6; 173/2.

a young castanet-player Mantitheos, a bearded lyre-player Eteokles, young Kallias and another youth unnamed. One of these painters did not know what Kydias looked like. The Ambrosios painter knew more names, and the same Kallias appears on another of his cups.[1] They were presumably both bespoke vases, but the instructions to one painter were inadequate.

The other poet is Anakreon, who, according to Dr Barron,[2] came to Athens at the age of fifty in 522 B.C. and died in Athens about 487 B.C. He is represented (with his name inscribed) on three vases, a cup by Oltos, 520–510 B.C., a red-figure lekythos by the Gales painter and a kalyx-krater by the Kleophrades painter, both a little before 500.[3] The Oltos cup, which was found at Vulci, has inside a woman tying her sandal and the inscription 'Memnon *kalos*', on the outside one side has Herakles and the Amazons, and the other Anakreon holding a lyre and dressed in a himation, approachêd by a youth called Nymphes and a youth or man called '. . . on'. One would say that Memnon, or someone giving a present to Memnon, found Oltos painting a komos on one side of a cup and had him write in the proper names. On the lekythos by the Gales painter, which was found at Gela, Anakreon walks with his lyre leaning slightly backwards, between two boys one with a skyphos and the other with a stick. Anakreon wears a long chiton, himation, perhaps shoes and sakkos. This is Anakreon in maenad dress, and was presumably a special commission. So was the Anakreon on the Kleophrades painter's kalyx-krater, but nothing remains of him except his lyre, ivy-wreath round his neck, himation, long chiton and shoes; the man dancing next to him certainly wears a sakkos on his head and carries a parasol. There were two other figures, one of whom had a long chiton and sandals and a name ending in *s*. This then was Anakreon's maenad dance and certainly a special commission. All except one of the twenty-nine other vases with 'Anacreontes' were painted after Anakreon's death and had no inscriptions;[4] the maenad dances of Anakreon became a stock subject with the vase-painter; they were a suitable

---

[1] This Kallias may also be the Kallias 'toasted' by the Taleides painter (cf. above) and be 'Kallias *kalos*' on a small b.f. amphora (*ARV²* 1588). The Kallias who goes with Euaion (cf. above) is much younger; he also goes with a much younger Mantitheos.

[2] *CQ* 14 (1964), 221.

[3] *ARV²* 63/86; 36/2; 185/32, Copenhagen 13365, *CV* pl. 333. Caskey–Beazley II, 55 ff.; Immerwahr, *AJA* 69 (1965), 152; Webster, *Greek Chorus*, 19, 24, 83.

[4] For the whole list, cf. below, p. 110.

subject for the symposion, because Anakreon was still sung and his maenad dress was still remembered in the late fifth century, as Aristophanes shows.[1] The one exception among the uninscribed vases is the plate by Psiax,[2] which is contemporary with the Oltos cup, and can be claimed as a special commission although the dancer is not named.

The symposion on the other side of the Kleophrades painter's kalyx-krater is also unique. It is very fragmentary, but one drinker wore a long chiton of very fine material and a himation with a border stripe, and a second wore the feminine sakkos, so that this was clearly felt as the symposion which preceded the maenad dance, and one reveller sings words which Professor Immerwahr has identified as the beginning of a four-line poem in the Theognidean corpus (1129 ff.). The Kleophrades painter was not only told that Anakreon was coming to the symposion but also what song was going to be sung.

Finally, two other simpler instances of symposion vases. A fragmentary cup[3] by the Euaion painter of about 460 B.C. has the name Lakedaimonios written by the head of a boy reclining with another on a symposion couch. This is the ordinary stock scene with a special name added, but the name is interesting because this was in all probability Lakedaimonios the son of Kimon, who was hipparch probably about 450 B.C. and later, in 433–432 B.C., strategos. The fragments have no provenance, but the cup would seem to have been a treasured possession as it was mended in antiquity. Finally a lekythos of the shape used by the Carlsruhe painter[4] has a girl dancing the pyrrhic, which was a favourite entertainment at the symposion; above her is written 'Zephyria *kale*'. This was, then, a little bottle of perfume presented to the dancer, Zephyria.

Another favourite scene to which names could be added is the assembly of athletes. As with the symposia, the best examples come from the Pioneer group. Beazley has discussed a psykter[5] by Phintias which was found in Orvieto. It has one group of wrestlers and four of acontists. The wrestlers Eudemos and Sostratos have trainers Hegias

[1] *Thesm.* 161, fr. 223K.
[2] *ABV* 294/21, Meggen, Käppeli; G. M. A. Richter, *Attic Red-Figured Vases (ARVS)* (New Haven, 1946), fig. 36.
[3] *ARV*[2] 791/42; *Dedications* 147, no. 135.
[4] *ARV*[2] 677/11 (no provenance), Cape Town 18, Boardman and Pope, pl. 14.
[5] *ARV*[2] 24/11; Caskey–Beazley II, 3; Jüthner *SB* (Vienna, 1968), pl. 98, Boston 01.8019. Here, pl. 5(a).

and Epilykos. Sostratos recurs again (unless Phintias ran short of names) with Eukrates and Ptoiodoros to form one of the groups of acontists. The other groups of acontists are Philon and Etearchos being instructed by Simon, and Xenophon being instructed by Phayllos. The most interesting of these names are Sostratos and Phayllos. This is the same Sostratos who is greeted on the hydria with a greeting to Euthymides, which we said might have been painted for a party before one of them went on a sea-voyage.[1] He also appears as a discus-thrower on a black-figure vase,[2] and there he is paired with an acontist Xanthippos, perhaps the father of Perikles. Professor Raubitschek[3] has identified him with the Sostratos, son of Petalos, who dedicated a chariot group on the Acropolis in the early fifth century and therefore had presumably won a chariot-race at the Panathenaia. Beazley[4] notes three and perhaps four other contemporary pictures of Phayllos as a diskos-thrower and once using the strigil. The amphora by Euthymides (Munich 2308, *CV* pls. 169–71) has Thorykion arming on the other side, so that it may have been a special commission for a party before Thorykion went on military service, and the three athletes on the back may have been his friends, Phayllos, Orsimenes and Pentathlos (is Pentathlos a real name or a personification of the Pentathlon in which Phayllos was an expert?). Peleus and Thetis, Theseus and Klytos on two of the Phayllos vases may be mythological paradigms for wrestling; Artemis and Apollo on a third have no obvious relevance. (A kalyx-krater from Capua by Euphronios[5] includes a Polyllos with the athletes Leagros, Antiphon, Hipparchos, Hippomedon, Tranion, Hegesias, Lykos; Polyllos may perhaps be a miswriting for Phayllos.) Phayllos has been identified with Phayllos of Kroton, a pentathlete who commanded his own ship at Salamis in 480 B.C. He may have trained as an athlete in Athens which was famous for its trainers in the late sixth century. He was given a statue on the Acropolis shortly after 480.[6]

Three athlete vases have pictures of members of the Alkmaionid family. The Megakles who won a Pythian victory in 486 while he was ostracized may be the Megakles who is *kalos* on vases by Phintias and

---

[1] Cf. above, p. 43.   [2] *ABV* 674 (no provenance), Louvre.   [3] *Dedications* 196.
[4] *ARV²* 168, 26/2, 28/11, 15/8; all from Vulci except the last, which has no provenance.
[5] *ARV²* 13/1, Berlin 2180; A. Lane, *Greek Pottery* (London, 1947), pl. 68; Noble, *Techniques*, fig. 152.
[6] *Dedications* 80.

Euthymides and on a white-ground plaque related to Euthymides.[1] The name on the plaque was partly erased and Glaukytes substituted, which suggests that some misfortune, like ostracism, befell Megakles. The Phintias hydria[2] shows boys getting water at a fountain, presumably for washing in the palaistra (before they go to the symposion, shown on the shoulder?); Megakles is written by the boy furthest from the fountain and *kalos* by the boy next to the spout, so that it is not unreasonable to claim that the left-hand boy is Megakles. Megakles won his Pythian victory with a four-horse chariot in 486 B.C., and Pindar, who composed the seventh *Pythian* to be sung at Delphi in celebration, mentions the one Olympian victory in the family. This was the chariot victory won by Alkmeon in 592 B.C. Beazley[3] finds a picture of this on a black-figure neck-amphora of about 480 B.C. found in South Italy: a charioteer inscribed [A]lkm[e]on is in a four-horse chariot with Athena on the far side, raising her hand in greeting. The other side of the amphora has Dionysos between two satyrs, a suitable subject for a symposion vase. 'About 480 B.C.' does not exclude a date in 486 or the next year, and it is tempting to suppose that this was a one-time vase made for an Alkmaionid party in Athens celebrating Megakles' Pythian victory by depicting his ancestor. The point would be even more telling if the Alkmeon who was *kalos* about this time on vases by the Berlin painter and Brygos painter[4] was a young relative of Megakles, as he almost certainly must have been with that name. Megakles had a son, a young Megakles who won a chariot victory at Olympia in 436 B.C.; he appears as an athlete on a fragment of a bell-krater[5] belonging to the group of Polygnotos about 440 B.C., and about the same time a bell-krater[6] by the Orestes painter found in Cyprus has on one side a two-horse chariot with the inscription 'Megakles *kalos*'.

Alkimachos appears as an athlete on a cup from Cervetri of about 430 B.C. by the Eretria painter.[7] This is probably a younger Alkimachos than the successful kitharode of whom we have spoken above. He is

[1] *ARV*[2] 1598 = 24/9, 28/12, etc.

[2] *ARV*[2] 24/9, London E 159, *CV* pls. 70, 1; 72, 1.

[3] *ABV* 401/6, Munich 1517; *A.E.* (1953–4), 205.

[4] *ARV*[2] 1563.   [5] *ARV*[2] 1054/58 (no provenance).

[6] *ARV*[2] 1113/10. 'Megakles *kalos*' also on a komos by the Kleophon painter, *ARV*[2] 1144/7 (no provenance).

[7] *ARV*[2] 1254/80, Louvre G 457; *AJA* 52 (1948), 340, pl. 35b; Immerwahr, *Studies in Honor of B. L. Ullman* (Rome, 1964), 20.

presumably the Alkimachos *kalos* of the inscription on a cup[1] from Spina by the Kalliope painter, who was a companion of the Eretria painter; the two cups may even have been ordered for the same symposion and then found their way to Italy. The Kalliope painter's cup has youths and women outside, one of the youths has a lyre and inside Apollo seated with a lyre and a Muse. Inside his cup the Eretria painter has painted Linos seated, unrolling an inscribed papyrus roll; in front of him stands Mousaios holding tablets; it looks as if the schoolmaster is going to read from the book and the boy is going to take notes. Beazley has suggested that the inscription marks the book as moral instruction in hexameters and quotes a tradition that Linos was the father of Mousaios. So the inside of the cup is a mythological contrast to the young athletes outside, and the purpose of the giver must have been to suggest that they were or should be as proficient in literature as in athletics. If the recipient was Alkimachos, the Kalliope painter's cup suggests that he was also proficient in literature.

A similar combination of athletics and literature appears on a cup from Orvieto by the Akestorides painter.[2] Inside is an athlete with jumping weights and his trainer. Outside, A. a boy unrolling a roll, a boy with a lyre and a man looking on, B. a boy with a writing case between a man and a youth. This is a school. The roll is inscribed with the first half of a hexameter which Beazley interprets as 'So my proud spirit sped further'. Here again, although no names have survived, the purchaser must have given the vase-painter the text for the roll. The cup combines the two activities of the Greek school, training in poetry and music and training in athletics, and was presumably made for a party to celebrate a schoolboy's triumph.

The best-known school cup is by Douris and was found in Cervetri.[3] Again the inside shows athletics, an athlete taking off his sandals, and the outside the school for poetry and music. The inscribed roll, which is held by a bearded teacher while the boy stands before him, reads 'Muse help me, I begin to sing of broad-flowing Skamander' – probably the beginning of an epic which the boy will recite. 'Hippodamas *kalos*' is inscribed on both the school scenes so that the cup was presumably a

---

[1] *ARV²* 1259/1, Ferrara T 617.
[2] *ARV²* 781/4, Washington 136373; *AJA* 52 (1948), 338, pls. 35a, 36–8; Immerwahr, op. cit., 22.
[3] *ARV²* 431/48, Berlin 2285; *AJA* 52 (1948), 337; Immerwahr, op. cit., 18; *PMG* 938e.

present to him. His name appears on a number of other vases,[1] and he may have been the strategos who was killed in 459/458 B.C. A cup by Makron (Berlin 2291), found in Vulci, has a man and a boy inside: the boy is inscribed Hippodamas; the subjects on the outside, A. the judgement of Paris, B. Paris leading Helen away, have a possible connection with the inscribed roll of the school cup. A pyxis from the Acropolis (560) also by Makron with men and women, all named, also has Hippodamas without *kalos*. The other ten vases with his name all have *kalos*, and there is nothing distinctive about the cups, but the aryballos (Oxford 1929, 175), which was found in Athens, has a very rare picture of boys racing sail-chariots: 'Hippodamas *kalos*' is painted in relief lines on the lip. This, the school cup and probably the cup with the Trojan stories were special orders; the rest may have been ready for firing when the name was put on.

The only other vase with an inscribed roll and also a name is a kyathos from Vulci by Onesimos with 'Panaitios *kalos*'.[2] The boys listen attentively as a third reads from a roll. The inscribed roll lies on the top of a chest: Chironeia is the title, the Precepts of Cheiron to his pupil Achilles, which was ascribed to Hesiod. The painter has written *kale* on the chest to show that he approves of this reading-matter. But the five other inscribed rolls on vases without *kalos* names are surely not the whim of the vase-painter (when he produced this sort of scene by himself he put imitation letters rather than an actual text on the roll)[3] but the will of the patron who, no doubt, gave him the text suitable for some particular recipient. They are (*a*) fragmentary cup[4] by Onesimos from Naukratis, a boy holding a roll with the beginning of a lyric poem, while a man plays the double flute and another apparently takes down dictation on a tablet; (*b*) lekythos[5] by a follower of Douris, a boy holding a roll with the beginning of the shorter hymn to Hermes; (*c*) cup by the Akestorides painter, boy with a scroll entitled 'Herakles' companions';[6] (*d*) fragmentary cup by the Wedding painter,[7] man holding a book roll: only the end of the inscription, . . . *ios*, survives;

[1] *ARV*² 459/4; 471/336, 337; 471/196, 314, 318; 431/67, 78, 89, 226–7; 450/23.

[2] *ARV*² 329/134, Berlin 2322; *AJA* 52 (1948), 337; Immerwahr, op. cit., 21.

[3] Immerwahr, op. cit., nos. 9, 10, 11, 14, 15, 16, 17, 20, 23, 26, 27, 29, 30, 37 (*ARV*² 923/28, 1208/38, 611/36, 1199/25, 1212/4, 1287/1, 1190/21; 1171/1).

[4] *ARV*² 326/93, Oxford G 138; *PMG* 938c; Immerwahr, op. cit., 19.

[5] *ARV*² 452 (bottom), *AJA* 52 (1948), 336, pl. 34; Immerwahr, op. cit., no. 5 (no provenance). [6] *ARV*² 1670. [7] *ARV*² 923/24; Immerwahr, op. cit., no. 8 (no provenance).

(*e*) red-figure hydria from Vari in Attica belonging to the group of Polygnotos.[1] Sappho sits holding an inscribed roll with 'winged words' written on the rolled part and 'Gods, airy words I begin' written on the open part. On the left Nikopolis holds a hand over her head, ready to take down a wreath from the wall; Kallis stands before her with a lyre, and another, unnamed woman stands beyond.

This is in a different tradition from the other vases with inscribed rolls, which may all have been inspired by the Douris school cup. Sappho is represented as a successful poetess (that is the meaning of the wreath and the name Nikopolis) and Kallis is going to sing her poetry. Nikopolis (victorious over fellow citizens) sounds like an invented name. Kallis may also be an invented name for the beautiful lyre-player, but might, on the other hand, be the real name of the lyre-player, for whom the purchaser ordered the pot. Long before this hydria, which was made about 440–430 B.C., Sappho had appeared on Athenian vases which were given to women.[2] The kalathoid vase[3] from Agrigento by the Brygos painter was presumably ordered by the Damas *kalos* whose name appears on it. It is a wine-container but the shape is modelled on a woman's workbasket so that quite apart from its subject it is likely to have been a present to a woman; the subject, Alkaios, characterized by his lyre as a poet, approaching Sappho with lowered head and Sappho moving away from him, must have been inspired by the poem[4] in which Sappho quoted Alkaios as saying 'I want to say something but shame prevents me' and answered him that if he had any desire for good, shame would not have prevented him. In ordering this vase for his girl, Damas was surely making an apology for a too fervid approach as well as urging his suit.

If we accept that the vases with inscribed book-rolls were special commissions, then we should probably also accept that the vases with a text coming out of a speaker's or singer's mouth were special commissions. I have already quoted the kalyx-krater[5] by the Kleophrades painter which has Anakreon on one side and on the other a reveller

---

[1] *ARV*[2] 1060/145, Athens 1260; Immerwahr, op. cit., no. 18; *PMG* 938d.

[2] The Sappho painter's name hydria, Warsaw 142333, *ARV*[2] 300, was painted about 500 B.C. [3] *ARV*[2] 385/228, Munich 2416, Schofold, *Bildnisse* (Basle, n.d.), 55.

[4] 137L–P; *Lyra Graeca Selecta*, 243.

[5] *ARV*[2] 185/32. Cf. also *ARV*[2] 1567/12, cup from Orvieto with 'Athenodotos *kalos*' reveller sings 'to the Panionian feast' (*PMG* 938b); *ARV*[2] 110/9 from Athenian agora, as interpreted by Beazley. Cf. also *ARV*[2] 317/16; 872/26; 1619/3 bis (above, p. 54).

singing the beginning of a four-line poem from the Theognidean corpus. Another good example is the rhapsode reciting the beginning of an epic on a neck-amphora[1] by the Kleophrades painter from Vulci. Presumably this was ordered to celebrate a recitation of the poem (at which the flautist on the other side perhaps provided the accompaniment), and the painter was given the text. Both here and on the Anakreon krater one expects the reciter to recite and the singer to sing. More surprising perhaps is a black-figure pelike with a picture of an olive-oil merchant: on one side he is receiving a customer and on the other side he is measuring out the oil; on one side he says 'Would I were rich' and on the other 'Already, already, more than half is gone', which I take to be a reflection on life rather than on his oil-stock.[2] Both reflections are in verse, and I should like to think that the owner of the olive-yard himself ordered the vase as a present for someone who would be amused by its philosophy. (On the other hand I do not feel certain that 'Call me that you may drink', said by a boy carrying a pointed amphora on an early red-figure cup,[3] is necessarily the sign of a bespoke vase; it can only be forced into verse by giving an unnatural quantity to one vowel.)

To return, however, to the vases where the names of contemporary Athenians are added to a stock scene, before the vase is fired, presumably at the wish of the buyer. An early fifth-century stamnos[4] has on one side a young warrior inscribed Menandros; a woman pours from a jug into his phiale and says 'Let my libation be good'. The boy is going to war and the vase was painted or at least inscribed for his final party. On the other side is a mythical parallel for a good libation, a satyr pouring a libation for Dionysos.

Women going to the fountain to draw water are an obvious picture for hydriai and are a feminine parallel to the athlete scenes. Sometimes the women are named: Simylis, Eperate, Kyane, Euene and Choronike are drawing water on a black-figure hydria[5] in the manner of the

---

[1] *ARV*² 183/15, London E 270, *CV* pl. 8, 2. Here, pl. 5(b).
[2] Vatican 413. Albizzati, pl. 61; D. von Bothmer, *JHS* 71 (1951), 42, no. 41; *PMG* 938 f.
[3] *AJA* 45 (1941), 593; Compiègne 1106; from Vulci; *PMG* 938a. The conversation about the first swallow on *ARV*² 1594/48 may also be attributed to the vase-painter, who at the last moment named one of the wrestlers on the other side Leagros.
[4] *ARV*² 246/8, Louvre G 54 bis, from Nola. Philippaki 95.
[5] *ABV* 261/41; London B 331, *CV* pl. 88/3. Two neck-amphorai with 'Hippokrates *kalos*' (*ABV* 321/9; *ARV*² 6/1) have similar subjects on both sides: A. chariot of Herakles, B. Dionysos.

Lysippides painter, which was found at Vulci. In the field above the women is written 'Hippokrates *kalos*'; this Hippokrates may have been the brother of Kleisthenes and the father of the Megakles who was ostracized in 486 B.C. (see above, p. 56). The hydria may have been bought by him or have been a present to him, and perhaps these were the names of the girls who danced and played at his parties. A similar but rarer scene is a picture of women picking fruit in an orchard, again a black-figure hydria by the A.D. painter found in Vulci;[1] the women are Philto, Rhode, Simyle, Tynnis, Korinno *kale* and two others unnamed (the *kale* may rather refer to one of the unnamed women than to Korinno). Here we have no indication of purchaser or recipient (unless it was Korinno); again the women were probably known at the symposion, and these painted hydriai were made for the symposion and then found their way to Etruria.

To sum up this section, again the vast preponderance of vases were found far from Attica: against five in Attica and one in Aegina, one was found in Cyprus, one in Naukratis, twenty-one in Etruria, four in the rest of Italy, two in Sicily (nine have no known provenance). Thus the evidence is again that these bespoke vases were put on the second-hand market after use at the party for which they were bespoke. Many of them were bespoke only in the sense that inscriptions were put on scenes which were part of the vase-painter's stock-in-trade, but the line here is impossible to draw; the fact that one can in fact trace Leagros growing older on the Leagros vases suggests that in some cases at least it wasn't a case of adding names or a longer inscription to a vase already painted and ready for firing but of painting a stock scene adapted to the particular customer. In some cases also a new bespoke picture may have set a fashion so that the scene became stock: it is tempting to think that the Kleophrades painter's Anakreon, Douris' school cup, and perhaps the Sappho hydria did this. One other point would bear further investigation; sometimes a mythological scene was chosen because it gave a parallel to the activity of the purchaser – the wrestling of Peleus and Thetis is a parallel to the wrestling of Phayllos and presumably the purchaser chose it as such.[2]

[1] *ABV* 334/6, Munich 1712; *AJA* 58 (1954), 189.
[2] Cf. below, p. 251.

3

Other Pictures with Contemporary or Special Names

A few more vases with names of contemporary Athenians are worthy of mention. One prize Panathenaic amphora carries a *kalos* name, Euphiletos. The name occurs with *kalos* on three contemporary vases and without *kalos* against Apollo playing the lyre before three Muses.[1] On the Panathenaic amphora[2] (which gives the Euphiletos painter his name) 'Euphiletos *kalos*' is written round Athena's shield. Beazley notes that Pheidias is said to have written 'Pantarkes *kalos*' on the finger of his Zeus at Olympia. Presumably, if the story is true, Pheidias commended his favourite to the keeping of Zeus. I do not feel clear that a similar explanation is satisfactory here, and wonder whether there may not have been some special connection between Euphiletos and this particular festival – he might have been the man who proposed in the Boule that this workshop should have the contract for making the Panathenaic amphorae or he might have been one of the athlothetai who were responsible for the conduct of the games (cf. above).[3]

I do not think the artist would have predicted the victory of Euphiletos in the pentathlon for which this amphora was one of the prizes, even if he was a favourite. But victory in the chariot-race may be the explanation of the 'Nikon *kalos*', written under the horses' legs and round in front of them, in a picture of a racing-chariot on a Panathenaic amphora of approximately the same date.[4] Here the inscription 'From

[1] *ABV* 666.　　　[2] *ABV* 322/1, London B 134, *CV* pl. 2, 2; *DBF* 91.
[3] On a red-figure Panathenaic by the Nikoxenos painter (*ARV*² 221/6) Nikoxenos is written on Athena's shield and *kalos* outside. Again Nikoxenos may have been a Panathenaic official and the vase painted for a symposion while he was in office.
[4] *ABV* 671, 716, brought up to date by *ARV*² 1602, Mainz University 74, *CV* pl. 35.

the games at Athens' is missing, and the amphora is therefore *not* a prize (although in all other respects it is identical with the prize amphora). The whole question of the 'non-prize' Panathenaic amphorai needs discussion, but for this one the obvious explanation is not that it was a competition piece but that it was made after the victory for a party in celebration. Nikon appears as a charioteer on another non-prize Panathenaic amphora,[1] where he is racing against Mynnon; this vase has the further inscription 'Hiketes seems *kalos* to me' so that presumably it was a present to Hiketes from someone who knew that he was interested in this particular chariot-race. (The prize amphorai do not show two racing-chariots but a single racing-chariot.)

Another non-prize Panathenaic amphora[2] by the Swing painter goes rather further from the canonical on both sides. On one side the canonical Athena is greeted by Hermes on the left and a bearded man with a staff stands behind her. On the other side a boy rides a horse preceded by a bearded man who announces 'The horse of Dysniketos wins' and followed by a youth carrying a tripod. This man is the herald; perhaps Hermes should be regarded as his counterpart, telling the news to Athena, and perhaps the man behind Athena (interpreted in *CV* as Zeus, but he does not look like Zeus) is Dysniketos, probably the father of the jockey. Beazley says that the tripod prize shows that the race cannot have been won at the Panathenaia. Yet the Athena is the canonical Athena and the shape of the vase is the canonical shape; is it conceivable that the Swing painter thought that a tripod, the traditional Homeric prize, made his meaning clear and was easier to draw than a number of Panathenaic amphorai? In any case the vase was an individual creation for this victory.

The practice of giving *kalos* names starts a little before the middle of the sixth century. It is a time when vase-painters used inscriptions very freely; they seem to take the place of the filling ornament used between the figures on geometric and seventh-century vases; and when the painter has nothing to write (or cannot write), he puts in a senseless jumble of letters. On Little Master cups *kalos* names vie with signatures and injunctions to drink well as suitable inscriptions for the bowl below the offset lip. It is difficult to suppose that they can have any other pur-

---

[1] *ARV*[2] 1584, Louvre F 283, *CV* pl. 2, 6–7. Cf. below, p. 193.
[2] *ABV* 307/59; *DBF* 92, London B 144, *CV* pl. 6, 2. Here, pl. 6.

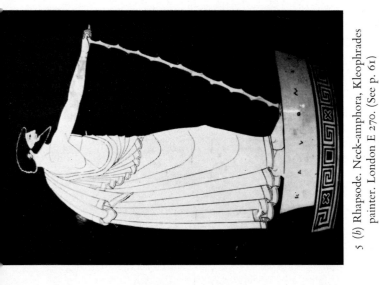

5 (a) Xenophon and Phayllos. Psykter, Phintias. Boston 01.8019. (See pp. 55 f.)

5 (b) Rhapsode. Neck-amphora, Kleophrades painter. London E 270. (See p. 61)

6 (a) and (b) Victor in horse-race. Panathenaic amphora, Swing painter. London B 307. (See p. 64)

pose here than to indicate the ownership of the cup, whether the name is that of purchaser or recipient. Two early *kalos* names which occur on other kinds of vases may be quoted. Stesias *kalos* may be the man commemorated by a grave epigram of the late sixth century.[1] Stesias *kalos* appears on three amphorai of group E found in Vulci, painted soon after the middle of the century, one of them signed by Exekias as potter.[2] Nothing marks these as out of the ordinary: the subjects are normal – Herakles and Geryon (twice), Ajax and Kassandra, Theseus and the Minotaur, warriors leaving home, Anchippos in a chariot leaving home. Even Anchippos, who is unknown but may have been an Attic hero, appears on another vase. If Stesias ordered these vases rather than earmarking them at a late stage before firing, he did not have exciting tastes.

Onetorides is more interesting: his name appears with *kalos* on nine vases, which cover a period from soon after 560 to at least 530.[3] Here again, as with Leagros later (cf. above), Onetorides is called *kalos* not only when he is a young beauty (if he ever was) but also a quarter of a century later: in fact 'Onetorides *kalos*' means 'bespoke by [or, less likely, for] Onetorides'. The vases are neck-amphorai, amphorai, hydriai and a kalyx-krater. They were found in Athens, Vulci and Ampurias (Spain); here it is interesting that the kalyx-krater, which is the earliest example of the shape known, was found on the north slope of the Acropolis and the excavators believe that it was a dedication, not a symposion vase. This and three other vases are by Exekias, the Ampurias fragment is near him; three more are by followers of the Lysippides painter (the successor of Exekias), but the ninth is by the Princeton painter. Onetorides seems to have had a particular interest in Exekias, and it is at least arguable that these four wonderful vases were special orders. The earliest is the neck-amphora in Berlin (1720) with A. Herakles and the lion and B. Demophon and Akamas (the sons of Theseus) with their horses. The neck-amphora in London (B 210) with A. Achilles and Penthesileia and B. Dionysos and Oinopion is rather later. Later still is the amphora, type A, in the Vatican (344) with A. Achilles and Ajax playing dice, B. return of Kastor to his family. The

---

[1] *IG* I², 287; Peek, *GVI* no. 154.
[2] *ABV* 133/9; 136/54; 136/49; *DBF* 63 f.
[3] *ABV* 143/1, 7, 13, 19; 148; 261/37; 264/2; 299/21; 693 foot.

latest of the Exekias vases is the kalyx-krater[1] with Herakles' introduction to Olympos on one side and the death of Patroklos on the other, a very rare subject. The subjects of the other vases with Onetorides *kalos* are Herakles and Hebe, Herakles and Kerberos, Herakles and Triton (twice), Hippomedon and Polykaste, horseman leading a void horse. Herakles subjects are so common in black-figure that we need not see his choice there (it is, of course, a problem why Herakles was so popular). The three scenes from the Trojan epic by Exekias may well be Onetorides' personal choice: all of them are connected with Achilles, and no earlier Achilles and Ajax dicing, death of Patroklos, or Achilles and Penthesileia is known to us in Attic. The Hippomedon scene[2] is unique and the legend is unknown: Hippomedon puts a flower on an altar invoking the god, ὦναξ, and Polykaste faces him holding helmet and girdle. Here again one may see Onetorides' choice. Lastly, three scenes have men with horses, Demophon and Akamas, the sons of Theseus, Kastor and the nameless men by the Princeton painter.[3] I am inclined to see Demophon and Akamas and Kastor as mythological paradigms of the Athenian knights, the class to which Onetorides probably belonged. The Dioskouroi appear similarly as a mythical paradigm to warriors setting out on a slightly later vase by the Edinburgh painter.[4] In the Onetorides vases we see something of his taste; he was probably one of the Athenian knights, a very high social class; besides Herakles, who was common property, he was interested in Achilles, and encouraged Exekias to use his exquisite art on new subjects.

Two black-figure vases with scenes of craftsmen have *kalos* names. It is impossible to say for certain whether the name belongs to craftsman, purchaser or recipient, but the scenes are unusual enough to be special orders. An oinochoe[5] of the Keyside class found in Vulci with a picture of a forge is inscribed 'Mys seems *kalos*. Yes.' The red-figure cup[6] with a sculptor's workshop making a statue of Achilles is inscribed

[1] Athens, Agora AP 1044. Here, pl. 7.
[2] *ABV* 693 foot, Villa Giulia.
[3] *ABV* 299/21, Bonn 365.
[4] *ABL* 220/87; London B 170, *CV* pl. 34, 2. On the Hippeis on archaic vases, cf. H. Metzger and D. van Berchem, *A.K.* Beiheft 4 (1967), 155.
[5] *ABV* 426/9; Cloché, *Classes et métiers* (Paris, 1931), 53, 107, pl. 23, 1, 3; London B 507.
[6] *ARV*[2] 400/1, 1573; H. A. Thompson, *Essays in Memory of Karl Lehmann* (New York, 1967), 323; Berlin 2294.

'Diogenes *kalos*'; as Diogenes *kalos* appears on five other vases with athletes and the like, his name on the foundry cup means that he ordered it or that it was ordered for him; he was not a sculptor himself but was interested in sculpture. Mys, on the other hand, sounds like a craftsman's name, and the picture illustrates the crucial moment when the furnace was opened. The jug may therefore be a special commission to celebrate a successful casting, and this Mys may be the grandfather of the famous Mys who decorated the bronze shield of Pheidias' Athena Promachos. The other black-figure vase is a small amphora type B by the Taleides painter with Theseus and the Minotaur on one side and men weighing goods on the other; the inscription 'Kleitarchos *kalos*' may mean that he was a merchant, and that it was ordered by or for him; Theseus and the Minotaur is common enough, but weighing goods only appears on one other black-figure vase.[1] On a red-figure amphora type B by the Dinos painter[2] a man selling oil is inscribed Alkimos. The subject is not uncommon, but here besides the man and a boy Athena appears, and on the other side Plouton, Demeter, Persephone. The amphora itself may have been used for oil, and the assembly of deities may have been meant to show that it was Attic oil from Alkimos' olive-yard. In any case Alkimos' name shows that this was a bespoke vase. It was found at Trachones in Attica.

It is clear that it often makes no difference whether a figure is given a name or a name with *kalos*. Either bespeaks the vase whether from its inception or at a late stage before firing. Thus we can set beside Alkimos selling oil, Nikarete written against a seated woman with two youths on a hydria[3] from Cumae in the manner of the Aegisthus painter, Antiochos against a flute-player on a neck-amphora[4] by the Berlin painter (the man on the other side is probably his trainer), Chorpheles against a dancing-girl on a stemmed dish[5] from Nola by the Dish painter. But a man dancing the pyrrhic on a cup[6] by the Eucharides painter has an abbreviated inscription, which seems to be 'Aristeides, you are *kalos*', and a citharode on a doubleen[7] by the Dutuit painter has 'Archinos *kalos*'. This vase has a twin which has no picture on the body

---

[1] *ABV* 174/1 (cf. 426/4, Keyside class), New York 47.11.5.
[2] *ARV*[2] 1154/38 bis.   [3] *ARV*[2] 508/6.   [4] *ARV*[2] 199/32.
[5] *ARV*[2] 787. Perhaps χορωφελὴς and the same for Tithonos on 1193/3.
[6] *ARV*[2] 231/78, Louvre G 136.
[7] *ARV*[2] 307/5–6, Naples 3155; Louvre G 137, *CV* pls. 33, 8–10.

but on the neck Nike on both sides; on one she pours a libation, on the other she runs or dances, pulling up her chiton with both hands. 'Archinos *kalos*' is written on both sides so that it is natural to suppose that the vases were a pair made to celebrate Archinos' victory in a contest for citharodes. Sometimes both formulae appear on the same vase: on a cup[1] from Vulci by Makron a bearded man labelled 'Antiphanes *kallistos*' approaches a woman; the outside has also pairs of man (bearded or beardless) and woman approaching or embracing; most of them have names, but only one, a woman Naukleia, has the addition *kale*. An interesting case, which surely must be a bespoke vase, is a chous[2] by the Trophy painter found in Athens. Athena stands by a column on the top of which is a child greeting her; the base of the column is inscribed '[TE]ISIAS dedicated', and in the field 'Sophanes *kalos*'. Beazley suggests that the child is Erichthonios, but it looks like an ordinary child greeting Athena. Is it not possible that Sophanes was Teisias' son and that Teisias had dedicated to Athena a statue on a column (not necessarily of him) to celebrate possibly his admission to the phratry at the Apatouria, and then had this chous painted for the Anthesteria when the child was three?

One last considerable group of vases with names should be briefly mentioned. A number of vases in the second half of the fifth century have pictures of satyrs and maenads, or of the women attending Aphrodite, and give them names. I have called them explanatory personifications and have suggested that the names tell the spectator what are the concomitants or conditions or results of Dionysiac ecstasy and of the fulfilment of desire; the impulse comes from outside, from tragedy and philosophy, and possibly through the medium of large-scale painting.[3] I give a considerable list, but only discuss a few examples where it may be justifiable to see special orders.

> *ARV*[2] 1037/2. Near Hector painter. Hydria from Nola, Brunswick 219. Fragmentary. Kleophonis *kale* seated; Kleodoxa sings to lyre; Euphemia plays flute. Also Kleodike; Panodike seated. (Cf. flute-girl at symposion, 1055/64.)

[1] *ARV*[2] 468/146, New York 12.231.1.
[2] *ARV*[2] 858/8, Louvre L 63. This is not necessarily the same Sophanes as on the other vases with 'Sophanes *kalos*' (*ARV*[2] 1609).
[3] Cf. *A.A.L.* 39 ff. (I must also acknowledge the help of Miss Valerie Land.)

ARV² 1045/6. Lykaon painter. Bell-krater, Warsaw 142355. A. Dionysos with satyr Oinopion and maenads Mainas, Polynika. B. Satyrs and maenads at herm. Alkimachos *kalos*, Axiopeithes *kalos* on A. Beazley, *VP* 56, suggests that the painter was thinking of the celebrations which followed a victory in the theatre of Dionysos.

1055/76. Polygnotos undetermined. Bell-krater from Nola, Compiègne 1025. Dionysos with satyr Komos, Ariadne and maenad Tragodia (B. satyr, maenad).

1055/78. Polygnotos undetermined. Fragment, Copenhagen, Thorvaldsen Museum 97. Dionysos with satyr playing the lyre, Dithyramphos.

1152/2. Dinos painter. Stamnos from Nocera de' Pagani, Naples 2419. Feast of Dionysos. A. Dione, Mainas. B. Thaleia, Choreia.

1152/8. Dinos painter. Kalyx-krater, Vienna 1024. Dionysos with maenads and satyrs, Eirene, Thyone, Opora, Oinanthe, Hedyoinos, Komos.

1155/1685. Manner of Dinos painter. Bell-krater from Athens, Agora P 9189. Maenads: Paidia, Thymedia.

1185/1. Kadmos painter. Volute-krater from Ruvo, Jatta 1093. A. Dionysos with Silenos, Simos, Sikinnis, Oinopion, Eudaimonia, Thyone, Oreia, Opora, Hebe. B. Marsyas. Neck: A. Sacrifice before a herm. B. Marsyas.

1188/1. Pothos painter. Bell-krater, Providence 23.324. Satyrs: Komos, Oinos. Maenads: Thaleia, Eudia. (B. 3 youths.)

1214/1. Kraipale painter. Chous from Vulci, Boston 00.352. Seated Kraipale; satyr Sikinnos, maenad Thymedia.

1248/8. Eretria painter. Squat lekythos, Kansas City 31.80. Mother and baby (Kephalos) with Eunomia, Paidia, Peitho, Antheia.

1253/58. Eretria painter. Cup, Warsaw 142458. I. Demon (satyr) and Choro (maenad). A. and B. Satyrs: Kissos, Lemnos, Aietos (dance); maenads: Tethys, Delos, Euboia, Kinyra.

1258/1, 2. Akin to Eretria painter. Choes, Oxford 534, Florence 22 B 324. Satyr Kissos and maenad Tragodia.

ARV² 1312/1. Meidias painter. Hydria from Populonia. Adonis. Note Chrysothemis (Hesperid), Eutychia, Erato, Eurynoe (?), Hygieia, Paidia, Pandaisia.

1312/2. Meidias painter. Hydria from Populonia, Florence 81948. Note Hygieia, Pannychia, Erosora (season of spring).

1313/5. Meidias painter. Hydria, London E 224. Note Hygieia with Hesperids.

1314/17. Meidias painter. Lekanis from Canosa, Naples Stg. 311. Antiochos, Pandion with Nikopolis, Nike, Klymene, Myrrhiniske *kale*, Epicharis *kale*. Cf. *AJA* (1935), 487.

1314/18. Meidias painter. Lekanis from Ruvo. Kallisto, Archestrate with Lysistrate, Myrrhine. Cf. *AJA* (1950), 319.

1316(a). Copy of the Meidias painter. Squat lekythos from Ruvo. Here, pl. 8. Hygieia, Pandaisia, Eudaimonia, Polykles.

1316/1. Group of Naples 3235. Panathenaic amphora from Ruvo, Naples 3235. B. Marsyas and Olympos with Tyrbas, Simos, Thaleia, Ouranie.

1316/2. Group of Naples 3235. Panathenaic amphora. A. Dionysos with Thyone, Simos, Dione.

1316/3. Group of Naples 3235. Pelike. Dionysos with Eirene, Polyerate, Erato, Pannychis, Batyllos, Sybas, Eurytion.

1318/1. Group of Boston 10.190. Chous from Vulci, Berlin 2658. Paian, Komos, Neanias.

1318/3. Painter of the Athens Wedding. Hydria, London E 226. Toilet of Helen. Kleio looks on.

1324/41 bis. Manner of Meidias painter. Oinochoe I, Budapest. Apollo, Eunomia, Eukleia.

1324/45. Manner of Meidias painter. Squat lekythos from Athens, London E 697. Aphrodite with Peitho, Eunomia, Paidia, Eudaimonia, Kleopatra.

1324/47. Manner of Meidias painter. Squat lekythos, New York 11.213.2. Aphrodite, Chrysippos, Pompe.

1324/67. Manner of Meidias painter. Tallboy. Goddess at her image with Eunomia and Thaleia.

1324/85. Manner of Meidias painter. Lekanis from Egnatia, Naples Stg. 316. Aphrodite, Klymene, Pannychis, Eunomia; Harmonia seated, Eukleia.

ARV² 1324/86. Manner of Meidias painter. Lekanis, Naples 2296.
Aphrodite, Klymene, Nesaie, Halie.

1324/87. Manner of Meidias painter. Lekanis, Mainz University
118. Paphie, Eunomia, Eukleia.

1324/92. Manner of Meidias painter. Pyxis from Eretria, London
E 775. Aphrodite, Eunomia, Paidia, Eudaimonia, Harmonia. Lid: Dionysos and maenads.

1324/99. Manner of Meidias painter. Pyxis, New York 09.221.
40. Aphrodite with Peitho, Hygieia, Aponia, Eukleia,
Eudaimonia, Paidia.

1330/7. Makaria painter. Squat lekythos, Reading 52.3.2.
Aphrodite, Eutychia, Makaria.

1330/8. Makaria painter. Squat lekythos, Baltimore, Walters
48.205. Eutychia, Eunomia, Paidia.

The hydria with Kleophonis (*ARV²* 1037/2) is not unlike the Sappho
hydria (cf. above), women with names making music. Here the addition of *kale* to Kleophonis suggests that she is a contemporary, and
Kleophonis is a flute-girl in a contemporary symposion. So presumably
the other names Kleodoxa, Euphemia, Kleodike, Phanodike are names
of contemporaries – perhaps professional names rather than real names?
On two squat lekythoi in the manner of the Meidias painter a contemporary man joins women-personifications. On one (*ARV²* 1316(a))
Polykles stands among women who belong to Aphrodite, called
Hygieia (health), Pandaisia (good cheer), Eudaimonia (happiness); the
perfume-vase was presumably a present to a girl, and said that union
with Polykles would secure these blessings. On the other (*ARV²*
1324/47) Chrysippos sits between Aphrodite, Eros, Pompe and another
woman. Pompe is the personification of a festival procession, and
Chrysippos is saying clearly enough that he fell in love with the girl
when he saw her in a procession.

Then there is a group of vases alluding to successful performances,
which were probably painted for the succeeding party. A bell-krater by
the Lykaon painter (*ARV²* 1045/6) has A. Dionysos with satyr Oinopion pouring wine into a mixing-bowl and maenads Mainas and Polynika, B. satyrs and maenads at a herm. Beazley suggests because of the
Doric form Polynika (much victorious) that the painter was thinking of

the celebrations which followed a victory in the theatre of Dionysos: the herm on the other side suggests a dithyramb.[1] On A. are two *kalos* names, Alkimachos and Axiopeithes. Beazley suggests that they were cousins because on other vases Axiopeithes is called 'son of Alkimachos'. This Alkimachos is the successful kitharode, whom we have already discussed. It looks as if he trained the chorus which his cousin Axiopeithes produced, and this vase was painted for their joint celebration. Like the maenad Polynika, the lyre-playing satyr Dithyramphos (dithyramb at the lesser Panathenaia was sometimes at any rate sung by lyre-playing satyrs, cf. above on Polion) on a fragmentary vase (*ARV*² 1055/78) probably alludes to a successful dithyramb.

An elaborate volute-krater by the Kadmos painter (*ARV*² 1185/1) has on B. Marsyas playing the flute against Apollo on the neck, and Marsyas converted to playing the lyre on the body, on A. a sacrifice in front of a herm on the neck and Dionysos with satyrs and maenads on the body. The decoration seems to be connected. In the large Marsyas scene Nike and tripod suggest that the vase was painted to celebrate a victory with a dithyramb, also celebrated by the sacrifice before the herm. And because Dionysos is the god of the dithyramb and of the wine drunk from the krater, he occupies one side of the vase (as also on the Pronomos krater celebrating a victory with a satyr play). Here his satyrs are named Simos, Oinopion, Sikinnos (alluding to the dance of the satyr-play), and his maenads Eudaimonia, Thyone, Oreia (alluding to the maenad's mounting dancing), Opora (autumn, the season of vintage) – conditions, concomitants and results of drinking wine.

A cup by the Eretria painter (*ARV*² 1253/58) has a pair of satyr and maenad dancing inside and further satyrs and maenads dancing outside. Their names are surprising: Demon and Choro (dance) inside; the satyrs outside are Kissos (ivy), Lemnos, Aietos (probably, as Beazley says, the name of a dance) and the maenads Tethys, Delos, Euboia and Kinyra (agitated sound). Kissos and Choro are known elsewhere[2] and Kinyra and Aietos are in the normal range. Tethys occurs rather earlier on a bell-krater by the Villa Giulia painter (*ARV*² 619/16) where the infant Dionysos is handed over to the maenads Mainas and Tethys (perhaps mother-ocean as an escape from the hostility of Hera? The

---

[1] Cf. Webster, *The Greek Chorus* (London, 1970), 93.
[2] Cf. *ARV*² 1247/1, 57 for both of them (Eretria painter).

72

role played by Thetis in the *Iliad*.). But Tethys here must be the mother of the islands, Delos, Euboia and Lemnos (one can only suppose that the painter made a mistake in making Lemnos a satyr instead of a maenad). Demon is an ordinary Athenian name. The painter connected him with dancing islands. It is possible that he wrote or produced a comedy with a chorus of islands (like the comedy of Aristophanes or Archippos, cf. 388 K) and had this cup painted (or at least named) to celebrate its success.

Lastly, because the names so obviously fit with those that we have been discussing, the most famous of the so-called 'Lenaian' vases, the stamnos by the Dinos painter (*ARV*² 1152/2)[1] names two of the maenads dancing before the image of Dionysos Dione and Mainas and two of the maenads on the other side Thaleia and Choreia. Choreia (like Choro on the Eretria painter's cup) alludes to the dance, Thaleia – a Muse name, used as early as Oltos (*ARV*² 64/104) for a maenad – to the good cheer which results from successful service of Dionysos. Dione was called the mother of Dionysos in Euripides' *Antigone* (fr. 177 N), which was produced later than this stamnos, but the identification may have been already made in the song which these women sang and is perhaps a reason for regarding this very good vase as a special order.

[1] A. W. Pickard-Cambridge, *Dramatic Festivals of Athens*, 2nd rev. ed. (Oxford, 1968), fig. 22.

4

Some Rare Scenes

The following vases for the most part do not have *kalos* names to indicate that they are bespoke vases. Yet the scenes are sufficiently rare to
make this a possibility. There is first a small batch connected with the
Persian Wars.

The self-immolation of Kroisos. Myson painted a magnificent amphora
type A (ARV^2 238/1)[1] which was found in Vulci. On one side Kroisos
sits on the pyre with a laurel wreath on his head, pouring a libation,
while a man Euthymos lights the pyre with two torches. On the other
side Theseus carries off Antiope and is followed by Peirithoos, who
looks round for pursuers; this seems to be an excerpt from his slightly
earlier psykter (ARV^2 242/77), as von Bothmer pointed out. There are
two questions: the source of the Kroisos scene and the relevance, if any,
of the Theseus scene. The style of the vase suggests a date at the very end
of the sixth century, so that it must be earlier than Bacchylides' Ode to
Hiero, which was written in 468 B.C.: in Bacchylides Kroisos is trans-
ferred from the pyre to the Hyperboreans by Apollo; on the vase
Kroisos' festal garb and the name of the servant, 'Of good cheer',
implies salvation. Whatever in fact happened to Kroisos when Sardis
was captured by Kyros in 546 B.C., this was the story put out by Delphi
to save Apollo's face. It is a possible guess that the Alkmaionidai, who
derived their wealth from Kroisos and had at this time won Delphi's
favour by rebuilding the temple of Apollo in marble instead of lime-
stone, would be the natural vehicle for this story in Athens. It has been
suggested also that the expansion and great popularity of the Theseus
saga in the last two decades of the sixth century was due to the Alkmai-

[1] Langlotz, *Zeitbestimmung*, 84; Louvre G 197, *CV* pl. 35; *Enc. Phot.* iii, 10–11; D. von
Bothmer, *Amazons in Greek Art* (Oxford, 1957), 128. Here, pl. 9.

onidai, so that the rape of Antiope is not so irrelevant as it seems.[1] There may be a further link in Apollo: the rape of Antiope appears on the pediment of Apollo Daphnephoros at Eretria. If this story was somehow connected with Apollo in the recent *Theseid* which gave the new version of Theseus' adventures, then it is also suitable here on a vase with a main scene celebrating Apollo's loyalty to the Eastern king who sent him so many gifts. The vase may then be a special commission by one of the Alkmaionidai.

Iris and Kallimachos. The winged striding marble figure from the Acropolis, no. 690, was connected by A. E. Raubitschek[2] with an epigram describing Kallimachos' victory at Marathon. This was the memorial erected to the polemarch by some member of his deme after his death in battle. R. Hampe had suggested that a bronze herald's staff belonged to the figure, and the epigram describes her as 'messenger of the immortals', Iris. Hampe further thought that the statue was illustrated by a black-figure stand in Eleusis (*ABV* 400/3). This is attributed by Beazley to the Dikaios painter, a member of the Pioneer group painting about 515 B.C., and it seems therefore necessary to give up either the connection of the statue with the epigram of 490 B.C. or the connection of the vase with the statue. In fact another vase, a lekythos by the Diosphos painter,[3] which could have been painted in 490 B.C. or so, fits the statue better; the right hand with the *kerykeion* comes further across the body and the left hand is extended holding a writing-tablet. This suits the balance of the statue: the tablet contains the news of the victory. The little lekythos may have been specially painted as an offering to the dead general.

Aphlaston vases. These have been collected by Beazley and Wade-Gery,[4] and I can only repeat their list. Wade-Gery's argument is that the aphlaston, the curving high stern of the trireme with a standard in front of it,[5] represented the capture of an enemy ship, so that the vases

[1] K. Schefold, *MH* 3, 60. I find this suggestion more convincing than K. Friis-Johansen's attribution of the *Theseid* to the influence of Peisistratos (*Medd. Danske Selskab.* (1945), 59).

[2] *Dedications*, no. 13; H. Payne, *Archaic Marble Sculpture from the Acropolis* (London, 1936), pl. 120/1-2.

[3] *ABL* 235/76, pl. 38, 4.

[4] *JHS* 53 (1933), 100; Beazley, *Panmaler* (Berlin, 1931), 20. Cf. also *Charites Langlotz*, pl. 20; Noble, *Techniques*, fig. 243.

[5] On the terminology, K. Friis-Johansen, *Medd. Danske Selskab.* (1959), 21.

which date in the twenty years after the Persian Wars echo the naval victories of the Athenians. The list is:

1 *ARV*² 384/211. Brygos painter. Lekythos from Gela. Athena with aphlaston.
2 *ARV*² 423/125. Painter of the Paris Gigantomachy. Lekythos. Nike with aphlaston.
3 *ARV*² 535/6. Recalls the Alkimachos painter. Votive shield from Athens. Nike with aphlaston.
4 *ARV*² 539/48. Boreas painter. Votive shield from Athens. Woman with aphlaston.
5 Acropolis 516. Graef–Langlotz, pl. 40. Fragment of skyphos from Athens. Wade-Gery says like in style to no. 4. *AS* is the end of a name; Wade-Gery suggests Aias, but it may be an ordinary Athenian name like Kallias.
6 *ARV*² 550/4. Pan painter. Column-krater from Binetto (Apulia). A. Poseidon with aphlaston. B. Youth playing the flute.
7 *ARV*² 650/1. Nikon painter. Neck-amphora from Nola. A. Athena with spear and aphlaston. B. Woman running. On both sides, 'Heras kale'.

It is obvious that the time range and number of the vases is small. The two votive-shields (3–4) are likely by their very nature to be special commissions. The neck-amphora (7) suggests certainly that it celebrates offensive action if the woman running away is rightly interpreted as Asia. It is difficult to say who the woman with the aphlaston is on the Boreas painter's votive-shield (4): could she perhaps be the Athenian tribe (*phyle*) to which the successful trierarch belonged? Poseidon (6) and Athena (1, 7) are obviously relevant to any Athenian naval operation. Nike (2, 3) can be victory against the enemy but could also be victory in some naval competition like a race. Probably all the vases,[1] except the votive-shields, were commissioned for a party to celebrate a trierarch's success whether in war or peace, and nos. 1, 6 and 7 found their way to the West by the second-hand market. It is intriguing that the Nikon painter's neck-amphora (7) has a feminine *kalos* name. The

---

[1] A black-figure oinochoe with white ground by the Athena painter (*ABL* 259/115), found at Rhitsona, has Nike and a ship. It obviously belongs in this context, but I should not claim it as a special commission.

lady is known from two and possibly three other early classical vases.[1] The most interesting is a fragmentary pyxis found in Athens with a picture of a bride and above it . . . *on kalos, Heras Kale*.[2] Can we guess that she was the wife of the victorious trierarch, who had her name put on the neck-amphora celebrating his victory, and that the pyxis was a wedding present?

Death of Hipparchos. Beazley[3] has discussed four vases representing the death of Hipparchos, the tyrant who was killed by Harmodios and Aristogeiton in 514 B.C. Again they fall close together between 475 and 460 B.C. They are a stamnos by the Copenhagen painter (ARV^2 256/5, Würzburg 515, Langlotz, pl. 182), a black-figure lekythos by the Emporion painter (ABL 264/39, pl. 48, 4) found in Athens, a skyphos by the Pan painter in Agrigento (ARV^2 559/147), and an unattributed skyphos fragment in Gela (*JHS* 68 (1948), 27, fig. 1). The statues of the tyrant-slayers were removed by Xerxes in 480 B.C., and a new group was made by Kritios and Nesiotes in 476 B.C. All the vases are inspired by this new group, and the Copenhagen painter's stamnos, which was probably found in Etruria, was, if not a special commission to celebrate it, at least a very quick reaction to it. All the vases show the painters' awareness of Athenian pride in Athenian democracy soon after the Persian Wars. The fragment from Gela was found in the sanctuary of the hero who founded the city. Beazley makes the attractive suggestion that the Sicilian who dedicated it and the other Sicilian who bought the Pan painter's skyphos had their local tyrant in mind.[4]

Special athletic scenes. A black-figure amphora of group E[5] has been much discussed because of its inscription. The scenes are a hoplite on one side, and a man carrying a tripod on the other. The inscription, which was painted before firing and runs down beneath the hoplite's spear, is interpreted by Amyx as 'Two obols, and you have me' and by

[1] ARV^2 1614.

[2] ARV^2 890/172. Cf. L. Robert in *Entretiens Hardt* 14 (1969), 340, on seeming hetaira names belonging to respectable women.

[3] *JHS* 68 (1948), 26. The Aristogeiton is possibly reflected on ARV^2 272/8, Harrow painter, now in Stanford.

[4] A black-figure lekythos of about 510 B.C. with a symposion has the painted inscription 'HIMERA'; as it was found at Gela, this should refer to the Sicilian town or its nymph, and the inscription at least must have been commissioned by a Sicilian in Athens (*ABL* 49; Lippold, *Neve Beiträge*, 136).

[5] ABV 136/50, New York 56.171.13; D. A. Amyx, *California Publications in Classical Archaeology* 1 (1941), 179; *Hesperia* 27 (1958), 300. Here, pl. 10.

Beazley as 'Two obols, and hands off'. Palaeographically, Kretschmer followed by Amyx, μ' ἔθιγες, is slightly easier than μὴ θίγῃς, Naber followed by Beazley. Syntactically Beazley's rendering is easier than Amyx. But 'worth much more than two obols' as a boast on a bespoke pot is parallel to Euthymides' 'As never Euphronios', and is much more likely than Amyx's price-tag. But Amyx is surely right in connecting the two sides of the vase, so that we have a unique contest as well as a unique inscription, and that surely means a bespoke vase. The hoplite has been victorious in a contest, and his success is represented by the man carrying the tripod. It may not be certain that a tripod was the prize for the contest if, as suggested above in connection with the Swing painter's victor in a horse-race,[1] a tripod-bearer is a stock-figure which simply denotes a victory in a contest, whatever the prize. Amyx has suggested that the contest was a duel of hoplites, and has collected the evidence for this practice, which seems to be sufficient. Perhaps it was not a standard contest but only took place when participants offered themselves.

Another performance which was not standard but took place sometimes at the Panathenaia was trick-dancing. This is probably the meaning of *thaumata* in an inscription recording the winning of a 'tripodiskos' (small tripod?) and its dedication to Athena on the Acropolis.[2] A black-figure amphora of Panathenaic shape has a man with helmet and two shields leaping on to the back of a horse while a flute-player plays and the audience on a grandstand applauds.[3] The vase was painted about 550 B.C. The inscription is not quite clear: probably it says 'a fine tumbling display!', and the vase-painter so conceived the mind of the audience. The Panathenaic shape suggests that the performance took place at the Panathenaia. The vase may have been specially painted for the party to celebrate the tumbler's success, and as it was found at Kameiros in Rhodes it is conceivable that the tumbler was a Rhodian visitor, who took it home with him after his success. Two other black-figure vases show armed acrobats, a cup of about 530 B.C. and a lekythos of about 480 B.C. from the workshop of the Athena painter.[4] The

[1] Cf. above, p. 64.

[2] *Dedications*, no. 322.

[3] Paris, Cab. Med. 243; *CV* pl. 88 and pls. 89, 1–2; Beazley, *BVAB* 14 (1939), 11, fig. 9; Kretschmer 88.

[4] *ABV* 236; Beazley, *BVAB* 14 (1939), 11, fig. 8; *ABV* 524/1.

lekythos is roughly contemporary with a fragmentary red-figure pelike[1] by Myson which also has an armed acrobat. These may also be bespoke vases but nothing points certainly to it.

Finally a red-figure Panathenaic amphora[2] by the painter of Palermo 1108, who is a follower of Makron, has an interesting scene. It was found in Vulci, so that it may well have been a special commission which reached Etruria by the second-hand market. On one side it has a youth carrying a Panathenaic amphora, and on the other a youth with sprigs in one hand and a plaque in the other. It seems an obvious conclusion that the vase was painted for a celebration after a victory at the Panathenaia, and its own shape alludes to this. On one side the victor is carrying away one of the prize Panathenaic amphorai; on the other he is bringing a plaque to dedicate to Athena after his victory. The figure represented on the plaque is shown by club and lionskin (which appears on his head, under his left arm and on his back) to be Herakles, and a plaque of Herakles is a suitable dedication to Athena.

A special cup for a young knight. A magnificent cup[3] by the Penthesileia painter was found in Tomb 18C in the Necropolis at Spina in Etruria. The other vases found in the same tomb were a good volute-krater by the Boreas painter, two quite ordinary cups, two rhyta and an oinochoe.[4] They presumably came to the dead man piecemeal over more than twenty years. The Penthesileia painter's cup must originally have been specially ordered for a party in Athens. First, it is the largest surviving kylix with a diameter of 56 cm. Secondly, it has the rare additional zone of decoration round the tondo inside. Thirdly, the tondo scene is unique. The outside has fine versions of Achilles killing Memnon on one side and Odysseus quarrelling with Ajax over the arms of Achilles on the other. The zone round the tondo has a fine cycle of the Labours of Theseus. These were all popular mythical themes. There is no obvious connection between them, but presumably the purchaser liked them.

In the tondo itself a young man rides a horse up to an altar, which has a wreath on it. A second horse is behind his horse. Another young man walks towards the altar. Both have short cloaks round their shoulders.

[1] *ARV²* 238/10.

[2] *ARV²* 299/2; Munich 2315, *CV* pls. 191 and 190, 4–5.

[3] *ARV²* 882/35, Ferrara T 18; N. Alfieri, *R.I.N.A.S.* 8 (1959), 59 ff. Here, pl. 11.

[4] *ARV²* 536/4; 718/241; 766/5; 910/48; 1013/20; 1213/1. Cf. below, p. 293.

Both have spears in their left hands. Both have a long bit of cloth twisted round their heads which is held in place by a metal headband. Both, according to Alfieri's careful description, have reins running from their left hands through their right hands to the horses. The spatial arrangement is impossible, but the painter clearly wants to say that one youth remained on his horse and the other dismounted. Alfieri explains: Theseus at the end of his youthful triumphs arrives in a temple perhaps of Athena Nike to receive the victor's crown; he is accompanied by Peirithoos; the characterization of the heroes adds a reference to contemporary Athenian cavalry. The truth lies in the last sentence. The parallels quoted for the mythical scene are completely different, and neither of the youths in the tondo is in the least like the Theseus of the surrounding zone, and Peirithoos does not appear in any of the labours of the surrounding zone. Nor does any artist represent a triumphal coronation by merely having a friend pick a wreath off an altar. But these are Athenian horsemen, probably cavalrymen. And the natural explanation of the action is that one of them has dismounted and laid the wreath, his own or his friend's, on the altar as a dedication. Two of the numerous red-figure vases with altar scenes may help a little. A cup by Onesimos[1] from Falerii has a man at an altar praying to Hermes inside, and males and horses outside; the column on the outside may allude to the Stoa of Herms. It is worth remembering that the Herms in the Agora had a riding-school nearby where the young men could be seen mounting and dismounting.[2] The cup has Lykos *kalos* on it, so that it was presumably a bespoke vase for Lykos who was successful in the riding-school. (I feel too doubtful about a fragment[3] by the Boot painter to claim it as a young cavalryman visiting the altar in the Stoa of Herms.) The second vase[4] is a pelike by the Niobid painter from Capua: on one side it has Nike and a youth with a spear, at an altar. Clearly an offering is being made for a victory and the youth's spear may show that he is a cavalryman. Closer still is a black-figure lekythos[5] by the Emporion painter found in Athens, which has Nike flying

[1] *ARV*² 324/63, Bonn 1227. *CV* pl. 7. For the altar of Hermes, cf. *ABV* 531/2; *ABL* 219/65.
[2] R. E. Wycherley, *Athenian Agora* III, *Testimonia* (Princeton, 1965), no. 303 = Mnesimachos, 4K; E. B. Harrison, *Athenian Agora* XI, 108.
[3] *ARV*² 822/23; *Beazley Gifts* (Oxford, 1967), pl. 31, Oxford 1966.515.
[4] *ARV*² 603/46, Capua 1391. *CV* pl. 6.
[5] *ABL* 264/31, Louvre ED 61.

7 Dedication of Onetorides. Kalyx-krater, Exekias. Agora AP 1044.
(See p. 66)

8 Polykles and women. Squat lekythos, Manner of Meidias painter. London E 698. (See p. 70)

and a youth with horse at an altar. So the wreath laid on the altar on the Penthesileia painter's cup may be a token of victory, and here Alfieri's identification of the wreath as an oak-wreath is suggestive. The archaic head, which used to be known as the Rampin Zeus until it was joined by Payne to the Acropolis horseman No. 590,[1] wears an oak-wreath and has been explained as a Pythian victor: it is even possible, if an inscription[2] from the base bearing a horseman in fact belonged to this statue, that he was the first Athenian to win a Pythian victory. If one of these two young men also had won a victory in the horse-race at the Pythian games, this would be an occasion for the painting of a very special cup which showed that he had acquitted himself in a way worthy of Theseus and the heroes of the Trojan War.

[1] Payne, *Archaic Marble Sculpture*, 8, pl. 11a; 133, 4.
[2] *Dedications*, no. 61.

5

Some Special Stories

THESEUS

In discussing Myson's amphora with Kroisos on one side and on the other Theseus and Antiope I have already noted the explosion of Theseus scenes in the late sixth century and the possible connection with the Alkmaionidai. The theory is that the writing of a new *Theseid* which added to the old stories – Theseus and the Minotaur, Theseus and Ariadne, Theseus and Helen, Theseus at the marriage of Peirithoos, Theseus and Peirithoos in the Underworld – the whole story of Theseus' journey to Athens with the various adventures on the way, embellishments of the Cretan story, possibly Theseus and the Pallantidai and certainly Theseus' part in Herakles' battle with the Amazons, his abduction of Antiope and the Amazon invasion of Attica, was encouraged by the Alkmaionidai and particularly Kleisthenes with a view to creating a modernized Athenian Herakles. Whoever was responsible, Theseus was accepted as the hero of the new Athenian democracy. It must have helped this acceptance that the new stories were represented on the vases used in symposia and if it was the Alkmaionidai who encouraged the poem, it was presumably also the Alkmaionidai who commissioned the earliest representations. (We have already noted the Alkmaionids Hippokrates, Megakles, Alkmaion and a younger Megakles as patrons of potters.)

Let us look at these for a moment. It was a new idea to represent two or even three scenes involving the same hero on each side of a cup, and once invented the idea remains practically restricted to Theseus and his adventures on the way to Athens with the addition of the Bull of Marathon and sometimes the Minotaur. The earliest surviving examples

82

are two cups made by Kachrylion about 515–510 B.C.[1] Both were found in Etruria, which agrees with their having been special commissions for a special party. One has Sinis, the Minotaur and Prokrustes on one side and on the other Skeiron, Kerkyon and the Bull of Marathon. The other has Prokrustes, Kerkyon and the Minotaur on one side, and the Bull of Marathon and the Sow of Krommyon on the other.

The Minotaur, as I have said, is an old story. Kerkyon is first here in red-figure and does not occur in black-figure. Sinis occurs first here, in red-figure, and in black-figure on a skyphos and a lekythos by the Theseus painter in the early fifth century.[2] Prokrustes occurs also on the same black-figure lekythos and on a twin skyphos.[3] The same two black-figure skyphoi also have Skeiron. A red-figure cup by the Euergides painter,[4] contemporary with Kachrylion's cups, has on one side Herakles and the lion, Theseus and the Minotaur, Theseus and Prokrustes. It looks as if the painter followed the new scheme but substituted Herakles and the lion for another labour of Theseus. Another contemporary cup,[5] by Skythes, has on one side Theseus and the Sow of Krommyon and on the other side Theseus attacking a youth, whom Brommer identifies as Prokrustes, although Prokrustes should be bearded. This cup has the love name Epilykos: Epilykos appears as the trainer of Sostratos on Phintias' psykter,[6] and Sostratos is paired with Xanthippos, who married an Alkmaionid,[7] on a black-figure pelike,[8] so that Epilykos *kalos* at least brings us into the neighbourhood of the Alkmaionidai. Another route leads in the same direction; Robert[9] identified this Epilykos with the father of Teisandros, whose daughter married Perikles' son Xanthippos; the two families were at least friendly, if not connected by blood.

The only one of these themes which seems to occur earlier is Theseus and the Bull of Marathon: the kalyx-krater by Phintias, the cup by Oltos, with Dioxippos *kalos*, and the cup by the Euergides painter[10] are all contemporary with the Kachrylion cups, but besides several

[1] *ARV*² 108/27, Florence 91456; 115/3, London E 36.

[2] *ABL* 249/1; 252/58, pl. 43, 1, Athens 515.

[3] *ABL* 249/2. Cf. also *ABV* 560/517, Utrecht 34, Haimon Group, cup.

[4] *ARV*² 89/21, Louvre G 71.

[5] *ARV*² 83/14, Villa Giulia 20760, from Cervetri, *CV* pl. 23, 25, 26.

[6] *ARV*² 24/11. Cf. above, p. 55.

[7] W. G. Forrest, *CQ* 10 (1960), 233 puts the marriage in 508 B.C., which would fit.

[8] *ABV* 674, cf. above, p. 56.   [9] *RE*, VI.   [10] *ARV* 23/5; 58/53; 90/29.

black-figure vases of the early fifth century[1] an amphora by the painter of Würzburg 252[2] is dated by Shefton towards the end of the second quarter of the sixth century; it is a careful work but the painter may be old-fashioned; even so, it would, I think, be difficult to bring it below 530 B.C. There is no doubt about the scene, and we have to assume therefore that this story was already known then. This simply means that the *Theseid* built on local legends. Apart, however, from this one vase the black-figure pictures of Theseus' journey to Athens and its immediate sequel chiefly occur on skyphoi and lekythoi by the Theseus painter and his contemporaries and successors. The exceptions are two larger vases with Prokrustes: one is a pelike[3] of the late sixth century, contemporary with the Kachrylion cups, and the other a neck-amphora[4] by the Troilos painter painted about 480 B.C. It seems clear that after the initial introduction the scenes from Theseus' journey to Athens quickly became stock scenes which any patriotic Athenian would be glad to have on a symposium vase or a perfume vase.

The only theme from the story of the Pallantidai which occurs on vases at all is Theseus' wrestling with Klytos, son of Pallas. As we have seen, Euthymides put it on the neck of his psykter[5] as a mythological paradigm to the two athletes on the other side; one of the athletes is Phayllos who appears with Epilykos on Phintias' psykter. It is interesting that at just this time Euthymides should have picked, or been instructed to pick, just this rare scene as a mythological paradigm.

Theseus' abduction of the Amazon Antiope occurs first on later black-figure and early red-figure about 515, well before the two vases by Myson discussed above.[6] The earliest are probably two red-figure cups by Oltos. On the earlier cup (London E 41), which comes from Vulci, Theseus and Antiope with Peirithoos and Phorbas take part of the outside and the scene on the other half is irrelevant (man and woman between two boys on horseback); inside is Theseus and one of the rescued Athenian girls after the Cretan expedition. The later cup (Oxford 1927.4065, *CV* pl. 53) has a naked woman with cup and ladle inside, and the Antiope story takes the whole of the exterior. The two

[1] e.g. Theseus painter, *ABV* 519/6; Edinburgh painter, *ABL* 216/16–17.
[2] *ABV* 315/2; Shefton, *Hesperia* 31 (1962), 347; Cab. Med. 174, *CV* pl. 33, 3–7.
[3] Athens, Agora, P12561. Von Bothmer, *JHS* 71 (1951), 43, no. 23.
[4] *ABV* 400.   [5] *ARV*² 28/11. Cf. above, p. 56.
[6] Von Bothmer, *Amazons*, 124 ff.; *ARV*² 58/51 and 77; *ABV* 367/87 and 93.

black-figure vases, one from Vulci, are amphorai type A of the Leagros group, very little later than the Oltos cups. One has Dionysos, satyrs and maenads on the back, a natural decoration many times repeated on symposion vases. The other has Herakles and the lion, a stock scene since very early times, but here it balances the new story, just as the Euergides painter put on his cup Herakles and the lion as well as Theseus and Prokrustes, and Theseus and the Minotaur. This must surely mean that Theseus, as newly conceived in the *Theseid*, is to rank as an equal of the old hero Herakles. Whether the Alkmaionidai were responsible or not, someone saw to it that the new *Theseid* found its way on to symposion vases in the last two decades of the century and the effort was extremely successful.

For the next step we are well documented. Kimon, the son of Miltiades, the victor of Marathon, who married Isodike, daughter of the Alkmaionid Euryptolemos[1] and sister of Peisianax, brought Theseus' bones back from Skyros about 475 B.C. An enclosure was built in the Agora to protect them, and the walls of the enclosure still had in Pausanias' day three paintings, an Amazonomachy, a Centauromachy and Theseus recovering Minos' ring from the sea (this last attributed to Mikon).[2] At the Theseia banquets were held in sixteen dining rooms in the Agora.[3] The pictures in the Theseion were probably painted in the late seventies. Fairly soon after, the Stoa Poikile, which was originally called after Peisianax, Kimon's Alkmaionid brother-in-law, was built, as it was either finished or nearly finished in 462–461 B.C.[4] The paintings were: (i) The Battle of Marathon by Panainos (brother of Pheidias) or Mikon. This does not concern us but it may have had some slight late reflection on vase-painting.[5] (ii) The Sack of Troy by Polygnotos. This may have only contained the scene of the swearing of Ajax the son of Oileus after the rape of Kassandra, and does not concern us. But one should nevertheless note the Niobid

---

[1] This is presumably the 'Euryptolemos *kalos*' of three late sixth-century cups by Apollodoros (*ARV*² 120/1, 4, 5).

[2] Onesimos (*ARV*² 318/1) and Briseis painter (406/7) are too early for the Theseion. Kadmos painter (1185/6) is too late to include here, but may, of course, be a special commission for the Theseia.

[3] On all this, cf. H. A. Thompson, *Hesperia* 35 (1966), 40.

[4] L. H. Jeffery, *BSA* 60 (1965), 42. Texts in R. E. Wycherley, *Athenian Agora* III (1957), 30 ff., and 113 ff. for Theseion.

[5] Cf. Jeffery, op. cit., 44, n. 15 with ref. to *BCH* (1963), 579, figs. 14–15, and *ARV*² 1550/3–5, moulded vases in the form of a distressed Persian's head.

painter's great pictures of the Sack of Troy (*ARV*² 599/1, 8, 18). (iii) The
Battle of Oinoe. Dr Jeffery has argued very convincingly that this was
in fact a picture of the appeal of Adrastos to Theseus for aid in getting
the bodies of the Polyneikes' Argives buried. (iv) Amazonomachy. (The
picture of the suppliant Herakleidai was probably later and does not
concern us. The picture of Sophocles as Thamyras has already been
noted.)

A number of very fine early classical vases have always been connected with these paintings. They have been studied in detail recently
so that discussion can be brief.[1] They seem to be peculiarly near big
painting in composition and in individual figures. The question that I
want to ask here is whether this peculiar and short-lived phenomenon
is not best explained if they were special commissions either for the
banquets in the Theseion or for the private parties of Kimon or
Peisianax. The following lists are restricted to the earliest vases, for the
most part before 450 B.C., which are the most likely to be special commissions.

(1) *Amazonomachy.* It is impossible to distinguish between pictures inspired by the Theseion and pictures inspired by the Stoa Poikile.
What we are told is (i) that Mikon painted Amazons on horseback,
(ii) that Mikon painted both in the Theseion and in the Stoa Poikile.
A bell-krater from Spina by the vase-painter Polygnotos painted
well after 450 B.C.[2] has three Amazons on the front, two mounted,
one on foot. Their names are Hippomache, Peisianassa and Dolope.
Peisianassa is named after Peisianax, the founder of the Stoa Poikile,
and Dolope is named after the inhabitants of Skyros, from where
Kimon brought Theseus' bones. It is therefore a reasonable guess
that both pictures had the Amazon invasion of Attica defeated by
Theseus. The early vases are:

(a) Kalyx-krater from   Von Bothmer, 160, no. 1, pl. 74/1; *ARV*²
Bologna.   891, Bologna 289. Near the Penthesileia
                         painter.

(b) Volute-krater from   Von Bothmer, no. 5, pl. 74/3; *ARV*² 599/
Gela.   2, Palermo G 1283. Niobid painter.

[1] D. von Bothmer, *Amazons in Greek Art* (Oxford, 1957), 161; B. B. Shefton, *Hesperia* 31
(1962), 362; E. Simon, *AJA* 67 (1963), 43; K. Jeppesen, *Acta Jutlandica* 40, 3 (1968).
[2] *ARV*² 1029/21; von Bothmer, op. cit., 200, pl. 83, 7.

(*c*) Volute-krater from Ruvo. — Von Bothmer, no. 6, pl. 74/4; *ARV²* 600/13, Naples 2421. Niobid painter.

(*d*) Volute-krater from Bologna. — Von Bothmer, no. 8; Pfuhl, fig. 508; *ARV²* 612/3, Bologna 279. Painter of Bologna 279.

(*e*) Volute-krater from Numana. — Von Bothmer, no. 7, pl. 75; *ARV²* 613/1, New York 07.286.84. Painter of Woolly Satyrs. Here, pl. 12.

(*f*) Kalyx-krater. — Von Bothmer, no. 3; *ARV²* 615/1, Geneva MF 238. Geneva painter.

(*g*) Kalyx-krater from Numana. — Von Bothmer, no. 2, pl. 74, 2; *ARV²* 616/3, New York 07.286.86. Painter of Berlin hydria.

(*h*) Cup from Vulci. — Von Bothmer, 147, no. 30, pl. 71/4; *ARV²* 879/1, Munich 2688. Penthesileia painter.

All, except perhaps the last, give the impression of having been painted at nearly the same time from the same models and all except the first and last come from the Niobid painter and his immediate followers. The two kraters from Numana, although by different painters, have the most adventurous adaptations of motifs from big painting both in the positions taken by the figures and in details of clothing. The cup is perhaps the earliest but obviously belongs to the same heroic world. The Penthesileia painter was named after it, but we have no knowledge of a great picture of Achilles and Penthesileia in this style, so that it is probably better to call it Greeks and Amazons and to assume that its very close echoes of big painting in postures, added colours, costumes and sheer scale come from either the Theseion or the Stoa Poikile.

(2) *Centauromachy*. The new scheme for a Centauromachy which appears at this time places the action actually in the banqueting chamber so that the couches appear and tables are used as shields. Here five vases[1] are early, four of them by the Niobid painter and the painter of the Woolly Satyrs, whose volute-krater from Numana ((*e*) above) has the new Centauromachy on its neck. As the

---

[1] Dr J. R. Green tells me that they are all from the same workshop.

Centauromachy is only recorded for the Theseion, it would be naturally supposed that the Amazonomachy on this vase is also the Theseion Amazonomachy. The vases are:

(*a*) Column-krater.	Shefton, *Hesperia*, 31 (1962), 365, no. 1; *ARV*² 541/1, Florence 3997. Florence painter.
(*b*) Volute-krater.	Shefton, no. 2; *ARV*² 599/9, Berlin 2403. Niobid painter.
(*c*) Volute-krater.	Shefton, no. 3; *ARV*² 599/10, Erbach. Niobid painter.
(*d*) Volute-krater from Numana.	Shefton, no. 4; *ARV*² 613/1. Painter of Woolly Satyrs. Neck scene of (*e*) above.
(*e*) Volute-krater.	Shefton, no. 5; *ARV*² 613/2, Louvre C 10749. Painter of Woolly Satyrs.

All are mixing-bowls. The only recorded provenance is Numana for (*d*), but it is extremely likely that (*a*) and (*e*) came from Etruria, and there is nothing to say that (*b*) and (*c*) did not.

(3) *Adrastos' appeal.* Before Dr Jeffery had made her suggestion that what Pausanias calls the Battle of Oinoe was in fact Adrastos' appeal to the Athenians to assist in burying the Argive dead, Professor E. Simon[1] had interpreted the picture on one side of a volute-krater from Spina by the painter of Bologna 279, who painted one of the great Amazonomachies ((*d*) in our list on page 87), as Adrastos and the children of the Seven supplicating Athena and Theseus in the presence of the ghosts of their fathers. She suggested that the original picture had its place in the shrine of Poseidon Hippios and Athena Hippia at Kolonos and that the representation of the Seven on the other side of the volute-krater from Spina was inspired by the fresco of Onasias in the temple of Athena Areia at Plataiai. She also argued that the same shrine at Kolonos held the great picture which inspired the Niobid painter's famous kalyx-krater from Orvieto (*ARV*² 601/22); this she interprets as Theseus rising from Hades when Kimon brought his bones back from Skyros to Athens. Still later Professor Jeppesen[2] interpreted the Niobid painter's picture as an attempt by Eteokles with the help of Herakles to make an agree-

---

[1] *AJA* 67 (1963), 54; *ARV*² 612/1; Ferrara T 579.
[2] *Acta Jutlandica* 40, 3 (1968); Louvre G 341, *CV* pls. 1–3, *Enc. Phot.* iii, 22–3.

ment with Polyneikes, and assigned the original to the temple of Athena Areia at Plataiai.

What is clear is that these two vases are unique, and therefore are likely to be special commissions. The problems of interpretation may be too difficult to solve in default of new evidence. Simon's interpretation of the volute-krater has the advantage of making both sides pictures of Theban legend. Jeppesen's interpretation of the kalyx-krater has the same advantage since the slaying of the Niobids is a Theban story inasmuch as they were the children of Amphion. It is also clear that the kalyx-krater more than any other vase-painting has taken over its compositions from great painting; this seems to me rather to rule out an original as far from Athens as Plataiai. For the kalyx-krater at least the immediate source must be two great pictures, and preferably two great pictures in Athens, and it may have been painted for a party celebrating their dedication. The Niobid story only becomes popular in Athens from this time onwards, which again suggests a new great picture in Athens. The interpretation of the volute-krater is further complicated by the scenes on the neck; a satyr-play, which has been connected with Sophocles *Pandora*,[1] on one side and Herakles and Bousiris on the other. Possibly one should not search for any connection between the neck scenes and the main scenes. Herakles is always a welcome and a cheerful figure, and a satyr-play is a tribute to Dionysos in whose honour the symposion is held. But this picture of a satyr-play is individual in the sense that it includes the choregos, the rich man who was responsible for producing the chorus, and one would think that he ordered the vase. The satyrs have hammers and the satyrs had hammers in Sophocles' *Pandora*, but there are earlier hammering satyrs[2] and the woman rising from the ground may be Persephone rather than Pandora. Then we could conjecture an Aeschylean satyr-play on this theme, and Aeschylus' *Eleusinioi* has already been connected with the Stoa Poikile by Miss Jeffery; the scene of the Seven on the other side is a necessary anticipation of the story about the bodies of the Seven (Aeschylus' *Seven* was produced rather earlier in 467 B.C.). But then we have to account for a lapse of

---

[1] *MTS*[2] AV 18 and p. 150.
[2] e.g. on the Eucharides painter's stamnos, *ARV*[2] 228/32; *MTS*[2] AV 3.

some twelve years between the production of the *Eleusinioi* and the painting of the vase; this is not impossible if past dramatic triumphs were celebrated at the symposia of Sophocles' Association of Actors. But it is wisest to admit our ignorance, while asserting that this was a very special vase.

VASES MADE TO CELEBRATE DRAMATIC VICTORIES

If we cannot be certain that the volute-krater with the Seven against Thebes and the supplication of Adrastos celebrated or remembered a dramatic victory, we can be certain about a number of other vases having such an occasion. I have quoted already the vases[1] with the name of Euaion, son of Aeschylus, illustrating Aeschylus' *Toxotides* and Sophocles' *Andromeda* and *Thamyras* and the white kalyx-krater illustrating Sophocles' *Dionysiskos*, which cannot be separated from the Andromeda vases, and I have quoted the Pronomos vase with a picture of cast and chorus of a satyr-play produced at the very end of the fifth century. In these cases Euaion and Pronomos are known historical characters so that identification is easy. But one can observe other pointers on these vases which can be applied where the vase has no name or no certain name to assist identification. In all the story itself or its treatment is new. In all there is at least an allusion to stage costume – much more, of course, in the masks and costumes of the Pronomos vase – but in the *Toxotides* Lyssa is a stage figure, in the *Andromeda* vases the oriental costume of Andromeda was probably worn on the stage, on the *Thamyras* vases the double-sided mask of Thamyras is indicated and on the Phiale painter's hydria the face of Argiope is stylized on the mask worn by Euaion; the Papposilenos of the Dionysiskos scene recalls stage costume.

Dramatic vases have been fully exploited many times for the information that they give on dramatic production and the help that they sometimes render in reconstructing lost plays.[2] What needs emphasizing here is that the earliest example of each theme is almost certainly a special commission either to celebrate a first production or to celebrate

---

[1] Cf. above, p. 47.

[2] Cf. M. Bieber, *History of the Greek and Roman Theater*, rev. ed. (Princeton, 1961); Séchan, *Études sur la tragédie grecque* (Paris, 1926); A. W. Pickard-Cambridge, *Dramatic Festivals of Athens*[2]; A. D. Trendall and T. B. L. Webster, *Illustrations of Greek Drama* (London, 1971).

a revival or, as I have suggested above, for the symposia of Sophocles' association in honour of the Muses. We cannot except in rare cases be certain of the event which caused the special commission because, although we know that Aeschylus was revived in the fifth century and that a classical tragedy was revived at the City Dionysia every year after 386 B.C., we do not have any precise information as to what was played in any deme theatres that may have been already in existence in the fifth century. I have discussed most of the tragedy and satyr-play vases in *MTS*² 44 ff. and appendix, and A. D. Trendall has dealt with the comedy vases in *Phlyax Vases* (=*PH*). Here I only list a number of examples which seem to me likely to have been special commissions and note those which may have celebrated the first production.

*ARV*² 121/23; *MTS*² AV 7. Cup by Apollodoros from Cervetri, armed satyr-choreut. Perhaps Aeschylus, *Isthmiastai*. (First production.)

*ARV*² 495; *MTS*² AV 9. Fragments of oinochoe near painter of Munich 2413 from Athens, Agora. Maenad tragedy. (First production.)

*ARV*² 571/74; *MTS*² AV 13. Hydria by Leningrad painter from Corinth. Tragedy with Persian subject, probably Aeschylus, *Persae*. (First production.)

*ARV*² 571/75; *MTS*² AV 14. Hydria by Leningrad painter. Satyr-choreuts building couch. Perhaps Aeschylus, *Thalamopoioi*. (First production.)

*ARV*² 586/47; *MTS*² AV 15. Pelike, undetermined earlier mannerist. A and B. Tragic maenad with sword. The word *kalos* can only apply to the *man* playing the part. Cf. perhaps the Oltos cup, *AJA* 72 (1968), 383, pl. 129.

*ARV*² 652/2; *MTS*² 144. Neck-amphora, probably by the Nikon painter, from Kameiros. A. Phineus and harpy. B. Harpy. Phineus wears mask; the harpy is labelled *kalos*, i.e. the actor or chorusman. (Perhaps first production, cf. *MTS*² 144, for other vases with the same subject, approximately contemporary; *ARV*² 502/7 may give on the back Aeschylus and Perikles (as choregos) with Nike.)

*ARV*² 1030/33; *MTS*² 141 f. Kalyx-krater by Polygnotos from Vulci.

Two rows: above, Nereids with the armour of Achilles. Below: A. Achilles mourning for Patroklos. B. Ransom of Hektor. Alludes to all three tragedies of Aeschylus' Achilles trilogy. (Perhaps an earlier vase celebrated the first production; what is clear is that the representation of the Nereids riding on dolphins and sea-monsters when they bring the arms to Achilles starts in the early classical period and is due to Aeschylus.)

*ARV*² 1046/10; *MTS*² AV 22. Fragmentary bell-krater by Lykaon painter from Taranto. Aeschylus, *Prometheus Pyrkaeus*. The satyr is in stage costume, so that this probably celebrates a revival. It is the first of a long line of illustrations which do not have the stage costume, so that apparently the picture of the revival vase set a fashion for stock vases.

*ARV*² 1057/104; *MTS*² 153. Kalyx-krater from Lokroi, not far from Polygnotos. Euripides, *Aigeus*. (First production.)

*ARV*² 1072, 1562/4; *MTS*² 150. Volute-krater, Kensington class. A. Probably Sophocles' *Pandora*. B. Youth with spears pursuing woman. On B., Alkimachos *kalos*. This is the citharode, cf. above, but as his name is on B. we cannot claim that he had any part in the production of Sophocles' *Pandora*. (If Sophocles' *Pandora*, probably first production.)

*ARV*² 1112/5; *MTS*² 140. Column-krater by the Orestes painter. A. Orestes at Delphi. B. Komos. (Perhaps too late for first production of Aeschylus' *Eumenides*; three other vases are approximately contemporary.)

*ARV*² 1180/2–6; *MTS*² AV 23–4. Dinos from Kallithea near Athens, and fragments of four bell-kraters, discards of a potter's workshop near the Peiraeus station in Athens, by painter of the Athens Dinos. Chorus of a satyr-play. One would suppose that this was a set painted to celebrate a victory with a satyr-play, like the Pronomos vase, but the bell-krater fragments are said to be discards; perhaps this simply means that the painter of the Athens Dinos had a disastrous firing from which he saved at least the dinos which is preserved and gave him his name. Perhaps a revival of Aeschylus' *Amymone*, if 1180/10 belongs to the set.

ARV² 1301/5; *MTS²* 138. Skyphos by Penelope painter from Basili-
cata. Aeschylus, *Choephori*. (Like the *Eumenidus* vases perhaps too late for first production.)

ARV² 1338; *MTS²* AV 37. Fragments of a volute-krater from Taranto,
akin to the work of the Pronomos painter. Dionysos seated
with cast and chorus of a tragedy. Euripides' *Hippolytos* has
been suggested, in which case this would be a deme-
theatre revival, but the identification is by no means
certain.

ARV² 1335/34; *PH²* 3. Herakles in Centaur-chariot. Inspired by
comedy. Nikias painter.

PH² 9–13. Unglazed oinochoai type 3 with painted polychrome
decoration, four from a well of the end of the fifth century
in the Agora, the fifth said to have been bought in Athens.
Scenes from comedy. Probably part of a set made to
celebrate a first production.

These are all symposion vases. The comedy set with its unique technique may have been a rush job to celebrate an unexpected success. The
rest, including the Euaion and Pronomos vases, are of high quality
except perhaps the *Eumenides* set. Finds in Athens presumably mean that
the occasion was important and the vase treasured. Finds in Etruria
probably came there by the second-hand market. Finds in Taranto and
Ruvo (Pronomos vase) perhaps mean that someone from this dramatic-
ally minded area visited Athens, saw the production and secured the
vase, and the same may be true of finds in Corinth and Kameiros.

VASES MADE TO CELEBRATE VICTORIES WITH LYRIC,
PARTICULARLY DITHYRAMB

The dithyramb vases examined so far have been claimed as bespoke
pieces because they had inscriptions put on before firing: the maenad
Polynika, Alkimachos and Axiopeithes *kalos* (*ARV²* 1045/6); Phrynichos and his singers (*ARV²* 1145/35); singers at the Panathenaia (*ARV²*
1172/8). Each of the scenes could have been painted on the vase in the
hope that a successful choregos of a dithyrambic choir would buy them,
and we shall have to consider these stock dithyrambic vases later. There

are, however, a few vases without prefired inscriptions which were probably ordered to celebrate dithyrambic or other lyric triumphs.

The first is a stamnos by the Eucharides painter[1] which has already been quoted as an example of hammering satyrs earlier than Sophocles' *Pandora*. It was painted in the decade 490–480 B.C. The satyrs wear the loincloths of the satyr-play but are hairy all over. This is curious and it is possible that the painter is thinking of the men dressed as hairy satyrs who, according to the Polion vase, sang dithyramb at the Panathenaia. This is the more likely as the other side of the vase shows preparations to sacrifice a bull which was a traditional prize for the dithyrambic poet. Then the chorus must have sung of the rising of the earth-goddess when the satyrs hammered the ground. She is not represented, but her head appears with two hammering satyrs on a contemporary lekythos[2] by the Athena painter, which was conceivably ordered for the same celebration.

The Kadmos painter's volute-krater in Ruvo[3] has already been quoted chiefly for the named satyrs and maenads on the back. The sacrifice before the herm on the neck and the Nike and tripod in the larger of the two Marsyas scenes suggest that it was a special commission for a victory with a song about Marsyas. Mr Boardman[4] has recently published a fragmentary kalyx-krater by the Kleophon painter which must be about the same date as the volute-krater, and these are the earliest Marsyas scenes on vases; he dates the sculptural group by Myron before 450 B.C. and regards it as a dedication by the lyric poet Melanippides after a victory with his Marsyas. The dating of the Myron group seems to me too high but it would be difficult to bring Melanippides' victory much below 450[5] so that the time gap remains. What we have then is (1) Melanippides popularizing the Marsyas story in a successful lyric poem soon after 450 (we do not know that it was a dithyramb), (2) Myron's group possibly dedicated by him, (3) the Marsyas story popular with the vase-painters from about 425, and our vase seemingly painted to celebrate a victory with a Marsyas dithyramb. The mythological index of *ARV²* quotes no Marsyas before the clas-

[1] *ARV²* 228/32; *MTS²*, AV 3.
[2] *ABV* 522/87; Metzger, *Imagerie* 12, pl. 3/1 and 2, Cab. Med. 298.
[3] *ARV²* 1184/1. Cf. above, p. 72.
[4] *JHS* 76 (1956), 18, pl. 1; *ARV²* 1144/16.
[5] Cf. Pickard-Cambridge, *Dithyramb etc.²* 40.

sical period but thirteen instances in the classical period by the Kleophon painter, Dinos painter, painter of Munich 2335, Kadmos painter and Pothos painter. All of these are symposion vases, kalyx-kraters, bell-kraters, one volute-krater and a fragmentary stamnoid vase. Known provenances are Greece, Naukratis, Taranto, Camarina, Vassallaggi (also Sicily) and Bologna. Some of these may well have been ordered for the same party as the Kadmos painter's volute-krater (1184/1); in particular, his bell-krater (1184/13) includes the tripod on a column, and it is tempting to interpret the painted inscriptions over the heads of Artemis, Marsyas and Apollo – NOSS[OS], MOLKOS, ALKIS – as the names of chorusmen, but they are very strange names.[1] But the story must soon have become a popular stock scene, since on the Kadmos painter's kalyx-krater from Camarina it is an irrelevant other side to Theseus' departure from Ariadne under the encouragement of Athena and Poseidon, a scene possibly inspired by Euripides' *Theseus*.[2]

In the case of the Kadmos painter's volute-krater the existence of Melanippides' poem justifies us in taking the tripod as the sign of a victory with a lyric poem, and the sacrifice at a herm may suggest a dithyramb.[3] The Pronomos vase (*ARV*² 1336/1) and the fragments from Taranto (*ARV*² 1338) show that the tripod can be the sign of a victory with a satyr-play or with a tragedy. We have suspected already the use of a tripod as a sign of an athletic victory, even where it was not the prize, and I think we have to suppose a similar use of the tripod on base or column to indicate a victory with sung poetry. It is not always easy to distinguish this use from the use of a tripod to indicate a sanctuary,[4] but it is probably justifiable to suspect a special commission for a victory with a sung poem when there is no reason to suppose that the scene depicted took place in a sanctuary. I should admit here the following:

*ARV*² 1184/6, Bologna 303, *CV* pls. 79, 82, 83. Kalyx-krater by Kadmos painter from Bologna. A. Theseus brought to Poseidon under the sea. B. Herakles and deer. The tripods are on the

---

[1] Could they be satyr-names?

[2] *ARV*² 1184/4; E. Simon, *A.K.* 6 (1963), 14, pl. 5, Syracuse 17427, *CV* pl. 10.

[3] I must honestly admit that the satyr added to the Marsyas scene on the neck has a typical satyr-dance posture, so that a satyr-play is an alternative.

[4] Cf. Metzger, *Imagerie* 98.

side with Theseus. It is, I suppose, conceivable that Bacchylides' paian for the Keians on this subject was revived in Athens.

ARV[2] 1184/33, Berlin 2634. Hydria by Kadmos painter from Vulci. Kadmos and the snake. (Nike belongs here to the story; Athena sends her to crown Kadmos.)

ARV[2] 1334/16, London E 498. Bell-krater by the Nikias painter. Herakles, Nike, Dioskouroi, Athena.

ARV[2] 1318, Vienna 1771. Bell-krater from Orvieto, may be by painter of the Athens wedding. A. Judgement of Paris.

The wonderful kalyx-krater by the Dokimasia painter,[1] with the death of Agamemnon on one side and the death of Aigisthos on the other, is surely a special commission. The pictures have been much discussed because of their two most startling features, the enveloping robe of Agamemnon on one side and the lyre held by Aigisthos on the other. Dr M. I. Davies has made a good case for the earlier occurrence of the robe, and it is natural to think of Stesichoros as an author. It is possible that Stesichoros' *Oresteia* was revived in Athens in the early fifth century; we know that he was well known in Athens and we need not necessarily suppose that the revival was either choral or complete; it is possible that some citharode sang parts of it at a competition. We may have two other vases painted for the same celebration. Mrs Vermeule says that the kalyx-krater was made in the Berlin painter's workshop and a late stamnos[2] by the Berlin painter himself again shows Aigisthos as a lyre-player. These two may certainly have been ordered and painted for the same occasion; I do not feel certain that we can date precisely enough to exclude a cup by the Brygos painter,[3] which has partly preserved Klytaimnestra pulling the robe off the dead Agamemnon (whose name is inscribed). The moment depicted is different but the version of the story is the same. If it is possible to date this cup down to 480–470, it is worth observing that whereas the potting of the kalyx-krater links it to the Berlin painter's workshop, as a painter the Dokimasia painter is an associate of the Brygos painter.

[1] *ARV*[2] 1652, now Boston 63.1246; E. T. Vermeule, *AJA* 70 (1966), 1; M. I. Davies, *BCH* 93 (1969), 214.

[2] *ARV*[2] 208/151, Boston 91.227; *AJA* 70 (1966), pl. 4; *BCH* 93 (1969), fig. 11.

[3] Bareiss collection. *Metr. Mus. Bull.* (June 1969).

Some Special Stories

This is for the moment as far as we can go in distinguishing bespoke vases. We have now to start from the other end. We have to distinguish between the uses to which vases of different shapes were put and ask whether the painter would naturally predict that certain types of scene were acceptable on vases with certain uses – wedding scenes on marriage vases, symposion scenes on symposion vases. Then we can go further and ask how far the painter predicted the kinds of success which make a man order a new set of vases, the kinds of success of which an illustration would be welcome to him and his friends. Sometimes we shall be able to say that they were stock scenes, sometimes that they were specially commissioned. Then beyond that we shall be able to distinguish and shall have to account for two main classes of illustration: pictures of ordinary occupations and pictures of mythology.

6

Uses and Subjects

Sometimes a vase-painter chooses a subject suggested by the use of the vase. A simple case is the appearance of fountain scenes on hydriai. The hydria is a water pot, and was used for carrying water from the fountain, whether for ordinary use in the house or for the symposion, or for washing or laying the dust in the palaistra: so either men or women at the fountain are a suitable decoration (some of the hydriai with named figures have already been mentioned above, pp. 45/57, 61). Fountain scenes[1] both in black- and red-figure are more common on hydriai than on other forms of vase as the following lists show:

Women at the fountain: ABV 261/41; 267/2, 3; 276/1; 280/1, 2; 333/27; 334/1–5; 335/1; 365/70–4; 384/26 (also men); 387/18 (man molesting woman); 393/1; 393; 397/30–2 (men and women); ARV^2 28/13 (two naked women washing, satyr, one woman drawing water); 29/1; 30/2; 34/12 (woman and youth, on the shoulder youths at fountain); 34/16 (women and a man); 209/167; 506/29 (Thracian women); 565/40 (women and two men); 1130/150, 154 (with Eros).

The remaining hydriai (1130/162–3; 1137/35; 1139/4) are small, not water pots but perfume pots, but because going to the fountain is women's work it is a suitable decoration for a perfume pot. The other kinds of vase so decorated are probably also perfume pots: ABV 383/9 (women and man), neck-amphora; 426/5–6, oinochoai; ABL 207/36, 62 (three women and man), lekythoi; 220/85 (naked women washing at the fountain), neck-amphora; ABV 479/1, neck-amphora; 481, onos (not a perfume vase but certainly a woman's tool); 497/187 bis, 191, lekythoi; 534/39 ter, oinochoe; ABL 241/11

[1] Cf. Dunkley, *BSA* 36 (1936), 142.

(three women and man), lekythos; *ABV* 604/72–3 (women and man), pelikai; *ARV²* 223/6 (naked woman washing at fountain); 286/18, pelikai; 379/144, cup; 658/28, lekythos, 79, alabastron; 681/ 98–101 bis, 201–3, lekythoi; 772, cup; 827/1, cup.

Men at the fountain. The men who join women fetching water or who molest them are mentioned above with the women. Men by themselves at the fountain are extremely rare. Boys wash themselves on the black-figure hydria which gives the Antimenes painter his name (*ABV* 267/1), and boys, including Megakles, draw water on Phintias' hydria (*ARV²* 24/9). These are commissioned pots. Otherwise there are only the boys on the shoulder of a Pioneer hydria mentioned above (34/12).[1]

To go further we must classify vases under their uses and ask how far the painters chose subjects suitable to the use.

The use of most Attic vase-shapes is clear and can be briefly noted (in each case the name is the conventional name used by archaeologists; Richter and Milne[2] discuss the relation of the conventional names to the real names).

Symposion. Amphora and pelike (on which see below), stamnos (may be used as mixing-bowl, e.g. as seen on the Lenaian stamnos, *ARV²* 1151/2), krater (may also be used as water-bath for cooling wine, as on *ABV* 186, oinochoe), dinos (which was also used as a funerary urn), hydria (also used for water for other purposes, as voting urns, and as funeral urns, as prize in torch-race, and very small hydriai must have been used for perfumes), chalice, psykter, kalathos, oinochoe (see below), kylix, kantharos, skyphos, rhyton, mastos, kyathos, plate, standlet.

Perfume. Aryballos[3] (for men to carry oil for ablution), alabastron (for women, also for perfume used after washing, cf. *ARV²* 1051/18, and seen in scenes with women buying perfume, *ARV²* 285/1, 596/1), askos, plemochoe (=exaleiptron), lekythos (seen in scenes of men buying perfume (*ABL* 209/81, pl. 24/4; black-figure pelike, Vatican

---

[1] Cf. M. Robertson, *BSA* 62 (1967), 6, n. 10; *GRBS* 11 (1970), 25, n. 18.
[2] *Shapes and Names of Athenian Vases.* Cf. also Sandulescu, *Studie Classice* 4 (1962), 35; Sparkes and Talcott, *Pots and Pans*, Agora Picture Book, no. 1.
[3] Cf. Beazley, *BSA* 29 (1927–8), 193.

413, *Mon.* II, pl. 45, Cloché, *Classes,* pl. 32, 2) and offered at tombs, cf., e.g., on *ARV*² 1227/1).

Marriage vases. Loutrophoros and loutrophoros hydria for fetching water for the bride's bath (also used as funerary gifts for those who died unwed). Nuptial lebes, which preserves the shape of a cauldron set on a stand over the fire for heating water but has become purely ornamental (cf., e.g., *ARV*² 1250/34). Lekanis, perhaps a trinket box.

Wool-working. Onos (=epinetron).

Libations. Phiale, oinochoe.

Two of the symposion shapes, the amphora and the pelike, were used for wine, oil and perfume, and one, the oinochoe, was used for wine and perfume.

I *Amphora and pelike* (both could be used as funerary urns, see below, p. 287)

(*a*) Prize Panathenaic amphorai were used for oil, but it does not follow that non-prize Panathenaic amphorai were also used only for oil. One kind of Attic unpainted wine amphora is very like the Panathenaic amphora in neck and proportions (e.g. Agora P 1253, *Hesperia* 7 (1938), 379, fig. 14).

(*b*) Wine was sold in unpainted pointed amphorai, and presumably the rare painted pointed amphorai (e.g. *ARV*² 182/6) were also used for wine. But unpainted pointed amphorai were also used for oil as the picture of Alkimos shows (*ARV*² 1154/38 bis, see above): it has not been reproduced but is described as 'sale of oil: Alkimos filling an amphora from a pointed amphora'. Presumably the presence of Athena shows that it is a sale of oil rather than wine. It may be our only picture of the sale of oil as distinct from perfumed oil; at the next stage the stock of perfumed oil is kept in something smaller than a pointed amphora.

(*c*) Amphorai (as distinct from Panathenaic and pointed amphorai), neck-amphorai, and pelikai could be used for wine, oil or perfume. The telling evidence seems to me to be the following:

Wine. The psykter-amphora (e.g. *ABV* 109/29) and psykter-neck-amphora (e.g. *ABV* 307/62) prove the use of amphorai for wine. Dionysos carries a neck-amphora (probably of metal) on the François vase (*ABV* 76/1, Florence 4209). A neck-amphora is shown in the wine-selling scene on *ABV* 299/20, Brussels R 279, *CV* pl. 16, 5; it is probably relevant that the vase with the picture of wine-selling is itself an amphora type B.[1] On a wall in the same scene hangs a pelike. Wine-selling is also represented on two red-figure pelikai (*ARV*[2] 1162/17–18), on which a phiale is filled from an amphora. It is probably also relevant to note that vintage scenes occur on black-figure amphorai (*ABV* 140/2, 151/22, 217/10, 225/10, 306/33).[2]

Oil. The only probable scene of oil-selling (as distinct from perfume-selling) is the Alkimos scene, which fixes the amphora type B for oil. The ordinary household used a lot of oil for lighting, cooking, anointing, and probably bought its stock in unpainted pointed amphorai as the Alkimos scene shows; perhaps, however, if a present of oil was made, it would be made in a painted amphora like the Alkimos vase.

Perfume. In perfume-selling scenes the stock is kept in a pelike (*ABV* 393/16; *ARV*[2] 185/30, 285/1–2, 596/1) or a neck-amphora (*ABL* 209/81; Vatican 413, cf. above). The vases themselves which have these scenes are all pelikai[3] except for the lekythos (*ABL* 209/81).

II *Oinochoai*

They are very often depicted on vases with symposion or komos scenes, used both for dipping wine out of mixing-bowls and for carrying wine to drink (shape III is the chous, which was used at the Choes festival when each man drank from his own chous, and it appears commonly in the komos)[4] and in libation scenes to pour wine into the phiale. But shape I, at any rate, was also used for perfumes as it appears with lekythoi on the steps of tombs (e.g. *ARV*[2] 1227/1), and on the Nikoxenos painter's pelike with the sale of perfumed oil (*ABV* 393/16) the man who comes to buy carries a purse and an oinochoe, shape I. Shape X appears hanging on the wall (e.g. white lekythos, *ARV*[2] 998/157) in the gynaikeion so that it can also be a perfume vase.

---

[1] An amphora B also holds wine (or wine mixed with water) on *ARV*[2] 147/14, Noble, *Techniques*, fig. 84, cup by Epeleios painter, New York 96.18.71.

[2] Also on cups: *ABV* 256/20; 389; and black-figure plaque apparently dedicated to Athena, *ABV* 337/32. In red-figure satyrs vintaging are shown on symposion vases, cup, *ARV*[2] 104/5, kraters, 186/49 bis, 281/30, 569/39, 1089/19 bis, 1170/7.

[3] Add *ABV* 396/22, 25. Possibly amphora B, *ARV*[2] 604/51.

[4] The small choes with children were probably made for children's graves (cf. R. Green, *BSA* 66 (1971), 189, and S. Karouzou, *AJA* 50 (1946), 125).

Perfume Vases. The aryballos was used exclusively by men and the alabastron by women. The ordinary painted lekythos was not used exclusively by women but it was certainly very commonly used by women (it appears hanging on the wall in women's quarters and standing beside a laver),[1] and the squat lekythos, which starts at the end of the ripe archaic period (*ARV*² 264/55–6, Syriskos painter; 385/224, Brygos painter) and gradually supersedes both the small red-figure lekythos and the alabastron, was predominantly a woman's vase. Some special shapes may also be mentioned. Miniature Panathenaic amphorai[2] were made from the late fifth century, perhaps to contain the Athenian perfume, *panathenaikon*. There were similar miniature pointed amphorai, including red-figure and black-glaze amphoriskoi, from about 430 B.C. onwards. Beazley suggests that the small vases with mouth, neck and handles like the amphoriskoi but bodies formed like almonds were designed for almond-oil. Like them are the aryballoi with the body in the shape of cockleshells; the earliest of them were made by Phintias, but they go on much later.[3] The moulded almonds and cockle-shells bring us into the neighbourhood of the head-vases. The aryballoi with moulded woman's heads, negroes' heads, single or paired, and once with a head of Herakles paired with a head of a woman, and the oinochoai with negroes' heads, women's heads and sometimes Herakles or Dionysos and once a satyr, run from 520 to about 420 B.C.[4] The moulded aryballoi were certainly perfume vases. Beazley[5] says the negroes were made because it would be a crime not to make negroes when one had that magnificent black glaze; a negro slave appears walking with his old master on the Copenhagen painter's name amphora and even if the figures on the negro alabastra are reminiscences of a picture based on the *Aithiopis*,[6] they still attest the popularity of the negro. Herakles is a hero of feasting, and perfume was used by banqueters. It is this connection with the symposion, I think, that accounts for him, as well as for Dionysos and the one satyr of the moulded oinochoai; these head-oinochoai are mostly too small[7]

[1] Cf. *ABL* 129. [2] Beazley, *BSA* 41 (1941), 10.
[3] *ARV*² 25; *BSA* 41 (1941), 14 n. 3. [4] *ARV*² 1530 ff.
[5] *JHS* 49 (1929), 39. [6] Cf. *Manchester Memoirs* 89 (1947), 6; *ARV*² 267.
[7] They range in height from 9 to 25 cm with the majority about 18 cm, but they are much thinner than oinochoai II and III of the same height.

to be used for wine and have small mouths more suitable for perfume; they are perfume pots like some other oinochoai (see above, p. 101). *Kalos* names[1] appear on two of the earliest head-aryballoi, so that they must have been bespoken before they were fired. But one point of moulding vases must surely have been to produce them in quantity, and in fact we have replicas; they must, therefore, normally have been stock vases.

But there is the further question connected with this. Did you take your perfume vase to the perfume-seller and have it filled, or did you buy a vase of perfume from him? The pictures of perfume-sellers show the purchaser coming with his lekythos or her alabastron to get a fill, and we have seen a considerable number of perfume pots which we have supposed to be bespoke vases – the head-aryballoi with *kalos* names, the alabastron with 'Aphrodisia *kale*' (*ARV²* 306), Douris' aryballos (*ARV²* 447/274), the alabastron with Timodemos (*ARV²* 1610), the white lekythoi with *kalos* names, the Anakreon lekythos (*ARV²* 36/2), Makron's pyxis and aryballos (*ARV²* 479/336–7), the lekythos with the boy reading the hymn to Hermes (*ARV²* 452), the lekythos with the pyrrhic dancer Zephyria (*ARV²* 677/11), the squat lekythoi with Polykles and Chrysippos (*ARV²* 1316(a), 1324/47). Probably when we come to consider individual scenes, many will have to be added to these. The lekythos with the picture of perfume-selling certainly belongs here, and the pelikai with pictures of perfume-selling were presumably painted for someone who wanted a larger supply than could be contained in a lekythos. On our evidence we must suppose also that small pelikai, hydriai and neck-amphorai contained perfumes. These must all have been taken to the perfume-seller by the purchaser to be filled.

Professor Haspels[2] gives a unique example of a lekythos with *Irinon*, iris perfume, painted on the lip before firing. It was decorated by the Diosphos painter with palmettes only. I see no way of determining whether it was bespoke by purchaser or by perfume-seller. But the possibility that a perfume-seller had the idea of putting up his perfumes in labelled bottles is attractive. And if it is true that the miniature Pan-

[1] *ARV²* 1530/1; 1531/1.
[2] *ABL* 124, 235/66, Athens 12271, pl. 37/2.

athenaic amphorai[1] and the almond-lekythoi both indicated by their shape the name of the perfume that they contained, again they would naturally have been made for the perfume-seller and bought from him ready filled. We have therefore to reckon with both practices; you might either take your perfume pot (whether bespoke or not) with you to the perfume-seller or buy one there ready filled.

[1] Is it fanciful to suggest that a small hydria with an owl and a laver (*ABL* 248/2) was also made to contain *panathenaikon*?

7

Wedding and Funeral Scenes

One would naturally expect wedding scenes to occur on marriage vases, and from the early classical period onwards they do. Earlier the distribution is unexpected. The following list gives (1) the wedding scenes in *ABV* and (2) the wedding scenes in *ARV²*, both divided according to shapes.[1]

	Black-figure	Red-figure
amphora	20	—
loutrophoros	—	98
dinos	1	—
nuptial lebes	(3)	32
krater	3	1
chalice	1	—
hydria	24	5
oinochoe	4	3
lekythos	4	3
pyxis	—	6
onos	—	1
lekanis	—	1
cup	—	1

The surprising figures here are not the high figures of wedding scenes on loutrophoroi and nuptial lebetes in red-figure (they start with the

[1] *ABV* 82/3; 90/4; 98/34, 132, 133; 107/3, 57 bis; 119/4; 134/15; 141/1, 5; 142/2, 7; 260/30; 261/35, 37; 264; 264/1; 267/9–11, 132; 277/10; 281/10, 13–14, 17; 286/13; 288/22, 29; 296/1, 15; 298/6; 304/1; 322/15, 16; 324/31–35; 328/11; 330/1–2; 332/25, 29; 335/5, 7, 28; 337/1; 364/59–61, 85, 108; 419; 421; 431/4–5; *ABL* 216/13, 50; *ABV* 498; *ABL* 232/5; *ARV²* 261/27; 488/85–100; 513/16; 514/1–2; 519/24–8, 31, 31 bis; 526/61, 73; 539/40, 44; 540/6; 544/59; 545/8; 548/43–4; 551/27; 554/79; 571/76; 581/9–12; 582/1; 816/6; 841/70–111 bis; 890/172; 899/146; 958/64; 990/46; 1017/44–5, 50; 1031/51–2; 1053/31; 1079/1–2; 1080; 1098/35, 38, 46 bis; 1102/5, 2–3; 1103/1–6, 9–11; 1112/3; 1126/1–2, 4, 6, 9–92, 95, 196; 1133/1; 1135/1; 1147/59; 1155/42; 1172/10; 1178/1–4; 1179; 1191/2; 1224; 1225/1–2; 1225/3; 1249/15, 32; 1256/11; 1266/1–9, 12; 1277/23; 1313/10; 1317/1, 3; 1317/1; 1320/1–3; 1322/11–32 ter; 1326/71, 79; 1332/1, 4; 1335/31–2.

Syriskos painter at the very end of the archaic period) but the practical absence of these in black-figure and the high figures for amphorai and hydriai in black-figure. It looks as if there was a change of custom about 480 B.C.: before that date painted vases with wedding scenes were normally used in a symposion before the wedding in the bridegroom's house and were presents to the bridegroom; the scene was the wedding procession with the bride and bridegroom in a chariot. Herakles and Hebe (*ABV* 261/37) and Peleus and Thetis (*ABV* 260/30) in the same scheme are mythological paradigms. After that wedding vases were normally presents to the bride, and the scene was more often the dressing and preparation of the bride than the wedding procession (which in the pictures now usually went on foot) and men other than the bridegroom were seldom represented.

The loutrophoros, as we know, was also used as a funeral offering for those who died before marriage, and this accounts for a number of the black-figure loutrophoroi (*ABV* 110/35–6; 139/13–14; 177; 409; 519/8–9; *ABL* 229/59–60; 252/74–5).[1] We have noticed before Phintias' loutrophoros (*ARV*² 25/1) with men leading a sow to sacrifice, and supposed that it was a special offering to Demeter. A black-figure loutrophoros, also from Eleusis (*ABV* 309/97), has a procession of men (one with tripod), men and youths carrying baskets and men carrying dinoi and baskets; this also may have been a special offering to Demeter.[2] Similarly some of the other black-figure loutrophoroi with women in stately procession were probably ritual vases (*ABV* 86/6; 88/1–3; 89/1–5; 117/21).[3] In Athens itself the Shrine of the Nymph (or of the Bride?) under the south slope of the Acropolis received offerings of loutrophoroi from the seventh century to the Hellenistic period. The black-figure examples have not, as far as I know, been studied, but the red-figure loutrophoroi account for rather under half of the 92 wedding scenes included above. It is difficult to get exact figures because these large vases are fragmentary. But the fact that wedding scenes are attested on loutrophoroi in the Shrine of the Nymph from Hermonax in the early classical period (*ARV*² 488/84) to the Manner of Meidias

---

[1] *ABV* 137/66 with men carrying tripods was found in the Kerameikos and is therefore presumably a funeral vase; it probably takes with it *ABV* 139/15.

[2] A connection of Demeter with games is given by *ARV*² 650/9 bis, amphora, A. Demeter at altar, B. men at pillar of stadion.

[3] The last, however, is from the Kerameikos and therefore presumably a funeral vase.

painter in the late fifth century (ARV^2 1322/26) shows first that the ritual was connected with marriage and secondly that all the other fragments, which have pictures of women but without anything to define them as wedding scenes, do in fact belong to wedding scenes; this adds at least another 45 red-figure loutrophoroi with wedding scenes (ARV^2 215, 501, 502, 506, 515, 522, 531, 534, 554, 632, 648, 689, 717, 957, 1013, 1079, 1098, 1137, 1155, 1157, 1162, 1176, 1277, 1313). Three of these show mythical weddings instead of contemporary weddings: ARV^2 534/11, Manner of Alkimachos painter, wedding of Peleus; 632/1, Methyse painter, wedding (with chariot) of Alkestis; 1013/12, Persephone painter, wedding of Herakles and Hebe. These are mythological paradigms, and probably we should accept the more violent seizure of Oreithyia by Boreas (ARV^2 506/26, Aegisthus painter) and of Tithonos by Eos (ARV^2 957/45, Comacchio painter) in the same sense. This interpretation is suggested by the wonderful epinetron by the Eretria painter (ARV^2 1250/34),[1] which must be a wedding present: on the sides the marriage of Harmonia and the marriage of Alkestis, but on the end Peleus wrestling with Thetis, not the subsequent stately marriage. The other red-figure loutrophoroi in the ripe archaic period continue the black-figure line of funeral loutrophoroi, and red-figure and white-ground funeral loutrophoroi[2] run right on parallel with the wedding scenes.

Black-figure nuptial lebetes are not very common. The earliest, by Sophilos (ABV 40/20), was found in Smyrna. The scene is the wedding of Menelaos and Helen and is a mythological paradigm of an ordinary wedding like the marriage of Hektor and Andromache in Sappho's marriage song: one wonders if some Ionian in Athens commissioned it as a wedding present. The other examples in ABV seem irrelevant to marriage: ABV 80/2 Amazonomachy;[3] 87/20 frontal chariot; 125/32, frontal chariot. Perhaps these, like the funerary loutrophoroi, were presents to the dead. But there is a late-sixth-century nuptial lebes with a wedded pair in a chariot, the common black-figure wedding scene (London B 298, Richter and Milne, fig. 72), so that the use of this shape as a marriage vase is old, but painted examples were evidently much

---

[1] Athens 1629, Schweitzer, *SB* (Heidelberg, 1961), 6.
[2] Cf. L. Kahil, *AK* Beiheft 4 (1967), 146.
[3] Cf. von Bothmer, *Amazons*, 9, no. 40, pl. 19, 2.

rarer in the sixth century than later. Finally a small nuptial lebes ascribed to Douris (*ABV*, 400): the dances on either side are relevant, and this was probably a perfume vase presented to a bride.

Funeral scenes also naturally appear on funeral vases. We have noted that loutrophoroi may be funeral vases, and the possibility that nuptial lebetes were also sometimes funeral vases. Prothesis scenes have been examined in great detail by Zschietzschmann.[1] All vases which have them were surely designed for funerals. A few cups have been found (e.g. *ABV* 113/81, Lydos) and some curious one-handled kantharoi, which were perhaps made for the Etruscan market (*ABV* 346–7).[2] In addition, scenes of mourning occur in black-figure on the neck of a hydria (*ABV* 268/22) and on an alabastron (*ABV* 518/5) and in red-figure on a hydria (*ARV*² 617/13). Red-figure lekythoi, such as *ARV*² 720/19 with a man looking at a stele, and white-ground lekythoi of secondary shape, such as *ARV* 730/5 with a youth at a stele, look forward to the great series of white funeral lekythoi by the Achilles painter, his companions and successors, which run through the second half of the fifth century and are frequently decorated with visits to the tomb.[3]

[1] *MDAI(A)* 53 (1928), I.
[2] Poursat, *BCH* 92 (1968), 550 ff.
[3] Cf. also below, pp. 185 f., 217, 223, 230–3, 235–7, 239, 240, 243.

8

Symposion and Komos Scenes

The typical symposion scene shows one or more figures reclining on a couch. It is difficult to draw a clear line between the symposion itself with entertainers present and the succeeding komos when the revellers danced and sang on their way home or to intrude into another symposion. In the following list Beazley's distinction between symposion

	Black-figure		Red-figure
		alabastra	0 + 4
amphora	5 + 36		7 + 34
small amphorai	7 + 30		0 + 8
		chalice	1
cups (all shapes)	62 + 91		547 + 667
dinos	1 + 0		3 + 2
epinetron	1 + 0		
hydria	4 + 1		6 + 8
small hydriai	0 + 4		
krater	4 + 1		164 + 306
		lekanis	0 + 1
lekythos	67 + 33		1 + 14
oinochoai	10 + 35		10 + 16
pelike	1 + 5		1 + 50
small pelikai	0 + 2		
plate	1 + 2		1 + 4
psykter	0 + 1		1 + 2
pyxis	0 + 1		0 + 0
		rhyton	5 + 6
stamnos	20 + 9		11 + 19
standlet			1 + 0
		askos	7 + 0

and komos is followed: the first figure for each shape is the number of symposion scenes and the second the number of komos scenes.

In black-figure komoi considerably outnumber symposion scenes. Perfumes were used at the symposion and the komos was the sequel of the symposion so that it was natural that both should appear on perfume vases as well as on vases used for wine and water. The small amphorai, hydriai and pelikai are perfume vases like the lekythoi and pyxides, but it is noticeable that the large figures for perfume vases are made up by the rough and presumably cheap prefabricated lekythoi of the Haimon group. The only surprise is the 'men reclining and seated women' on the epinetron (*ABV* 480/2): it was a convenient scene for the space, and a hetaira would like to remember the symposion while working wool.

The distribution in red-figure is curiously different. It is true that again komoi outnumber symposion scenes, but the numbers of cups and kraters have gone up out of all proportion to other types of vase. It also looks as if in the fifth century the komos and symposion were not felt so suitable for perfume pots as before: small amphorai and lekythoi have dropped heavily and there are no small hydriai or small pelikai with these subjects.

Three special types of komos are omitted from the figures. Padded dancers and their successors are treated under Dances. Dancing on a wineskin, *askoliasmos*, is sometimes shown in early red-figure – the examples are *ARV²* 14/3, kalyx-krater; 43/178, cup; 94/104, cup; 124/13, cup; 166/3, cup; 169/6, cup. The other dance which is not included is the Anacreontic dance. In Anakreon's lifetime these were presumably pictures of the private-parties of a non-Athenian celebrity, and the Gales painter's lekythos (*ARV* 36/2) and the Kleophrades painter's kalyx-krater (*ARV²* 181/32) are special commissions. But as Anakreon died about 487 b.c.[1] the later ripe-archaic and early classical works can only remember him, and it is questionable whether we have a survival of the actual symposion dances or a survival of a pictorial tradition. The list is as follows:

Black-figure amphora: ABV 115/3; plate, *ABV* 294/21.

Red-figure: ARV² 36/2, lekythos; 82/17, cup; 181/26, pelike, 32 kalyx-krater; 273/18, column-krater; 280/11, amphora; 283/4, pelike; 290/25, stamnos; 305/1, lekythos; 372/169–70, cups; 414/30, cup; 427/132, 229, 244, cups; 508/4, amphora; 524/20, column-krater; 531/50, column-krater; 563/9, column-krater; 583/1, column-krater; 584/73, lekythos; 637/49, amphora; 672/7, amphora; 815/2, cup.

[1] Barron, *CQ* 14 (1964), 221. Cf. above, p. 54.

Symposion and Komos Scenes

References for the normal symposia and komoi are as follows:

Symposia. ABV 26 (two), 51 (twenty-one), 58 (five), 64, 83, 84, 91, 97, 104, 132, 152, 208, 209, 214 (two), 269, 324, 332, 343 (seven), 344 (eight), 381, 383 (five), 386, 388 (five), 390, 396, 448, 449, 474, 475; ABL 216; ABV 480, 483; ABL 222 (two); ABV 496, 502 (three), 504; ABL 252; ABV 520, 530 (two), 534 (two), 551 (fifty-six), 574 (three), 580 (three), 581 (three), 593 (two), 595 (two), 597, 612 (four), 624 (three), 627, 638; ARV 5, 20, 23, 27, 28, 29, 31, 33, 34, 36 (two), 48 (three), 52, 58 (twelve), 70 (nine), 79, 81, 85, 86, 88 (four), 96 (two), 97 (two), 98 (two), 103, 104, 105 (five), 106, 110 (three), 117 (four), 119 (two), 120 (four), 121, 124, 125, 129, 131, 133, 134, 137, 139 (forty-eight), 141 (two), 142 (four), 144 (five), 145 (two), 147, 148, 152 (four), 154 (nine), 165, 167 (two), 168, 171 (three), 173 (two), 175 (three), 176 (three), 185, 193 (two), 221, 223, 224, 225 (two), 227 (five), 234, 239 (nine), 260, 266 (three), 275 (three), 277, 278 (four), 279, 281 (two), 290, 316 (three), 320, 326 (eight), 330, 331 (four), 336 (eleven), 341 (seventeen), 348, 349, 351 (two), 353 (twenty-six), 359 (four), 364(five), 369 (two), 371 (nineteen), 386, 389, 393, 401 (four), 403, 404, 410, 418 (fifteen), 427 (twenty-four), 448 (three) 454, 455 (three), 456 (two), 466 (twenty-nine), 505 (three), 508 (two), 514, 517, 524 (five), 532, 536, 543 (five), 555, 563 (two), 567 (six), 572, 576 (four), 583, 584, 600, 602, 609, 612 (two), 613, 615, 625, 632, 644, 650, 684, 741, 781 (two), 785, 791 (twenty-two), 801, 803, 812, 818 (three), 831 (three), 832 (two), 834, 836 (six), 840, 856, 861, 863, 865 866, 868 (eleven), 871 (five), 894 (five), 899, 904, 906 (two), 907, 911 (thirty-three), 918, 926 (two), 931, 959 (twenty-eight), 964 (three), 965, 968, 970 (two), 980, 981 (two), 1020, 1028 (four), 1034, 1038, 1045, 1052, 1055 (six), 1064 (two), 1069 (two), 1071, 1083 (two), 1086 (two), 1089 (three), 1091 (four), 1095, 1097 (seven), 1101 (four), 1108, 1113, 1115, 1118 (five), 1120 (three), 1125, 1137, 1144, 1151, 1152 (two), 1164 (sixteen), 1170, 1171, 1184, 1186 (two), 1190 (two), 1249, 1267, 1276 (twenty-eight), 1282 (five), 1292, 1297 (five), 1323, 1333 (eight), 1342 (two), 1345, 1401.

Komoi. ABV 157 (three), 176, 186, 205, 206, 209, 210 (three), 214 (five), 219 (four), 225 (six), 248 (two), 250 (three), 276, 299, 339 (three), 340 (two), 343 (two), 344 (six), 367 (four), 382, 383 (seven),

385 (six), 386 (two), 387, 388, 390 (three), 393 (three), 395, 405, 426,
428, 429, 437, 447 (four), 449 (two), 450 (two), 455 (two), 469 (five),
471; *ABL* 206 (four), 215; *ABV* 474, 475, 479, 481, 482 (two), 483,
484, 488, 496 (three), 503; *ABL* 251 (eight), 253; *ABV* 519 (six);
ABL 256 (six); *ABV* 523 (two), 530 (two), 531, 532, 534, 535 (two),
536 (two), 537; *ABL* 241, 245; *ABV* 538, 556 (fourteen), 573 (four),
574 (four), 576 (three), 578, 580, 586, 589, 592, 593, 594 (eight), 596,
597 (five), 607, 612, 619 (eight), 627 (two), 628, 632, 633 (twenty-
seven); *ARV* 9, 15, 21, 27, 28, 29, 31, 32 (three), 34 (two), 40 (two),
43 (eight), 52, 55 (thirteen), 70 (twenty-three), 78, 79, 80 (three), 81,
82 (thirteen), 86 (two), 88 (twenty-four), 96, 97 (two), 98 (four), 104
(two), 105 (three), 108, 111 (two), 113 (two), 114 (two), 115, 120,
124 (five), 127, 128, 129, 134, 136 (three), 137 (two), 138, 144 (two),
145, 146 (seventeen), 148, 149, 150 (ten), 152 (two), 153, 154 (twelve),
156 (two), 161 (three), 165 (three), 166 (five), 168, 169 (four), 170
(two), 173 (two), 174 (five), 175 (two), 176 (two), 177 (five), 178,
179 (three), 181 (four), 195, 198 (twenty-one), 221 (two), 224, 225,
227 (two), 228 (eight), 233 (eight), 235 (seven), 236 (seven), 238
(forty-two), 243 (two), 245 (three), 252 (three), 258, 260 (three), 266,
272 (two), 273 (four), 277, 280 (thirteen), 285, 287, 290 (seven), 296
(three), 298, 301, 309, 315 (four), 316 (two), 318, 320 (two), 324
(nineteen), 328 (three), 330, 331 (two), 335 (eight), 337 (twenty-
nine), 342 (thirty-two), 348 (two), 349 (five), 352, 354 (eleven), 357,
358 (twenty-three), 359 (three), 361 (ten), 372 (forty-two), 387 (ten),
389 (four), 391 (five), 402 (four), 404, 405 (two), 409, 412 (five), 414,
416, 418 (fourteen), 427, 428 (seventeen), 448 (two), 449, 450, 454
(two), 455, 456, 461 (fifty-two), 483 (four), 488 (three), 494, 499
(four), 502, 504 (six), 506, 508, 510 (three), 513 (two), 515, 516 (four),
517 (six), 518 (six), 521, 525, 528, 531 (eight), 533 537 (seven), 539,
541 (eighteen), 546 (eleven), 550 (two), 551 (three), 561, 563 (ten),
566 (two), 567 (thirty-one), 572 (four), 575 (nineteen), 583 (four),
584 (seven), 609 (two), 615, 626 (three), 627, 629 (three), 632, 637
(two), 644, 648 (two), 672, 683 (nine), 691, 715, 775, 782, 784 (two),
785, 790 (seventeen), 797, 799, 800, 802 (seven), 809 (seven), 810
(twelve), 818, 824, 825 (three), 826, 830 (four), 833 (two), 837 (four),
863, 868 (four), 871 (four), 882 (seven), 897, 902 (nine), 907, 914
(two), 941 (eight), 945 (eight), 947 (two), 948, 950, 974 (three), 977,

978 (six), 979 (two), 1005 (two), 1023 (three), 1028 (six), 1034, 1036, 1045, 1047 (eight), 1052 (two), 1055 (four), 1064 (two), 1069 (two), 1071, 1075, 1077, 1088 (two), 1089 (two), 1092, 1095, 1098 (two), 1100, 1101 (two), 1104 (two), 1107, 1108 (three), 1112 (five), 1113 (two), 1115 (five), 1116, 1118 (four), 1120 (four), 1121 (two), 1122 (two), 1124 (two), 1136, 1139 (two), 1143 (nine), 1153, 1155, 1166 (two), 1171 (two), 1183, 1186 (three), 1190 (two), 1193, 1255, 1261, 1277 (three), 1278 (three), 1283 (six), 1284 (five), 1286, 1293 (two), 1294 (two), 1301 (two), 1305, 1318 (two), 1333 (two), 1401 (two), 1404.[1]

[1] These scenes are so numerous that I have only given the page numbers and the numbers of instances by the painter whose entries are on that page: the page number is usually the first with the painter's entries, rather than the actual page. I have included in the symposion the attendants, men with amphorai, men with couches, cup-bearers, even when they appear alone. (Vases in the addenda are entered under the page numbers of their painters.)

9

Dances

It is impossible to keep pictures of dances distinct from pictures of the symposion and from pictures of the komos which followed the symposion. Dancers performed at the symposion and the members of the symposion danced in the streets. Moreover there is one major class of ritual dance scenes which merges gradually into the komos, the dance of the padded dancers. At the beginning, in the early sixth century, their affinity with Corinthian padded dancers is obvious, and they are dressed in short chitons which suggest padding; but as the century advances they are represented, naked first with red chests and later as ordinary black-figure men, but steps and attitudes of the padded dancers continue and these komasts may take the place of satyrs or be included with satyrs as part of Dionysos' retinue. This phenomenon[1] has been frequently discussed and can be briefly interpreted here.

The connection with Corinth at the beginning is extremely close. Beazley[2] says of the KX painter, the chief painter in the Komast group, that two of his favourite shapes are borrowed from Corinth and the dancing komasts are Corinthian. The last statement needs qualification in one important respect: on Corinthian vases when women dance with the padded dancers they are naked, on the earliest Attic vases they wear the same short chitons as the men and they probably are men dressed up as women. This means that although the painters of the Komast group were probably inspired by imported Corinthian vases to represent padded dancers, the padded dancers that they represent are Attic and not Corinthian. Or, to put this as the patron would see it, the patron liked the Corinthian vases and said to the potter why should we

[1] e.g. GTP 29 f.; Webster, *The Greek Chorus* (London, 1970), 11 ff.
[2] DBF 20.

not have our own padded dancers, who dance in honour of Dionysos, on the cups that we use in the symposion? So the tradition was started and the subsequent development by which the padded dancers become normal black-figure men is due partly to the tendency of stock figures to lose their individuality, partly to the fact that the steps of the padded dancers were also the steps of other excited dancers at the symposion or the komos. We can trace the tradition down to the end of black-figure, and a very high proportion of the vases on which these dancers occur are symposion vases; a seeming exception is the tripod kothon in the manner of the KY painter, but probably this was really a lamp[1] which would be entirely suitable for the symposion.

The komast tradition in black-figure (references to *ABV*)

	Early	Middle	Late
amphora	95/21, 27, 31, 33, 41, 46, 52, 66, 72, 74, 82, 105, 106, 107, 112; 683/51 bis, 60 bis, 105 bis	110/32, 115/2; 120/21 bis; 138/3, 151/11, 225/4–9; 303/4; 304/7; 306/48, 94, 96	
small amphora		131/4	484/4
cup	26/22 ff.; 31/7 ff.; 33/2–3; 33/1–12; 34/1–5; 35/3–9; 36/1–4; 37; 63/3, 13, 35–6; 71/3, 4, 15, 17, 23, 34–7; 79	113/74–6; 151/77; 191; 209/1	614/3
dinos	82/3; 90/1		
hydria	91/2; 95/131	123/714	
krater	35/36; 36/1–5		
lekythos		111/38; 151/61	463 (*ABL* 203/1)
nuptial lebes			400
oinochoe	35/37 (680)	151/39, 45, 66	
pelike			339/1
plate		111/47; 131/4	
tripod kothon	33/1		

The table shows very clearly that this tradition gradually died out through the century and that in the earliest period cups predominate, but about 570 B.C. begin the large number of Tyrrhenian amphorai with komasts as one of their bands of decoration; then in the middle period komasts continue to be popular on amphorai from Lydos to the Swing painter.

[1] *ABV* 33/1; I have extended the suggestion of P. N. Ure, *AE* (1937), 259, to include the tripod kothon.

One early skyphos[1] is unique. It is by the KX painter and was found in Athens. The men are dressed as komasts but instead of dancing they walk behind a lyre-player and carry a variety of drinking vessels, rhyta, skyphoi of two types and a kantharoid cup. This must be some special ceremony in which drinking vessels were taken to a shrine of Dionysos, a ceremony like that on the Minoan steatite vase from Knossos.[2] The skyphos may have been specially painted for a subsequent party in celebration.

The earliest komast vases closely reflect the actual performance of the padded dancers but the performances were not unique. However, there are later representations of pre-dramatic dances which probably were unique or at least were only revived at long intervals, so that there is some reason to regard the vases as special commissions. Those listed in *ABV*, *ABL* and *ARV²* are as follows:[3]

AVB   66/57. Cup by Heidelberg painter. A. and B. Anacreontes'. From Greece.

       297/17. Amphora, type B, by painter of Berlin 1686. A. Chorus of 'knights'. B. Satyr and maenad. From Cervetri?

ARV² 1622/7 bis. Psykter by Oltos. Sifakis, *BICS* 14 (1967), Warriors riding dolphins.

ABV   434/3. Oinochoe, group of Vatican G48. Three men running in long chiton, himation and helmet.

       473/187. Oinochoe, Gela painter. Chorus of cocks.

       518/2. Lekythos, Theseus painter. Warriors riding dolphins. From Athens.

       586/67. Lekythos, Beldam painter. Hoplites carrying severed heads.

       587/4. Lekythos, Beldam painter. Dance of Amazons.

It is not easy always to draw the line between pre-dramatic dances and other dances. The 'Anacreontes' on the Heidelberg painter's cup with their formal grouping and their flute-players who wear the same costume certainly look like a public performance, however they should be

---

[1] *ABV* 26/21, Athens 640, *MDAI(A)* 62 (1937), pl. 57, 2 and 58.

[2] Nilsson, *Gesch.* pl. 3/1.

[3] These and further examples are discussed in *The Greek Chorus*, 13 f., 20 f. Cf. also the illustrations and the list in Pickard-Cambridge, *Dithyramb etc.²*, 301 ff., esp. nos. 24, 28, 30, which are not in *ABV*. Perhaps also the Minotaurs, *ARV²* 54/9; 66/125, 132; 75/62.

interpreted. But the 'Anacreon' on the amphora type C (*ABV* 115/3) is taking part in a private party and is a forerunner of the Gales painter's Anakreon:[1] this may be a very early reaction to Anakreon's arrival in Athens; here there is no inscription, only the curious male figure in female clothing. Three other black-figure scenes may be pre-dramatic rather than ordinary dances:[2]

ABV 305/31. Amphora, type B, by the Swing painter. A. Theseus and Minotaur. B. Men in long himatia running towards flute-player. From Orvieto? *MDAI(R)* 53, pl. 25, 2. (With the Swing painter we cannot argue for any connection between the sides: the old men did not necessarily sing of Theseus and the Minotaur.)

ABV 305/26. Amphora, type B, by the Swing painter. A. Herakles and the lion. B. Procession: men headed by flute-player. From Etruria. Naples 2503, *CV* pl. 3, 1–2.

ABV 522/1–2. Skyphoi, near the painter of Rodin 1000. A. and B. Old men in long chitons and himatia, walking to the right. From Rhitsona and Tanagra. Ure, *Sixth and Fifth Century Pottery from Rhitsona*, pl. 18, 5.

From these we turn to what we may call recurrent official dances where we only suspect a bespoke vase when the figures are named. The most obvious are dithyrambs, 'Lenaian' maenads and pyrrhics. I have already noted two special vases with dithyramb singers because of their inscriptions: they represent two separate types and each has a number of earlier vases behind it which are in no way marked as special vases.[3] The first type is the slow dithyramb of draped men or boys, of which the Kleophon painter's bell-krater with the named singers is a late and splendid example (*ARV*[2] 1145/35, Copenhagen 13817). This tradition starts for us with the Amasis painter in the third quarter of the sixth century: *ABV* 153/36 (oinochoe), 63 (lekythos), 66 (oinochoe); then in the fifth century: *ARV*[2] 407/18, 416/3 (cups); 529/3 and 6 (neck-amphorai: A. dithyramb singer, B. pyrrhicist); 957/38 (small pelike, A. dithyramb singer, B. Lenaian maenad); 1138/41 (small hydria, A.

---

[1] Cf. above, p. 54.

[2] Perhaps also *ARV*[2] 213/238; 345/78; 837/10; 861/14, which may have some connection with the phallophoroi.

[3] Cf. *The Greek Chorus*, pp. 20, 22.

dithyramb singer, B. woman with torch). These are dithyrambs sung and danced in honour of Dionysos at his festival. (I omit here another class of representation: the vase which represents the actual victory by including Nike in the scene.)[1] The other type is the dithyramb danced by men dressed as satyrs: the bell-krater of the late fifth century by Polion (*ARV*[2] 1172/8, New York 25.78.66, cf. above, p. 48) is proved by its inscription to be bespoke. The earlier examples are black-figure: *ABV* 285/1, amphora, circle of Antimenes painter; *ABV* 495/158, lekythos by the Gela painter. Possibly *ARV*[2] 228/32[2] also belongs here, with its hairy satyr-choreuts using mallets.

The so-called 'Lenaian' maenads have been much discussed.[3] I doubt if we can be certain what the festival is, but at some festival in Athens women dressed as maenads shared wine from a mixing-bowl, and danced and sang before the mask of Dionysos. A late and splendid example, the stamnos by the Dinos painter (*ARV*[2] 1151/2), has already been quoted for its names. The whole list in red-figure is as follows.

ARV[2] 98/1. Alabastron, Pasiades painter. Woman with phiale, heron, woman dressed as maenad, running, with sprigs in her hands. From Marion, Cyprus, London B 668.

462/48. Cup, Makron, from Vulci, Berlin 2290.

499/10. Stamnos, Deepdene painter, from Capua, Warsaw 142351, *CV* pl. 27.

569/40. Column-krater, Leningrad painter, from Ruvo, Milan.

595/71. Oinochoe (i), Altamura painter. Two women holding branches of ivy at flaming altar with herm of young Dionysos(?). Hobart, Hood, *Greek Vases in Tasmania*, pl. 16.

621/33–42. Stamnoi, Villa Giulia painter, from Falerii, Vulci, Capua, Gela. Cf. Pickard-Cambridge, *Festivals*[2], fig. 18.

628/4–6. Stamnoi, Chicago painter. One from Capua.

672/14. Lekythos, near London E 342, from Athens, Cracow 1252, *CV* pl. 10, 2.

957/38. Small pelike. Comacchio painter. A. ?Lenaian maenad, B. ?dithyramb singer. From Nola.

[1] Cf. above, p. 72, and below, pp. 132 f.
[2] Cf. *MTS*[2], AV 3, and above, p. 94. Cf. *The Greek Chorus* 20, fig. 3.
[3] Cf. *The Greek Chorus*, 18 f., 81 f.

1019/82–4. Stamnoi, Phiale painter (83 from Suessula). Cf. Pickard-Cambridge, *Festivals²*, fig. 20.

1072. Stamnos, recalls Barclay painter, New York 21.88.3, Philippaki, pl. 42/4; Noble, *Techniques*, fig. 121.

1073/9–11. Stamnoi, Eupolis painter, 9 and 10 from Vulci. No. 11 shows thyrsoi planted in the sanctuary. Cf. Pickard-Cambridge, *Festivals²*, fig. 23.

1151/2. Stamnos, Dinos painter, from Campania, Naples 2419. Cf. above p. 69.

1249/13. Oinochoe (iii), Eretria painter. Mask in liknon (from Anavysos, Attica).

In this list the Altamura painter's oinochoe falls rather outside: the dance, the idol and the wine are missing, but the women are performing a Dionysiac ceremony. Similarly the early alabastron[1] gives preparations in the house (indicated by the heron), one woman pours a libation, the other practises her steps in the maenad dance. What is most noticeable is the large number of stamnoi, twenty-two, all whose provenance is known found in the West, running from about 460 to about 420. It looks as if they were painted in answer to a known demand, possibly, as stamnoi occur on the table under the idol in the Dinos painter's picture (and on others), for use in the festival itself rather than at a party to celebrate it, and a large number went overseas afterwards. The black-figure vases do not add anything to the picture.

ABV 395/3. Neck-amphora from Vulci, painter of Munich 1519. Women seated and women bringing them wine (B. boxers). Munich 1538, Nilsson, *Gesch.* i, pl. 36, 2.

ABL 222/27. Lekythos, Marathon painter. Four women at image of Dionysos.

ABV 488/3 (=*ABL* 222/26). Lekythos, group of Brussels A 1311. Same subject.

502/96. Lekythos, class of Athens 581. Maenads at image of Dionysos.

---

[1] Cf. Schneider-Hermann, *BVAB* 42 (1967), 75, lekythos by Bowdoin painter. Probably many other pictures of maenads by themselves really represent Athenian women as maenads, e.g. *ABV* 201/1; 627/7, 10; *ARV²* 73/31; 501/6 ter (1656); 725/2; 769/4; 1015/19; 1200/2; 1220/1, 11; 1303/1; 1304/4; 1324/43; 1350/25.

504/18. Lekythos, Kalinderu group. Women dancing at idol of Dionysos (from Eleusis).

ABL 250/44. Skyphos, Theseus painter. Satyr and maenad at an image of Dionysos. (From Athens?)

ABV 553/392–4. Lekythoi, Haimon group. Women at idol of Dionysos. (392–3, from Athens.) Athens 498, *CV* pl. 4.

560/518. Cup, Haimon group. Women dancing at the image of Dionysos. Stockholm, Nilsson, *Gesch.* i, pl. 37, 3.

573/2. Oinochoe. Woman at image of Dionysos in cave. Painter of half-palmettes. Berlin 1930. *MDAI(A)* 53, 89.

(Probably the following which show women in a vineyard with drink or food should be added: *ABV* 320/6, 366/75, 377/235, 380/287.)

They are all late. The earliest is not before 500 and the latest probably about 480. They are all very ordinary vases, perhaps all made for the ordinary home demands of women who performed in this festival, as rather later the red-figure oinochoe (*ARV*² 595/71) and the red-figure lekythos (*ARV*² 672/14). On the other hand the wonderful cup by Makron (*ARV*² 462/48) is surely a special commission. The very delicate and beautiful alabastron by the Pasiades painter (*ARV*² 98/1) one would expect also to be a special order; as it is an alabastron it should be a present for a woman, and the subject agrees with this. But the lip has a pre-fired inscription: ὁ παῖς καλός. Presumably this must be taken as the boy's description of himself, put on as a reminder to the girl. And how did it come to Cyprus? The other very good small vase is the chous by the Eretria painter (*ARV*² 1249/13) with the unique picture of the mask in the *liknon*; this too one would expect to be a special present for one of the women who took part in the festival.

The pyrrhic, the male war-dance with shield and spear, was performed in competition at the Panathenaia and may be already represented on geometric Attic vases.[1] As the list shows, it appears in red-figure in the last quarter of the sixth century and in black-figure at the beginning of the fifth century. It scarcely lasts after the early classical period as the only later example is the Academy painter's hydria (*ARV*² 1125/19). In red-figure all the vases are symposion vases except for a

[1] See *The Greek Chorus* 22, 26, 52; Poursat, *BCH* 92 (1968), 550.

single lekythos; but there are a number of late black-figure lekythoi and a single alabastron. The last must be a present to a woman illustrating her lover, but the rest may be either presents to women or perfume vases for the symposion. It looks rather as if for the period 520–450 B.C. young men took the same sort of pride in dancing the pyrrhic as they took in athletics, and then it fell out of fashion as an athletic dance[1] and so out of demand as a vase-picture.

alabastron	*ABL* 263/17
amphorae	*ARV*² 529/3 and 6 (contrasted with dithyramb singer)
cups	*ABV* 345/1; *ARV*² 57/40; 73/27; 136/10; 231/78; 354/23–4; 822/21
hydria	*ARV*² 34/14; 1125/19(?)
krater	*ARV*² 601/19; 602/28
lekythoi	*ABL* 252/66, 258/90; *ABV* 523/9; 584/18; *ABL* 267/27, 46, 72; *ARV*² 694
oinochoai	*ABV* 531/5–6
pelike	*ARV*² 578/69

Dances of women also go back to geometric times as pictures on Attic vases,[2] and this subject must have been in great demand particularly by women. The dances were cult dances although we cannot often say which particular cult is in the painter's mind. I give first a list which is divided by shapes and is roughly chronological:

amphora, small	*ABV* 483/3–4; 661/15
alabastron	*ABV* 584/2
astragalos	*ARV*² 765/20
cup	*ABV* 90/7; 620/73–84; *ARV*² 373/47; 390/1701; 914/142
hydria, small	*ARV*² 1138/41
krater	*ABV* 1/1; *ARV*² 618/1 (partheneion); 551/17, 1018/68, 1074/1 (mantle dancers)
lekythos	*ABV* 154/57 (shoulder); *ABL* 269/66; *ARV*² 1314/14
oinochoe	*ABV* 530/85; *ABL* 249/16
plate	*ABV* 119/7
pyxis	*ABV* 90; 622/125, 127
tripod kothon	*ABV* 45/26

[1] Perhaps, cf. *Ar. Nub.* 988.   [2] Cf. *The Greek Chorus* 5, 21, 25.

The majority of these can only be called 'women dancing' but some tell us rather more, and I take these in the order of the list.

ABV 661/15 is one of the miniature Panathenaics of the fourth century which are thought to have held the ointment Panathenaikon. From the picture it looks as if Athena on one side is matched on the other by a woman dancing with arms raised in greeting – a dance which summoned Athena to appear.

ARV² 765/20, London E 804, *CV* pls. 26–7, from Aegina. The Sotades painter's astragalos is surely a special commission, and must illustrate some special dance in which dancing women are met by an uncouth man, possibly Hephaistos. This seems to have some memory of a real dance behind it and not to be simply an illustration of mythology.

ABV 90/7, London 1906.12–15.1, *JHS* 66, 8, pls. 2–3. This dance of five women and a boy to an altar with Demeter on one side and probably Persephone on the other has been interpreted by Ashmole as the Thesmophoria. It is a unique scene and an elaborate cup, and is surely a special commission.

ARV² 390/1701; *ABL* 269/66, pl. 54/1. Both the inside of this cup, a rather special cup with white ground, and the very ordinary black-figure lekythos by the Beldam painter show women running, and the black-figure lekythos adds an altar. The cup was found at Brauron, where a number of chalices of special shape with women racing and dancing at an altar were also found. Evidently the Brauron Artemis created a special demand for a vase of a special shape illustrating the races and dances in her sanctuary. Our two vases repeat the theme on ordinary shapes and were presumably purchased by worshippers for their own purposes; the white cup may well have been a special commission.

ARV² 1138/41, London E 212, *CV* pls. 89/4, from Nola. The woman with torch, who matches a boy dithyramb singer, may be a member of a torch-chorus of women.

*ARV*² 551/17; 1018/68; 1074/1. Beazley takes the earlier krater by the Pan painter as an anticipation of the later kraters. The mantle-dancers probably danced in honour of Dionysos, and so their picture was suitable for any symposion.

*ARV*² 618/1, Villa Giulia 909, *CV* pls. 21–2, from Falerii. The Villa Giulia painter's superb kalyx-krater with a partheneion of women with linked hands is also certainly a symposion vase and perhaps a special commission for a symposion of women.

*ARV*² 1314/14, Louvre MNB 2110, from Attica. The presence of Aphrodite and Eros among the dancing women may mean that the painter was thinking of a dance in the cult of Aphrodite, which would suit a perfume pot.

ABV 154/57, from Vari, Attica, New York 31.11.10, Karouzou, *Amasis Painter*, pl. 43. The main scene of the Amasis painter's lekythos is women weaving a peplos. The shoulder has a dance of women up to a seated goddess whom the leading woman greets. Mrs Karouzou naturally suggests the Panathenaia. It is one of the few dance pictures which shows a change of tempo between running and dancing; another is the wedding dance on another very fine lekythos by the Amasis painter.[1]

As far as we can see, these dances all have a single line of dancers very often with linked hands, but there are a few vases where the dancers seem to be represented either in two lines or in pairs going in different directions, and here we must suppose the dancers to be divided into two ranks:

Men: *ABV* 305/22, amphora, New York 41.162.184, *CV*, Gallatin, pl. 36, 1. The pairs of men are ivy-wreathed and probably dance in honour of Dionysos.
ABL 199/12, lekythos.
*ARV*² 941/36, cup, Vienna University 503.37–8, *CV* pls. 37–8.

---

[1] Von Bothmer, *AK* 3 (1960), pl. 7; *The Greek Chorus*, fig. 5.

Women: *ABL* 199/20; 244/66–8, 71–2; *ABV* 706/399 bis and ter;
ABV 553/395–9 lekythoi.

ARV² 261/19, *Délos* 21, pl. 6, nuptial lebes by the Syriskos
painter from Rheneia. This is a very special vase which was
originally buried in a grave on Delos. The subject is Apollo
and a double-line dance of the Muses or the Delian women.
We cannot tell whether it was a wedding present preserved
till death, or a funeral gift for a woman who had died before
marriage.

Outside these pictures of cult dances numerous pictures survive of
duets and solos from the symposion. The duets are two boys or two
girls:

alabastron	*ABL* 263/13 (youths), 15 (women)
amphora	*ABV* 244/47 (men); 325/1 (women, ?maenads)
small amphora	*ABV* 343/8 (women, ?maenads)
cup-skyphos	*ABV* 567/629 (women); cup *ARV²* 1283/16, perhaps youths disguised as women
hydria	*ARV²* 1019/86, 1110/40 (women), 1131/164 (women)
lekythos	*ABV* 293/11; 584/21(709); 1323/68 (women)
oinochoe	*ARV²* 1353/3, 6 (women); 1313/12 grotesque dancers (men)
small pelike	*ARV²* 555/94 (women)

(The lekythos *ABV* 496/170 has exceptionally youth and woman
dancing.)

The solo dancers are more frequently girls than boys. Girls dancing the
pyrrhic at the symposion are recorded from the early classical period
and Zephyria, who is named, is as early as any. The Persian oklasma
dance is first seen in the free period.

solo boys:	small amphora	*ARV²* 554/45
	cups	*ABV* 209/1; *ARV²* 365/54; 381/179; 661/93; 904/79, 98; 907/5
	lekythos	*ABV* 502/118
	oinochoe	*ARV²* 1321/2; 1335/33
	pelike	*ARV²* 1119/28

solo girls:	alabastron	*ABL* 265/4–5; *ARV*² 99/14, 30; 100/28; 163/13. Pyrrhicist: *ABL* 263/17; *ARV*² 751
	amphora	*ABV* 217/9; *ARV*² 1016/37
	cup	*ABV* 209/1; 560/521; *ARV*² 7/8; 55/16, 68, 93, 129–30; 68; 80/10; 85/2; 88/1; 135/11; 149/8; 157/86; 378/121; 468/145, 158, 319; 1278/33
	dinos?	*ARV*² 1061/160 (kalathiskos dancer)
	dish	*ARV*² 787/5 (*Choropheles*)
	hydria	*ARV*² 500/38; 1019/87, 88; 1032/61;[1] 1061/159. Pyrrhicists 1060/144; 1085/35
	krater	*ARV*² 246/7; 564/21; 1125/18; 1186/25. Pyrrhicists: 1045/9; 1084/12; 1154/34; 1164/57–8; 1346/3. Oklasma: 1333/11, 25 Girl disguised as Eros: 1118/24 Girl disguised as Athena: 1190/30
	lekythos	*ARV*² 303/3; 311/2; 680/112; 1019/118. Pyrrhicists: 677/11 (*Zephyria*); 1019/121
	oinochoe	*ABV* 439/7; *ARV*² 1019/98; 1139; 1323/35; 1353/6. Pyrrhicist: 1094/103
	pelike	*ARV*² 232/10 bis; 500/32. Girl disguised as Eros: 1113/43 bis
	phiale	*ARV*² 1019/146, Boston 97.371. Noble, *Techniques*, fig. 141
	plate	*ABV* 659/11; *ARV*² 1305/1
	pyxis	*ARV*² 934/75
	rhyton	*ARV*² 930/101; 1278/26
	stand	*ARV*² 84/25; 163/14

These solo performers were performers at the symposion so that their pictures were suitable on symposion vases and on perfume vases which could be presented to the performer.

1 This may be a special commission. Lippold (*Neue Beiträge* 137) points out that Elpinike (Kimon's sister) plays the flute for girls dancing a Laconian dance, which would suit Kimon's pro-Spartan views. The hydria is Naples 3232, Furtwängler-Reichhold iii, 320–1.

10

Cult Scenes

We have already quoted a number of cult scenes both in discussing stock vases and in discussing special vases. In particular we have noticed pictures of weddings and of cult dances of various kinds.[1] And we have noticed some special scenes of sacrifice and prayer – to the Pythian Apollo by Kallias and his friends, by Archenautes and Diomedes, and to Hermes by horsemen – and two of the special vases were connected with the Panathenaia.[2] The potters must have known that scenes of sacrifice, prayer and libation were popular. The patron might want such pots to dedicate to the god to whom he had prayed or sacrificed, or for the symposion which followed the meal after the sacrifice, and, of course, libation was also part of the symposion. Or again a pot with such a picture could be a present to someone who had partaken in the ceremony itself or its celebration. In most cases we cannot distinguish between vases which were dedicated and vases which were used in the symposion or given as presents. Excavation in a shrine may tell us in some cases, and we can at least use the negative criterion that a vase dedicated in a shrine in Athens or elsewhere in Greece is unlikely to be found in an Etruscan tomb.

To survey this considerable material I make a first division into scenes of sacrifice, altar scenes (which are often sacrifices or cult dances cut down to the essential to fit the available space), herm scenes, and figures with torches and/or phialai. These are arranged under shape and black-figure precedes red-figure in each case; red-figure is divided into ripe archaic, early classical, classical and late fifth century.

Let us ask for a moment whether these figures tell us anything. If we look first at the scenes of sacrifice, the high figures are black-figure

[1] See above, pp. 117 ff.   [2] See above, pp. 49 ff.

	sacrifice					altar scenes					herm scenes			torch and/or phiale					total
	Bf	RA	EC	C	F	Bf	RA	EC	C	F	Bf	RA	EC	Bf	RA	EC	C	F	total
amphora	7	10	6	2			1	7							1	11	1		46
small amphora	1	1				1			1		1	1	3						9
alabastron			1			1	5	1							1	3			12
cup	3	16	11	2	1	2	40	52	9	2		6	1	1		6		1	150
hydria	2			2	1			3											8
small hydria	1					2		1	2								1		7
krater			5	18	4		2	4	1	1		1	3			4	2		45
lekythos	18	2	7	1	1			71	5				8		4	24	1		142
loutrophoros		1														2	1		4
nuptial lebes																1			1
oinochoe	7	1	2	3	2	3		3	2	2	3	1	1				1		31
pelike	1	2	2				4	5	1			2	3				1		22
small pelike				1				1	15							2	7		26
plaque	1																		1
pyxis									1								1		2
stamnos		1		5				1											7
stand																1			1
TOTAL	41	32	34	34	9	9	52	149	36	5	4	11	19	1	6	55	16	1	514

lekythoi, ripe archaic cups (and it must be remembered that these are largely contemporary), early classical cups and classical kraters. The number of black-figure lekythoi is remarkable but they have, of course, been preserved in quantity, and black-figure painters had much less inhibition than red-figure painters about running the scene right round the vase. One might suspect that most of them are dedications. Sacrifices are normally long scenes and so suitable for the outsides of cups and for kraters: six of the bespoke vases with sacrifices discussed earlier are bell-kraters of the classical period. The altar scenes do not occur till late black-figure and blossom enormously on ripe-archaic and early classical cups and early classical lekythoi. The abbreviated scene is very suitable for cup interiors and for lekythoi, but in the classical period small pelikai, which are also perfume pots, to some extent take over from the lekythoi. The herm vases (as distinct from sacrifices to Hermes or at Herms)[1] are a small class; it looks as if herms were interesting in themselves roughly from the time of Hipparchos, who made the milestone herm, to rather after the date of the building of the Stoa of Herms in the Agora. The women with torches present rather the same picture as the altar scenes – considerable popularity particularly on lekythoi in the early classical period and then in the classical period a take-over by small pelikai. (Probably the loutrophoroi and nuptial lebetes should be omitted as these women belong to marriage scenes.)

We can then look at the subject-matter in greater detail. In some of the scenes of sacrifice we can say to what god the sacrifice was performed.

ATHENA

The potters had their own special link with Athena as their patron. Paseas inscribed a plaque with Athena and a worshipper 'of the drawings of Paseas'.[2] A fragment of a kalyx-krater[3] by the painter of the Louvre Centauromachy found on the Acropolis has a picture of a pottery above and below youths leading a ram to sacrifice. It seems reasonable to suppose that the sacrifice was to Athena and that the potter dedicated his kalyx-krater to her. (Some of the potter dedications mentioned

---

[1] The later vases discussed by Metzger, *Imagerie* 77, belong to these kinds.
[2] *ABV* 352, from Athens.   [3] *ARV*[2] 1092/76, Acr. 739, *PP* pl. 5, 2–3.

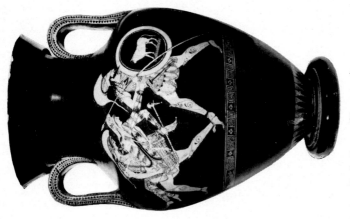

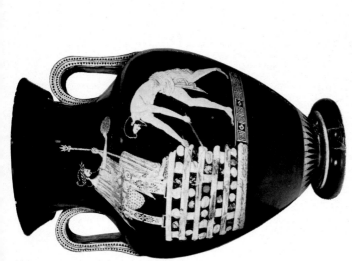

9 (*a*) Kroisos. (*b*) Amazonomachy. Amphora A, Myson. Paris G 197. (See p. 74)

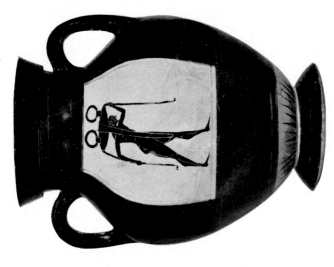

10 (a) and (b) Victor. Amphora B, group E. New York 56.171.13 (Fletcher Fund). (See p. 77)

above, p. 4, belong here because they have pictures of Athena, *ARV*[2] 240/42, 499/17, 1556 *Kallis*.)

The ordinary Athenian also had his link with Athena as the patron goddess of his city. He sacrificed and prayed and dedicated offerings to her, and if he was successful, he celebrated the occasion. His needs for dedication and celebration the potters could probably anticipate, and in the following cases we cannot often tell whether the vases came from stock or were special commissions. Probably we tend to associate too much with the Panathenaia, but at least all that follows can reasonably be associated with Athena.

A lekythos by the Amasis painter,[1] already quoted for its dances to a seated goddess on the shoulder, has a scene of weaving on the body, and it is natural to connect the two scenes and suppose that these are the girls weaving the peplos for the Panathenaia and that the lekythos was painted for one of them to dedicate at home.

A black-figure amphora[2] from Vulci has three men leading a bull and preceded by a priestess holding sprigs in both hands to an altar behind which stands an armed Athena; on the other side of the vase two men play flutes and two men play lyres. This solemn sacrifice is surely the main sacrifice at the Panathenaia. Also about 550 B.C. a Panathenaic amphora[3] of unknown provenance not only shows the Panathenaic Athena at her altar and a flute-player but also a woman with the peplos. The king and men and women on the other side perhaps belong to the mythical time when the ceremony of the peplos was supposed to be instituted.[4]

A later Panathenaic amphora of the Leagros group[5] has a procession to sacrifice and men carrying Panathenaic amphorai. This may be either a sacrifice associated with the transference of the prize amphorai from the Acropolis to wherever they were put for the Panathenaic games, as on the specially commissioned red-figure Panathenaic

[1] *ABV* 154/57, from Vari, Attica; Karousou, *Amasis Painter* (Oxford, 1956), pl. 43. Perhaps cf. also 320/5, Louvre F 224, *CV* pls. 57, 4, 9 and 11, where the other side has Athena, seated, Hermes, a goddess, Poseidon, a goddess.

[2] *ABV* 296/4, Berlin 1686. The decorative inscriptions are nonsense, which would perhaps be unlikely if the vase were bespoke.

[3] *ABV* 298/5, New York 53.11.1. Here, pl. 13.

[4] Three other black-figure processions in honour of Athena cannot be tied to any particular festival: *ABV* 393/20, hydria from Etruria; *ABV* 443/3, oinochoe from Attica (Vraona); *ABL* 216/8, lekythos from Athens; cf. also *ARV*[2] 617/12, hydria.

[5] *ABV* 369/119, from Athens.

amphora described above (p. 51), or more simply a victor removing his prizes and preparing to celebrate his victory, again as on a specially commissioned red-figure Panathenaic amphora (above, p. 79). A lekythos by the Athena painter[1] has Athena and two trainers or officers at the Panathenaic games; one of them holds a sprig which is inscribed with a miswritten *hieropoios*. It was found in Gela and perhaps came there by the second-hand market.

Then there are nine red-figure Panathenaic amphorai which were probably painted with the Panathenaia in mind:

*ARV*² 506/25. Aegisthus painter. A. Youth playing flute, man with hand raised and a sprig in his other hand, Panathenaic amphora between them. B. Man with sprig and boy with long branches; both muffled like dithyramb singers. Did the man perhaps win a victory with a chorus at the Panathenaia and does the amphora merely indicate the festival?

221/8. Nikoxenos painter. A. Athena with 'NIKE' written. B. Jumper and flute-player. Athletic victory at Panathenaia. Munich 8728, *CV* pl. 190.

249/9. Syleus painter, from Vulci. A. Youth with sprigs and skaphe (as on the Parthenon frieze). B. Youth with sprigs. New York 20.244, *AJA* (1923), 269.

361/14. Triptolemos painter, from Vulci. A. Athena with stylos and tablets. B. Acontist. Munich 2314, *CV* pls. 197–8.

226/7. Eucharides painter, from Vulci. A. and B. Man with sprigs and pinax.[2]

261/28. Syriskos painter, from Etruria. A. Man with branch. B. Youth.

604/52. Niobid painter, from South Russia. A. Athena and warrior. B. Man with sprig and youth with oinochoe and kantharos. The shape and Athena suggest the Panathenaia; perhaps the man won in an armed contest (cf. above, p. 78), and the vase came to South Russia either by the second-hand market or it was bought by a visitor. Leningrad, *Niobidenmaler*, pl. 10a.

---

[1] *ABV* 522/34, Buffalo G 479, *AJA* 48 (1944), 123.

[2] Cf. the contemporary Panathenaic amphora illustrated in *Münzen und Medaillen*, 40, 1969, 57, no. 95, now Stanford.

ARV[2] 1146/48.[1] Kleophon painter, from Nola. A. Priest pouring from a kantharos on the remains of the victim; acolyte. B. Youth and boy. The shape suggests that the artist thought of a sacrifice to Athena.

> 221/9 and 10. Nikoxenos painter. A. Athena. B. Priest on 9; priestess on 10. Louvre G 60, 61, *CV* pls. 31–2.

An armed Athena standing on a column must have been a well-known dedication. It appears on an oinochoe[2] of the group of Berlin 2415 with a man standing before it in greeting or prayer. It was found in Sicily, perhaps taken back as a memento of a well-known monument.[3] A neck-amphora[4] by the Nikon painter from Italy with 'Glaukon *kalos*' has Athena on one side and a priestess on the other, a present perhaps from Glaukon to the priestess of Athena.

Sometimes Athena is represented by her owl. The common red-figure skyphoi[5] and lekythoi[6] with the owl between two olive branches were an obvious selling line for Athenians and visitors. I have noted already (above, p. 44) a cup specially commissioned for dedication on the Acropolis with this on the inside, and have suggested also (above, p. 104) that the owl with a laver on a small hydria may indicate that the vase contained the perfume *panathenaikon*. A cup connected with Hermonax[7] has the owl between olive sprigs inside, and three owls with plants between them on each outside surface. A variant is the owl and pointed amphorai (for oil) on the inside of a cup of the Haimon group;[8] the two Herakles scenes on the outside have the relevance that he was a favourite hero of Athena. But on two late black-figure vases[9] by the Theseus painter, a cup and an oinochoe, owl and altar signify a sanctuary of Athena.

Professor Corbett[10] has argued that a stamnoid vase, which recalls the Dinos painter and has A. torch race, B. sacrifice of bull at altar with herm in celebration of victory, refers to the torch-race at the

---

[1] Metzger, *Imagerie* 109/9.
[2] *ARV*[2] 776/3, New York 08.258.25, Richter and Hall, pl. 88. Here, pl. 14.
[3] Cf. *ARV*[2] 529/12, London 1928.1.–17.57, *CV* pl. 46, 2, neck-amphora by Alkimachos painter. The Athena repeats Akr. 140 (*Dedications*, no. 22). She is approached by Hermes as on the Swing painter's amphora of Panathenaic shape, cf. above, p. 64.
[4] *ARV*[2] 650/2.   [5] *ARV*[2] 982.   [6] *ARV*[3] 677/14.
[7] *ARV*[2] 492/1656, no provenance.   [8] *ABV* 560/522, probably from Athens.
[9] *ABL* 250/14, from Athens; *ABV* 519/15, no provenance.
[10] *Hesperia* 18 (1949), 349; *ARV*[2] 1190; Metzger, *Imagerie* 112.

Panathenaia because in that torch-race the tribe (*phyle*) whose team was victorious received a bull. (It may not be irrelevant to note that the herm also appears on vases that have been associated with dithyramb at the Panathenaia.) This vase was evidently kept as a treasured possession by its owners. Another rather later example is *ARV*[2] 1347/3, bell-krater by the Kekrops painter from Spina, which also has the torch-race on one side and the sacrifice on the other.[1]

Before leaving Athena, two special cases must be mentioned, the Panathenaic prize amphorai which were a major commission for each Greater Panathenaia, and the curious jugs from the Agora published by J. R. Green.[2] They date from the end of the fifth century, are of a special type with moulded breasts below the neck and are decorated with Athena in a chariot on the body and on two examples a Panathenaic Athena on the neck. They were evidently commissioned for some special ceremony in honour of Athena and then preserved.

DIONYSOS

The dithyramb at the great Dionysia was performed by choruses of men and boys from each tribe (*phyle*) and the first prize was a bull for the poet and a tripod for the tribe. We have seen vases painted for special dithyrambic victories,[3] and also pictures of dithyramb singers.[4] There are others which have no names to single them out as special commissions and which belong here because they mostly represent the sacrifice of the bull to Dionysos; they are very like the torch-race vases and cluster in the same period, but they are perhaps anticipated by vases of the first half of the fifth century, with Nike either flying to a tripod, or with a bull, or with a dithyramb singer, or with satyrs clad in himatia.[5]

---

[1] The other torch-race vases in *ARV* only show the race, not the sacrifice after the victory. On the Prometheia, cf. above, p. 44.

[2] Class of Agora P 15840, *Hesperia* 31 (1962), 82, *ARV*[2] 1697. On the competition for painting Panathenaic amphorai, cf. above, p. 11.

[3] *ARV*[2] 1045/6, and probably 1581/20.

[4] Cf. above, p. 117.

[5] *ABV* 429/9, oinochoe; *ABL* 208/52, lekythos; 245/88, small hydria; *ARV*[2] 205/122, kalyx-krater from Gela; 214/1, Panathenaic amphora from Nola; 229/41, hydria from S. Russia; 527/80, cup; 884/73, cup.

*ARV*² 1036/5. Stamnos from Vulci by Hector painter. A. Nike watering bull at tripod. Personification of successful tribe. B. King and women (? the subject of the dithyramb). Munich 2412, *CV* pl. 247.

 1107/7. Amphora B by Nausikaa painter. A. Two women preparing oxen for sacrifice before tripod. B. King, woman, man and woman (? again an allusion to the subject). London E 284, *CV* pl. 17, 3.

 1123/3. Pelike from Athens by painter of Athens 1183. A. Nikai leading bull to sacrifice, and satyr at a tripod. B. Youth with spears pursuing women. Athens 16260.

 1158/iii. Kalyx-krater, probably from Etruria, near the Dinos painter. A. Nike, tripod, Nike leading bull, Dionysos, Maenad (*Bakche*), satyr (*Simos*). B. Boy singing and boy playing the flute, with two Nikai. As the singer is a boy, the vase was designed for a team of boys, *not* men. The flautist is the accompanist. Bologna PU 286.

 1185/17. Bell-krater by Kadmos painter. Dionysos, Nike, young satyr, satyr (no tripod here). Madrid 11074, *CV* pl. 14, 3.

 1276/2. Kalyx-krater by Marlay painter. A. Youth with lyre, Nike flying with sash to tripod and satyr dancing at it. B. Man with sceptre and two women, one holding a chaplet, the other a sash. This should strictly be excluded because it does not show the sacrifice, but Nike, tripod and satyr fix the subject and associate it with the rest. The lyre-player was perhaps the poet, as the accompanist at the performance was a flute-player. Again B. Alludes to a mythological theme. Oxford 1942.3, *Ashmolean Report*, 1952, pl. 2; here, pl. 15.

 1324/37. Oinochoe in the manner of the Meidias painter from Greece. Youth decking a tripod, boy holding a lyre. As the last; perhaps a boy's chorus and the poet. Boston 10.206.

A hundred years before this group, the Amasis painter[1] painted an oinochoe which was found in Orvieto with a goat led to sacrifice accompanied by a dithyramb singer: the goat was the third prize in the dithyrambic contest.

[1] *ABV* 153/43.

The procession which brought Dionysos in a ship on wheels, possibly at the Anthesteria, is illustrated on two skyphoi by the Theseus painter and a colleague,[1] and is associated with a procession of men bringing a bull to sacrifice led by a woman(?) carrying a basket (*kanoun*) and a youth with a thurible. A black-figure lekythos of the Cock group [2] has a curious picture of men prostrating themselves before the image of Dionysos. The Polygnotan volute-krater from Spina is explained as votaries before Dionysos, in his determination as Sabazios, and Kybele.[3]

We then come to some more problematic pictures. A column-krater by the Pan painter from Etruria[4] has a youth at a herm on one side and a woman carrying a large phallos on the other. The boy has a sprig in his hand; the head of the herm is wreathed with ivy so that it may be right to suppose that it is a herm of Dionysos, not Hermes. The woman is also ivy-crowned so that she is presumably a votary of Dionysos in some sense. A cup by the Pan painter probably from Etruria[5] has a boy in a long chiton and a very elaborately decorated himation holding a very large branch as he passes a laver in front of a column: he wears a complicated wreath and raises his right hand in prayer. It is unique and probably bespoke. It has been connected with a festival of Dionysos, the Oschophoria, which is the reason for including it here. But although this boy may be wearing female dress like the boys in the Oschophoria, he does not, like them, carry grapes; the clue is lost.

A black-figure hydria[6] of the Leagros group from Vulci has a normal picture of women at the fountain but here a man and a seated woman are decorating the fountain with branches and on one side Dionysos and a seated woman are looking on, on the other side are Hermes passing by and a seated woman. The decoration is presumably in honour of nymphs to whom the fountain is sacred and they are represented by the seated women (one nymph may decorate her own fountain). Dionysos' presence is sufficiently explained by the fact that the Greeks drank wine with water and good water was essential; the hydria is a symposion vase. On the other hand, here and on *ABV* 333/27 (London B 332, *CV* pls. 88, 4, and 91, 2), Beazley suggests that the fountain is between a

---

[1] *ABL* 250/29–30; 253/15; 250/29 was found in Athens.
[2] *ABV* 470/103, no provenance.
[3] *ARV²* 1052/25, Ferrara T 128.   [4] *ARV²* 551/10; Metzger, *Imagerie* 81; Berlin 3206.
[5] *ARV²* 560/156, Villa Giulia 50422, Beazley, *Panmaler*, pl. 6, 5.
[6] *ABV* 365/71, London B 334, *CV* pls. 90, 2 and 91, 4.

shrine of Dionysos and a shrine of Hermes. I do not feel certain about this or about the interpretation of *Dionysia Krene* on the fountain-house on a kalpis by Hypsis (*ARV*² 30/2); is it a fountain near a precinct of Dionysos or a fountain sacred to Dionysos and *his* nymphs? It may be right to connect the subject with a red-figure pointed amphora from Vulci by the Copenhagen painter:[1] on one side Dionysos pours wine from a kantharos while a woman Nymphaia holds an oinochoe; on the other side are two women, one muffled and the other holding a flower, whom Beazley interprets as nymphs. I do not see the justification for identifying Nymphaia (cf. Roscher and L.S.J. *s.v.*) with Ariadne. Is she not rather a personification of the Nymphaion, the place where the Nymphs, who appear on the other side, produce the good water which is essential for appreciating the good wine;[2] the *kalos* name Karton shows that this was at least in its last stages a bespoke vase.

Two vases may be used as links between Dionysos and Demeter. An amphora B by the Amasis painter from Etruria[3] has on one side a procession to sacrifice: a *kanephoros*, a man carrying a myrtle branch, a man carrying a pig, a man carrying a wineskin; on the other side the typical komasts of Dionysos. Perhaps the painter thinks of a sacrifice to Demeter, since the pig seems to belong to her rather than to Dionysos, but puts a typically Dionysiac scene on the other side to suit the symposion which will take place after the sacrifice. Similarly, the priest with a *liknon* (winnowing-fan) who moves in procession on the neck of a pointed amphora(?) from Athens by the Pan painter[4] may be a priest of Demeter, but it must also be remembered that the mask of Dionysos lies in a *liknon* on a chous by the Eretria painter.[5]

DEMETER

Besides the two vases just mentioned, which may refer to Demeter rather than Dionysos, a black-figure pelike near the Rycroft painter[6] has a very curious picture which Metzger interprets as a preliminary ceremony in the Eleusinian mysteries. A man with cup, wineskin and

[1] *ARV*² 256/2, London E 350, *CV* pl. 18.
[2] Cf. Athenaeus 465a on the Anthesteria.
[3] *ABV* 151/11, Berlin 1690, Karouzou, *Amasis Painter*, pl. 9.
[4] *ARV*² 553/31, Acropolis 618.
[5] *ARV*² 1249/13; cf. above, p. 120.
[6] *ABV* 338/3; Metzger, *Imagerie* 28/64, pl. 9/3; Naples 3358.

sprig speaks words to two young men seated behind a table loaded with food which has a basket of bread(?) beneath it; behind is a stylopinax with a picture of the Dioskouroi. The two young men are labelled *mysta* (the dual) and there is another, illegible inscription by the table leg. The difficulty that I feel in the interpretation is that all analogy suggests that the man with the sprig is a mortal approaching gods; I wonder whether the two young men can be the Dioskouroi worshipped here as initiates (they were, according to Attic legend, initiated in the Eleusinian mysteries). In any case, there is no connection between this picture and the scene of Ajax and Odysseus disputing over the arms of Achilles on the other side of the vase.

Two black-figure vases show a sacrifice with two seated women who are probably Demeter and Persephone. One is a lekythos from Eleusis by Elbows Out.[1] A procession comes up with a bull for sacrifice; on either side of a flaming altar sits a woman elaborately garlanded holding a wreath; they are the goddesses. On the other, a lekythos by the Haimon painter from Athens, the scene is reduced to a woman playing the flute and a ram between two seated women.

Undoubtedly Eleusinian is a red-figure stamnos[2] in the undetermined group of Polygnotos. On one side the *dadouchos* with a torch in each hand is followed by a youth wreathed with myrtle and carrying the *bakchos* (a bundle of branches) and by a woman carrying a torch (Persephone according to Beazley, and this seems to be right as she does not herself belong to the procession but gives it a greeting);[3] on the other side a youth and women with torches. Nothing of the secret rites could be put on a vase, and here the allusion is primarily to the arrival of the great procession at Eleusis by torchlight. The vase-painters must have known that there would be a demand for such vases by the initiates both for dedications and for their private symposia when the ceremonies were over.

Torchlight is so much a feature of the Mysteries and of their goddesses that perhaps a picture on a bell-krater[4] by the Eupolis painter from Camarina with a priestess holding torches and a bull may be claimed as a picture of a sacrifice to Demeter.

---

[1] *ABV* 251/1; Metzger, *Imagerie* 21/42, pl. 5/2; Athens 493. *ABL* 243/48, Athens, *Deltion* (1927–8), 91.
[2] *ARV*² 1052/23 from Eleusis, Eleusis 636, *AE* (1937), 227 ff.
[3] Cf. Picard in *RA* (1941), 257.   [4] *ARV*² 1073/3, Syracuse 22886, *CV* pl. 17, 1.

HERMES

We have noticed already that herms, sometimes with an altar and sometimes in a Stoa, occur on vases connected with dithyramb, and we have noticed a 'cavalry' cup with a man praying to Hermes inside.[1] The vases show that there was a herm, an altar and a pillared building in the Agora by the end of the sixth century. The literary evidence[2] about the Stoa of Herms in the Agora and the three herms erected to commemorate Kimon's victory over the Persians in 475 B.C. is not particularly clear, but a small pelike by the Pan painter[3] shows the three herms on one side and on the other a girl with a sacrificial basket and a youth putting down a hydria. This is evidently a sacrifice to the herms. I am not sure why the youth has a hydria; a late black-figure oinochoe by the painter of Half-Palmettes[4] has a woman with a hydria at an altar, but this again is unexplained. Probably also the two herms on another small pelike[5] by the Pan painter are the same herms; on the other side a boy catches a pig by the leg in front of a herm; was it a sacrificial animal that escaped? So also perhaps are the two herms with a boy praying to one of them on a late black-figure olpe.[6] And a youth prays to two herms on a neck-amphora by the Pan painter,[7] while on the other side a warrior leaves home: he may be a cavalryman. The Stoa of Herms in the Agora is the place where the young horsemen went, and we can add to the 'cavalry' vases quoted above:

ABV 525/10. Oinochoe of Sèvres class. Horseman; behind him a herm.

ARV² 147/19, Würzburg 475. Cup by Epeleios painter from Vulci. I. Naked youth at herm. A. Youth and horse (jockey). B. Warriors and horses (cavalry).

ARV² 292/32, Hague 2026. Amphora by Tyszkiewicz painter. A. Man making prayer to herm. B. Man on stick, youth with spear and chlamys (cavalryman). (In both these cases it is reasonable to suppose a connection between the herm scene and the other scene or scenes on the same vase, but in a great many pictures of man, youth or youths at a herm

---

[1] Cf. above, pp. 80, 93.   [2] Cf. E. B. Harrison, *Athenian Agora* XI, 108.
[3] *ARV²* 555/92. Here, pl. 16(a).   [4] *ABV* 573/3, Cab. Méd. 267, *CV* pls. 62, 11; 64, 2.
[5] *ARV²* 555/91 bis (1659).   [6] *ABV* 448/2.
[7] *ARV²* 553/33, from Nola? Perhaps, cf. also 654/9, 'Charmides *kalos*'.

there is no such connection to show the meaning of the herm scene: *ARV*² 275/65; 285/8, 9; 366/87; 378/116; 439/159; 563/12; 697/14, 15.)

A number of vases show sacrifices at a herm and I suspect that when there is no reason to suppose another reference the herms in the Agora are meant:

ABL 219/65. Small neck-amphora by Edinburgh painter. Man with oinochoe and man with phiale before altar and herm. London WT 220, *CV* pl. 45, 6.

*ARV*² 367/97. Skyphos by the Triptolemos painter from Nola. A. Herm. B. Youth at altar. Cab. Med. 839. (We can add to this the not infrequent pictures of herms alone.)

*ARV*² 367/98, 101, 104; 685/162–4; 697/16–17; 701/13; 779/10.

*ARV*² 523/9, Naples 3369. Column-krater by the Orchard painter in Naples. A. Procession of three women and a girl to herm. B. Man, youth and woman. (Women at a herm occur also on *ABV* 530/7; *ARV*² 931/4.)

*ARV*² 551/15, Naples, *Mon. Linc.* 22, pl. 80. Column-krater by Pan painter from Cumae. A. Man and two boys sacrificing to wreathed herm. B. Komos of three boys (after the symposion which followed the sacrifice).

*ARV*² 581/4, Berlin 2172. Pelike by the Perseus painter from Etruria. A. Herm, bird and altar. B. Acolyte and herm.

*ARV*² 1158/iv, Athens 1456. Bell-krater. (Perhaps Boeotian.) Wreathed youth and man before a herm.

*ARV*² 1172/17, Louvre CA 1860, Metzger, *Imagerie* 80, pl. 29/2. Oinochoe by Polion from Greece. Bearded herm, altar, splanchnopt.

*ARV*² 1276/9 bis, Ferrara T 876 B, Valle Pega. Bell-krater by the Marlay painter from Spina. Youth leading bull to herm.

But three scenes have nothing to do with the Agora herms. On *ARV*² 311/2, ionochoe by painter of the Leningrad Herm-Mug, the libation to a herm takes place in the country; on a bell-krater by the Nikias painter, *ARV*² 1334/14, the herm to which sacrifice is being made is in a naiskos, and on another, 1334/15, Metzger, *Imagerie* 80, pl. 32/1, the herm is beardless.

A few vases fall outside these categories. A cup by the Dokimasia painter from Capua[1] has a youth with a wreath which he intends to put on a herm; to his left is a column without a capital, which K. Friis-Johansen compares to the inscribed columns found from the archaic period. On the outside the cup has a boar hunt on one side and a deer hunt on the other. One would suppose that the decoration of the herm is thought to accompany a prayer for successful hunting. Then a pelike in the manner of the Pig painter from Perachora (on the gulf of Corinth)[2] has on one side a man holding a sprig in front of a herm which is decorated with a red wreath; on the other side is a boy with a lyre and kothornoi (cf. the type worn by revellers) before a herm decorated with a white wreath and an altar. Here the point seems to be the contrast between the rather solemn man on one side and the reveller on the other. I do not know why in particular a herm should be thought of in connection with a reveller, but the connection occurs on two other vases.[3] A different contrast can be seen on a column-krater from Bologna by the Boreas painter:[4] a woman prays to a black-haired herm, and an old man by a dead tree prays to a white-haired herm. The painter seems to have given the herms the characteristics of their worshippers. (Athletes are commonly shown standing by the herm in the palaistra, and these are listed below, pp. 208 ff.)

APOLLO

A tripod may indicate a sanctuary of Apollo, and this may be its function on three black-figure amphorai. Two[5] of them have on one side a procession to a tripod: one has the ransom of Hektor on the other side, and the other a komos. The third[6] has two bearded men approaching two tripods in front of a palm-tree, which suggests Apollo's sanctuary at Delos. Here too the other side of the vase is seemingly irrelevant – Herakles and the Nemean lion.

A number of sacrifices to Apollo[7] are found in red-figure from about 450 B.C.:

ARV^2 603/41, Istanbul 2914. Bell-krater by Niobid painter from Samaria. (B. Youth pursuing woman.)

[1] ARV^2 413/16, Copenhagen 6327, CV pl. 143.
[2] ARV^2 566/7, Athens, JHS 56 (1936), pl. 10.   [3] ABV 531/2; ARV^2 564/30.
[4] ARV^2 537/12, Bologna, 206, CV pl. 27.   [5] ABV 95/7, 112.
[6] ABV 305/24, Munich 1395, CV pls. 28, 1 and 29, 3.   [7] Cf. Metzger, $Imagerie$ 108 ff.

1028/9, 10. Stamnoi by Polygnotos from Cervetri. Bespoke vases: Archenautes and Diomedes, cf. above, p. 50.

1051/17. Stamnos, Group of Polygnotos, from Cervetri. Bespoke vase: Diomedes, cf. above, p. 50.

1113/31 bis (1683), Frankfurt. Bell-krater by Hephaistos painter from Nola. Metzger, *Imagerie* pl. 47. Sacrifice. Apollo statue on pillar behind altar.

1124/4 bis (1684). Small pelike by Academy painter in Catania. Sacrifice, laurel.

1143/1. Ferrara, T 47 Valle Pega. Volute-krater by Kleophon painter, Spina. Youths leading bulls. B. Return of Hephaistos. Metzger, *REG* 71 (1964), 114.

1144/14, Leningrad 774. Kalyx-krater by Kleophon painter. Sacrifice, palm-tree. B. Satyrs and maenad.

1149/9. Bell-krater. Manner of Kleophon painter, Capua. Bespoke vase; Kallias, cf. above, p. 50. B. Satyrs and maenad.

1159, iii. Bell-krater. Near the Chrysis painter, Capua. Probably commissioned with the preceding. Cf. above, p. 50.

1182/2. Bell-krater, Port Sunlight. Petworth Group, Capua. Sacrifice, Apollo.

1190/24. Bell-krater, Louvre G 496, *CV* pls. 35, 2 and 4. Pothos painter. Sacrifice, Apollo.

1333/12. Bell-krater, New York 41.162.4. *CV* Gallatin pl. 25, 5–6. Nikias painter. Sacrifice, laurel.

1334/13. Bell-krater, Lecce 630. Nikias painter, from Rugge (South Italy). Sacrifice, laurel.

What is noticeable about this list is first that the time range is comparatively short, secondly that they are all symposion vases except perhaps the small pelike by the Academy painter, thirdly that there is no evidence that any of them was found in Greece, fourthly that three, which do not have the standard three youths or the like on the other side, have Dionysiac scenes, but this probably means no more than that such scenes were felt relevant for a symposion vase. We cannot, I think, suggest an obvious recurrent occasion for a symposion after a sacrifice to Apollo, and in fact three different occasions have been suggested for some of these vases: a Pythian musical victory for the Archenautes–Diomedes vases, a political occasion for the Kallias vase and a Pythais for the Spina vase.

OTHER GODS

*Adonis. ARV*² 1313/3, Athens 1179. Hydria by the Meidias painter from Attica. Festival of Adonis. (Cf. also 1175/11, acorn lekythos by Aison from Athens, woman watering Adonis plant, with women and naked youth.)[1]

*Aphrodite. ARV*² 1325/51, Oxford 1966/714; *Beazley Gifts*, pl. 41, 277. Squat lekythos said to be from Olympia. Image holding two phialai flanked by two Erotes, one with spray. A woman approaches on each side. Catalogue says 'Visit of mother and bride-to-be to sanctuary of Aphrodite and Eros'. I suspect that the women are dancing and the Eros with sprig is praying to the image of Aphrodite for them.

*Aphrodite Genetyllis. ARV*² 1204/2, Athens 1695; Rumpf, *BJ* 161, 208–9. Lekythos near the Group of Palermo 16. Women with puppy and basket before three torches in the ground.

Bendis. Cf. Beazley on *ARV*² 1023, 147–8.

Dioskouroi. Theoxenia. *ARV*² 1049/53. Hydria by Christie painter from Athens; 1187/36. Hydria by Kadmos painter, from Bulgaria.

Herakles. ABV 519/33. Cup by Theseus painter from Bari. I. Statue of Herakles, A. and B. Symposion. The painter probably thought of a symposion at some feast sacred to Herakles.

*Hestia. ARV*² 708/12, Leningrad St. 1575. Squat lekythos from Nola. Woman seated with torch, perhaps Hestia. Cf. Hampe and Simon, *GL* 28 on *ARV*² 1224/2 pyxis of Oppenheimer group: two women bring offerings to Hestia who is also approached by two dancers: a seated woman with maid might be a bride, and the whole a wedding present.

Three black-figure vases show images of goddesses: *ABV* 308/66, neck-amphora, goddess with two children between columns with owls; 326, standing goddess in shrine; *ABL* 269/73 bis, seated goddess with phiale between columns.

[1] Cf. N. Weill, *BCH* 90 (1966), 664.

UNDETERMINED

In many pictures of sacrifices the god is not indicated; most of these can be treated briefly, but two careful pictures should be mentioned first because here it is our knowledge, not the painter's presentation, which is deficient. The scene on one side of a cup by the painter of Bologna 417[1] has been explained as the purification of a boy; the other side has women dancing and the inside Dionysos and a maenad; perhaps therefore the rite is Dionysiac. A cup by the Pan painter[2] from Cervetri has on one side a priest pouring a libation over an altar on which flesh is burning. On the other side are a man with a stick and writing-case, a table on stones on which a boy is placing objects and on which stands a large kotyle filled with objects, a man with stylus and writing-tablet and a boy with a bowl (*skaphe*) full of objects. Inside a boy with a *skaphe* full of objects approaches a table, and there is a man with a writing-case. Conceivably the sacrifice is unconnected with the other scenes, but it seems more likely that it is being made to ensure the success of the other operation. The table has evidently been specially set up in the open air. The objects are the same in all cases; they are small irregular things rendered in added red. The three men with writing instruments must be recorders; the three boys are porters. No satisfactory suggestion has been made; I do not think that they can be the sacred olives, but it seems to me conceivable that the objects are pot-sherds and that we have here the counting in an ostracism. (I do not think that they need be the same as the single small object held by the priest on the Pan painter's stamnos[3] from Cervetri: that may be sacrificial grain, and one would expect the sacrifice to be connected with the success of the flute-player on the other side.)

The rest can be roughly classified as follows:

Bull and ram	*ARV*[2] 1674 (under 903).
Ram	*ABV* 243/44 (priestess).
Bull	*ABV* 54/70; 391; 438/2 (woman); 441/5; 496/175;
	ABL 207/46, 78, 84, 96, 168, 178, 185, 250/60,
	ABV 519/34; 532/15–16;

[1] *ARV*[2] 914/142, Florence 3950 and Greifswald 340.
[2] *ARV*[2] 559/152, Oxford 1911.617, *CV* pls. 2, 9 and 7, 3–4. Here, pl. 16(*b*).
[3] *ARV*[2] 552/23.

	*ARV*² 35/1; 146/3 bis; 517/4; 686/205 (woman); 1144/21.
Pig	*ARV*² 117/7; 226/8; 658/31 (women).
Undetermined	*ABL* 226/8; 247; 267/14, 15, 63, 64;
	*ARV*² 108/26; 146/3; 173/10; 231/86; 472/210; 558/142; 1145/26–7; 1190/25–6; 1214/2 (*Pythodelos kalos*), 3.
	*ARV*² (all include women) 363/27; 384/212; 355/92 bis; 652/32; 714/170; 1323/36; 1324/47 (cf. above, p. 71).
Extispicy	*ABV* 270/52, 71; 278/30; 286/8 (all amphorai with mythological scenes on the other side).
	*ARV*² 181/1; 220/3 (both amphorai continuing the black-figure tradition).
Splanchnopt	*ABV* 390/6 = *ARV*² 225/3; *ARV*² 170/3; 898/132 (all cup-interiors).
Suppliants	*ABV* 551/338; *ARV*² 435/87; 465/92; 962/63.

G. Bakalakis[1] has interpreted six vases with bulls in a sanctuary as the Dipolieia, but generally we have no clue. Sometimes, although we cannot say to what god the sacrifice was made, the collocation of these scenes with other scenes tells us a little of what the painter had in mind. When he has athletes in another scene on the same vase, he is thinking of a sacrifice in which athletes take part.

ABV   54/70. Cup by C painter from Taranto. A. Bull led to sacrifice, B. procession, according to H. R. W. Smith, spectators or partisans of victory. I. The succeeding symposion.

*ARV*² 108/26, London 97.10–28.2. Cup made by Kachrylion from Orvieto. A. Boy with basket (*kanoun*), woman with phiale, B. Athletes, I. Greek archer. Was one of the athletes to serve as an archer and this cup was made for his farewell party?

*ARV*² 170/3, Florence 3930, *CV* pls. 76 and 116, 4. Cup by the Winchester painter in Florence. I. Splanchnopt, A. and B. Athlete.

Naturally departure on a campaign is an occasion for a sacrifice and a party.

[1] *AK* 12 (1969), 57, including Gela painter *ABL* 207 ff., nos. 78, 84, 96, lekythoi; 178, small neck-amphora; 185, oinochoe.

ABL 226/8, pls. 33/1 and 35/2, Athens 595. Lekythos by the Sappho painter. Goddess mounting chariot. Shield and helmet. Man sacrificing. Perhaps a sacrifice at dawn before departure?

ABL 250/60, pl. 43/2, Louvre CA 1837. Lekythos by Theseus painter. Sacrifice of bull before man seated in house (or is he the god in his temple, Zeus or Poseidon). One of the men with the bull holds spears, a cavalryman?

*ARV*² 173/10, Würzburg 474, Langlotz, pl. 143. Cup by Ambrosios painter, from Vulci. A. Kallias with cup, Lysistratos with cup and oinochoe, man with basket and incense by altar, Antileon with kantharos. Old man, who says 'Hither, too' (an appeal to the divinity). B. Dionysos on donkey with satyrs and maenad. I. Warrior. B. is included because wine is to be drunk in the cup. The painter was perhaps told to paint A., at any rate to add the names. The warrior is relevant if he is one of the men on A. who is going to war.

*ARV*² 181/1, Würzburg 507, Langlotz pl. 175. Amphora A by Kleophrades painter from Vulci. A. Warrior leaving home (extispicy). B. Komos – the revel succeeding the symposion after the sacrifice.

*ARV*² 220/3, Louvre G 46, *CV* pl. 31. Amphora A by Nikoxenos painter. A. The same as 181/1. B. Dionysos with satyrs and maenads.

*ARV*² 558/142, Athens 2038. Fragments of kantharos from Menidi by Pan painter. A. Sacrificial procession. B. Shield, and therefore presumably a warrior.

*ARV*² 568/28, Trieste 993. Column-krater by the Leningrad painter. A. Warrior leaving home. B. Procession: women with torches. The connection is rather different here. The warrior's departure is contrasted with a typical scene of peace, part of a night celebration by women (*pannychis*) which took place in many festivals.

Sometimes, however, the painter simply alludes to the symposion and/ or komos which follow the meal after the sacrifice:

*ARV*² 146/3. Cup by Epeleios painter. A. Sacrifice. I. Symposion. B. Komos.

11 Two knights. Kylix, Penthesilea painter. Ferrara T 18C. (See p. 79)

12 Amazonomachy, Centauromachy. Volute-krater, painter of the Woolly Satyrs. New York 07.286.84 (Rogers Fund).
(See p. 87)

*ARV*² 225/3. Cup from Vulci by painter of London E 2. I. Splanchnopt.
A. and B. Komos.
*ARV*² 517/4. Column-krater by painter of Bologna 235. A. Bull led to
sacrifice. B. Komos.

ALTAR SCENES

The majority of altar scenes have a single figure, usually a youth or
woman; they are admirably adapted for the inside of a cup or for a
lekythos, and little more can be said about them. But a certain number
of vases have more figures:

ABL 239/141. Small neck-amphora by Diosphos painter. A. Young
warrior and old man with sceptre at altar. B. Gigantomachy.
*ARV*² 99/8, 100/17. Alabastron of Paidikos group, one with man and
woman, the other with two women.
267/1. Pelike near the Syriskos painter. A. Two women at altar.
B. Woman in himation and woman with phiale – to pour a
libation at the altar.
288/12. Pelike by Argos painter. A. Man with phiale, woman
with oinochoe. B. Jumper. Libation for athlete?
290/13. Column-krater by Tyszkiewicz painter from Selinus. A.
As 288/12. B. Youth.
292/35. Panathenaic amphora by Tyszkiewicz painter. A. Man
and woman at altar. B. Zeus pursuing woman.
368(1649). Kantharos by Brygos painter from Menidi, Attica. A.
Symposion? B. Woman(?) at altar, male approaching.
486/43. Pelike by Hermonax (N. Weill, *BCH* 86 (1962), 93).
Woman with tainia, youth with flutes(?) at altar. Has he
played successfully for a sacrifice?
501/2–4. Stamnoi by painter of Yale oinochoe from Nola and
Capua. Altar scenes perhaps mythical as mythical scenes on
other sides.
504/6. Kalyx-krater by Aegisthus painter from Bologna. A. Two
youths at altar. B. Youth and woman at altar.
591/25. Kalyx-krater by Altamura painter. Warrior and woman
at altar.

*ARV*² 599/8. Volute-krater by Niobid painter from Bologna. Neck
   B. Men and women (including two goddesses?) at altar.
   Perhaps mythical and connected with Neck A. as on 502/
   2–4.

   616/1. Volute-krater from near Licata (Sicily) by painter of
   Berlin hydria. A. Apollo with Artemis and Leto. B.
   Priestess, woman with oinochoe and sprig, woman praying.
   ?Prayer to Apollo of Delos.

   827/7. Cup by Stieglitz painter. A. and B. Women; on left of A.
   an altar. I. Woman preparing wool, woman with mirror.

   834/140. Small hydria by Sabouroff painter. Two women at
   altar.

   852/4. Pelike in manner of Sabouroff painter. A. Man and
   woman, both with oinochoe, at altar. B. Woman with
   alabastron.

   1090/49. Bell-krater from Athens by painter of Louvre Centauromachy. Women at altar, and boy.

   1129/114–15. Pelikai by Washing painter. A. Youth and woman
   at altar. B. Youth. (115 from Cumae.)

   1129/125. Pelike by Washing painter. A. Two women at altar.
   B. Youth.

   1130/133. Pelike by Washing painter. A. Two youths at altar, one
   with phiale. B. Youth.

   1132/187. Squat lekythos by Washing painter. Two women at
   altar.

   1136/11. Small pelike from Etruria by Hasselmann painter. A.
   Youth and woman with phiale at altar. B. Youth.

   1141/2. Small pelike related to painter of London E 395. A.
   Athlete and youth at altar. B. Woman.

   1342/1. Pelike by painter of Louvre G 433 from Al Mina. A.
   Woman with right hand raised. Youth leaning on stick with
   right hand on altar. Is he swearing fidelity?

   1355/26. Oinochoe 4 by painter of Ferrara T 28. Three women at
   altar: one with phiale, one with torches.

There is nothing surprising in this list. From the sacrifice scenes we
expect to find in these shorter scenes libations, athletes, warriors.

Cult Scenes

The single figures by altars can be briefly summarized: I have noticed where the other side or in the case of a cup the outside may be relevant.

1 Men or undetermined males (as distinct from youths): *ARV*² 221/11; 332/23 (*Kanoun*); 366/88 (praying with cup); 396/34; 416/9; 464/81 (Komos on A. and B.); 466/109 (libation; Komos on A. and B.); 604/57 (libation); 667/25; 697/10 (leaning on stick with flower); 803/47 (extending right hand over altar); 1268.

2 Warriors: *ABL* 249/18; *ARV*² 305/5 (Athena on the other side); 413/19 (fights outside the cup); 415/1 (outside perhaps mythical scene of warriors leaving home); 435/92 (outside warriors leaving home); 486/46 (A. man at altar, B. woman bringing warrior shield and spear; sacrifice before going on campaign? But N. Weill, *BCH* 86 (1962), 71, suggests that this is the arming of Theseus, in which case the 'man at altar' belongs above as a separate scene); 610/26 (Pelike in the manner of the Niobid painter from Gela. A. warrior leaving home, libation, B. women and man at altar, libation); 1069/1 (Oxford 1965.134, warriors at altar, old man with stick, Nike with helmet); 1128/99 (warrior and man at altar); 1192/1; 1271/28 (cup, athletes outside).

3 Youths:

   (*a*) Komast: *ARV*² 626/105 (A. and B. Komos).

   (*b*) Athlete: *ARV*² 364/41 (A. and B. hoplitodromoi); 720/16; 779/4; 788/4; 809/39; 838/63; 866/2, 38 (athletes, A. and B.); 868/44 (athletes, A. and B.); 947/5; 1399/5 (athletes, A. and B.).

   (*c*) Libation: *ARV*² 214/185 bis (*Alkmeon kalos, Nikostratos kalos*); 684/140; 1201/4; 1207/32; 1249/22.

   (*d*) Running to altar: *ARV*² 392/6; 396/35; 707/4; 718/243 (perhaps abbreviated pictures of a race?).

   (*e*) Unspecified: *ABV* 519/27; *ARV*² 120/10; 373/47 (dance on A. and B.); 394/10; 395/1–3; 396/29, 29 bis; 396/30–2; 397/1; 423/115, 118 (with stick and purse); 530/16 (with lyre; perhaps explained by 565/33, youth with lyre and youth at altar, as music for a cult dance?); 818/28; 822/18; 865 (A. and B. symposion); 866/12, 33; 868/77; 875/8, 15; 959/54 (A. and B. symposion); 980/2 (from the Kabeirion at Thebes; therefore a dedication, perhaps by the woman Akridion, whose name is inscribed); 1025/7; 1128/106.

4 Women (cf. also below, pp. 230, 232, 235, 241):
  (*a*) Three vases include an unspecified goddess besides the woman at the altar: *ARV*² 100/18; 640/65; 1070/6.
  (*b*) Pouring a libation, or with phiale or oinochoe: *ARV*² 101; 380/161; 561/10; 624/83; 674/20; 676/18; 680/75 (no altar); 686/204 (from Sparta, a fawn behind the woman); 690/9; 691/28 (snake by altar); 698/35–6; 719/3–4; 719/11; 721/6; 722/3; 751/2 (she holds a sceptre); 820/2; 843/130 and 160 (no altar); 843/134; 862/25 (with sceptre); 951/1 (no altar); 1261/56; 1362/10.
  (*c*) With thurible: *ARV*² 667/12; 724/7.
  (*d*) With basket (*kanoun*): *ARV*² 651/31; 690/10; 698/37; 732/42; 815/2; 1023/148 (pairs with 147, which has Bendis inside, cf. Beazley *ad loc.*).
  (*e*) With olive branch: *ARV*² 774 (altar has flute and sprays). Perhaps a flautist who has dedicated her flute and prays to Athena; the white-ground cup found in Athens is itself probably a dedication.
  (*f*) With wreath: *ARV*² 176/1 (woman naked); 724/7; 758/97.
  (*g*) With girdle: *ARV*² 644/135. Klonis leaves bed to put girdle on altar. Presumably a marriage dedication, and the altar is in fact some way from her house. (Cf. the maenad noted above, p. 119, n. 1.)
  (*h*) With flute or lyre: *ARV*² 377/114 (lyre); 698/38 (flute); 751/1 (lyre). Perhaps the musicians who provide music for dance at the altar.
  (*i*) Running to altar: *ARV*² 377/151, 164; 392/24; 642/99 (with oinochoe and phiale); 691/11 (with spear or sceptre); 703/46–8; 706/4–5, 7; 1201/5–7; 1220/8, 10; 1221/1. Probably the leading figure of a race or dance to the altar.
  (*j*) Dancing with krotala at altar: *ARV*² 444/232.
  (*k*) With torches: *ARV*² 264/63 (walking); 651/10; 677/12; 680/74 (running); 690/8; 720/23 (running); 831/25; 844/159 (walking); 1221/13 (running). The women walking or running are presumably the leaders of a torchlight dance; the others could possibly be goddesses (Demeter or Persephone) or women at a marriage, or women who will light a fire on the altar.

It seems logical to add the women with torches here, although there is no altar. The omission of the altar is a further abbreviation, and here too a variety of interpretations are possible. An obvious division is into women running with torches and women standing with torches:

(i) Running: ARV^2 211/203 (with phiale also), 206, 213; 409/52 (B. King; or god to whom the service is performed?); 514/2 (probably in a marriage); 519/19; 582/15; 624/84; 642/104; 655 (on the other side man with phiale and woman with oinochoe); 680/74; 703/50, 51 (with basket also): 712/94–6; 720/1; 726/8 (on the other side Nike; above, woman seated and woman – Nike suggests that the torch-running was competitive, and the upper scene shows the home); 726/21; 727/2 (on the other side, woman praying); 732/35–7; 838/12 (with phiale also); 838/31 (with branch also); 853/1 (on the other side, Eros dancing and woman playing the kithara, *kalos* name DION (without *kalos*)); 853/2 (on other side warrior and man with *kalos Dion*. Perhaps pairs with 853/1; here war and peace, cf. 568/28 above, and 853/1 shows that Dion fell in love with the woman for whose torchlight dance the kithara-player played); 951/2 (the chair shows that the woman starts from home); 973/14 (?maenad); 977/1 (the woman on the other side runs with a mirror); 1002/14; 1194/2 (on the other side youth leaving home, war and peace); 1215/6; 1219/1 (with sprig also; on the other side boy with sprig, so a scene of sacrifice); 1219/2 (on the other side a woman running with basket, so a scene of sacrifice); 1220/5 (on the other side woman running with phiale, so a scene of sacrifice); 1221/12–13 (in both Eros on the other side, cf. 853/1).

(ii) Standing: ABV 560/517; ARV^2 452/3; 488/70 (on the other side Zeus, as recipient of sacrifice?); 490/124; 500/30; 514/2 (perhaps stand for marriage vase); 525/36 (with sprig also, and man with stick, commanding sacrifice?); 525/37; 525/40 (on the other side woman with phiale and shield, and two men. Sacrifice for departure?); 531/37 (marriage vase); 535/4 (on the other side Nike with *Nikon kalos*; sacrifice for Nikon's victory? cf. 624/78, Nike and woman at altar, *kalos Nikon*); 556/111 (perhaps Hekate); 636/7 (on the other side, Artemis with *kalos Glaukon*; Glaukon's sacrifice to Artemis?); 650/4 (A. Nike with two torches, B. woman with one torch; victory in a woman's torch dance?); 671/7 (woman with torch, woman with alabastron and box leaves bed or stool; the torch-dancer at home, cf. 951/2, above); 674/27; 722/1 (with sprigs also, on the other side woman with cock: sacrifice?); 726/15 (on the other side, maenad or woman dressed as maenad); 730/6; 1006/2 (on the other side horsemen, cf. 1108/22, 28; sacrifice for cavalrymen?); 1108/23 (on the other side, chariot and Nike; sacrifice for successful chariot-race); 1136/15; 1138/41 (paired with boy dithyramb singer); 1361/27.

(*l*) Maenads: ARV^2 691/12; 710/28–31 (28 bis–30 with phiale or oinochoe; 31 with torch; all at mound altar, see below); 724/11; 730/2; 1220/1; 1357/6. These are probably all Athenian women dressed as maenads whether for the 'Lenaian' or some other festival, cf. above, p. 118.

(*m*) Unspecified: ARV^2 100/19; 392/25; 396/22; 558/126; 667/19; 680/60; 698/39; 707/7–8; 710/33–4; 732/43 (sceptre); 732/44; 758/98; 758/1; 803/58; 810/22 (A. and B., youths and women with sprigs); 829/3; 834/1 (A. and B. symposion), 2; 838/16 (outside of cup which has woman holding helmet and garment inside; perhaps sacrifice for warrior's departure); 959/2; 1132/195; 1293/3.

(*n*) Women at mound altar (cf. maenads above): ARV^2 642/110; 646/2; 686/206; 710/35–49 (39, with phiale).

(*o*) Women at block altar: ARV^2 686/230.

(*p*) Eros (cf. above under (*k*) 853/1, 1221/12–13): ARV^2 1130, 134–9 (four small pelikai by the Washing painter with Eros flying to an altar on one side and a youth with a phiale on the other: a libation to secure success in love and the prayer granted is a suitable picture on a perfume pot given to a girl); 1133/199; 1224/1 (youth with lyre and Eros playing the flute at altar; woman seated with lyre, Eros and two women. It is not clear to me what this painter intended; perhaps the scenes should be taken separately: the boy is a musician and he hopes that Eros will play for him while he plays for a chorus at the altar; the women who are themselves musicians will see him and fall in love with him? The pyxis comes from Greece and was probably designed to be a present for a woman.).

(*q*) Nike also frequently appears at an altar; sometimes she has torches, sometimes a thurible, sometimes she pours a libation. Nike takes the place of the victor or victorious team which makes the sacrifice to celebrate the victory, and the vase with Nike has some connection with the celebration; it is used in the symposion or dedicated or given as a present. In the scenes where she has torches, thurible or phiale the altar is often omitted. Where she has torches and the altar is omitted, she may sometimes represent a victorious torchlight chorus rather than the lighting of the fire on the altar, and this is clearly the case when she holds a lyre as well (*ABL* 264/44).

Nike at altar: *ABL* 264/35, 38, 42 (with lyre); *ARV*² 210/184, 214 (thurible, no altar); 229/46; 302/20 (thurible, no altar); 310/2, 3, 9; 379/141; 393/42 (with torches); 624/78 (cf. above); 625/90; 649/46 (with oinochoe and *kanoun*); 650/6–7; 651/16 (Nike and youth with sceptre, *Nikon kalos*), 24 (thurible, no altar); 655/3; 656/21–2; 657/8, 38, 43 (all thurible only); 667/13 (thurible); 671/1, 3 (with torch and *kanoun*); 672/2; 673/16 bis (with *kanoun*); 678/13–39, 45–62, 68–70, 181–197, 227–9, 247–8; 697/22–7; 699/ 63 (thurible only); 699/66–7; 700/3, 14; 702/10–19, 79; 707/1–3; 1706; 709/15–17; 717/229; 721/2; 725/1; 731/12; 735/105; 740/2; 828/20; 844/1672; 929/86; 1003/19; 1071/3; 1197; 1202/8; 1220/3.

Nike pouring libation (without altar): *ARV*² 446/268; 493/2; 642/ 103; 659/47; 662; 701/1; 709/20; 717/220; 721; 734/94; 844/148; 852/6.

Nike with torches: *ABL* 264/44; *ARV*² 197/79, 102, 209 (running); 272/9 (running); 527/71 (running); 531/29 (running, with torch and thurible); 679/40 (running), 41 (running, with torches and phiale); 702/20 (running); 706/1 (standing at wool basket, sacrifice to celebrate success in competition in spinning or carding?); 1070/3; 1218/2.

A shape count for these Nike vases was not given at the beginning of this section: neck-amphorai 12, cups 4, hydria 1, small pelikai 3, oinochoai 6, lekythoi 134, alabastra 2. Here the preponderance of perfume vases (lekythoi) is enormous.

11

Victorious Athletes

An obvious cause for celebration was victory in the games so that quite apart from special commissions[1] the potter could count on a market for pots with pictures of victorious athletes, both pots for the symposion and perfume vases for dedication. The list starts early in the sixth century with a cup by the C painter.[2] On one side the victor carries a tripod on his head and is met by a bearded flute-player and bearded men with drinking horns and phialai. The painter has telescoped three moments in the celebrations, the victory song, the libation before the sacrifice and the symposion afterwards. On the other side riders with spears probably indicate cavalry, the class to which the victor belongs, and inside the winged running goddess is presumably Nike. From this time onwards Nike is common in vase-painting and we have always to ask what her relevance is. It is very likely that there was a famous statue in Athens, probably by Archermos, of a running (or rather flying) Nike, and some black-figure vases[3] simply illustrate this or a later statue. These are small vases, lekythoi, oinochoai or cups, mostly found in Greece. The figure was pleasing and the purchaser could interpret it as he wished.

The victor carrying a tripod recurs on a number of other vases, and we cannot say either what victory he won or indeed what the prize was, since the tripod merely means 'prize'.

ABV 135/33. Amphora B of group E from Vulci, Copenhagen 109, *CV* pl. 101, 2. Victor with two youths with wreaths on either side (B. Fight with chariot).

---

[1] Cf. above, pp. 63 ff.   [2] *ABV* 51/1, Heidelberg S 1, *Metr. Stud.* 5, 96–7.
[3] e.g. *ABV* 400/3; 452/3; *ABL* 194/6–8; *ABV* 532/3; 707/594 bis; 580/9; 582/13; 647/213; 653/5.

135/40. Amphora B of group E from Vulci. Same as last. B. Chariot wheeling round. The painter had a chariot-race in mind.

135/40 bis. Amphora B of group E. Same as last. B. Frontal chariot.

135/50. Amphora B of special type, group E, from Orvieto, New York 56.171.13, here, pl. 10. Cf. above, p. 77.

265/2. From Samos. Male with tripod under foot of large band-cup.

309/97. Loutrophoros from Eleusis by the Swing painter. Cf. above, p. 106.

ARV² 256/3, from Athens, Panathenaic amphora by Copenhagen painter. A. Victor with tripod. B. Nike. Probably Panathenaic victory.

On three vases the tripod is carried by a follower behind the victor:

ABV 149/1. Amphora A, near Exekias, from Nepi. Villa Giulia 8340, *CV* pl. 17. Both sides.

149/2. Amphora B, near Exekias. B. Ajax with the body of Achilles. The athlete on A. is a great brawny man so that Ajax may be a mythological paradigm.

Another scheme is to put the tripod between or near the contestants:

ABV 86/7. Amphora of Panathenaic shape by the painter of London B 76, Bonn 589, *AA* (1935), 40. A. Horsemen on either side of tripod. B. Frontal chariot. The shape of the vase alludes, of course, to the prize Panathenaic amphorai. The frontal chariot is a common decoration but perhaps here one may see an allusion to a chariot-race.

96/13. Ovoid neck-amphora of Tyrrhenian group. Horse-race to tripod.

137/60. Neck-amphora of group E from Vulci. A. Hoplito-dromoi. B. Foot-race. Tripods under the handles are the prizes. Herakles and the lion on the shoulder is a mythological paradigm for the effort involved.

214/49. Stemless cup in Florence. Two males with tripod between.

217/8. Nicosthenic amphora by painter N from Cervetri. Boxers with tripod between.

The tripod appears on one other vase:

ABV 299/17. Amphora type B of the Princeton group from Vulci, Munich 1378, *CV* pls. 10–12. A. The family with the tripod. B. Herakles carrying his prize tripod. Here again the Herakles scene is a mythological paradigm.

A few black-figure vases show a victorious horse and jockey being led in:

ABV 260/27. Prize Panathenaic amphora by the Mastos painter, Nauplion 1, *DBF* pl. 37. Two men greet him with elaborate sprays.

    306/59. Panathenaic amphora (not prize) by the Swing painter from Vulci, London B 144. Here, pl. 6. Cf. above, p. 64.

    454/1. Lekythos by painter of New York 07, from Attica, New York 07.286.41, Richter and Milne, fig. 94. Shoulder: horseman conducted by naked youths to seated men. Main scene: goddess mounting chariot.

In red-figure the victor is commonly shown adorned with wreaths, sprays and sashes. This is rare in black-figure[1] and scarcely begins before the red-figure period:

ABV 312/6. Neck-amphora by painter of Vatican 365. A. Victor and two women. B. Warrior and two women.

    604/65. Small neck-amphora from Orvieto by Red-Line painter. A. Wrestlers and victor. B. Herakles and lion. Again the Herakles scene is a mythological paradigm.

The red-figure scenes are so numerous that I simply list them under shapes, noting any interesting cases:

Panathenaic amphora: *ARV*[2] 183/9, Kleophrades painter.
Nikosthenic amphora: *ARV*[2] 53/2, Oltos, victor on each handle.

amphorai:	*ARV*[2] 262/29, Syriskos painter; 487/65 by Hermonax from Nola, B. Nike; 553/40, Pan painter, from Cumae, B. scene after sacrifice; 646/9, Oionokles painter, A. Nike, B. jockey.
stamnos:	*ARV*[2] 296/5, Troilos painter, B. Zeus, Poseidon, Hera.

[1] *ABV* 110/33, Florence, *DBF* pl. 18, Lydos prize Panathenaic amphora from Orvieto, is a special case: the victor approaches the Panathenaic Athena with a tainia.

pelikai: *ARV*² 183/25, Kleophrades painter; 238/3, Myson, from Gela, B. komos; 286/12, Geras painter, from Nola, with Nike; 873/1, painter of Florence 4021; 1040/15, Peleus painter, from Taranto, with Nike; 1140/4, small, by painter of London 395, from Sicily, A. victor and Eros; 1342/1, painter of Louvre G 539, from Nola, A. victor with Nike.

kraters: *ARV*² 564/23, 23 bis, Pig painter; 1054/56 bis, Polygnotos, undetermined, from Tutogi, Spain, A. victorious jockey and Nike; 1108/23, 26, Nausikaa painter (cf. above, p. 150); 1164/47, painter of Munich 2335, victor in horse-race with Nike.

hydria: *ARV*² 32/3, Pezzino group, from Vulci.

cups: *ARV*² 43/71, eye-cup from Vulci; 47/150, eye-cup from Rome; 55/17, 73, 97, 116, Oltos (73 from Orvieto, 97 from Chiusi; 97 *Memnon kalos*); 113/4, Thalia painter; 114/1, painter of Louvre G 36; 331/15, manner of Onesimos; 357/73, Colmar painter; 363/36, Triptolemos painter; 407/12, Briseis painter; 430/33, 38, 59, 263–4, Douris (263–4 A. Nike; 59 from Vulci; 263 from Capua); 450/18, manner of Douris (Nike and victor); 455/10, Ashby painter; 464/79, Makron; 625/102, Villa Giulia painter, from Corchiano, Etruria; 784/20, painter of Munich 2660, from Vulci; 792/60, Euaion painter, from Vulci; 809/6, follower of Makron, from Orvieto; 809/20, follower of Makron (inside, boy with toy chariot); 868/36, Tarquinia painter, from Vulci; 1270/18, Codrus painter, Nike crowning athlete; 20 from Ampurias, Nike and athletes; 1301/14, Penelope painter from Chiusi, A. wrestlers, Nike on stele, B. Nike and trainer.

lekythoi: *ARV*² 446/267, Douris, Nike and victor, *Diogenes kalos, Memnon kalos*; 684/153, Bowdoin painter, from Sicily; 714/164, Aeschines painter, Tel Aviv.

oinochoe: *ARV*² 308/2, by Terpaulos painter, from Cervetri.

plate: *ARV*² 78/97, by Epiktetos, from Vulci.

bobbin: *ARV*² 890/175, Penthesilea painter, from near Athens. Probably not victorious athlete but a boy-dancer holding an ivy-spray crowned by Nike. B. Eros and boy, lyre-player? Present for participant in a victorious boys' chorus.

From the beginning with the inside of the C painter's cup and increasingly in red-figure, Nike may appear with the victorious athlete. But there is another whole group of vases where the athletes themselves are not marked as victors, but victory, or the hope of victory, is shown by the presence of Nike. In another band of the Nicosthenic amphora with boxers and tripod (*ABV* 217/8, cf. also 4) Nike appears with runners. On a late black-figure cup (*ABV* 627/1) Nike also appears with runners. On a lekythos by the Emporion painter (*ABL* 264/31) she appears with a rider at an altar,[1] and on an oinochoe (*ABV* 530/70) she appears with a ship, whether a victory in war or in a naval competition.[2] Several times she appears in a scene termed 'departure of chariot'; this is perhaps a departure for the *apobates* race in the Panathenaia; the instances are *ABL* 213/174; 245/85; *ABV* 567/631. The chariot-race at the Panathenaia may be indicated by Nike with Athena in chariot, *ABV* 555/429.

The scenes of Nike and athletes are common in red-figure. I simply list them noting any points of interest: *ARV*² 197/45, A. Zeus and Nike, B. two athletes; 251/30, A. Poseidon, Amphitrite, Nike, B. boxers and trainer; 309/1 bis, akontist; 405, white alabastron from Tanagra, present to a girl from a victor?; 519/20, from Gela, A. Nike, B. youth running, perhaps to be taken together; 547/27, racing-chariot with Nike and trainer, from Bologna; 593/41, from Spina, A. Dionysos and Oinopion, B. Nike, akontist and flautist; 673/17, from Gela, Nike with helmet,

[1] Cf. above on the Penthesileia painter cup.   [2] Cf. above on the aphlaston vases, p. 76.

running to pillar, victory for a hoplitodromos; 716/235, from Nola; 803/58 bis (1670), from Athens; 1016/35, Nike and hoplitodromos; 1040/18, from Athens, A. chariot and Nike with Panathenaic amphora (therefore victory at Panathenaia), B. king and Nike; 1097/13–14, A. racing-chariot with Nike, 13 from Camarina, 14 from Spina; 1101/1–2, the same, 1 from Bologna; 1104/4, from Spina, Nike in chariot, and warriors; perhaps the *apobates* race?; 1112/2–4, A. chariot and Nike, B. komos; 1113/8, from Camarina, A. horseman and Nike; 1115/20–2, racing-chariot and Nike, 20 from Rugge (S. Italy), 21 from Spina, 22 from Cumae; 1118/22–3, chariot with Nike, 22 from Etruria; 1120/4, chariot and Nike; 1122, the same, probably from Sicily; 1155/5, the same, from Eleusis; 1163/40, A. Herakles and Athena, with Hera and Iris, B. jumper, Nike and trainer; 1166/97 bis (1685); 1186/24, discus-thrower, flute-player, Nike and man; 1194/1; 1333/1, Nikias painter, from Greece, torch-racer at altar, with Prometheus, Nike, etc. (cf. above, p. 44, and 1345/10–12, 12 from Al-Mina); 1340/5, Modica painter, perhaps Pythian victory, from Spina; 1350/1, from Spina; 1393/33, 34 from Athens, 42, 45, 50 (45 and 50 from Ensérune), 56 from Le Cayla; 1400/1, from Ruvo; 1401/7, from Spina.

The total list of vases with athletic victories, which have been considered above, consists of 2 prize Panathenaic amphorai (both abnormal in showing the victor instead of or as well as the competitors), 115 symposion vases, 7 lekythoi and 1 alabastron, 1 loutrophoros and 1 bobbin (which should probably be excluded), a total of 127. Many provenances are unfortunately unrecorded, but the following figures give some idea of the distribution:

Athens	5	Eleusis	2
Greece (elsewhere)	3	Samos	1
Sicily	7	South Italy	3
Campania	7	Rome	1
Etruria	34	Asia Minor	2
France	3	Spain	2
		TOTAL	70

For Sicily it is worth remembering that Pindar (fr. 124) expects Thrasyboulos of Akragas to use Athenian cups at his symposion, and for Asia Minor the dedication of a Panathenaic amphora to Zeus in Labraunda in the mid-fourth century by a citizen of Herakleia.[1]

[1] P. Hellström, *Act. Inst. Ath.* V, ii (1965), 7, no. 1.

12

Concerts

We have already noticed a number of vases with pictures of musical performances which, because of the inscribed names or texts, can be claimed as vases commissioned to celebrate a particular performance; but there are over 150 more which have no identifying names (except for a very few with *kalos* names, which might perhaps have been included among the commissioned vases). They may be divided into (1) Panathenaic amphorai, where the choice of shape may show that the painter was thinking of the Panathenaic festival, (2) vases where there may be a connection between the concert and the mythical scene on the other side, (3) vases with kithara-players, (4) vases with lyre-players, (5) vases with flautists, (6) miscellaneous.

	black-figure	red-figure: archaic	early classical	classical	free	total
amphora	17	25	12	5		59
cup	1	4	11	4		20
hydria	1	3		1		5
krater		4	10	14		28
oinochoe	3	1	4	2	3	13
pelike	3	4	2	8		17
stamnos			4	2		6
phiale				1		1
lekythos	4	1	1	4		10
TOTAL	29	42	44	41	3	159

The shapes show an even heavier preponderance of symposion vases over perfume vases than in the case of victorious athletes but with an extraordinary falling off in the late fifth century. Within the symposion shapes, amphorai give ground to kraters in the fifth century.

We know the distribution of about 60 per cent of the concert vases as against 55 per cent of the vases with victorious athletes. Athens,

Greece and the Greek islands account for a considerably higher proportion and Etruria for a rather smaller proportion. It looks as if the concert vases were more highly prized by Greeks and went less readily on to the export market. In Sicily, South Italy and Campania the proportion is almost exactly the same for both types.

DISTRIBUTION

	black-figure	red-figure	total
Athens	7	7	14
Greece		9	9
Greek Islands	2	4	6
South Russia	2	2	4
Bulgaria		1	1
Sicily	3	6	9
South Italy		5	5
Campania		9	9
Etruria	7	33	40
TOTAL	21	76	97

PANATHENAIC AMPHORAI

Only one prize Panathenaic amphora[1] has a concert scene on the obverse; this was painted 430–420 B.C. and was found in South Russia; it has a kithara-singer, a judge and a seated man. One of the fourth-century inscriptions listing[2] Panathenaic prizes gives the victorious kitharoidos gold and silver instead of Panathenaic amphorai filled with Acropolis oil. Whether the award of oil was exceptional or whether there was a change of practice we cannot say because we have only the inscribed amphora as evidence. At least the prize amphora is evidence that oil was sometimes given as a prize for musical performance at the Panathenaia, and therefore the relation of prize Panathenaic amphorai to non-prize Panathenaic amphorai is presumably the same in vases with musical scenes as in vases with athletic scenes.[3]

Black-figure Panathenaic amphorai without the inscription 'from the Athenian games', particularly when they have the Panathenaic Athena or even the Panathenaic Athena between cock columns on one side, must surely carry an allusion to the prize amphorai, and it is a reasonable conjecture that they were designed to hold wine at the victor's

[1] *ABV* 410/2 from Tanais, Leningrad 17295, *AA* (1912), 374.
[2] Discussed by J. A. Davison in *JHS* 78 (1958), 36. Aristotle and an inscription probably of 402 B.C. agree on the award of gold and silver.   [3] Cf. above, p. 64.

subsequent celebration.[1] They are: *ABV* 139/12, near group E, from Orvieto, kithara-singer; 396/9, Eucharides painter from Athens, flute-player; 396/12, Eucharides painter, from Athens, flute-player and singer; 403/3, Sikelos, from Athens, ?flute-player. A variant is the neck-amphora *ABV* 405/20, Kleophrades painter, from Vulci, A. kithara-singer, between columns with cocks, B. Dionysos with maenad on donkey. Apparently he wanted to include a Dionysiac scene suitable for a symposion, and therefore omitted Athena but put the kithara-singer between the cock columns which on the prize amphorai flank her.

An early ovoid amphora from Athens,[2] in style near Kleimachos, has a flute-player with two men listening on one side and a horseman and a trainer on the other. The shape is certainly like a Panathenaic amphora, and it is possible that this celebrates a double victory in a flute competition and a horse-race. The date is so early, about 570 B.C., that it may anticipate the institution of the Greater Panathenaia.

I have assumed that the vases quoted so far show three forms of music, song to the kithara with the singer accompanying himself (*kitharodia*), song to the *aulos* (flute) with the singer accompanying himself (*aulodia*), and song accompanied by a flautist[3] (*auletike*). The fourth-century inscription on the Panathenaia adds also *kitharistai*, which I take to mean 'playing the kithara as an accompaniment to a singer', and this the painter would have shown if he had wanted to represent it. The vases suggest that three, at any rate, of the types of competition antedate the fourth century at the Greater Panathenaia.

The red-figure Panathenaic amphorai are none of them prize vases; the following have concert themes: *ARV*[2] 197/10, Berlin painter, from Vulci, A. kithara-singer, B. judge or trainer; 221/7, Nikoxenos painter, from Nola, A. Athena with kithara, B. kithara-singer; 221/29 bis, Nikoxenos painter from Lokroi, kithara-singer, possibly Athena; 553/30, Pan painter, from Vulci(?), A. kithara-singer, B. judge; 987/3, Achilles painter, A. kithara-singer (Apollo), B. Nike. All these may be painted for celebrations of Panathenaic victories as the use of this shape

---

[1] An uninscribed Panathenaic amphora in Bonn (*AA* (1935), 453, fig. 31), which is not in *ABV*, has A. singer and flute-player with audience, B. the Panathenaic Athena faced by a girl with lowered hands; she is perhaps one of the *arrhephoroi*, who were concerned with the festival.

[2] *ABV* 85/1, Athens 559, *AJA* 42 (1938), 496 ff.

[3] Cf. Davison, op. cit., 37, with further examples not in *ABV*; Webster, *The Greek Chorus*, 56.

13 Offering to Athena. Panathenaic amphora, Princeton painter. New York 53.11.1 (Rogers Fund). (See p. 129)

14 Man at statue of Athena. Oinochoe 4, group of Berlin 2415.
New York 08.258.25 (Rogers Fund). (See p. 131)

hints; the Athena on the two by the Nikoxenos painter especially suggests this. The Achilles painter paints Apollo and Nike instead of the mortal victor.

VASES POSSIBLY SHOWING THE THEME OF A SONG

In discussing Euphronios' kalyx-krater with the flute-player mounting the platform to play for Leagros and his friends[1] (*ARV*[2] 14/2) I suggested that the story of Herakles and Antaios on the other side was the theme of the *aulodia*; on other vases the presence of a tripod in a mythical scene indicates that the myth was the subject of a song.[2] On black-figure vases, roughly contemporary with the Euphronios krater, we can probably see the same scheme: *ABV* 311/2, 4, amphorai by painter of Munich 1410, A. duel of Ajax and Hektor; A. Amazonomachy; on both, B. flute-player; 319/10, neck-amphora, A. kithara-singer, B. Ajax with the body of Achilles; 375/211, neck-amphora, Leagros group, A. Athena and giant, B. kithara-singer; 393/14, pelike by Nikoxenos painter, A. Dionysos with Athena and Herakles both seated, B. kithara-player. The scheme is also used in red-figure; *ARV*[2] 3/2, amphora by Andokides painter, A. fight watched by Athena and Hermes, one warrior has Boeotian shield and one a shield decorated with a scorpion,[3] B. kithara-singer; *ARV*[2] 3/4, *JDAI* 76 (1961), 48, fig. 2, amphora by the Andokides painter, A. Herakles and the lion, B. singer and flautist with audience; 274/39, column-krater by the Harrow painter, A. Poseidon and Theseus, B. kithara-singer; 574/2, column-krater by Agrigento painter, A. goddess mounting chariot and Nike with kithara (cf. also 574/1); 589/1, volute-krater by Altamura painter, Gigantomachy on the body; on the neck, A. Triptolemos, B. victorious kithara-singer; 589/3, volute-krater by the Altamura painter, on the body A. Zeus giving the infant Dionysos to his nurses, B. athletes; on the neck A. victorious kitharode (crowned by two Nikai), B. men, youths and boys.

Of course it is only a possibility that the two sides are connected, and even if the connection is granted, in some cases other explanations are possible. For instance the Gigantomachies may not be the subject of the song but simply an allusion to the Greater Panathenaia because the

---

[1] Cf. above, p. 49, Louvre G 103.   [2] Cf. above, p. 95.
[3] I do not know what story opposes Echion, son of Hermes, to a hero protected by Athena.

Gigantomachy was woven into the peplos. The scene with Dionysos, Herakles and Athena may rather be an allusion to a cult which perhaps included a competition of kitharoidoi, but we do not know enough to say this.[1]

The column-krater by the Harrow painter (ARV^2 274/39, Harvard 60.339, from Ruvo, *CV* Robinson, 2, pls. 31–3) has naturally been connected with Bacchylides' paian for the Keans at Delos (*Dith.* 17); Robinson pointed out that the cast is similar: Nereid, Nereus, Poseidon, Theseus (perhaps holding the box with Minos' ring) and Amphitrite with wreath, and Gentili identified the elaborate hem of Theseus' chiton with the *aion* which Amphitrite gives him in Bacchylides. In our vase and the vases[2] contemporary with it the emphasis is on Theseus' meeting with Poseidon as well as, or instead of, his crowning by Amphitrite. This can hardly come from Bacchylides, who merely says that the dolphins brought Theseus to the house of his father, god of horses, and then goes on to the Nereids and Amphitrite. In this respect the cup by Onesimos,[3] which is too early for Bacchylides, illustrates him better than this group of vases, which is contemporary with the supposed date of his paian (478–470 B.C.). If we want to say, and it is very attractive to say, that our kithara-singer sang Bacchylides' paian in Athens very soon after its choral production in Delos, we must, I think, also say that the Harrow painter painted the scene as he knew it from the epic[4] and added details like Nereus and the special chiton of Theseus from the new performance. The most we can safely say is that this vase and the Kadmos painter's later vase[5] may celebrate Athenian revivals of Bacchylides' paian. If we could only prove this, it would be valuable evidence as to how the Athenians became so well acquainted with foreign choral poetry.

KITHARA-SINGERS

There are many other pictures of kithara-singers besides those mentioned in the previous sections and the commissioned vases for

---

[1] A number of vases connect Herakles and Dionysos in a symposion, and I suspect that they allude to an Athenian cult: *ABV* 390/5; 430/18, 23; 520/32; ARV^2 257/14; 281/33; 451/2; 809/2; 866(?); 1186/31. Cf. I. K. Raubitschek, *Hearst-Hillsborough Vases* (Mainz, 1969), no. 12.

[2] ARV^2 202/80, 260/2, 362/19, 406/7; cf. K. Friis-Johansen, *Mededelingen Ny Carlsberg* (Copenhagen, 1969).

[3] ARV^2 318/1.   [4] Cf. above, p. 82.   [6] ARV^2 1184/6; cf. above, p. 95.

Alkimachos, Nikomachos, Archinos, Diomedes and Archenautes.[1] They start in the time of Exekias, about the middle of the sixth century, and run through to the end of the fifth. Sometimes the performer is shown with listeners, sometimes he is alone or a trainer or judge balances him on the other side of the vase. From the early classical period (which includes late vases of the Berlin painter) Nike is commonly added; sometimes she holds the kithara, sometimes a wreath or tainia or phiale; perhaps two Nikai mean that the kithara-singer has already won one victory; similarly on *ARV*[2] 1163/32 Nike holds two phialai and this surely implies libations for two victories.

I only note in the list any interesting variations. Black-figure: *ABV* 148/1 (A. concert, B. alone); 212/1; 300/15; 310/105; 318/5; *ARV*[2] 232/1 (A. Hermes seated playing the flute, goat dancing, satyr, B. kithara-singer and man – perhaps a contrast between country music and town music?); *ABV* 401/2 (A. kitharode, B. athletes; the painter evidently thought of a festival with both musical and athletic contests, perhaps the Panathenaia); 451/8; *ABL* 200/17 (Phanyllis painter); 208/ 73–5 (Gela painter); *ABV* 496/169; *ABL* 239/134 (Diosphos painter, neck-amphora, A. kithara-player and man; B. flute-player and man). Red-figure: *ARV*[2] 7/7; 10/4; 31/3 (A. warrior leaving home, B. kithara-singer, a stock vase which could be bought for either occasion?); 190/ 92–3 (perhaps both from the same vase); 197/3, 22–3, 26, 68, 93 (clearly a favourite subject with the Berlin painter, who also painted the Panathenaic amphora noted above and on late vases 74–5, 100, 104 adds Nike with kithara, so that they were certainly meant to celebrate successes); 248/3; 249/5 (A. kithara-singer and man, B. jumper and trainer, cf. above *ABV* 401/2); 250/13; 250/17 ter (cf. *ARV*[2] 1632, 1639 pelike by Syleus painter with Etruscan graffito, said to have been found with another pelike by the Syleus painter with the same graffito and with two stamnoi by the same potter, one painted by the Kleophrades painter, one by the Troilos painter; the subjects have no obvious connection and it looks as if the merchant picked them up from the shop in Athens; they do not seem to have been a bespoke set which got to Etruria by the second-hand market); 280/21, 39; 288/8, 11 (on 8 I assume that Dionysos and maenads is a stock scene relevant to the use of the pelike rather than the theme of the song; but 11 has on A. negro

[1] Cf. above, pp. 49, 50, 67.

leading camel; it is perhaps conceivable that the kithara-singer on B. sang a song on some Eastern subject); 295/76; 310 (1); 383/199; 486/52; 499/14; 502/8; 551/19; 568/47, 57, 70; 590/8 bis (kithara-singer[1] with two Nikai, the same subject as on the neck of 1 and 3, cf. above); 590/9 (A. kithara-singer with Nike and judge, B. flute-player); 590/18; 593/46 (cf. below for subject on reverse); 595/67 (with the two volute-kraters this makes seven vases by the Altamura painter with this subject); 600/15 (on the back of the handle of a volute-krater by the Niobid painter); 635/2; 637/29 (neck-amphora by Providence painter, A. Nike with kithara, B. youth; on A., *Timonides kalos*; Timonides is the successful player and the name was added to commission the vase for him); 638/50 (the shape is uncertain, and it is possible that the fragments come from a Panathenaic amphora); 646/10 (A. Nike with kithara, B. kithara-singer); 650/5 (A. Nike with kithara, B. youth with oinochoe at vessel, the symposion after the victory); 657/34, 36 (lekythoi, Nike with kithara, perhaps for dedication after the victory); 1039/7 (bell-krater, concert, Nike with wreath, woman with tainia – either wingless Nike or the kithara-singer's mother?); 1041/2 (kithara-singer with Nikai); 1054/57; 1058/119 (as 1041/2); 1062/1 (the same, but B. youth holding lyre with boy and male, perhaps a school scene); 1084/17 (kithara-singer with judge and Nike); 1093/91; 1095/2 (as 1041/2); 1098/33 (perhaps the same); 1123/1 (the same); 1144/17 (fragment of kalyx-krater by the Kleophon painter, from Pheidias workshop at Olympia; kithara and Nike with wreath; Pheidias or one of his assistants must have brought the krater with him from Athens after a symposion to celebrate the victory of a friend who was a kithara-singer); 1144/65 (kithara-singer and Nike); 1163/30 (jumper and trainers on the reverse, cf. above 249/5); 1163/31 (as 1041/2); 1163/32 (Nike with a phiale in each hand, kithara-singer, judge); 1212/1 (with woman); 1324/39 (oinochoe, shape 3, kithara-singer mounting a platform with Nike and youth; it is always a question whether a chous does or does not carry an allusion to the Anthesteria; K. Friis-Johansen[2] has suggested on other grounds that on the third day the *chytrinoi agones* may have included a contest for kithara-singers, and so this chous may have been made for a victor or prospective victor there).

---

[1] As above, *ARV²* 987/3, and below, *ARV²* 638/50, the singer may be Apollo.
[2] *Act. Arch.* 28 (1967), 192.

Concerts

Flautists may perform, as we have seen, in *aulodia* when they sing and play themselves or in *auletike* when they accompany a singer or a chorus in dramatic or non-dramatic choruses or when they play the flute for a sacrifice. The flautist on the Euphronios krater (ARV^2 14/2) is an *aulodos*; Pronomos on the volute-krater named after him (ARV^2 1336/1) was engaged to accompany the chorus of a satyr play. We are here primarily concerned with flautists who are performing as *aulodoi* or as accompanists to solo-singers, but we have also two examples of a flute-duet.

In the list here the flautist is an *aulodos* unless otherwise stated. Black-figure: *ABV* 387; *ABL* 219/64 (neck-amphora by Edinburgh painter, London B 188, *CV* pl. 45, 10, A. and B. flautist and singer on platform with man watching); *ABL* 239/134 (A. *aulodos*, B. kithara-singer); *ABL* 252/61 (lekythos by Theseus painter, flautist and singer).

Red-figure: ARV^2 114/2 (unclear whether kithara-singer or *aulodos*; athlete inside the cup); 199/32 (the scene is unclear; on the side with the flautist, the inscription *TIOCH* might possibly be *Antiochis* rather than *Antiochos*, and then the flautist would be accompanying the dithy-rambic chorus of the tribe, *phyle*); 207/136, 176; 400 (cup-fragments, lyre-player and flute-player, probably school); 432/50, cup by Douris, inside, boy singing and man playing the flute; outside, A. school; 552/23 (B. sacrifice, presumably after the victory of the *aulodos*, cf. above, p. 142); 553/32 (*JDAI* 76 (1961)), 48 ff., fig. 24, neck-amphora by Pan painter, A. two flautists, Beazley takes as duet, *synaulia* (perhaps they sang and played alternately), B. herald and two women, Beazley suggests that he brings them the news of victory); 553/43 (neck-amphora by Pan painter, A. youth seated playing, youth listening hold-ing flutes, B. youth walking away); 558/128; 586/51 bis (pelike by the same painter as 586/51, A. flute-player at tripod and judge, B. the like; it has been suggested above[1] that the tripod generally indicates a choral or dramatic performance, so that this is probably the flute-player for a chorus); 589/9 (the flautist here merely seems to indicate a different kind of music from that provided by the victorious kithara-player on the other side); 589/46 (similarly here, but this is a rather special

[1] See p. 95.

performance considered below); 595/67 bis (flute-player with Nike and judge); 781/3 (cup by Akestorides painter, inside, boy singing and youth seated playing the flute; this like 553/43 is not an agon but a private performance; I am inclined to include it (like 892/7, on which see below) under the general heading of 'pictures of school'; the outside has a komos on both sides); 1084/16 (boy singing and youth playing the flute with Nike and judge); 1104/8 (similar but without judge); 1119 (u 59) (flute-player and Nike); 1119/5 (boy singer giving the note to his flute-player; he may be a soloist or the leader of a chorus); 1123/2 (flute duet, *synaulia*, with two Nikai); 1186/24 bis (singer and flute-player with youth and Nike).

LYRE-PLAYERS

The heavy kithara with its wooden box and elaborate arms was practically restricted to the virtuoso, concert performer. The lyre is much more an all-purpose instrument and it is correspondingly more difficult to interpret the pictures of lyre-players. It is used by the singer in the symposion and the komos, and to accompany male and female choruses; it is the instrument on which the boy learned to play at school. On the Pronomos vase the poet of the satyr-play has a lyre hanging behind him, and it seemed probable that the youth with a lyre in a picture[1] of Nike flying to a tripod and a satyr dancing at it was the poet of the victorious dithyramb.

A black-figure chous by the Amasis painter (*ABV* 154/48)[2] has a youth, ivy-crowned, holding a lyre decorated with ivy and an ivy spray in his other hand coming up to a bearded man, also ivy-wreathed, seated on a chair holding out a flower; the scene is flanked by a woman with a pet fawn and a boy with a dog. Beazley and Mrs Karouzou interpret this as a family scene but the boy must have played at a Dionysiac contest, perhaps for a male chorus as illustrated on an amphora by the Swing painter.[3]

When Nike is included, we can be certain that the performance was competitive and successful. The series starts with the Pan painter, and it is easiest to take them in the order of *ARV*[2], commenting where necessary.

[1] *ARV*[2] 1276/2, above, p. 133. Here, pl. 15.
[2] Vatican 432 from Vulci, Karouzou, pl. 41. Compare also the mastoid cup, *ABV* 154/76, with A. woman handing lyre to youth, B. libation to celebrate victory.
[3] *ABV* 305/22, New York 41.162.184; *CV* Gallatin, pl. 36, 1.

Concerts

ARV^2 553/35, Taranto. Neck-amphora by Pan painter from South Italy. A. Nike with lyre and three phialai. B. Youth in himation. This should imply that the youth was three times victorious with the lyre, perhaps in playing for a chorus.

553/102, Oxford 312, CV pl. 33, 2. Lekythos by Pan painter from Gela. Nike with lyre.

565/36, Cambridge 37.22, CV RS pls. 10 and 17. Neck-amphora by the Pig painter. A. Theseus and Prokrustes. B. Winged goddess pursuing youth. Beazley writes 'Eos and Tithonos, one might have said, but the goddess holds the lyre and the youth a sprig'; Eos and Tithonos was in fact the interpretation of Winifred Lamb in the Cambridge *Corpus Vasorum*. I see one possible explanation that the painter indeed intended Eos and Tithonos, but at a late stage someone required a vase to celebrate a victory with a lyre, and the Tithonos was given the kind of sprig that competitors carry when they pray for or give thanks for success, and Eos was converted into Nike by holding the lyre of the victor; if a rush demand is the explanation, it is probable that the Theseus and Prokrustes has no relevance to the victory. Three other early classical vases have the same ambiguity; in them the boy holds the lyre, as does Tithonos normally, but the winged goddess has a tainia which must mean that she is Nike; here too a last-minute transformation seems the most likely explanation: ARV^2 671/13, lekythos not far from painter of London E 342; 975 and 975/2, skyphoi in the manner of the Lewis painter.

568/32, Florence 81268, CV pls. 36 and 44. Column-krater by Leningrad painter, from Chiusi. A. Boy with lyre, and two Nikai. B. Youth running and others. Perhaps a contrast between athletics and music such as we have noticed before. It is worth remembering that Sophocles at the age of fifteen or sixteen was the leader of the paian after Salamis: he was naked and played the lyre[1] (*Vita* 3). But this boy may merely have been successful at school.

[1] Perhaps, cf. also Anakreon 386, *PMG*.

*ARV*² 571/72, Munich 2323, *CV* pl. 213. Neck-amphora by Leningrad painter, from Vulci. A. Youth with lyre, Nike, woman. The woman is explained as a wingless Nike as she holds a tainia. But is she rather his mother?

580 (u 41), Vatican. Pelike by Oinanthe painter, from Etruria. Gods and goddesses and Nike holding a lyre at an altar. To celebrate a victorious hymn?

659/37. Lekythos by painter of the Yale lekythos. Nike with lyre.

838/19. Cup by Sabouroff painter. Inside, Nike and boy with lyre. Outside, women.

871/95. Chous by the Tarquinia painter. Youth moving to the right with cup and lyre, Maltese dog, Nike with chous. Here the lyre belongs to the komos; the victory is for drinking the jug of wine.

891/1. Cup by the Splanchnopt painter, New York 26.60.79, Richter and Hall, pl. 81. Inside, Nike and boy with lyre. Outside A. Nikai, male with spear, and youth. B. Arming. The contrast here seems to be between war and peace and also a contrast of age. Success at school and success in the cavalry.

892/7. Cup by the Splanchnopt painter, Melbourne 1644.4, Trendall, *Felton Vases* (Canberra, 1958), pls. 8 and 10. The whole cup shows school scenes: inside a boy playing the flute and a boy ready to sing; outside A. paidagogos, boy, boy with lyre, paidagogos, man playing the flute for boy ready to sing, B. paidagogos, boy with lyre, paidagogos walking off left, Nike holding wreath for boy who is also walking off left, man with stick. The interpretation is not entirely clear, but is at least certain that Nike is here a victory at school, and as the boy whom she prepares to crown has no instrument he has presumably won a competition in singing. I take him to be following his paidagogos away from the man on the right who may be the master of the school. The cup celebrates successful graduation.

918/3. Cup in the manner of the painter of Bologna 417. Inside

Nike and youth with lyre; outside A. and B. Nike and women. The painter is perhaps thinking of a successful women's chorus for which the youth played the lyre.

1019/79, Geneva 14987. Bell-krater by the Phiale painter. Youth with lyre, Nike and judge. Nothing suggests anything other than a solo performance here.

1254/88–9. Cups by the Eretria painter. 88, Villa Giulia, from Todi. Inside, youth with lyre and youth offering him a wreath. A. and B. Youth with lyre and youths. 89, Athens 17539, from Attica. Inside, two youths. A and B. Nike crowning a youth; youth and youth with lyre. The youths wear wreaths, and both cups probably celebrate the victory of a chorus (although the youths are not obviously singers): on 88 it is the musician and on 89 the singer who are crowned.

1282, Athens 12961, from Piraeus. Chous recalling the Marlay painter. Boy with lyre approaching a tripod. Here there is no Nike but the tripod is the symbol of victory with a chorus and the boy must have played for a boys' chorus. The chous does not necessarily allude to the Anthesteria.[1]

1290/12–13. Cups in the manner of the painter of Heidelberg 209. Insides, Eros flying to right, with a lyre, woman seated on a rock. Outsides: 12, Nike with lyre, youth and male; 13, Nike with lyre and youths. Beazley suggests that the woman seated on a rock is a Muse, and we should probably see Nike with a Muse on an early classical neck-amphora (*ARV*[2] 669/1) and possibly the Nike seated on a rock on a white-ground squat lekythos which recalls the Shuvalov painter (*ARV*[2] 1213/3)[2] symbolizes a victory with poetry or music. If the Muse is involved, perhaps the successful youths are poets rather than musicians or members of the chorus.

1302/23, Naples, *Mon. Linc.*, 22, pl. 89, 2. Skyphos by the Penelope painter, from Cumae. A. Nike holding a lyre. B. Youth. Compare the following.

[1] Cf. p. 164.
[2] Cf. also *ARV*[2] 722/1, Athens 2025.

*ARV*² 1324/37 and 40. Choes in the manner of the Meidias painter. 37,
youth decking a tripod, boy holding a lyre, and another
male. 40, two Nikai, one of them holding a lyre, at a tripod.
Beazley says the lyre must belong to the youth and compares 1276/2. I suppose that in all three the victory is for a
chorus and the lyre indicates the poet. The chorus may be
dithyrambic but did not necessarily perform at the Anthesteria, although both vases are choes.

All these are pictures of successful performances, and the success is
shown either by the presence of Nike or because someone else is pre-
senting the lyre-player with a wreath: the success is of various kinds –
at school, in a komos, as a poet, playing for a male chorus or female
chorus or singing in a male or female chorus.

MISCELLANEOUS

First, a stamnos by the Altamura painter,[1] already mentioned for its
victorious kithara-player, has on the other side four youths with lyres
and a man with a flute. The man with the flute is in the middle; he is
not playing but he is conceivably conducting the three youths who are
playing their lyres; the fact that the fourth is not playing the lyre may
merely mean that lyre-playing and flute-playing alternated in this performance. Purely instrumental music is unlikely; the youths then are
singers to the lyre. It may be right to recall the succession of pictures of
satyrs singing to the lyre which ends with Polion's 'singers at the Panathenaia';[2] on Polion's vase the three singers advance towards a flautist
who has lowered his flutes. It is, of course, possible that the youth on
the stamnos who does not play his lyre is not one of the chorus but the
poet. In that case the stamnos is even more like the Polion krater. We
could then conjecture that dithyramb-singers at the Panathenaia did not
always wear costume and that both sides of the stamnos referred to
contests at the Panathenaia, but this is only a possibility.

There are two different kinds of women musicians, first of all women
singing and playing in choruses and secondly women who sang and
played at the symposion. We have already noticed a number of instances of women's choruses. In particular a cup[3] with Nike and youth

[1] *ARV*² 589/46; Philippaki, pl. 47, 2–3, Lyons.   [2] *ARV*² 1172/8; cf. above, p. 48.
[3] *ARV*² 918/3; cf. above, p. 168.

with lyre inside and Nike and women outside was interpreted as a women's chorus; three other cups,[1] probably by the same painter, have two women inside and Nike and women outside, and these may also be women's choruses.

A phiale by the Phiale painter found near Sounion[2] has youths visiting a school where entertainers were trained, a dancing-girl and a flute-girl: on the protuberance in the middle is Nike. It may be a special commission, as painted phialai are not common, for pouring a libation for success in graduation in the school. So also the women with lyres, accompanied by Eros and women, on two kalyx-kraters[3] by the Cassel painter are probably professional entertainers, a suitable decoration for a mixing-bowl for their own parties or for a party of men; so also a pelike[4] by the Orpheus painter with a woman playing the flute and a man listening. We have already noticed a very fine pair of hydriai[5] with professional entertainers, possibly with professional names, Kleophonis, etc.

We have also noticed the Kleophrades painter's neck-amphora[6] with a rhapsode and a flute-player on the other side. I see no way of saying for certain whether the artist thought of two forms of performance or one, the flute-player accompanying the rhapsode, since two other contemporary neck-amphorai by the same painter (16 and 17) have on their two sides, one of them acontist and jumper, two forms of performance, and the other discus-thrower and trainer, a single performance. I do not think we can be certain that a rhapsode was never accompanied by a flautist, but it is the *communis opinio* that he was not, and two other vases which may show rhapsodes have no flautist: *ABV* 386/12, black-figure pelike, manner of Acheloos painter, A. youth standing on platform between two listeners, B. Gigantomachy (subject of poem or allusion to Panathenaia?); *ARV*[2] 272/7, red-figure neck-amphora by Harrow painter, A. man on platform and man, B. youth.

---

[1] *ARV*[2] 907/1–3, painter of Bologna 417; 1 and 2 from Bologna.
[2] *ARV*[2] 1023/146; cf. above, p. 125.
[3] *ARV*[2] 1084/11, 14; 11 from Spina.
[4] *ARV*[2] 1104/13, from Rhodes.
[5] *ARV*[2] 1037/2–3; above, p. 71.
[6] *ARV*[2] 183/15; above, p. 61. Here, pl. 5(*b*).

13

Other Pictures of Nike

We have seen Nike as a sign of athletic victory and as a sign of victory in music, but there remain a large number of other pictures of Nike where it is sometimes impossible to determine the nature of the victory.

Three red-figure Panathenaic amphorai have Nike on one side so that the allusion is presumably to a Panathenaic victory, but the other side is unenlightening: *ARV²* 197/7 (woman with oinochoe and phiale), 15 (youth) from Vulci; 638/51 (man).

Seven red-figure vases have *kalos* names on the side with Nike, so that presumably they were bespoken late for someone who won a victory, but the other side (or sides) of the vase does not clarify the victory. The names are:

Archinos: ARV² 939/1, cup from S. Agata de Goti. Inside, Nike and youth. A. and B. Nike and youths. Archinos is the youth on the inside of the cup.

Hippon: 641/90–1, lekythoi by Providence painter. 91 has Nike alone and was found in Gela. 90 has Nike with a prize hydria. (Cf. *ARV²* 1586 for eight other vases with this *kalos* name.)

Hippoxenos: 637/28, neck-amphora. B. Goddess.

Kallias: 654/2, neck-amphora from Corinth. B. Man. (Cf. *ARV²* 1587 for seven other vases with this Kallias as *kalos*; his vases are some thirty to forty years earlier than the Kallias vases discussed above.)[1]

Lichas: 530/15, neck-amphora. B. Youth. (Cf. *ARV²* 1594 for eleven other vases with this *kalos* name.)

Sokrates: 207/134, column-krater by the Berlin painter. B. Youth. It is attractive to connect this with a Panathenaic amphora (198/12)

[1] Cf. p. 50.

from Vulci by the same painter with the same *kalos* name, which has a discus-thrower on one side and a youth on the other, and to suppose that he won a Panathenaic athletic victory. He may be the Sokrates who was strategos in the Samian War.

Then a number of vases besides the one with 'Hippon *kalos*' have Nike with a hydria. Here one cannot always distinguish between various possibilities: a hydria was the prize in the torch-race and probably other competitions, and Hippon's hydria is called a prize hydria. So when on a neck-amphora by the Berlin painter (202/89), the only vase of this group which is not a lekythos, Nike with a hydria on one side is balanced by a youth running on the other, one naturally thinks of a prize in a race, and Nike carrying two hydriai (385/222, lekythos from Italy) would naturally be interpreted as carrying two prizes. But when she seems to be going to lift a hydria from a fountain (sometimes the water is represented), the painter probably thinks of her as taking water either for the sacrifice after the victory (cf. p. 133 on 1036/5) or for the symposion after the sacrifice: lekythoi, 680/71–73 bis, 199; 697/20–21 (known provenances are Gela, Agrigento, Locri and Attica).

On a large number of vases Nike is associated with a warrior or warriors: here again there are possibilities besides prayer for or celebration of victory in war. The victory may be in a duel in the games[1] or the painter may be thinking of hoplitodromoi or apobatai, who competed in arms. The list is a long one. Black-figure: *ABV* 645/182, 248. Red-figure: *ARV*² 310/1; 347/99 (cup, I. youth with armour, A. Nike and youths); 428/21–2 (a pair of cups from Vulci made by Kleophrades and painted by Douris, I. Nike and warrior, round the tondo chariot race, A. and B. athletes; *Panaitios kalos* inside 21, *Chairestratos* inside 22; were the pair having a party before they set out on a campaign?); 500/26–7; 515/10; 576/41 bis (column-krater by the Orchard painter, warrior about to leave home; his shield device Nike flying with a sash); 583/5; 585/24; 599/6; 603/46;[2] 616/6; 631/3; 637/26–7; 659/35; 798/148; 881/29; 891/1 (cf. above); 941/31; 990/50, 91; 1003/19 bis; 1011/15; 1070/4; 1096/7; 1114/10; 1119/3; 1128/98; 1157; 1249/18, 40; 1391/4, 18. The majority of them are symposion vases: 11 kraters, 4 neck-amphorai, 1 pelike, 1 hydria, 1 oinochoe, 11 cups, but they include

[1] Cf. p. 78.   [2] Cf. above, p. 80.

also four lekythoi and three small pelikai, which are perfume pots. Known provenances are: Athens 1, Thebes 1, Olynthos 1, Kameiros 1, Sicily 6, S. Italy 1, Campania 4, Etruria 8.

A few vases associate Nike with satyrs and/or maenads or with maenads without satyrs. We should perhaps think that the maenad dances performed by Athenian women were competitive and success was celebrated by these vases. Black-figure: *ABV* 555/427, alabastron, Haimon group, A. satyr and maenad, B. Nike. Red-figure: *ARV*² 705/2, lekythos by painter of London E 673, Nike with thyrsos; 715/171 from Camarina, lekythos by the Aischines painter, Nike and maenad; 766/4, pygmy rhyton in the manner of the Sotades painter, Nike, satyr and maenad; 1185/17, bell-krater by the Kadmos painter, Dionysos seated with Nike, young satyr and satyr. The last two should perhaps rather be referred to dithyramb.

The three lekythoi and a cup on which Nike is associated with writing-tablets (*ARV*² 697/28, probably from Campania) or a book-roll (*ARV*² 838/27, 1199/20 from Skopelos) were perhaps prizes for success, but except in the case of the cup (838/27), where it is a woman who is seated with the book, we cannot say whether it was success in a boys' school or in a girls' music school.

On a hydria by the Leningrad painter (*ARV*² 571/73, from Ruvo) Athena and Nikai bring wreaths to craftsmen decorating metal vases;[1] this must have been for a special occasion when the workshop had won a state competition for making metal vases. Another unique vase is a lobster claw askos from Greece by the Splanchnopt painter (*ARV*² 899/ 147) decorated with Nike and fish; presumably it celebrates a special catch. An astragalos (264/67) signed by Syriskos as potter, painted by the Syriskos painter with Nike, Eros and a lion, with the *kalos* name Timarchos, was perhaps a prize for successful competition in throwing knucklebones but it was found in Etruria. A large and rather clumsy lekythos (663) signed by Mys as painter was found at Tanagra; it has Nike on the neck and two Nikai on the shoulder; the body has Apollo with Artemis, Leto and Hermes; presumably it is a dedication for some victory connected with them, and one wonders whether this Mys has any connection either with the earlier bronze-worker[2] or with the contemporary toreutic artist.

[1] Cf. J. R. Green, *JHS* 81 (1961), 73, pls. 6–7.   [2] Cf. above, p. 66.

Other Pictures of Nike

We have knowledge of women's beauty competitions in Lesbos[1] and of competitions in carding wool at Taranto.[2] Some of the Nike vases suggest that there may have been similar competitions in Athens. We have already thought of this solution for a lekythos from Camarina which has Nike with torch standing at wool basket (706/1, above, p. 151). Others are *ARV*² 397/50, lekythos probably from Athens, Nike running with mirror (beauty-competition?); 655/2, neck-amphora from Nola, A. Nike, B. woman at wool basket, *Kallikles kalos* on A. may mean that Kallikles ordered it for the successful wool-worker; 705/1, lekythos, Nike with mirror (beauty-competition); 705/5, squat lekythos, Nike at wool basket with mirror (combines both); 705/1–4, flying with mirror; 707/4, lekythos, Nike at wool basket; 726, the Two-Row painter, alabastra mostly with two rows of pictures, 1 below, A. woman seated at wool basket, B. Nike; 3 probably from Athens; above, A. Nike, B. woman spinning, below, A. woman seated at wool basket, B. woman; 944/84, pyxis from Penthesileia workshop, Nike in gynaikeion.

The winged female-figure who appears very commonly on loutrophoroi and nuptial lebetes with marriage scenes is called Nike in *ARV*² and elsewhere. I believe that she should rather be regarded as Aura. Nike has, as I see it, no place in preparation for the wedding, but Aura as the bringer of health is eminently desirable, and the healthy garden from which she comes is symbolized by the flower or tendril which she often carries.[3] It is difficult to arrive at an accurate figure for the Aurai on marriage vases in *ARV*² because many of them are fragmentary but it is in the neighbourhood of seventy. A few winged goddesses on other vases I should be inclined to regard as Aurai rather than Nikai: *ARV*² 217/2, lekythos of late school of Berlin painter, from Taranto, Nike flying with torch (on the assumption that Nike kindling an altar runs or stands rather than flies, and that this is a marriage-torch); 558/141, fragment by Pan painter from Greece – Beazley's comparison with 554/79 shows that it probably comes from a loutrophoros; 653/7, neck-amphora by Charmides painter, A. Nike flying and picking a plant, *kalos Charmides*, B. Nike (possibly a wedding-present from Char-

---

[1] Cf. Alkaios 130, 32 (L–P).
[2] Black-figure eye-cup, New York 44.11.1; *CV* 2, pls. 25, 39.
[3] Cf. *AJA* 69 (1965), 64; *Hellenistic Art*, 25.

mides); 695, lekythoi by painter of Athens 1308, 2, Nike flying with tendril, probably from Sicily, 5, Nike flying with a flower; 731/11, lekythos from Athens by the Carlsruhe painter, Nike flying with basket; 799/1, hydria near the latest works of the Euaion painter, woman with phiale standing at altar with Nikai and women – this sounds very like a preparation for a marriage.

This leaves two further groups. First, there is a large number of vases where, as far as I can see, we have no way of telling what competition, if any, the painter thought of. The subjects are Nike alone and without attributes,[1] or Nike with youth, youths or man, or Nike with woman or women. I have noted the few which have *kalos* names and the few where something tells us a little more.

ABV 434/4; 530/71; *ARV*[2] 85/21; 199/31, 35, 135, 188–9, 195, 201 bis, 208; 215/14, 19; 249/17 bis; 271/3; 276/73; 301/6; 303/10; 307/7, 16, 17; 309/13, 14; 310/2, 4; 376/87, 111–2; 384/215; 389/32; 393/ 33–5; 397/50–1; 407/16; 410/54–6; 423/121–2, 126–8; 447/269 (*Pythaios kalos*); 450/35; 486/41; 496/8–9; 505/16 (man reclining and Nike serving him with wine); 505/18; 513/22; 517/3; 520/46; 523/10; 527/70; 530/14, 28; 541/6, 21; 547/19; 553/104–6; 560/6–8; 624/79; 628/2; 641/80, 81, 92, 102, 114, 118 (114, 118 both *Glaukon kalos* and from Athens); 644/3; 1702; 645/1, 9; 1663; 647/11; 651/27; 655/4 (*Kallikles kalos*); 656/24; 657/9, 22, 48, 661/81, 87, 91; 666/15; 667/8, 14–18, 43–4; 670/15; 671/2; 1665; 673/16, 18, 19; 674; 676/19 (*CV* Norway, pl. 39/2); 687/228; 695/1, 3, 4, 6–8; 696/4; 699/64, 68–70; 700/2; 702/31–2, 34–35 bis; 705/3; 705; 705/5; 706; 706/11–13; 707/ 1–3, 5; 708/1; 709/1–14, 18–19, 211–2; 718/236; 719/13 (Nike at mound: perhaps conceived as mound altar?), 13 bis, 14; 720/28; 724/1; 726/5–7, 9, 13, 18, 25; 728/2, 9–16, 20; 1706; 730/1; 731/8–10, 16–17, 89, 93; 775/3; 777/1; 822/28; 830/2 (A. and B. Amazonomachy); 842/114, 132, 147, 154, 158, 161; 853/1, 3; 857; 881/31, 164; 895/80–3; 903/50–3; 907/1–5; 918/208–9; 921/32; 924/32; 925/9; 931/1; 939/2–5, 9, 20; 951/4 (with Eros); 954/3; 955/5, 21; 963/102; 970/87; 973/17; 975; 990/39, 63, 73; 1044/8; 1071; 1082/3; 1083/3; 1096/3; 1117/4; 1136/10; 1138/52; 1192/2; 1193/2 (top); 1193/1; 1194/3; 1197/6–9; 1200/1, 3; 1202/9; 1703; 1204/5; 1220/1; 1220/2,

---

[1] In some cases attributes may have been omitted from the description. The black-figure vases are quoted above, p. 152, n. 3.

15 Victory with dithyramb. Kalyx-krater, Marlay painter.
Oxford 1942.3. (See p. 133)

16 (a) Three herms. Pelike, Pan painter. Paris C 10793. (See p. 137)

16 (b) Recording. Cup, Pan painter. Oxford 1911.617. (See p. 142)

4–5, 9; 1221/1–2; 1222/1; 1223/4; 1263 (bottom); 1297/6, 14; 1321/3 (Nike in chariot and two little boys, presumably a version of a chariot victory for children); 1345/8 (symposion); 1363/10; 1364/1–2; 1365/1 (ball-game); 1368/3–4; 1692; 1369/1; 1370/3–4; 1396/8–9; 1550/2, 5, 14.

The known provenances are: Attica 45, Corinth 3, Thespiai 1, Eretria 6, Olynthos 1, Greece 8, Rhodes 4, Sicily 42, South Italy 10, Campania 15, Etruria 32. The shapes are: 30 amphorai, 47 cups, 3 moulded rhyta, 8 hydriai, 11 kraters, 5 pelikai, 2 stamnoi, 7 oinochoai, 1 plate. Probably some of the small amphorai, hydriai and pelikai should be reckoned as perfume vases rather than symposion vases. Undoubted perfume vases are: 8 alabastra, 157 lekythoi, 4 askoi and 3 pyxides. The proportion found in Attica itself and Greek settlements overseas as distinct from Etruria is very high, and lekythoi account for over half the total. These are the small vases that the Athenians made to celebrate their own private successes, both as presents and dedications.

The other group to be dealt with is the vases where Nike appears in the company of gods and heroes. She appears with Athena, Zeus, Hera, Poseidon, Apollo, Hermes and with pairs or larger companies of gods and goddesses. It is impossible to tell whether she is appearing as herself, an immortal, signifying the power of the god or gods with whom she associates, or whether, particularly when she appears with a single god, she represents a victory which the mortal won under the auspices of the god. Perhaps the vase-painter did not mind which interpretation his purchaser made. She appears also with Herakles, with Kekrops, with Theseus, with Tereus and with a number of unidentifiable kings and women. In these scenes too several interpretations are possible: she may be the victory which the hero wins; she may conceivably be a victory which the mortal wins with a poem about the hero; sometimes it may be that we misname her and she is rather Iris (which Beazley often puts as an alternative) or Pheme, the news of the heroic action. In one particular case, the Achilles painter's bell-krater with A. Tereus and Pandion, B. Nike and youth with 'Hegeleos *kalos*', it is tempting to suppose that Hegeleos won a victory connected with Tereus, perhaps in a chorus which sang the Tereus story (as it is an early work of the Achilles painter, it is probably too early for Sophocles' *Tereus*). In another, the

Sotades painter's Kekrops, Nike pours a libation for Kekrops and signifies his fame.

> Selected list: *ABL* 208/86–8; 246/6; *ABV* 555/444, 503; 560/510;
> 587/6; *ARV*² 198/25, 73, 103, 148; 215/10; 250/16, 38; 265/80; 286/
> 17; 288/5, 6; 292/38, 44, 63; 306/2; 361/8; 384/206–7; 399; 410/57;
> 484/18; 487/63; 515/3, 4, 13; 519/16; 537/13, 14; 579/1; 580/3; 585/
> 28–9; 603/34; 611/37; 614/7, 9; 638/52–4, 62, 77; 673/11; 736/114,
> 123, 126–7, 134–142, 150–1, 153; 764/8 (Kekrops); 852/1; 939/6;
> 991/56; 991/61 (Tereus and Pandion, *Hegeleos kalos*); 993/79; 1043/4;
> 1174/4; 1339/3; 1345/9.

The known provenances are: Attica 1, Naukratis 1, Sicily 3, South
Italy 2, Campania 13, Etruria 16, Spain 1. The shapes are: amphorai 15,
hydriai 3, kraters 16, pelikai 6, stamnoi 3, cups 19, moulded rhyta 5,
lekythoi 9. Distribution and shapes are very different from those of the
last group: here Campania and Etruria overtop all other sites and there
are only 9 lekythoi to counter-balance 67 symposion vases. These are
primarily symposion vases and when the symposion is over they go on
the export market.

14

Horsemen and Chariots

A very large number of vases have pictures of horsemen and this is natural enough if the potters' patrons frequently belonged to the class of Hippeis. It was a reasonable assumption that they and their friends would like to see their activities on the vases used in the symposion. These vases also found a ready market both in the Greek world and outside it as the following distribution shows:

	black-figure	red-figure
Athens and Attica	33	13
Boeotia	3	2
Corinth	7	2
Greece	16	2
Euboia	2	3
Thasos	1	
Delos	1	
Rhodes	16	2
Bulgaria	1	
Cyprus	4	1
Xanthos	1	
Egypt	6	
Sicily	14	9
South Italy	13	6
Campania	11	10
Etruria	89	93
Spain	1	1
Albania		1
Yugoslavia		1
South Russia		1
TOTAL	219	147

The distribution alters between black-figure and red-figure: a much higher proportion of red-figure goes to Etruria. This may mean that a higher proportion of red-figure are vases bought for a single symposion in Athens and then put on the second-hand market.

The actual number of vases are about 50 per cent higher for black-figure, which looks as if the subject became less popular. Amphorai, neck-amphorai, hydriai and lekythoi have high numbers in black-figure and very low numbers in red-figure. On the other hand cups and kraters, particularly column-kraters, are remarkably more numerous in red-figure. Apart from specially commissioned vases of which a number have been noted already, it looks as if in red-figure horsemen were stock scenes on cups and column-kraters, which were not particularly interesting but a good selling line. In the black-figure period,

	black-figure	*red-figure*
amphorai	69	9
neck-amphorai	98 (incl. 11 Nikosthenic)	9
cups	130	180
hydriai	24	2
kraters	9	58
pelikai	0	7
dinos	2	0
stamnos	1	2
tripod kothon	2	0
oinochoai	18	6
alabastron	2	1
aryballos	0	1
pyxis	1	1
lekythoi	81	6
loutrophoroi		3
plates		2
TOTAL	437	287

however, the horsemen were more self-conscious so that besides stock vases, among which the numerous black-figure lekythoi, running till about 470, must be included (and in addition the use of horsemen on reverses and in subsidiary scenes), a number of very fine vases were produced particularly round the middle of the sixth century.

The scenes with horsemen can be broken down into a number of subjects, some connected with war, some with games[1] and some with cavalry training. The pictures are so numerous that only a small selection can be described. It is natural to start with the great horsemen amphorai of the early sixth century.[2] A very fine amphora from Attica by the painter of Acropolis 606 (*ABV* 81/4,[3] Berlin 4283, Metzger and van Berchem, *AK*, Beiheft 4 (1967), 155, pl. 56/3) has on both sides two horsemen riding side by side, one heavy-armed and the other light-armed, above them flies an eagle and below them run on one side of the vase a hare and on the other a hound. Hunting and war are two aris-

---

[1] Cf. above, pp. 154 ff., on victorious athletes.   [2] Cf. *DBF* 39.
[3] *ABV* 81/5 heavy-armed horseman alone; 98/47 mounted warriors; 484/8.

tocratic occupations. Van Berchem and Metzger suggest that the kind of warfare in which the heavy-armed man dismounted to fight and left his horse with his squire was already out of date some time before this vase was painted. This may be true, but perhaps the squire–knight relationship remained as a method of training after the invention of the cavalry phalanx. Certainly the tradition persists on vases.[1] They also suggest that the eagle stands for Zeus, in whose honour the Athenian Hippeis held a procession (*pompe*) every year (Plut. *Phoc.* 37). Sometimes the heavy-armed man is shown dismounting[2] and sometimes the light-armed man is an archer (*ABV* 119/9).[3] Exekias has a very attractive variant of this on an amphora from Orvieto: on one side the hoplite grazes his horse, on the other side the archer grazes his (*ABV* 145/16, Philadelphia 4873, *DBF*, pl. 31, cf. 292/3). Another variant is to omit the squire and have the warrior dismount, leading at the same time a void horse: *ABV* 55/91, 57/114; 681/122 bis.[4] Then there are warriors leaving home accompanied by horsemen. An early and clear instance is a Siana cup related to the C painter which has a fight with cavalry[5] on one side and on the other side woman, mounted man, man, warrior and mounted youth (*ABV* 681/60/11 bis): here the woman and man are presumably mother and father and the fight on the other side shows that the departure is for war and that the warriors will fight on horseback.[6] Essentially Exekias' picture of Demophon and Akamas in full armour leading their horses, belongs here as a mythological paradigm (*ABV* 143/1, Berlin 1720; cf. above, p. 65; cf. also *ABL* 206/15, 37, 50; *ABV* 475/28; 504/1).

A number of riders are only equipped with spears, and it is difficult to be certain whether they are thought of as cavalrymen, hunters or jockeys. The last seems to be a real possibility, as one of the riders by a tripod on an early amphora of Panathenaic shape carries a spear.[7] On

---

[1] e.g. *ABV* 39/8, 109/23; cf. 109/25, the squire leaving home; 273/112; 456/2; 479/2 (squire in chlamys with spears).

[2] *ABV* 61/9; 152/24; 227/17; 311/5.   [3] Cf. *ABV* 514/39, 525/1; *ABL* 257/55; 529/61.

[4] Cf. also *ABV* 55/92; 174/2; 241/26, 27, 28; 299/21; 529/65.

[5] Cf. *ABV* 81/1; 263/8; 383/7; 512/10–12; 513/31; 647/221.

[6] Cf. *ABV* 69/2; 97/26; 129/686/9; 141; 174/8; 216/690/37 bis; 243/45; 257/691/5 bis; 283/13; 289/25; 300/9; 336/22; 391/1. Cf. also 150/8; 277/21; 304/5, 10, 11; 312/3, 7; 323/19; 336/16; 368/103; 386/10 (also archer); 429/3 (variant); 490/38, 39; 499/13; 504/2; 505/4; 510/19; 511/8; 644/68–181, 185, 247. Abbreviated, 217/5; 326; perhaps also 217/10, 45.

[7] *ABV* 86/7, Bonn 589. Cf. above, p. 153; J. M. T. Charlton, *AJA* 48 (1944), 257; cf. also *ABV* 478/1.

the early cup by the C painter with Nike inside, and outside A. a prize-winner coming home and B. riders with spears the natural assumption is that the prize-winner had won a horse-race in which he carried a spear.[1] So a good many other riders with spears can be similarly interpreted.[2] A complicated example is the cup by Sakonides in Taranto (*ABV* 171, *N.Sc.* (1903), 34–5) where the riders with spears are separated by other figures, including Nike and a seated 'king' with a woman with bridal gesture behind him: I do not feel clear whether they are the parents of the rider, or the judge of the race and Athena, or a god and goddess (Zeus and Hera?) in whose honour the race is run. A hydria by Lydos shows the jockey leaving home, represented by two women, two bearded men and the owner of the horse (*ABV* 108/13; cf. 41; 174/8; 301/2). On the other hand where the man has a chlamys and two spears, whether he leads two horses or one, I am more inclined to regard him as a cavalryman leaving home for training or action (e.g. *ABV* 271/80(?), 272/95; 277/12; 289/25, 30; 316/6, 8; 330/2; cf. also *ABV* 236/7;[3] 499/15; 396/27, 35; *ABL* 205/47, 115; *ABV* 478 = *ABL* 220/85).

Then there are the riders without spears or other military equipment. They appear on a cup by the C painter with bearded men in himatia between them who raise a hand in greeting (*ABV* 54/55).[4] Probably they were jockeys and the bearded men own the horses. (On a hydria by Lydos (*ABV* 108/12) the men appear leading horses without riders.) On a neck-amphora of group E (*ABV* 137/62, Berlin 1716) the jockey has two horses[5] and rides between the trainer and the owner; on the other side a hoplite leaps off a chariot and is, therefore, presumably competing in the *apobates* race, and the shoulder has wrestlers on both sides, so that here all scenes are athletic. The jockeys actually appear galloping on a number of vases,[6] whether in a race, or in training as the presence of a bearded man on a krater by Lydos suggests (*ABV* 125/28). On an amphora by the Bucci painter the scene of youth leading horse

---

[1] *ABV* 51/1; cf. above, p. 152.

[2] *ABV* 51/3, 4, 11, 12, 103; 92; 223/65; 239/5; 282/1; 366/84; 391/2; 468/42; 573/2.

[3] Kastor leaving home on Exekias' amphora, *ABV* 145/13, Vatican 344, is a mythological paradigm for this. Cf. above, p. 65.

[4] Cambridge 29.20, *CV* 2, pl. 23–4; cf. perhaps 54/54, 57, 59 (youth), 62 (women and youth), 63, 95 (women); 533/3–4 (jockeys led by grooms).

[5] Cf. (*a*) with man and youth: *ABV* 214/56; 226/7; 596; 613/48; (*b*) with youths, 128/91; 303; 698/452.

[6] e.g. *ABV* 99/49, 77, 93; 217/10; 189/7, 15, 16; 433/1 (hunters); *ABL* 237/114.

and another youth is varied by the insertion of a cock on a column, in allusion to the Panathenaic festival (*ABV* 715/315/1 bis). Other indications of racing are the presence of Nike[1] between men and horsemen (*ABV* 71/2) and the presence of a seated man or men, who are probably judges (*ABV* 216/2, 454/1); on an amphora (338/1) a man on horseback holding a cup, preceded by a woman playing the flute, is probably celebrating a victory. The other common scenes with horsemen (without spears) divide into three classes. (*a*) Horseman or horsemen and youths: here the youths are presumably the friends of the jockey or cavalryman (*ABV* 61/2; 71/4, 5, 14; 128/90; 129/4; 157/85; 194/2; 200/5–6; 212/3; 219/22, 28, 34; 226/6, 8; 229; 241/30 (man); 263/6; 268/22; 270/77 (man); 276/3; 278/37; 318/2 (men); 323/18; 420/9; 453/5; 464/11–12; 468/43–5; 490/43; 496/181; 512/16–18; 514; 515/7; 515/1). (*b*) Horseman or horsemen with draped figures, male or female or both, as well as undraped youths. Here the jockey or cavalryman is thought of as arriving home or leaving home. The draped man, if bearded, may be either the father or the owner of the horse (or both) (*ABV* 131/6; 228; 281/13(?); 303/2, 3; 305/12, 13, 47(?); 320/2(?); 325/40; 590/3; 693/22 bis). (*c*) Horseman alone (*ABV* 160/1; 162/1; 167; 210/1, 5; 1, 2). Probably also 56/98; 60; 61/8–9; 62; 65/33; 67/2; 74/10; 81/6; 226/4; 239/8–12, 14, 20, 26, 40, 47, 50, 51, 58; 265/3; 317/3; *ABL* 235/78; *ABV* 510/20; 578/55; 580/11; 597/16; 599/5; 609/2; 635/43–5.

The Swing painter twice paints a man fallen on the ground: *ABV* 693/25 bis, in a scene with horseman, three youths and old man; 305/23 in a scene with horses rearing; on the other side, chariot wheeling round. He presumably thought that the purchaser's pleasure would be enhanced by seeing the disaster in the same spirit as Pindar speaks of the vanquished slinking home by backstreets (*P* 8, 86).

Two other schemes are (1) frontal horsemen and (2) a pair of horsemen usually with something else between them. The frontal horsemen do not need any special interpretation; they fall into the same schemes as the horsemen in profile. They appear alone (*ABV* 67; 258/6; 322/13; 516/7; 590), once helmeted (300/14), between warriors (135/41; 288/10; 298/2; 341/1–2; 431),[2] with hoplites and members of the family (287/2, 307/51, 368/111), and simply with members of the family, sometimes

---

[1] On Nike, cf. above, p. 156. The winged youth, who appears with horsemen on *ABV* 53/45, 152/50, probably also indicates victory. Cf. also 191/7; 311; *ABL* 264/31.

[2] Warrior between frontal horsemen, *ABV* 481/1, *ABL* 220/86; old man, *ABL* 220/80.

men, sometimes youths, sometimes women, sometimes all three (63/7, 272/88, 104–5; 307/45, 76; 315/3; 341/1, 2; 453/12; 478/1; 483/2; *ABL* 230/11). Once Athena appears between frontal horseman (298/3), presumably in allusion to the Panathenaic contest. It is conceivable that a woman between two frontal horsemen (e.g. 272/88, Dunedin 48.231) should be interpreted as Helen and the Dioskouroi but there is nothing to fix the interpretation.

The pairs of profile riders are rather more enigmatic. There is a scheme with files of horsemen meeting, presumably in combat (123; 268/28–9). Two riders flanking boxers (*ABV* 219/20) and two riders flanking a frontal chariot (683/124 bis) link horse-racing with other sports. So probably pictures of a chariot and horsemen (64/27, 280/55) allude to both a horse-race and a chariot event. The unclear scenes are siren between horsemen (106/4), a maenad between two horsemen (219/19), an Amazon archer between two horsemen (219/21)[1] and two men reclining between two youths on horseback, both facing right (638/82, late cup of the Leafless group); should one perhaps think of a theoxenia with the Dioskouroi, Dionysos and another god?[2]

Many of the black-figure schemes continue in red-figure, and it must be remembered that the two styles overlap for something like sixty years, and the overlap period accounts for nearly half the red-figure examples. Frontal horsemen do not appear, but pairs of riders are found three times in archaic red-figure: twice with a chariot between them, but a chariot in profile, not frontal (*ARV²* 30/1, 182/4), and on the outside of a cup by Oltos (*ARV²* 63/87) flanking Herakles and Kyknos on one side and Theseus and the Minotaur on the other; Herakles and Theseus are heroes whom the young knight emulates.

The heavy-armed warrior appears on horseback (61/71) or leading a horse (228/25) or with a horse (57/44, 49, 70; 74/38; 77/94; 91/45; 147/23–4; 149/22, 25; 1628/22 bis; 228/33; 301/2). Two early vases (like

---

[1] Perhaps cf. 434/8, warrior between two horsemen; *ABL* 231/6, archer; 234/40, hoplite; *ABV* 511/5, hoplite.

[2] The following I do not know enough about to classify: *ABV* 31/2; 33/1; 52/13, 14, 48–54, 57–8, 60–1, 64–6, 93–4, 102, 107; 58/1–2, 4–5, 17; 60/6; 82/4; 85/714; 95/6; 96/16, 23, 24, 32, 40, 48, 51, 57, 60, 68, 85, 110, 124; 105/3; 123/5; 689/1–2; 191/8; 270/64; 276/8; 277/39, 45; 284/10; 304/1; 346/10–12; 365/63, 65–7; 366/104, 209; 386/15; 387; 426/3; 429/19; *ABL* 195/18–20; 205/1; 206/72; 218/43; 220/85; *ABV* 476/8; 478/2; 485/1; 490/40; 499/14, 16; 504/3; 505/4; *ABL* 230/5, 9; 232/63–5, 93, 100; 257/84; 268/35–6; *ABV* 512/16–18; 523/10; 539/10; 600; 635/41.

some in black-figure) add an archer to a warrior with horse or to a
warrior and a horseman (3/3; 35/2). A variant on the archer is a peltast
in Oriental dress (with a horse 155/38). The mounted warrior continues
in the early classical period, but there they appear in pairs (537/18; 547/
16).[1] Similarly other horsemen appear in pairs (sometimes more): 537/
16–17; 547/18–21; 1658/19 bis; 568/30; *classical*, 1108/22; 1115/18–19;
1116/1; 1119/2; 1124/6–7; 1263/2; 1277/12. Some of these are certainly
cavalrymen. In the second half of the fifth century battles between
horse and foot appear on funeral loutrophoroi (990/45; 1146/51–2) and
on a white lekythos (1384/2).[2] The old theme of warriors leaving home
accompanied by horsemen continues: *archaic*, 1625/44 bis; 125/16;
134/5 (on this cup a warrior and a youth with a horse is a link between
the warriors on the other side and the athletes on this side and on the
inside); 149/8 (with *apobatai* on the other side); 20, 21; *late archaic, 402/*
24 (the horseman has the Thracian cloak, and a similar cavalryman
appears on the other side); *early classical* 860/9 (again the horseman is
Thracian; inside, a youth who may be the young Glaukon, riding with
two spears, petasos and Thracian cloak); 880/8; *classical*, 1039/12, two
warriors, Thracian riding; 1270/14; *late fifth century* 1344/2, cavalryman,
old man and warrior.

In late black-figure already (e.g. *ABV* 499/15) the rider with chlamys,
sometimes petasos and two spears is distinguished from the mounted
hoplite. In the red-figure period he appears sometimes in ordinary
chlamys, sometimes in Thracian cloak, sometimes with petasos, sometimes with Thracian headgear. He is the cavalryman *par excellence*. I
have noted him above in the scenes with warriors, but there is also a
series of cavalrymen leaving home and another of cavalrymen with
horses. The cavalrymen leaving home start with *ARV²* 414/34, Oxford
1965.121, Philippaki, pl. 28, by the Dokimasia painter: youth with two
spears, petasos, chlamys leads off his horse; his father pats its neck; his
brother stands behind (perhaps the muffling himation characterizes him
as a boy choreut, and there is a contrast between school and military
service). Then *early classical*: 601/21; 623/68; 869/55. (I suspect that the
following also belong, but I have not seen pictures of them: 523/7; 537/
19; 547/23; 1658/21 bis; 861/11; 880/11–13, 20; 961/43.) *Classical:*
1056/88; (perhaps 1069/1, 1073/5); 1683/34 bis; 1090/34; 1092/70, 86–7

---

[1] Cf., however, 769/3.   [2] Cf. the grave monument of Dexileos, and above, p. 108.

(the horses omitted); 1095/7; 1108/21; 1119; 1155/41; 1222/1. The series of cavalrymen with their horses starts in the late archaic period with a cup by the Eleusis painter which has 'Leagros *kalos*' inside and outside (315/6); the decoration is connected, war and peace: inside, warrior and archer; outside, A. fight, B. two youths with cavalry cloaks and horses, one horse stands by a shaft, which is conceivably the shaft of a herm.[1] Other *late archaic* examples are 323/59 and 402/24, which has a hoplite and cavalry on the other side of the cup. *Early classical:* 860/2, 21 bis (on the latter the cavalryman is seated and his horse tied to a pillar); 880/20 (combines the two scenes). *Classical:* 1068/1; 1095/3; 1276/3, youth with chlamys riding horse, cavalryman.

Single horsemen are very common in red-figure, partly because they admirably fill the interior of cups. Euphronios' Geryon cup (*ARV*² 16/17)[2] about 515 B.C. has a young rider with petasos and Thracian cloak, labelled 'Leagros *kalos*', on the inside, and this sets the style for subsequent figures.[3] Epiktetos' black-figure horseman (*ARV*² 70/3) has a simpler chlamys, a wreath and two spears.[4] The Pedieus painter's horseman (86/4) is presumably a jockey as the outside of the cup is decorated with a horse-race, and the jockey often appears again.[5] The series of single horsemen runs through to the end of the fifth century. It is an interesting link across about forty years that the young Euphronios paints the young Leagros as a cavalryman and the old Euphronios makes the cup on which the Pistoxenos painter paints Leagros' son, Glaukon, as a cavalryman (860/2).[6]

Among the predominant cups and the vases of other shapes with single horsemen are a few lekythoi. The classical white lekythos loosely connected with the Achilles painter (1008/1), which was found in Greece, raises the question whether these were funeral vases. They are

[1] Boston 10.196, from Cumae, Caskey-Beazley, ii, Suppl. pl. 5–6; cf. above, p. 139. Not a column as in 337/30.

[2] Munich 2620, from Vulci, Richter, *Handbook of Greek Art* 327.

[3] *ARV*² 154/9; 327/30; 860/9; 860/15.

[4] *ARV*² 324/60, cf. 769/1, 2, 4; 880/32; 1005/1; 1006/2, 4. I suspect that the following belong here also but I have not seen pictures: *ARV*² 11/6; 110/1; 155/40; 201/61; 212/217; 215/6; 402/24; 684/159; 875/12; 880/7; 899/2; 903/45; 932/20; 960/20, 21; 988/15–16; 993/95; 1008/1; 1108/24; 1263/2; 1351/9; 1398/1, 3; 1403/3.

[5] *ARV*² 148/3; 159/1; 172/1; 324/66; 449/7; 688/244; 862/24; 962/84; 964/7; 1031/47; 1137/22; 1138/45, 49; 1173 (bis). Add the winning jockeys: 56/31; 57/41, 72.

[6] Glaukon is a jockey on 860/1, presumably a cavalryman on 860/2, the boy with the warrior on 860/5, and, I suspect, the cavalryman on the inside of 860/9, all by the Pistoxenos painter, the first two signed by Euphrhnios as potter.

301/2, warrior checking a prancing horse, white lekythos by the Diosphos painter, found in Sicily (where many Attic funerary vases have been discovered): 684/159, horseman, red-figure lekythos by Bowdoin painter found in Magna Graecia; 993/95, horseman, red-figure lekythos by the Achilles painter. Another red-figure lekythos by the Achilles painter (993/96), which was found, like many funerary lekythoi, in Eretria, has a youth riding to a tomb, so that in its case there is no doubt. A red-figure lekythos in his manner (1003/20), also found in Eretria, has a youth with horse at a tomb. Probably then all the lekythoi were painted to be tomb offerings, like the loutrophoros, found in Greece, by the Kleophon painter (1146/50), which has two warriors, an old man and a cavalryman, divided by three tombs. (I have already mentioned the funerary loutrophoroi and lekythoi with battles between horse and foot.)

To the jockeys by themselves a few pictures can be added where father, mother, trainer, owner or friend is included: 58/51; 64/102; 223/1; 281/31; 1649/23 bis; 403/25; 1083/4; 1274; 1276/6. A large number of vases show youths or a youth with a horse or horses, and they follow the black-figure groups of youth leading horse and horseman with youths. We can perhaps distinguish (*a*) youth leading horse, (*b*) youth with horse or horses, (*c*) youths and horses, (*d*) youths and horse. Sometimes we can say that a youth is a cavalryman.

(*a*) Youth leading horse (cf. black-figure: *ABV* 451/12; 511/7; 529/660 624/6, 8; 630/2): *ARV*² 15/11, 1625/110 bis; 1628/25 bis; 162/2 (boy with spear and chlamys); 264/57 (man); 324/64; 324/72 (male with two javelins); 324/73; 337/28 (with a seated youth also); 412/1–2, interpreted as an inspection; the youths have spears, petasos and chlamys, two bearded men, one seated, by a tree are the officials (Berlin 2296, *CV* pl. 75). *Early classical:* 816/2 (also a man; inside, a cavalryman without a horse); 887/137; 968/50 bis. *Classical:* 1067/10; 1172/15; 1183/4; 1293/5.

(*b*) Youth with horse or horses: 7/3; 72/15; 77/84; 88/1; 90/35; 97/1; 108/25; 137; 164 (man with horse); 150/25; 165/1; 407/14 (also B. man and horses); 412/6 (man also). *Early classical:* 880/8, 25 (inside; A. youths with horse, B. youths with horse and man); 936/7, 945/23; 960/26, 36–7. *Classical:* 1284/32.

(c) Youths and horses (cf. in late black-figure *ABV* 426/3): 91/50; 324/
  62; 324/67 (one youth has spear and chlamys); 880/5 (one youth in
  Thracian costume), 6, 28; 891/2 (also man); 960/24, 30 (also man),
  36, 41.

(d) Youths and horse (already in late black-figure *ABV* 292/1, 294/25,
  295/2; 329/1; 330/2; 474/20): 8/13; 91/51; 104/6; 114/3; 125/16;
  138; 147/20–21; 148/3; 1700; 149/19; 150/27, 29; 152/2; 155/38;
  221/17; 239/1638; 324/61, 63,[1] 65 (2 spears lean against the wall), 69,
  71, 73; 337/29; 374/56. *Early Classical:* 860/4, 8 bis; 873/1; 875/12;
  879/1 (the boys with spears, petasos, chlamys and horse share the
  outside with boys arming, so that they are certainly cavalrymen), 3,
  4 (boys with chlamys, petasos); 899/2; 914/147; 934/56, 66; 960/
  27–9, 31–5, 40.

This leaves a very few comparatively uncommon scenes. In black-
figure a warrior is painted about to mount (*ABV* 339/2; *ABL* 238/129);
a youth with Thracian cloak mounts his horse on *ARV²* 173/1; a youth
with chlamys and petasos mounts on 1134/8. A youth grooming a horse
appears on *ARV²* 76/76; 108/24; 155/41; 243/4; 329/125 bis, and then
much later on 1109/29. The other scenes are unique: *ARV²* 159/1,
Adolphseck 29, *CV* pl. 22–4, cup by the painter of the Vatican Horseman, A. Dionysos seated and maenad, B. horseman holding an ivy-
branch and woman. Presumably the horseman is doing honour to
Dionysos but the scene is unclear. The other two are early classical and
need no special explanation: 934/66, cup by the Curtius painter, inside,
youth resting with his horse in front of him; in a zone round this youths
and horses; 960/24, painter of London D 12, inside, boy seated with
lyre, outside A. man holding horses and seated youth, B. youths and
horse (B. is noted above).

It is clear that there is a change in the dominant type of cavalryman:
the mounted hoplite dominates in mid-sixth-century black-figure;
with Leagros and his son, the youth with Thracian cloak is the popular
type. But there is a fairly steep falling off after the early classical period
and it would be interesting to know why. Perhaps interests have
changed and the generation of Alkibiades is more interested in chariot-
racing with professional charioteers?[2]

---

[1] Cf. above, p. 80.
[2] Cf. the very interesting study by Anna Simonetti, *Rendiconti Ist. Lombardo* 103 (1969),
  273.

The agonistic performances of horsemen are shown on other vases which we have now to consider. In addition to those quoted under victorious athletes and horsemen, horse-races occur on many other vases: eight survive on prize Panathenaic amphorai (*ABV* 369/114, 395/1–3, 407/1–2, 408/2, 413/1), and there may be an allusion to a Panathenaic victory on an early ovoid amphora in Athens (*ABV* 85/1, Athens 559; cf. above, p. 160). A cup by the C painter (*ABV* 53/46, Louvre F 64, *CV* pl. 77) pairs a horse-race on one side with a foot-race on the other, and the winged youth inside may be an allusion to victory (cf. above, p. 183). A horse-race is the main subject of a white-ground lekythos by the Diosphos painter (*ABL* 232/14). Otherwise in black-figure horse-races are relegated to minor zones on large vases (*ABV* 82/1–2; 90/2; 96/12, 17, 22, 71, 75, 123; 263/2), and this tradition continues in the Nikoxenos painter, neck of volute-krater (*ARV*² 221/13). In red-figure horse-races occur on a number of cups (*ARV*² 86/4, 332/30, 348/1, with the prizes indicated, 373/49–50, 859/1) and a few other vases (*ARV*² 532/51, column-krater; 587/70, hydria; 619/13, kalyx-krater; 1054/56, column-krater; 1090/39, column-krater; 1324/41, chous). We should perhaps add the rather rare rider with a javelin; he is seen on three prize Panathenaic amphorai (*ABV* 411/1, 414/1, 417/2) and on a few fifth-century cups (*ARV*² 770). (Perhaps some of the horsemen with spears discussed above should be so interpreted.)

Harnessing the chariot naturally precedes the various types of chariot-race. As a scene from everyday life, it only occurs in black-figure, and there it is not always clear whether the painter thinks of myth or everyday life. In the departure of warrior in chariot, which is sometimes associated with harnessing scenes, the painter is often demonstrably thinking of myth, and it is arguable that he must be thinking of myth since chariots were not used in sixth-century Attic warfare; probably then all the departures should be classed as mythical paradigms for the contemporary scene of the cavalryman leaving home. Both scenes have been treated very fully by Wrede,[1] and I can be brief on the harnessing scenes here. The earliest is undoubtedly mythical: the harnessing of Achilles' chariot on the kantharos from the Acropolis signed by Nearchos as potter and painter. He has joined the harnessing of the chariot with the arming of Achilles and apparently an assembly of gods

[1] *MDAI(A)* 41 (1916), 250 ff.

on the other side.[1] The elements of this scene: man standing at the head
of the horses (here Achilles), pole-horses already harnessed, one or both
trace-horses being led up, recur constantly. The names of the horses are
not the *Iliad* names, and perhaps Nearchos took them from his client
who dedicated the kantharos after his success.

Shapes and distribution of the rest are as follows:

Amphorai A: 1 from Etruria.

Amphorai B: 1 from Athens, 1 from Etruria, 1 unknown.

Neck-amphorai: 1 from Etruria, 1 unknown.

Dinos: 1 from Sicily.

Hydriai: 11 from Etruria, 7 unknown.

Lekythoi: 3 from Athens, 1 from Rhodes, 1 from Delphi, 2 from
Sicily, 4 unknown.

Oinochoai: 1 from Delphi, 1 from Ruvo, 1 from Etruria.

Pyxis: 1 from Athens.

The proportion of hydriai and lekythoi is very high and the proportion
of large vases found in Etruria is very high.

The list is as follows: *ABV* 144/4, 147/3 (Exekias, and manner of
Exekias; in both the horses are excited; the scene extends to both sides;
one trace-horse is closely associated with a warrior, so that the scene is
either a mythical warrior's departure or preparation for an *apobates*
race); *ARV*² 1699, *Ergon* 1961, 38, Exekias; *ABV* 175/12 (Taleides
painter); then a large number of Antimenes painter, manner of Antimenes painter, and related to Antimenes painter, 266/4, 5, 6 (on 5 the
owner is Hippotion and the charioteer Zeuxidemos; on 6 the figures
are named Kallippos, . . . hippos, Harmippos, Ephippos, which is too
much of a good thing, but fictitious names here do not necessarily cast
doubt on the names on 5, and charioteers may have adopted speaking
names), 266/7, 8, 34 (shoulder picture), 129 (warrior behind, perhaps
apobates), 133 (probably undefined mythical because combined with
warrior mounting chariot and arming); 276/2 (a warrior behind one
horse, and a man with a sword at the head of the front horse, perhaps
mythical therefore); 280/3; 293/8 (by Psiax, Simon standing behind the
chariot, Sikon leading up the trace-horse, Euthoos the charioteer behind
the pole-horses, a boy in front unnamed; Euthoos again is a speaking

---

[1] Acropolis 611, *ABV* 82/1; *DBF* 40; K. Friis-Johansen, *The Iliad in early Greek Art*
(Copenhagen, 1967), 115, 259.

name; the Simon, who is addressed with Panaitios as one of the knights in Aristophanes (*Equ.* 242), is presumably a descendant of this Simon), 9; 296/2; 307/63 (Swing painter, young warrior mounting a two-horse frontal chariot, which is being harnessed, Athena; perhaps mythical); 315/1; 337/27 (shoulder scene, two chariots each with bearded long-robed charioteer mounting, clearly preparation for a race); 337/24 (ephebe mounts chariot, two warriors and boy bring the trace-horses; should one think of the warriors as elder brothers?), 25; 342/2 (warrior mounting chariot, Oriental archer with trace-horse, charioteer in long robe, warrior at front of horses; the collocation of warrior, horse and archer recalls the pictures of horsemen mentioned above and the scene should be contemporary; then the warrior mounting the chariot may be thought of as an apobates). Then four hydriai from the Leagros group, 360/4 (shoulder picture, youth or man mounting chariot); 364/56 (man with sword mounting chariot, woman with spear, dog in front of horses; the inscriptions suggest that this is contemporary, the man is called *Simos*, the woman *Kleita*, then beyond her *Tellou hyys*, and in front of the horses *Klonou*; the man may be 'son of Tellos', and Klonou is the common genitive after some such word as *eikon*; Klonos could be the name of either horse or dog, probably horse as the name starts from the nose of the nearer pole-horse; perhaps we should think of the painter equating his client with the mythical heroes by putting him into a mythical scheme); 365/64; 386/14 (the chariot is a war-chariot, therefore probably mythical); 429/2; *ABL* 204/3; 206/4, 63 (bearded man behind chariot, bearded man with two spears, charioteer, boy at horses' heads), 79, 180 (same scheme as 63); *ABV* 474/21; *ABL* 222/30; 229/1 (warrior with Boeotian shield mounts chariot, mythical); 241/14–15, *ABV* 539/11; *ABL* 251/55; *ABV* 572/1 (lekythos, close to Pholos painter, woman with dinos on her head behind the trace-horse, charioteer in long robe with inscribed letters (unclear), Hermes leading the way; possibly the dinos is a prize, and the picture a kind of prayer to Hermes for safe-conduct to victory).

Four-horse chariot-races go back to Attic geometric art and may have taken place in the celebration of eighth-century funerals and hero-cults.[1] It is not clear in geometric art whether they derive from the epic or real life.[2] Two early chariot-races in Attic black-figure are certainly

[1] H. A. Thompson, *AA* (1961), 228.
[2] Webster, *From Mycenae to Homer* (London, 1964), 173 f.

mythical, the funeral games of Patroklos on the fragment by Sophilos (*ABV* 39/16) and on the François vase (*ABV* 76/1, Florence 4209). For the rest we can perhaps only be certain that they are contemporary when they appear on the reverse of Panathenaic amphorai (*ABV* 110/ 33, Lydos; 322/3, Euphiletos painter; 396/19, Eucharides painter; 404/ 1–6, Kleophrades painter; 410/1, 5; 411/3; 412/1; 416/15; and four which were not prize amphorai, 369/116, Leagros group; 394/9, painter of Munich 1519; *ARV*² 1584 (*Hiketes*), 1602 (*Nikon*), see above, pp. 63 f. The natural assumption is that the painter and purchaser do think of contemporary chariot-races. Of the vast majority nothing need be said; I only describe here a few that are interesting:

ABV   95/8, Florence 3773 and Berlin 1711. Tyrrhenian ovoid neck-amphora from Tarquinia. A. Departure of Amphiaraos. B. Chariot-race: a crash on the left, then two chariots racing, then a grandstand flanked by the prizes, a dinos on a column and a tripod, perhaps mythical.

324/39, London B 300, *CV* pls. 74–5. Hydria by Euphiletos painter from Vulci. Shoulder: turning post, galloping horseman, galloping chariot, marshal; combines horse-race and chariot-race.

332/17, Madrid 10920, *CV* pls. 8 and 10. Hydria by Priam painter from Etruria. Shoulder: chariot-race. Main scene, harnessing Priam's chariot. Two *kalos* names: Tellos, Nikias. Perhaps charioteer and owner in a successful race? The mythical subject is clearly felt as relevant.

332/20, London B 345, *CV* pls. 94–5. Hydria by Priam painter from Vulci. Shoulder: winged goddess between two facing chariots – Beazley suggests that she is Eris (Strife).

360/92, San Francisco 243.24874, *CV* pls. 8–10, 30. Leagros group: lid of an amphora type A with chariot-race, from Vulci. So also the black-figure lids of the Kleophrades painter's amphorai type A, *ARV*² 181/1, 4, from Vulci.

401/6, Munich 1517. Late neck-amphora. Alkmeon with chariot and Athena; cf. above, p. 57.

435/1, Copenhagen 108, *CV* pl. 122, 2. Painter of Oxford 224. Oinochoe from Vulci. Chariot-racing with Athena run-

ning beside, an allusion to the Panathenaia. So also the
Haimonian lekythoi, *ABV* 545/184–94.

ABL   206/195. Gela painter. Oinochoe. Chariot with winged horses
racing past a dinos. The dinos is the prize, and the winged
horses are metaphorical rather than mythical.

ARV²   429/21–2, Berlin 2283 and 2284. Two identical cups painted by
Douris and made by Kleophrades, celebrating Panaitios
and Chairestratos, from Vulci. Outside, athletes; inside,
Nike and warrior, and round the tondo chariot-race. It
looks rather as if fighting and chariot-racing are the successful conclusion of young athleticism.

      507/33, Louvre CA 2955, *Enc. Phot.* iii, 20b. Loutrophoros(?)
by the Aegisthus painter. Chariot-race above; main scene,
valediction to the dead. Here, as in geometric, the chariot-
race is part of the funeral games, whether in fact funeral
games were held or not.

      547/27, Bologna 215, *CV* pl. 44. Early classical column-krater
from Syracuse by painter of London E 489, racing chariot
with Nike and judge. This is the common scene from now
onwards, and they have been discussed above under victorious athletes (15 column-kraters, 1 bell-krater).

      1110/43 bis. Hydria by the Nausikaa painter, found in Attica.
Chariot at the gallop and Athena. Beazley suggests that the
young charioteer is Erichthonios, in which case this would
be the mythical foundation of the Panathenaic games.

On the whole the chariot-race vases give the impression of being
stock scenes. Very few can be claimed as special orders: the non-prize
Panathenaic amphorai with Nikon and Hiketes, the hydria with Tellos
and Nikias, and the two Douris cups, although on them the chariot-
race is the least important scene. But there are a considerable number of
chariot-races in black-figure against only 22 in red-figure. Does this
mean that after about 450 chariot-racing had become so professionalized
and expensive that even the class which commissioned fine pottery for
special parties did not indulge in it and therefore did not want it represented on vases?

Excluding the red-figure pictures of victorious charioteers, shapes
and distribution of the vases already discussed are as follows:

Panathenaic amphorai: 16 prize amphorai of which 2 are from Athens, 1 from Sparta, 1 from Al Mina, 1 from Sicily, 1 from South Italy, 2 from Cyrenaica, 2 from Etruria. 4 non-prize amphorai, of which 2 are from Etruria.

Amphora, type A. Lid: 3 from Etruria.

Hydriai: 3 from Etruria. 1 red-figure from Attica.

Loutrophoros(?): Unknown.

Cups: 2 red-figure from Vulci.

Lekythoi: 2 from Athens, 2 from Greece, 1 from Rhodes, 1 from South Russia.

Oinochoai: 1 from Vulci, 1 unknown.

The other chariot-races are as follows:

Neck-amphorai: *ABV* 360/182; 388/6 (shoulder); 598/33–4. No provenances.

Hydriai: *ABV* 360/3, 9, 10, 37, 54, 66, 75, 83 bis; 384/25; 386/15 (all shoulder scenes of Leagros group; 5 from Etruria); *ARV*² 1621/12 bis (Pioneer group, shoulder).

Column-kraters: *ARV*² 537/20 from Cumae; 547/26 from Syracuse.

Stamnoi: *ABV* 343/3, 388/1, 2, 2 bis. 1 from Etruria.

Cups: *ABV* 61/12; 67/1; 160/2; 166/1; 193/1; 195/2; 196/1–2. All early to middle. Provenances: Athens, Greece, South Italy, Campania, Etruria. Late black-figure skyphoi and cups: *ABV* 560/516, 610, 625–7, 644–8, 664 bis, 696–7, 580/10; 654/11–12. Provenances: Athens, Greece, Rhodes, Al Mina, Campania, Etruria.

Lekythoi: *ABV* 345/2; *ABL* 206/6–8; 215/2; *ABV* 500/58–9; *ABL* 226/25; *ABV* 509/11; *ABL* 242/28; *ABV* 543/142–8; 706/210 bis; 545/195–210; *ABL* 247/2; 266/5. Provenances: Athens, Greece, Rhodes, Clazomenae, Etruria.

Oinochoai: *ABV* 427/1; 430/21; 526. One from Greece.

Pyxides: *ABL* 226/55; 237/119.

Again the impression is that this is a popular stock scene, particularly (apart from the early cups) in the late sixth and early fifth centuries, which found a wide market abroad as well as at home.

A few additions can be made. The chariot wheeling round gives the painter an interesting problem in perspective drawing,[1] and the painter must have seen this in the chariot-race. The series starts with group E and continues to the end of black-figure; in the vast majority of cases the scene is mythical – sometimes Athena or Herakles is in the chariot, sometimes the charioteer himself is armed or he conveys a militant warrior, very often the wheeling chariot is included in a fight. The only instances where the wheeling chariot certainly belongs to the chariot-race are two prize Panathenaics (*ABV* 369/112–13, Leagros group, included in the total given above) and a small neck-amphora by the Red-Line painter (*ABV* 602/38) where the charioteer is quite young and unarmed. The group must have come from the race-course but it is normally used as a kind of mythical paradigm: 'this skill was useful in the battles of gods and heroes'.

Other chariot events appear occasionally. The *apobates* race, in which a fully armed warrior leapt from the moving chariot and ran to a mark, is illustrated in late black-figure and two red-figure column-kraters: *ABL* 234/61–2, lekythoi by Diosphos painter from Corinth; *ABV* 544/ 149–83 bis, lekythoi in the manner of the Haimon painter, 6 from Athens, 7 from Greece, 1 from Paestum, 4 from Ampurias; 568/643, shallow skyphos of the Haimon group, from Greece; *ARV*[2] 1097/ 15–16, column-kraters by Naples painter, one from Sicily. These are all stock scenes which obviously sold well at home and abroad. On the earliest Panathenaic amphora, of the Burgon group, from Athens, *ABV* 89/1, London B 130, *CV* pl. 1, the victor drives a cart with two horses; this was known as *synoris*. On two other prize Panathenaics, close to the Kleophrades painter, from Vulci, *ABV* 405/4–5, the victor drives a cart with two mules. (The bearded man on a mule-cart attended by two other bearded figures on a lekythos close to the Pholos painter, *ABV* 572/2, is probably not racing; Plaoutine interprets him as Dionysos.) Two-horse chariots occur on a doubleen by the Berlin painter (*ARV*[2] 1701/50 bis) and on a column-krater by the Orestes painter, found in Cyprus, which has been already mentioned because of the *kalos* name, Megakles (*ARV*[2] 1113/10; cf. above, p. 57).

[1] Cf. J. White, *Perspective in Ancient Drawing and Painting* (London, 1956), 11 ff.

15

Athletics

This chapter is concerned with stock athletic scenes as distinct from the victorious athletes already discussed. They are very common.[1] At first single events are represented; in the last third of the sixth century several events are shown together, and here the artist is probably thinking of the palaistra rather than competitions elsewhere.

First, the foot-race. Foot-races are found on Panathenaic amphorai: *ABV* 69/1, from Greece; 109/34, from Athens; 120 (Jüthner, pl. 3a); 274/122, from Vulci; 125 (Oxford 1966.934); 276/46, from Athens; 286/11; 314/5, from Athens; 322/4, 6 (Jüthner, pl. 5), 7, 8 all from Vulci, 11, 12, from South Italy; 403/1, from Vulci, 2 from Samos; 403/2, from Athens; 404/13–16, of which two from Athens (15, Jüthner, pl. 10a); 406/4–5, one from Vulci; 408/1, 3, 10–11, 715, of which one from Athens, two from Cyrene, two from Vulci; 409/1–2, 5, of which two from Bologna (Jüthner, pl. 10b, 35b), one from Athens, one from Attica; 409, from South Italy; 410/1, 3, from Vulci and Athens; 412/2, from Cyrenaica; 413/2–3, from Cyrenaica; 414/1, 3, 5–8, all from Cyrenaica. All of these are probably or certainly prize amphorai except 274/122, 286/11, 322/12, which were presumably made for a celebration after the Panathenaia.

Very few of the other vases need discussing. I note where other athletic events are included either on the other side of the vase (here noted as B.) or in the same scene; also where the foot-race is a subsidiary, normally shoulder, scene: *ABV* 53/46 (Louvre F 64, Jüthner, pl. 8b), cup from Taranto, B. horsemen; 60/7, cup; 61/2 lekythos, shoulder, from Tanagra; 98/36, Tyrrhenian ovoid neck-amphora; 109/

---

[1] A very useful collection of illustrations in *SB* (Vienna, 1968), abbreviated below as Jüthner.

19 hydria, shoulder, 41, lekythos, shoulder, 72–3 cups, from Taranto; 120/2, from Greece; 127/62, 65–7, amphorai; 141/7, neck-amphora, shoulder, from Vulci; 686/8, Vulci, neck-amphora, shoulder, boxers, runners; 151/21, amphora from Etruria, subsidiary frieze with jumper, acontist, discobolos; 223/65 (Jüthner, pl. 1), cup, in same band as wrestlers, boxers, javelin-thrower, discus-thrower, from Vulci; 227/15, 16, cups; 228/5, neck-amphora, B. wrestlers, from Etruria; 248/2, neck-amphora, shoulder; 282/20, 21 (New York 56.171.27), stamnos, with jumper, discobolos, acontist; 304/2, hydria, shoulder; 306/48, amphora type B, from Ialysos; 343/2 (Jüthner, pl. 6), stamnos, with acontist, boxers, jumper; 6 (Oxford 1965.97), B. boxers; 344/1, stamnos, with boxers, from Vulci; 345/2, with boxers, jumper, discus-thrower, acontist, from Vulci; 362/28, hydria, shoulder with boxers, acontist, discus-thrower, from Vulci, 64, shoulder with boxers, discobolos, 65, hydria, shoulder with boxers, main scene, horsemen with *kalos* names, *Leagros* and *Olympiodoros*, from Cervetri; 213 (Würzburg 215, Langlotz, pl. 59), neck-amphora, with jumper, B. discus-thrower, acontist, from Vulci (the sprinters have an inscription, 'You are winning, Polymenon', so that this may be a commissioned vase); 214, neck-amphora, A. with discus-thrower, jumper, B. with discus-thrower; 215, A. with boy boxers; 384/16, amphora, A. with discus-thrower, B. jumpers; 460/1, cup, inside, boxers, with foot-race round tondo, A. and B. foot-race, from Thebes; 460/2–3, lekythoi; 461/19–20, 32, lekythoi, one from Campania, one from Sicily; 461/38–43 ter, oinochoai; 462/56, amphora; 470/89, lekythos; *ABL* 213/173, lekythos, from Greece; *ABV* 516/4–5, lekythoi; 589/3, neck-amphora, B. boxers; 599/43, B. wrestlers; 661/10, 12, miniature Panathenaics, from Greece.

Here we need only say that the foot-race is a stock scene, popular with purchasers who were athletes or interested in athletics, conveniently adaptable for any vase shape and good in the export trade. The multiple palaistra scene, including one or more runners, is perhaps first represented for us by the late Amasis painter (151/21) and on the Nicosthenic cup by painter N (223/65) then picked up by the Perizoma group (343–5) and the Leagros group (362–386). The Perizoma group gets its name from the large loincloths worn by athletes and revellers; where we can check, these vases with athletes wearing loincloths were found in Etruria and were possibly designed for that market.

In red-figure the palaistra scenes dominate: runners normally appear singly rather than in a race. ARV^2 32/3, hydria, from Vulci, with boy victor; 38/5, cup from Cervetri; 43/71, cup, from Vulci, 142, cup; 54/20 bis, cup, both sides, *Memnon kalos*; 70/1, cup, from Orvieto; 88/10, cup, from Vulci with discobolos and acontist (Jüthner, fig. 68), 11, cup, from Vulci, A. and B. runners, I. jumper, 56, cup with jumper, discobolos; 161/2, cup, from Vulci; 165/5, cup, from Vulci, I. runner, A. hoplitodromos, B. athlete with sprig, a victor or praying for success, 6 cup, A. runner, B. hoplitodromos, 9 cup; 166/4, cup, A. boxer, B. athlete; 221/14, volute-krater, neck, A. boxers, acontists, discobolos, runner, B. satyrs as athletes; 271/1, hydria, runner, jumper, discobolos; 316/10, cup, I. jumper, A. runner, acontist, B. jumper, acontist; 345/69, cup, A. runners, 72, I. boxer; 353/12, cup, I. jumper and acontist, A. and B. runners; 454/1, jumper, acontist, runner; 868/45, cup, I. runner; 1171/2, volute-krater, neck, runners, jumper, discobolos, boxers. The number is small and very few show actual races; it is, of course, possible that there are some runners also among the large number of scenes simply labelled athletes. But the totals over a long period show a remarkable decline: black-figure 52; red-figure, early 14, late archaic 7; early classical 1; classical 1.

Two special kinds of race and their contestants may be considered before the other kinds of athlete; races in armour and torch-races. Racers in armour, hoplitodromoi, cannot always be distinguished from warriors running and I have not distinguished them in the following list which starts with a cup by Lydos: ABV 111/70, cup, from Taranto; 137/60, Munich 1471, Jüthner pl. 39, neck-amphora, group E (see above, p. 153); 300/16, fragments from Athens, A. Athena, B. hoplitodromoi, certainly the race at the Panathenaia, possibly from a Panathenaic amphora, in the manner of the Princeton painter (the inscription 'MNES' is possibly part of a signature by Mnesiades, potter colleague of Andokides); 322/5, Panathenaic amphora, from Vulci, possibly a prize amphora; 346/7–8,[1] one-handled kantharoi, from Vulci, with a funeral scene (does this mean that the custom of funeral games survived in Athens or were these vases painted for Etruria?); 371/151, neck-amphora; ABL 195/7, lekythos, from Samos; ABV 415/11, 12, 417/1, fourth-century prize Panathenaic amphorai, one from Cyren-

[1] Poursat, *BCH* 92 (1968), 550 ff.

aica, one from Etruria; *ABV* 468/39, lekythos, from Alexandria, warrior crouching between two males (possibly better explained as pyrrhic dancer?); 479/3, amphora B; 490/36, lekythos; 531/3, oinochoe I by the Athena painter, from Kameiros, bearded man holding long branches and with elaborate wreath greeting statue of a young hoplitodromos[1] – it is one of our few pictures of contemporary statues, and the man is perhaps the father of a victor; *ARV²* 9/2, cup from Vulci; 48/159, cup; 53/1, Nicosthenic amphora, handle; 83/12, cup from Tanagra, 13, cup from Greece, 16, *Epilykos kalos*, 23, cup, *Krates kalos*; 90/38, cup; 104/2, cup, from Vulci (Jüthner, pl. 26b); 111, cup from Agora, *Hippomedon*; 129/21, cup; 136/7, cup, from Taormina; 139/ 10–16, cups, from Athens, Rhodes, two from Gela; 149/9, 23, cups from Vulci; 161/5, 6, cups, one from Orvieto; 165/2, cup, from Vulci, B. discobolos, 5, 6, (6, Jüthner, pl. 32c) cups, one from Vulci, B. runners (cf. above), 7, cup, 11, cup, from Vulci, B. jumper, acontist, discobolos; 166, cups, 2, B. acontist, 5, from Cervetri, A. B. jumpers, 10, from Vulci, A.B. acontists; 169/3, cup, A. jumper; 170/2 (Jüthner, pl. 45b), cup, *Antimachos kalos*, I. jumper; 178/1, cup, from Corinth.

Late archaic: 198/19, Panathenaic amphora, Berlin painter, from Vulci, A. and B. hoplitodromos, presumably alludes to Panathenaic festival; 198/96, Nolan amphora (Jüthner, pl. 16), from Nola; 258/23, stamnos, from Vulci; 260/14, column-krater, from Orvieto; 271/1, hydria, with runner, etc. (cf. above); 279/1, column-krater; 1641/8 pelike; 280/25, pelike; 316/4, cup, from Vulci, with named wrestlers and boxers, A. *Ambrosios, Euagoras, Antias, Antimachos*; *Kephisophon, Dorotheos* and *Olympiodoros kalos* (therefore probably bespoke); 323, cups, 55, from Greece, 56, *Panaitios kalos*, 57; 336, cups, 15, from Orvieto, *Lykos kalos*, 75, with discobolos, 76, 77, from Tarquinia, 78, from Athens, 79, 80, from Populonia, 81; 342, cups, 13–14, *Lysis*, 14 from Orvieto, 15, 28–9, 63, 78, B. boxers; 346, cups, 86–90; 353, cups, 15–19, 16 *Lysis kalos*, 48, from Vulci, *Lysis*; 363, cups, 35, B. jumper, 41, inside, youth at altar, cf. above, p. 147, 42; 401, cups, 3, with boxers, pancration, 10, with acontists and boxers, 18 bis; 412/10, cup, B. wrestlers; 418, cups, 28, B. acontists, 97.

Early classical: 533/62 (Jüthner, pl. 15d), cup, from Vulci; 1706/155

[1] Jüthner, *SB* (Vienna, 1968), pl. 30; cf. *ARV²* 177/3, cup in Baltimore from Chiusi by the Kiss Painter, I. boy athlete and man. The boy seems to be a statue and 'Leagros *kalos*' may refer to him. Cf. *CV* Robinson, 2, pls. 5–6; A. E. Raubitschek, *Hesperia* 8 (1939), 162.

bis, cup; 561/11, skyphos, from Capua; 565/37, neck-amphora, from Capua; 861/12, cup, A. and I. acontists; 875, cup, near Ancona painter, I. judges, A. wrestlers and boxers, B. hoplitodromoi; 914/146, cup.

Classical: 1016, Nolan amphorai, 32–5, 33 from Nola, B. athlete, 35 with Nike; 1059/127 Nolan amphora; 1074/4, column-krater, from Bologna; 1089/20, column-krater, with athlete and trainer; 1135, pelike, B. athlete.

Late: 1334/18, bell-krater, Nikias painter, hoplitodromoi casting lots before statue of Athena.

The hoplitodromos is a stock picture; he fits easily alone in the tondo of a cup or multiplied on its sides or on the sides of a bigger vase. The few with *kalos* names or names without *kalos* were bespoke vases in the sense that the names were put on before firing and the youths concerned may have competed in the race. The distribution is wide, both in the Greek world and outside it. Here the numbers startlingly alter from 13 black-figure to 97 red-figure, again falling off sharply in the fifth century.

The earliest pictures of torch-races are early classical. The literary evidence also is fifth century: Herodotos says that after Marathon the Athenians honoured Pan with yearly sacrifices and a torch (VI, 105); this may be a torchlight procession rather than a torch-race. In the *Agamemnon* produced in 458 Klytaimestra compares the beacon-chain to a relay torch-race; it is at least plausible to suppose that the institution of torch-races at the Prometheia were celebrated in Aeschylus' *Prometheus Pyrphoros*, which was probably written in 457. Herodotos refers to relay torch-races (*lampadephoria*) which the Greeks hold in honour of Hephaistos (VIII, 98). Regulations for the Hephaistia in Athens in 421–420 B.C. (*L.G.* I² 84) refer also to torch-races at the Panathenaia and Prometheia. We have already noticed late fifth-century vases illustrating the torch-races at the Panathenaia (*ARV²* 1190 from the Agora, 1347/3) and the Prometheia (1333/1, from Greece), and an undefined victory in a torch-race (*ARV²* 1345/11, 12). The rest are: *ARV²* 1660, Berlin 1962.33, Greifenhagen, *Führer*, 147, pl. 83, chous by Altamura painter, torch-race of satyr-boys before Dionysos, this is a parody – satyrs doing what ordinary boys do – and has nothing to do with the satyr-play; 688/255, oinochoe shape 1, Bowdoin painter.

Classical: 1041/10, bell-krater, Harvard 60.344, *CV* Robinson ii, pl.

47–8, manner of Peleus painter, from Gela, two runners, prize hydria, altar, priest, behind an olive-tree (signifying the Acropolis); 1166/105, chous, by painter of Munich 2335; 1171/1, volute-krater by Polion, Ferrara T 127, Jüthner, pl. 40a, from Spina, the torch-race on the neck may well be the torch-race at the Hephaistia as the main scene is the return of Hephaistos (B. Thamyras); 1214/5, pelike from Nola, B. two athletes, *Diphilos* on both sides; 1272 cups, 6 with athletes, 8, 10; 1286, cup from Spina.

Late: 1333/2, bell-krater by Nikias painter from Troy; 1352/4, oinochoe 2, from Spina, athletes, one with racing-torch; 1356/1–3, oinochoai 2, from Spina; 1404/1, cup, A. torch-racer and two athletes, B. three athletes. The only torch-racers on black-figure are on the fourth-century miniature Panathenaics and here the reference is clearly to the Panathenaia: *ABV* 661/1 from Cumae, 2 from Greece, 3, the torch-racer is seated on the prize-hydria, 7 from Greece, 9, 11 from Greece, 13, 14 from South Russia, 23 from Eretria, 26, and one other on p. 662.

The other events commonly represented on vases are jumping, boxing, wrestling, javelin-throwing, discus-throwing. I take them in this order, putting the Panathenaic amphorai first where these are relevant and noting other events where they occur. (These are not repeated later, i.e. if an acontist appears with a jumper, he is not noted also in the acontist list, nor have I usually repeated vases already discussed in earlier chapters.)

(1) The jumpers do not appear before the third quarter of the sixth century but are frequent from then onwards: *ABV* 201, skyphos, from Athens; 210/3, cup, outside acontist and discobolos; 228/6, neck-amphora, A. with acontist, B. wrestlers; 344, Panathenaic amphora, not prize, with acontist and discobolos; 345/1, lekythos, with acontists, discobolos; 381/2, neck-amphora, A. with discobolos, B. boxers; 383/8, neck-amphora, from Vulci, with discoboloi; 386/8, neck-amphora, from Perugia, with discobolos; 386/9, neck-amphora, with acontist, B. discobolos, acontist; 401/2, neck-amphora, Louvre F 264, A. with discobolos, B. kitharode (cf. above, p. 163); 461/14, lekythos, from Vulci; *ABL* 219/67, doubleen, A. with acontist, B. discobolos, athlete; *ABV* 509/2–3, lekythoi, with discobolos and acontist, 3 from Athens; 514, lekythos with acontist, etc., *Kephisophon kalos, Chaireleos ari(stos)*, New York 08.258.30, Jüthner, pl. 52b; 561/528, cup; 574/1. Cup from Greece.

ARV² 21/4, pelike; 27/9, pelike, A. with discobolos, B. acontists; 50/198, cup, B. discobolos; 200, B. athlete; 54/7, psykter from Campagnano, with acontist, discobolos, boy victor being given tainiai; 54, cups, 84 from Vulci, 98 from Chiusi, *Memnon kalos*; 70/12, cup; 78, cup, from Vulci; 80/2, cup; 83/10, cup from Vulci, with acontist, discobolos, *Epilykos kalos*; 88, cups, 21, 38, 44 bis, 51, from Vulci, with A. athletes, B. youths with horses, 55, with athletes, acontist, 130, from Adria; 131, from Vulci, *Paidikos*; 103/8, cup, from Populonia; 104/5, cup; 105/2, cup; 113/2, cup, jumper, B. and I. acontist; 124/3, Jüthner, pl. 48a, cup, B. acontist, 4, cup, from Naukratis, 23, cup from Tarquinia, with acontist, discoboloi; 130/30, cup, from Greece; 134/5, Jüthner, pl. 24, cup, I. jumper, A. jumper, hoplitodromos, discobolos, hippacontist; 138/1–2, plates, from Athens; 145/2, cup; 149, cups, 20, 21, from Vulci, 39, Jüthner, pl. 58, 85, from Vulci, I. jumper, A.B. discoboloi, acontists; 39 bis, I. discobolos, A. discobolos, acontists, B. jumper and two youths, 49, with acontist, 61; 152, cups, 4, from Vulci, I. discobolos, A.B. discoboloi and jumper, 8, from Capua; 153, cup, from Athens; 153, cups, 2, Jüthner, pl. 58, 62, from Tarquinia, A.B. athletes, 4, from Cervetri, 48, with acontist; 166/7, cup, from Cervetri, B. athlete using pick; 168/1, I. acontist; 170, cups, 1, 2, with I. discobolos, 3, with I. splanchnopt; 171, cups, 1, I. discobolos, 2; 178/4, cup; 179, cup; 180/2, cup.

Late archaic: 197/6, Panathenaic amphora (probably to celebrate victory in Panathenaic games), Munich 2310, *CV* pl. 192 and 198, from Vulci, B. discobolos; 221/24, hydria, from Greece 28, fragment, from Athens; 236/19, column-krater, from Athens, with acontist; 239/23, column-krater, Jüthner, pl. 93c, from Falerii, with acontist and discobolos, 44, column-krater, from Orvieto, with acontist; 243/2, pelike, from Nola; 249/5, amphora C, B. kitharode; 274/43, column-krater; 280/16, pelike, Jüthner, pl. 48a; 281/34 ter, column-krater; 288/12, pelike, B. prayer for victory? (cf. above, p. 145); 291/14, pelike, with discobolos; 297/11, column-krater, Jüthner, pl. 60, with acontists, discobolos; 309/1 bis, Nolan amphora, Nike and acontist; 1645/1, hydria, with acontist, discobolos; 316/10, cup from Orvieto, A.B. athletes; 320, cups, 20, with athletes, *Athenodotos kalos*, 21, from Orvieto, with acontists, *Athenodotos kalos*, 22, from Orvieto, with discoboloi, *Panaitios kalos*, 26, with boxer and athletes, 27, with acontist and athletes, 32, 42, with acontists, 48, with acontist, 49, with boxers and athletes, 53 with acontists; 331/16, cup; 335, cups, 11, 12 from Chiusi, 14 bis, 57, from Vulci, 74; 342/61, cup, 83, cup, both A.B. athletes; 348/5, cup, from Chiusi; 350/1, cup; 351/8, cup, with acontist, discobolos; 352/2, cup, from Tarquinia, I. with acontist, A.B. wrestlers; 361/9, column-krater; 33–4, cups, 33 with discobolos, acontist, athletes, 34, the same, without discobolos; 381/173, skyphos, from Greece, with athletes; 401/10 bis, cup, with discoboloi; 419/44, cup, from Adria, 59, cup from Numana; 427/31, cup, with acontists, *Chairestratos kalos*, 270, lekythos, *Chairestratos kalos*, replica of jumper on 31; 452, cup; 479/ 328, cup.

Early classical: 529/10, neck-amphora, from Campania; 560/157, cup, from Chiusi; 568/64, pelike, from Bologna, B. acontist; 578/71, pelike, with acontist, discobolos; 584/40, pelike; 643/127, skyphos; 684/145– 50, lekythoi, three from Sicily, one from Athens; 237, squat lekythos, from Athens; 720/18, 1668, lekythoi, one from Gela; 782/9, cup; 792/ 73, cup, A.B. athletes; 799/11, cup; 799/2, skyphos, from Salonica; 822/26, cup, with athlete; 834/5, cup, with athletes; 868/58, cup, 66–9, cups, from Spina, Orvieto, Bologna; 872/20, 21, cups, from Bologna, Spina, 33, chous; 882/36, cup, with acontist, discobolos; 903/57, cup, from Bologna, with athletes, 96 bis, cup, 97, cup, from Spina; 946, cup; 948/5, cup, from Falerii.

Classical: 1022/134, lekythos; 1060/135, pelike, Jüthner, pl. 46a; 1084/8, bell-krater from Cyrenaica; 1129/198, cup, with Erotes; 1134/ 15, pelike; 1140/3, pelike; 1163/30, bell-krater, B. citharode, 41, with youths, 49, from Cervetri; 1176/34, 35, pelikai; 1216/1, oinochoe 2 from Spina; 1253, cups, 81 from Adria, 82 from Athens, 87 from Ensérune, all with athletes; 1261/59, rhyton, from Beirut, with acontist, ball-game; 1270/27, cup, from Todi, with boxers; 1273, cup, A.B. athletes; 1290/15, cup, from Orvieto; 1304/1, skyphos, from Suessula, with discobolos; 1307/4, plate.

Late: 1351/9, cup; 1401/3, cup with boxer, from Ruvo.

(2) Boxers are found already in geometric. Here I put the boxers on Panathenaic amphorai first: *ABV* 260/28, no inscription but otherwise identical with prize Panathenaics, perhaps a competition piece, cf. p. 64; 274/123–4, 286/12, 307/61, 327/1, from Vulci, none of these are prize amphorai; 338/2, from Athens, probably a prize; 394/10, not

prize; 403/3, from Athens, probably a prize; 405/3, *ARV*² 1632, *ABV* 407/1, from Vulci, 407, from Ruvo, 410/4, from Attica, 411/2, from South Russia, 412/3 and 412, from Olynthos, all inscribed prize amphorai; 414/5, from Cyrenaica, uninscribed, perhaps a competition piece; 414/3, from Eleusis, 415/2, from Capua, 4, from Cervetri, 9, from Cyrenaica, all inscribed prize amphorai.

Then the black-figure and red-figure boxers, other than those already mentioned, in roughly chronological order: *ABV* 57/107, cup; 64/27, cup, from Greece, with wrestlers; 67/2, cup, with wrestlers; 70/1, cup from Greece; 70/2, cup, from Rhitsona, B. acontist; 70/4, lekythos, from Attica; 81/2, column-krater, from Athens; 120/3-4, skyphoi; 131/5, neck-amphora; 141/6, neck-amphora, from Perugia, shoulder, with wrestlers; 152/24, neck-amphora, from Vulci, neck, with wrestlers, 65, fragments from Naukratis; 190/4, cup; 201/2, cup; 217, Nicosthenic amphorai, 12, 20, from Cervetri, shoulder, 36, from Cervetri, neck, 41, minor frieze, with wrestlers, 48, neck; *ARV*² 122/6, 1700, neck; *ABV* 223/59, neck-amphora, from Tarquinia, neck; 225/1, 9, Nicosthenic amphorai, from Cervetri, neck; 226/1, neck-amphora, from Agrigento, neck and body, B. wrestlers; 228/3, cup; 248/4, neck-amphora, shoulder, 22, cup, B. wrestlers; 306/22 bis, 44-6, amphorai B, from Etruria; 343/7, stamnos, from Tarquinia; 344/4, stamnos; 370/129, neck-amphora; 375/212, neck-amphora, from Vulci, B. discobolos, 217, neck-amphora; 381/1, neck-amphora, B. pankration; 382, lekythos; 384/19, pelike; 386/6, neck-amphora, with discoboloi; 388/1, stamnos, from Vulci, wrestlers under handle, 7, lekythos, from Taranto, with wrestlers; 401/1, neck-amphora, B. acontist; 445/7, olpe; 451/11, olpe, from Athens; *ABL* 203, lekythos, from Megara Hyblaea; *ABV* 466/1-2, lekythoi; 470/90, lekythos, from Perachora; 471/1, lekythos, from Vulci; 478/1, neck-amphora; 480, volute-krater, neck, from Athens; 482/1, neck-amphora, B. discobolos, acontist; 496/174, lekythos; *ABL* 251/43, skyphos, B. wrestlers; 593/3, neck-amphora, 7-8, 13 with wrestlers, discobolos; 609/2, kyathos, from Vulci.

*ARV*² 36/1, Panathenaic amphora, from Aegina, A. Athena, *Pythoklees kalos*; 70, cups, 15, Jüthner, pl. 90b, from Vulci, with acontist, discobolos, B. youth with horses, 41, cup, from Chiusi, 82, cup, from Athens; 79/5, cup; 106, cups, 1 from Athens, 2 from Bologna; 117/6, cup, *Epidromos kalos*; 124/2, cup; 134/4, cup; 146/28, cup; 150/44, cup,

I. athlete, B. wrestlers; 153/3 ter, cup, A. and B. athletes; 174/15, cup from Cervetri, with wrestlers.

Late archaic: 182/4, amphora A, from Vulci; 221/23, hydria, with athletes; 221/29, fragment, from Athens; 235/8, column-krater; 236/9, column-krater, 14, fragment from Eleusis; 251/30, stamnos; 280/27, column-krater; 295/178, fragment(?); 296/9, stamnos; 320/14, cup *Athenodotos*, 37, cup, B. pankration, *Panaitios kalos*, *Lykos kalos*; 1646, cup; 339/64, cup, *Lykos kalos*, with athletes; 352, cups, 1, from Orvieto, 8, B. wrestlers; 363/36 bis, cup, with acontists, 37, cup, with athlete, 79 bis, cup, with athlete; 374/58, cup; 401, cups, 6, 8, with acontist, 8 bis, with athletes; 404, cups, 3, from Tarquinia, with discobolos, acontist, 4, 5; 418, cups, 25, from Vulci, 26, with acontist, discobolos, 29, from Tarquinia, with athletes, 30, 31, with athletes, 32–41, 34–5, from Orvieto, 39–41, from Adria; 427/29, cup, from Vulci, boxer at altar, *Chairestratos kalos*, 37, 230, from Chiusi; 449/11, cup, from Chiusi; 467, cups, 132, with athletes, 135-9, with athletes, 139, from Orvieto.

Early classical: 814/100, stamnos, with wrestlers; 815/4, cup, from Spina, with acontists; 817/4, cup; 823/14, cup; 835, cup, from Falerii, with wrestlers; 868/46, cup; 904/64, cup, with wrestlers.

Classical: 1089/59, bell-krater, from Eleusis; 1111/2, pelike, from Tarqunia; 1253/79, cup, with athletes; 1270/23, cup, with wrestlers; 40, cup, 46, cup-skyphos.

Fourth century: ABV 662/24, miniature Panathenaic, from Thespiai.

(3) Wrestlers are a much shorter list. But many of them have already been quoted; in particular, they tend to pair with boxers. Panathenaic amphorai with wrestlers are: *ABV* 396/20, from Athens; 403/1, from Taranto; 406/6, from Athens; 407/2, from Vulci; *ARV*² 214; *ABV* 410/2-3, from Attica; 412/1, from Athens; 414/4, and 415/10, from Cyrenaica; 416/16. All are prize amphorai except two fragmentary ones and they may well be also.

The black-figure wrestlers start in the second quarter of the sixth century, paired with boxers. The others are *ABV* 64/26 cup; 113/80, cup, from Italy; 137/62, neck-amphora, shoulder, from Orvieto; 310, lekythos; 315/3, neck-amphora, shoulder; 344, stamnos, from Populonia; 375/216, neck-amphora, B. acontist and discobolos; 424/15, oinochoe I; 470/91, lekythos; 484/18, neck-amphora.

Red-figure: *ARV*² 3/1, amphora A, from Vulci; 33/7 bis, amphora B, B. two athletes. *Late archaic:* 320/19, cup; 331/17, with athletes; 339/65, cup, from Cervetri, A. pankration; 342/57-8, 64 and 65, both with athletes, 64 *Lykos*, 65 *Lysis*, cups; 357, cup; 388/6, cup, with athlete; 407/11, cup, with acontist; *early classical:* 866, cup with athletes; *classical:* 1005/7, neck-amphora, from Capua; 1054/59, bell-krater; 1163/47 bis, 48, bell-kraters; 1270/22, cup from Vulci, *Xenon kalos*, 41, cup from Todi; 1282, cups, 8, 24, from Lanuvium; 1301/28, oinochoe 8; *late:* 1342/3, pelike.

(4) Acontists belong mainly to the palaistra scenes which start in the third quarter of the sixth century; they are very common in red-figure. Panathenaic amphorai with acontists are: *ABV* 369/117, with disco-cobolos, probably a prize amphora; 369/118, with discobolos, not prize; 411/4, from Cyrenaica, prize; 438, with discobolos, not prize. Otherwise all the black-figure acontists have been entered except the lekythoi *ABV* 476/2 from Taranto; 497, with discoboloi, one from Greece, one from Taranto.

Red-figure: *ARV*² 10/2, oinochoe from Cervetri, *kalos Melieus*; 15/10, neck-amphora, from Vulci, B. discobolos; *Antias*; 13, hydria, *Leagros, Antias, Smikythos kalos*; 23/1, amphora A, from Vulci, with discobolos, *Sostratos kalos, Chares, Hail! Demostratos*; 43/68, cup, 165; 54/13, cup, from Etruria, B. discobolos, 22, cup; 69, mastoid, *Memnon kalos*; 70/83, cup from Vulci; 88/1, cup, from Capua, B. youth with horses; 106/2, cup, from Adria; 112/1, cup, from Vulci; 113/5, cup; 148/29, cup, A. and B. athletes; 150/48, cup, from Chiusi, A. and B. athletes; 163/2, plate; 167/9, cup, 10 bis, cup, B. athlete; 169/4, cup, from Vulci; 169/1, cup from Vulci, *Dorotheos kalos*; 170/4, cup.

Late archaic: 182/6, Jüthner, pl. 57a, pointed amphora, from Vulci, neck, with discobolos, 19, neck-amphora, 35, Jüthner pl. 84, kalyx-krater, from Tarquinia, B. discobolos; 203/95, Nolan amphora, from Cervetri; 226/5, Jüthner, pl. 100, neck-amphora; 236/10, column-krater, with discobolos, *Aphrodisia kale*; 239/41, column-krater, 54, column-krater from Gela, B. athlete; 272/13, neck-amphora; 1641, pelike, B. discobolos; 279/1, amphora C; 280/28, Jüthner, pl. 93a, column-krater, with discobolos; 295/79, fragment; 309/5, Nolan am-phora, from Ruvo, 16, lekythos, from Gela; 316/12, cup; 320/28, cup from Vulci, I. with discobolos, *Panaitios kalos*, A. and B. athletes, 30, cup, 31, cup, 34, cup, 38, 39, cups, from Etruria, A. and B. athletes, 54, cup, 331/31, cup; 339/73 and 85 bis, cups, from Vulci, *Diogenes kalos*; 352/66, cup; 361/14, Panathenaic amphora, A. Athena with stylus and tablets; 363/40, cup, from Adria; 390/1, alabastron, *Chairippos kalos*; 401/9, cup, with athletes; 404/9, cup; 418/117, cup, from Tarquinia; 452/6, lekythos, from Eretria.

Early classical: 562/23 ter, column-krater; 1659, pelike; 584/42, pelike; 775/4, oinochoe 7; 1670, cup; 788/1–2 cups; 792/139, cup; 814, oinochoe 1, from Spina; 826/29, cup, from Tarquinia; 897/134, cup, from Tarquinia; 979/1, cup, with athletes.

Classical: 1054/85, bell-krater, from Athens; 1102/4, column-krater, with discobolos, from Spina; 1253/84, cup, with discobolos; 1261/65, pelike, with discobolos; 1270/21, cup, 28 bis, cup; 1274/4, Jüthner, pl. 54c, cup; 1298, 1–6, acontists, two from Campania.

Late: 1348/1, oinochoe 4, from Spina, *kalos philos Mikion*; 1396/7–9, cup or cups, from Veii; acontist and Nike.

(5) Discoboloi have been mentioned many times with acontists and other light athletes. Two prize Panathenaics (*ABV* 409/3, from Cumae; 416/13, from Cyrenaica) and two non-prize Panathenaics (*ABV* 397/3, 406, from Rhodes) have discoboloi. Otherwise there remain in black-figure a lekythos, 496/173, and a cup from Athens, 574/6.

Red-figure: *ARV*² 10/3, cup; 10/1, oinochoe, from Cervetri; 43/146, cup, from Selinus; 54/19, cup, 27, cup, from Vulci, B. discobolos, *kalos Memnon*, 38, cup, from Chiusi, B. athlete; 70/6, cup; 82/7, cup, from Athens, 11, cup from Vulci; 88/23, cup, from Cervetri, 108, cup from Athens; 96, cup, from Vulci; 97/6, cup; 101/1, cup; 118/1, cup, *Kleomelos kalos*; 139/9, cup from Camiros; 145/1, cup, from Vulci; 146/26 bis, cup, A. and B. athletes; 150/25, cup; 150/41, cup, A. and B. athletes, 47, cup, from Vulci, A. and B. athletes, 52, cup; 153, cup; 154, cups, 5 from Marseille, 6; 163/1, plate, with athlete, *Xenophon* and *Dorotheos*; 167/8, cup; 178/3, cup from Locris.

Late archaic: 182/17, neck-amphora, 20, Nolan amphora, from Gela; 197 Panathenaic amphorai, 4, 12, from Vulci, *Sokrates kalos*, 13 from Vulci, Jüthner, pl. 88, 46–7, doubleens; 215/3, Nolan amphora from Capua; 239, column-kraters, 52, 53, from Athens; 320/24, cup, A. and B. athletes, 40, 41, cups, A. and B. athletes, 73 bis, cup; 342/62, cup, 71, 73, cups, with athletes; 366/78, cup, 390, pyxis D; 416/10, cup; 418/119,

Nolan amphora from Nola; 427/4 (from Tarquinia), 449/20, cups, *Chairestratos kalos*; 452/2, lekythos, from Eretria.

Early classical: 638/44, neck-amphora; 684/152, lekythos, from Gela; 918, cup, discobolos.

Classical: 990/40, Nolan amphora; 1089/57, bell-krater, from Rhodes; 1140/1-2, pelikai, 2 from Nola; 1156/20, dinos, Jüthner, pl. 93d; 1177/1, pelike, with athletes; 1261/40, cup, from Bologna; 1263/1, cup, with athletes; 1281/71, cup, from Athens; 1286/12, skyphos, from Athens; 1287, cup, from Vulci, I. discobolos and athlete at altar, A. and B. athletes; 1290/18, cup, A. and B. athletes; 1299/1, cup, from Marne; 1304/3, from Spina.

Late: 1400/3, cup.

Outside these there is a large general class of athletes and a few very specialized performances. The general class may include some athletes which, had I been able to see pictures, I could have classified, but the majority of them are athletes at rest, distinguished by strigil and aryballos, sometimes taking off their cloaks, sometimes washing at a laver, sometimes indicated by the stele or pillar at their side, sometimes by a herm, or by the presence of a trainer. I give first the small number of black-figure vases which Miss Haspels calls 'palaestra'; they certainly belong with the scenes discussed above but it is not clear which sports are shown: *ABL* 207, lekythoi, 41 from Greece, 77,[1] 98 from Delos, 99 from Gela, 183 oinochoe; 217, lekythoi, 34-5, 53 from Camarina; 234/38, lekythos, from Greece.

Then the large general class of athletes: black-figure, *ABV* 100/70, neck-amphora, subsidiary frieze; 113/83, cup, from Greece; 127, amphorai B, 62 from Cervetri, 63 from Rhodes, 65-8; 130/1, plate, from Delos; 279/53, (?) stand of nuptial lebes; 308, neck-amphorai, 75, from Vulci, 85, 93, from Locri; 313, hydria, from Greece; 339/1, small Panathenaic amphora, A. Athena; 345/3, one-handled kantharos, from Cervetri; 360/16 bis, hydria, shoulder, 140, neck-amphora, 293, lekythos; 396/5, Panathenaic amphora, from Samos; 453/8, neck-amphora, from Nola; 461/17-18, lekythoi, from Athens, 55, amphora; 463/2, lekythos, from Camiros; 465/33-6, lekythoi, from Taranto, Siena, Carthage; 466/1-2, lekythoi, from Lucania; 466, lekythos, from Athens; 466/2, lekythos, from Campania; 469/76-82, lekythoi, three

[1] Now Allard Pierson Stichting 3331, Haspels, *Mélanges Michalowski* (Warsaw, 1966), 437.

from Athens, three from Rhodes; 471/2, lekythos from Cyprus; 502/101, lekythos, from Attica; 519/12, amphora from Greece; *ABL* 256/76, lekythos; *ABV* 661, miniature Panathenaics, fourth century, 4–8, 16–19, 22, 25, 27; 662; one from Athens, Eretria and Tanagra, five from Greece. Noticeable in this list is the large number of lekythoi.

Red-figure: *ARV²* 7/4, alabastron, from Athens; 15/16, fragment, *Antias*; 23/3, pelike; 32/3 bis, psykter; cups, 43/149, 163; 54/41, A. and B. jockey, *Memnon kalos*, 44, 56, from Vulci, 100, 128, *Memnon kalos*; 70/63; 79/11, from Camiros, *Hipparchos*; 1624/4; 82/1, from Cervetri; 86/3, from Cervetri; 86, from Orvieto, *Epilykos kalos*; 88/15, 52, from Etruria, 53, 54 from Vulci, 57–9, from Athens, 103, from Tarquinia, 106, from Athens, 103/9; 104/1, 6; 108/26, from Orvieto; 109; 111/17; 114/1, 2; 115/1, 2 from Athens; 118/3, aryballos, from Cumae; 121/2, cup from Cervetri; 127/30, pyxis; cups, 130/31, from Greece; 134; 134/2, from Cervetri, 3, 6; 136/2, from Italy, 3, from Vulci, 9; 142/6 from Medma; 144/22, lid, from Athens; cups, 144/3, from Athens; 146/20, 27, 30; 148/2, from Vulci, 11, from Chiusi, 22 bis, from Cervetri; 150/40, Jüthner, pl. 58e, 85, from Vulci, 42, 43, 45, 46, from Selinus, 50, 51, 62, from Vulci; 152/2; 153/1, from Orvieto, 3, from Ruvo, 3 bis, 4 bis, from Locri, 7, 14; 157/77–80, oinochoai 8A, from Tarquinia (2), Suessula, Athens, 85 ter, alabastron; 162/2, cup, from Vulci; 163/9, plate, *Epidromos*; cups, 165/1, from Vulci, *Menis kalos*; 169/2; 171/1; 174/17, from Orvieto, *Ambrosios*, 24, *Tleson kalos*; 177/3, from Chiusi, inside *Leagros kalos*, A.B. komos, *Epidromos kalos*.

Late archaic: 184/27, pelike, 34, kalyx-krater, from Corinth, 60, stamnos, 61, stamnos, from Athens; 206/128, volute-krater, 131, volute-krater, from Cervetri, 187, chous from Sicily, 243, cup from Athens; 215/11, stamnos, from Orvieto; 226/9, amphora B, from Agrigento, 17, kalyx-krater, from Athens, 34, stamnos, 81, cup; column-kraters; 235/9; 236/5; 239/21, 25, 55, 55 bis; 246, pelike; 251/29, stamnos, from Nola; 257/6, stamnos, from Vulci, *Nikostratos*; 260/4, volute-krater, neck, from Athens; 263/52, psykter, from Tarquinia, 76, kantharos, from Veii; 267/2, fragment; 271/1, kalyx-krater, from Spina; 272/29, pelike, from Agrigento, 34, pelike, 44, column-krater, from Spina, 84, fragment, from Athens; column-kraters, 278/5; 281/31–2, from Spina, 34, from Chiusi, 34 bis; 282/41, lekythos, from Gela; 282, column-krater, from Capua; 286/30, column-krater; 291/14, stamnos, from

Cervetri; cups, 320/17, from Taranto, 23, from Italy, *Panaitios kalos*, 25, 29, 35, 36, 43, 44–7, 50, 51, 51 bis, 52, 64, Jüthner, pl. 45c, from Orvieto, 69, 95, 99, 113, from Cervetri, *Panaitios kalos*, 128, 129; 1646, aryballos; cups, 331/13, 14; 335/1, Jüthner, pl. 50, stand, from S. Italy, *Antiphon kalos*; cups, 335/13, *Lykos kalos*, 13 bis, 14, from Vulci, *Laches kalos*, 48, from Orvieto, *Laches kalos*, 62–72 (70 from Orvieto); 342/11, *Lykos kalos*, 20, 47, 59, 60, 64–6, 67, *Laches kalos*; 68, 70, 73–7, 79–82, 84–5, 103, 108, 114, 115, skyphos, from Athens; cups, 353/6–7, 9, Jüthner, pl. 100c, 10, 11, from Vulci, 13, 14, from Athens, 22, from Cervetri, 23, *Panaitios kalos*, 51, 71, from Tarquinia; 358/1; 361/10, column-krater, from Sicily, 24, hydria from Vulci; cups 38, 39, 79, 80–1; skyphoi, 102, from Vulci, 103, from Fratte; cups, 374/59, 61, 71, 93, 138, 227, oinochoe 8A, from Taranto; cups, 387/2 ter (with victors); 396/10, 39, from Bologna; 401/4, 5, 31–2, 33 from Cervetri; 407/13, from Orvieto; 412/7, from Chiusi, 11, from Spina; 414/1; 416/8; 416/1, from Orvieto; 418/27, 42–3, from Adria; 45, from Orvieto, 46, from Bologna, 47, from Falerii, 48–56, 57, from Nola, 58, 94; 427/13, from Etruria, 15, 21, from Vulci, 22, from Vulci, 30, from Chiusi, *Chairestratos kalos*, 32, 34, 35, *Chairestratos kalos*, 39, 187, from Vulci, 224 bis, 226, from Orvieto, *Hippodamas kalos*, 243; 449/12, 13 and 14, from Orvieto; 453, from Chiusi; 454/2, 10 (I. victor); 455/1, from Vulci; 457/3, from Attica; 467/131, 133, from Vulci, 134, 140, from Orvieto, 141–2.

Early classical: 486/47, pelike; neck-amphorai, 529/11 from Bulgaria, 11 bis, 51, column-krater, from Rhodes; column-kraters, 537/19, 21, from Spina; 562/1–5; 568/24, from Nola, 39, from Rugge, 43; 584/20; 589/3, volute-krater from Spina, 52, pelike; kalyx-kraters, 618/5–6, one from Marzabotto (Etruria), 11, from Taranto; bell-kraters, 14, from Corinth, 16, from Nola, 18, from Rhodes, 26; 54, pelike; 101, cup from Tarquinia; 631/39, oinochoe 4, from Gela, *Alkimachos kalos*; neck-amphorai, 650/9 bis, 17, from Nola, *Kallias, Charmides kalos*; 658/23, oinochoe 2; 77, aryballos, from Attica; 674/28–9, lekythoi, from Boeotia, Agrigento; 684, lekythoi, 154, from Rhodes, 154 bis, from Sicily, 155–8 (one from Spina); squat lekythoi, 238, from Nola, 239; 242, oinochoe 1, 256, oinochoe 3; lekythoi, 690/13 from Eretria; 693/1; 714/163, from Camarina; 720/17; 778/7, pelike, from Etruria; 779/2, oinochoe 8B; 781/10, 11, cups, 13, oinochoe 8C; cups, 785/13, 788/3,

5, from Athens; 789; 789; 792/61–2, 63, from Vulci, 64–6, 67–8, from Orvieto, 70, from Athens, 71–2, 72 bis, from Aleria, 74, from Vulci, 75, from Numana; 799/9; 800; 801/10, from Bologna, 33, 38, 48, 70, skyphos, from Vulci, 79 mug, from Athens; cups, 809/8, 18, 19; 815/5, oinochoe 8B, *kalos Hiketes*; cups, 817/5–10, 11, from Adria, 12, from South Russia, 13, 14, from Capua, 15, 25, from Chiusi (outside, youths and herm), 46, 49, 51 rhyton from Sicily; cups, 820; 822/12, from Athens, 13–17; 823/1–15 (four from Etruria), 23 (herm), 24, rhyton, from Bologna; cups, 824/1, 2, from Orvieto, 3, 4, from Ruvo, 14, from Orvieto, 16, from La Monédière, 28, 31, skyphos; cups, 1671/4 bis, from Bologna; 835/1, from Cesa, 3, 4, from Greece; 836/2, from Orvieto; 866/3, 6, 8, 39–40, 41, from Athens, 42–4, 61, 64, from Vulci, 65, 70, 71, from Adria, 72, skyphoi 84, 87, from Tanagra, 88, from Athens; cups, 872/22, from Adria, 23 *kalos Lykos*, 24; 874/4, from Vulci, 18, from Vulci (herm); 882/37, from Greece, 38–9, 74, from Bologna; 897/112 (herm), 133; 901/10 (herm), 58, 59, from Falerii, 60, from Chiusi, 61, from Orvieto, 62–3, 67, 71–2, 77, from Adria, 78, 85–6 (youth at herm), 91, from Nepi, 93, from Falerii, 102–3, from Ampurias, 104–5, 107 ter; 907/2; 908/6–7 (youth at herm); 919/1–15 (one from Campania, eight from Etruria); 923/27; 926/13 (youth at herm), 65, from Greece, 66, from Tarquinia; 934/57–8, 63, from Cervetri; 935/4; 935, from Spina; 940/22, from Spina, 44, from Chalandri, 45, 46–7, from Spina, 48, 49, from Orvieto, 49 bis, 60, from Adria, 68, 73, skyphos; cups, 944/1–26 (12 from Etruria, 2 from Athens, 1 from Brauron); skyphoi, 35, from Suessula, 39, from Athens, 40, from Adria; cups, 946/1, from Athens; 946/1, from Athens, 2–3, from Spina; 947/3–5, 14, from Al Mina, 15, 16, skyphos, from Spina; 948/4 cup, 6, skyphos, from Spina; 948, cups, 1, 2–5, from Etruria, 6, from Attica, 7, 9–23 (2 from Athens, 7 from Etruria, 1 from Delos); 949, from Ampurias; 950/1, from Chiusi; 1–5 (1 from Corchiano); 6–7, skyphoi, from Spina; 1–4, cups, from Spina; 951/1–3, cups (1 from Etruria, 1 from Campania); 957/37, pelike (youth at herm); cups, 961/55, from Spina (youth at herm); 967/12–17; skyphoi, 976, youth between pillar and altar taking an oath, 981, from Taranto.

Classical: 990/77 bis, chous, *Euaion kalos*; 1005/6, neck-amphora, from South Italy; 1013/14, chous, *Dion kalos*, 15, oinochoe 4, from Athens; 1030/29, kalyx-krater; 1059/134, pelike, *kalos Kallias Eunikos*,

166, cup, from Bologna, 167, Oxford 1966.705; 1066/1, oinochoe 7, from Vulci; 1103/10, column-krater, 15 pelike, from Sicily; 1120/2, column-krater, from Marzabotto; 1125/17, bell-krater, from Greece; 1129/110, pelike; 1134/13, 14, pelikai; 1139/3, pelike, youth bringing votive tablet to herm; 1141/2, pelike; 1141/1, pelike, from South Italy; 1145/34, bell-krater, from Vulci; 1163/50, bell-krater, from Spina; 67, from Israel, 96, column-krater, from Spina; 1171/13, oinochoe 1, 21, cup-skyphos, from Athens; 1175/16, oinochoe 1, 17 chous from Capua, 36, 38–41, pelikai (two from Suessula), 44, youth at herm; 1177/1, cup from Todi; pelikai, 1177/2; 1178, from Cumae; 1184/2, column-krater, from Spina, 23, bell-krater; 1203/1, lekythos, from Nola; 1216/3, oinochoe 2, from Spina; 1216/1, oinochoe 2, from Spina; 1217/7–9, oinochoai 4 (one from Egnatia); cups, 1253/72–4, 75, from Falerii, *Kissos*, 76–7, from Spina, 78, from Brauron, 82, from Greece, 83, 85, from Spina, 86, 97, from Brauron, 98, from Vilafranca; 1255/1, 2, from Athens, 8, rhyton from South Italy, 10 bis, oinochoe 8C; 1256 cup, from Cervetri; 1258/2 skyphos; cups, 1261/39, 41–2, 57, from Numana; pelikai, 66–9, 69 bis, 70, from Salonica, 71, from Tel Aviv, 72, from Suessula; oinochoai 4, 78, 79; oinochoe 6, 80; 1264, oinochoe 2; 1264/1, neck-amphora, 3, neck-amphora from Greece, 13, oinochoe 4, from Peiraeus, 14, oinochoe 4, Jüthner, pl. 46b, 16 and 18, cups; cups, 1270/19, from Vulci, 24, 25, 26, 26 bis, 28, 29, from Ruvo, 30, from Ampurias, 31, 32, from Taranto, 33, 35–7, 38, from Ampurias, 39, 42, from Corchiano, 43, from Ampurias, 44, from Orvieto, 45; 1272/1–5, 7, 9; 1273/1–3, one from Vulci; 4–5, plates from South Italy; 1273 cup; 1273 cup; cups, 1274/1–2, from Etruria, 5, from Cumae; 1281; 1287, from Spina; 1287, from Eretria; 1288/2, from Vulci, 17–19, 24, from Populonia; 1289/5, 10; 1290/17, from Vulci; 1291/1–3, 4–6, from Orvieto, 7, 8, from Orvieto, 9, 10, from Vignanello; 1292/1–2, from Orvieto; 1292; 1294/11; 1295/18–19, from Todi, 21–2, from Ampurias; 1296/1, from Spina, 2, from Athens, 3–5, from Spina; 1297/1, from Todi, 2, from Spina; 1298/7–9; 1298; 1298; 1298/1–3; 1299/1, 2 (with sprig), 3, from Athens, 4–7; 1299; 1299/2; 1299/1, from Athens, 2; skyphoi, 1303/2; 1304/1–2; 1304/2, from Athens; stemmed plates, 1305/2, from Italy, 3, from Ruvo; 1307/5, from Spina, the trainer, companion to 1307/4, jumper.

Late: 1333/3, bell-krater, 35, rhyton, from Nola; pelikai, 1342/2, 2 bis, 3, from Spina; 1342/2, from Cyrenaica; 1345/14, kalyx-krater, from Spina; oinochoai 4; 1349/7-8, from Spina; 1350/4, oinochoe 2, 11, cup, from South Russia; 1352/2-4, oinochoai 2, from Spina; 1354, skyphos, from Spina; oinochoai 2, 1354/1, 6, 11, 21, all from Spina; 1356/4-5, from Spina; 1359/6, pelike, from Vulci; 1361/18-19, kantharoids; cups, 1392/6-7, from Etruria, 8, from Athens, 9-10, from Etruria, 35-38, 39, from Cervetri, 40, 41, from Bologna, 43, 44, from Chiusi, 46-9, from Ensérune, 51-5, from Ensérune, 58, 62; 1397/4, from Ensérune; 1398/2, 3, from Adria, 4, from Orvieto; 1399; 399; 1400/1; 1400/1-2, 3, from Nola; 1400/2; 1402/10; 1403/1-5 (four from Etruria), 6, skyphos, from Adria; cups, 1404/1-4, 5, from Spina, 6, 8-9, 11, skyphos, from Athens.

The two specialized performances which appear chiefly on Panathenaic amphorai are the pankration and the pentathlon. The pankration is a combination of boxing and wrestling; the Panathenaic amphorai are *ABV* 404/8-9, from Vulci; 405/2; 413, from Cyrenaica; 417, from Capua, all prize vases. In addition to these it appears on a late black-figure neck-amphora *ABV* 381/1 and late archaic red-figure cups *ARV²* 322/37, 339/65, 401/3, 404/4, 1651. The pentathlon (jumping, running, discus, javelin, wrestling) appears on Panathenaic amphorai: *ABV* 322/1-2, from Vulci, both with four athletes; 344, from Vulci (discobolos, acontist, judge); 404/7, from Vulci (jumper, acontist, judge), 405/1 (discobolos, jumper, judge).

Lastly, the rare pictures of ball-players may be included here: *ABV* 306/42, amphora, *ABL* 216/2, lekythos, both, man with ball, boys riding on shoulders of youths; *ARV²* 114/1, cup, inside, ball-player, outside, athletes including victor; 867/32, cup, from Chiusi, inside, youth with ball; 1262/59, rhyton, from Beirut, ball-player with athletes.

The number of stock vases with athletes is so large that it is worth while looking at the breakdown into shapes and provenances. In the following table all the vases in this chapter are included except the prize Panathenaic amphorai and the fourth-century miniature Panathenaic perfume vases. Most of the vases which can be accounted special commissions have been discussed earlier, and the victorious athletes have been treated earlier. Of the vases in this chapter rather over seventy have either *kalos* names or names attached to one or more of the athletes on them, and these names were put on before firing; they are about 4 per cent of the total, so that these are largely pots not specially made to order. The total list is as follows:

Shapes	black-figure	red-figure early	late archaic	early classical	classical	late fifth century
amphorai	14	3	3			
neck amphorai (including non-prize Panathenaics)	69	3	20	7	10	
cups (all types including rhyta)	31	223	312	305	145	60
hydriai	6	2	6			
psykter		2	1			
kraters (including dinoi)	2	0	40	21	28	4
pelikai	1	3	10	10	32	5
stamnoi	10		10	1		
oinochoai	6	3	2	11	23	15
kyathos	1					
alabastron		2	1			
aryballos		1		1		
lekythoi	59		5	23	2	
squat lekythoi				2		
pyxis		1	1			
lid		1				
stand		1	1			
plates (including stemmed)	1	5				
TOTAL	200	250	412	381	240	84

A glance at the figures for shapes shows the immense preponderance of cups in red-figure, only kraters and pelikai showing some continued signs of popularity among the larger symposion vases; of the smaller vases oinochoai show a considerable increase from the early classical period. Alabastra, which are normally used by women, are naturally rare, and squat lekythoi are also usually women's vases. It is interesting to compare the figures quoted above for horsemen. 437 black-figure vases have horsemen and 287 red-figure vases; 199 black-figure vases have athletes, and 1371 red-figure vases. One would suppose that the same young men bought both, and in fact the scenes are often paired. The choice of shapes looks much the same: more amphorai and neck-amphorai in black-figure, more kraters and pelikai in red-figure, a large number of lekythoi in black-figure and a very large number of cups in red-figure. The distribution in the home market of Attica on the one hand and the export market of Etruria is also similar: in black-figure about 15 per cent of the horsemen with known provenances go to Attica and 40 per cent go to Etruria and 13 per cent of the athletes go

Distribution	black-figure	red-figure early	late archaic	early classical	classical	late fifth century
Attica	13	13	13	20	12	2
Greece and Greek islands	25	9	7	12	6	
Sicily	5	5	8	10	2	
South Italy	12	4	2	4	7	1
Campania	3	4	8	12	12	2
Etruria	34	80	83	112	55	33
Corsica				1		
France		1		2	2	10
Spain				2	6	
Egypt	2	1				
Africa	1				1	1
Syria						1
Cyprus	1					
Asia Minor					4	
South Russia				1		
Bulgaria				1		
TOTAL	96	117	121	177	107	50

to Attica and 34 per cent to Etruria; in red-figure about 9 per cent of the horsemen and just over 10 per cent of the athletes go to Attica and 60 per cent of the horsemen and 60 per cent of the athletes go to Etruria. Again, as far as our figures allow us to conclude (and again we only know the provenances of half the black-figure athlete vases and well over a third of the red-figure vases), a considerably higher proportion of red-figure vases than black-figure go for export (whether by the second-hand market or not) and a considerably higher proportion of them go to Etruria. But against this common pattern of favourite shapes and local distribution where we seem to see common tastes in nearer purchasers and more distant purchasers, we see the change in popularity; horsemen in the black-figure period and athletes in the red-figure period; partly this must be a change of interest and partly perhaps the increasing expense of keeping horses; it may be that if you are rich enough to keep a horse or horses, you are also rich enough to have decorated metal symposion ware and so cease to buy special pots for the symposion.

16

Men and Women

Many vases have pictures of men and women, and it is not always easy to interpret the scenes, although, as they are stock scenes, their meaning must have been clear and desirable. The categories seem to be A. men and women conversing, B. men visiting women, C. men kissing or embracing women, D. men watching women, E. women in a man's house. The following lists are as accurate as possible, but the pictures available are comparatively few, and the short description in *ABV* or *ARV²* cannot always fix a vase in a category.

A. This is the earliest type as it appears already with the C painter. On a skyphos (*ABV* 57/118, Louvre MNC 676, *Metr. Stud.* 5, 99) four pairs of men and women face each other. The men are bearded and have long white chiton and red himation, two of the women hold their himation out from their faces in what is usually called the bridal gesture. The other two women have their himatia round their shoulders in the penguin scheme. Perhaps the essential feature is the greeting of the bride. The same scheme may have occurred on the loutrophoros hydria of Kleimachos (*ABV* 85), but too little is left to be certain. Certainly on a band-cup near the BMN painter (*ABV* 227/1, New York 14.147.3, *CV* pl. 16, 26) a bride is greeted by draped and undraped youths and on one side she holds a large wreath (here she could conceivably be Ariadne).

B. In the scenes of men visiting women the woman is normally seated, which implies that she is at home, and the man is often leaning on his stick. An alabastron or mirror hanging on the wall emphasizes that the woman is in her house. *ABV* 321/2, New York 56.171.121, 696/2 bis (the woman is seated in a vineyard), 396/24, 34, *Robinson*

Studies, ii, pl. 49b (the woman is seated in a building with a wreath hung on a beam), 440/4 (again vines behind, she holds wreath and flower, he holds a flower), 698/3 bis (olpe, near the Amasis painter, naked youth with ivy branch, woman with ivy branch and flower, man leaning on stick, youth with ivy branch; perhaps here a man watching preparations for a Dionysiac ceremony); *ABL* 208/90; *ABV* 480 (onoi: 1, 3, 4, 5, seated woman or women and seated youths, the youths have visited the women and sit talking to them; α, a man talks to a woman while she sits spinning), *ABV* 496/184 (men and women both seated), 530/77–80; 554/424; 560/592 bis, 618 bis, 619 bis, 678; 578/47–52 (on 47 the woman has a lyre and so is presumably a musician); *ABL* 263/4 (youth giving alabastron to seated woman), 11; 265/1, Bonn 311 (man leaning on stick with wreath, woman with flower; the house is shown by wool basket, mirror, chair, boots, heron); *ABV* 584/1 (youth and woman with flute, again a musician); 585/5–7, 603/63, 82, 622/125–6 (men and women seated in pairs).

C. Man kissing or embracing woman: *ABV* 496/171; 554/420, 420 bis; 560/514–15, 616, 673–4; 585/8–9.

D. In comedy the young man often falls in love with the girl because he sees her in a procession. I think we can recognize this theme where we have one, or more often two, young men leaning on their sticks watching a girl walking: *ABV* 401/4, London B 275, *CV* pl. 68, 1 (late neck-amphora: the girl is walking between columns), 409/696 (neck of a loutrophoros by the Achilles painter, the girl carries a sacrificial basket, but this may be a visit to the tomb); *ABL* 195/32.

E. The mark of these is that the man is seated. Sometimes certainly this means that it is his house, but the woman need not be visiting: she may be the wife or daughter of the house. *ABV* 452/1, 2, 10, 11, 14, 454/1, 2 (all same general scheme: man seated, woman standing, naked youth behind him); 463/2; *ABL* 237/157 (woman crowning seated youth); *ABV* 621/101, 102, 112, Reading 29.xi.4, *CV* pl. 10, 14 (youth seated between women: on 112 two naked youths flank the women, and the seated youth is draped and holds a sceptre; conceivably he is Dionysos and they are his votaries); 625; 625, Berkeley 8.3350, *CV* pl. 18, 1 (bearded man seated with sceptre;

woman with right hand raised – possibly she is praying to a god).

The following black-figure vases I do not attempt to classify:

ABV 52/15, 16, 36, 115; 59/15; 89/1; 90/5; 103/113; 119/8; 131/1–2; 305/28, 93; 397/1; *ABL* 195/2, 208/58; *ABV* 496/172; *ABL* 237/110, 113; *ABV* 519/14; *ABL* 246/2; *ABV* 554/412–19; 560/523, 544–5, 617–18, 676–7; *ABL* 263/6; 265/1–2; *ABV* 585/4, 20; 586/3–4; 586–7/709.

Many of the black-figure vases belong to the red-figure period and some run as late as the second quarter of the fifth century: only about a fifth can be dated securely before 530 B.C. It is therefore natural that the black-figure schemes should be found also in red-figure. In red-figure too the difficulty of classifying the pictures from descriptions is considerable and the unclassified category is large:

*ARV*² 27/3, 99/9–12, 13, 24, 32, 115/2; 226/24 bis; 253/58; 255/1–2; 257/18; 260/15; 272/3; 278/1, 2; 280/19–20; 283/1; 283/1; 293/44, 49, 50, 52, 57; 296; 386/4; 396/12; 405; 408/32–3, 41; 421/81; 428/5, 110, 145, 186; 449/4; 468/143, 145, 149, 155, 159, 160, 164, 180, 185, 193, 195; 485/30–1, 35–6, 50, 54–6; 495/10; 499/14, 31; 502/8, 506/20; 509; 509; 512/6, 19; 515/4, 14; 517/5; 520/34, 38, 42, 50; 523/1–9, 11–17, 19–24, 28, 44, 46–52, 54, 56, 59; 528; 528, 531/31, 42, 47, 49 bis, 50; 536/5, 10, 12, 28, 32 ter; 541/7, 23, 33–5, 41–2, 44, 47, 52, 52 bis, 53, 53 bis, 60–1, 67; 545/5–7; 546; 546/11, 12, 17, 19 bis, 30, 38, 41, 45, 46; 565/39; 566/9; 570/63; 586/49, 57, 60, 61; 603/35, 38; 617/2; 622/52, 91, 92, 108; 633/1; 668/30, 31; 673/4; 714/174, 175, 187, 222, 239–42; 723/4; 738/148; 769/1–3; 782/1; 784/23; 786/2; 795/101, 148; 805/80; 810/23–5, 27, 29, 33; 814/2; 819/39–41; 821/1, 6, 7, 8; 825/12; 827/3, 26; 838/28–30, 32–4; 860/3; 874/6; 876/1–3; 880/15, 76–9, 81; 892/8–15, 17–18, 20–1, 23; 908/9–12, 14, 16, 17–20 bis, 22, 26, 27 bis, 28, 30–2, 34, 35, 64–6, 69–72, 75–7, 79–83, 87–8; 919/1; 925/1–2, 4–18, 21–8, 104; 935/76; 938/12–16; 940/6, 8, 23; 955/1–3,

11, 22, 35–6, 63, 70; 962/73; 966/8, 30–1; 969/81 bis, 85; 973/4; 980/1;
993/91, 1018/69; 1059/131, 134, 139; 1071/3; 1077/2–3, 5; 1079/2;
1080/1, 2, 6; 1082/2; 1083/4; 1095/1; 1096/8, 11–15, 17–20, 21 bis,
23–4 bis; 1104/1, 5, 7, 9, 11; 1107/10, 28, 31, 35, 37; 1110/1; 1111/2;
1113/10; 1113/3; 1122/2; 1129/111, 185; 1136/13, 14; 1140/5–11;
1145/38, 39; 1162/11–12, 32, 35, 46, 49, 53, 57; 1165/73, 80, 85, 87,
92, 95, 97–8, 107; 1170/4–8, 10; 1170; 1176/28; 1220/1; 1250/24, 29,
31; 1259/19, 23; 1262/75, 75 bis, 77; 1264/2; 1267/10, 20; 1276/7; 45,
1282/34; 1287/2; 1288/1, 3, 6; 1327/89; 1352/1, 7–10; 1354/3; 1369/
1–2; 1392/11, 29, 56, 68; 1404/2.

A number of red-figure vases can, however, be classified although
there may be doubts about detailed interpretation. These are given
below period by period. Scheme A does not appear in anything like its
black-figure form.

Early red-figure

B. Men visiting women: *ARV²* 22/4, 99/23 (girl holding apple greeting
   youth leaning on stick), 101/3 (youth, boy with food, woman spinning), 102/1.
C. Men kissing or embracing or making love to women: *ARV²* 22/
   1620; 76/70; 80/12; 113/7; 118/14; 175/35; 177/1–2; 179/1631;
   180/1.
D. *ARV²* 99/15, youth watching two hetairai walking.
X. *ARV²* 153/85 bis, youth courting a boy, woman.

Late archaic

B. *ARV²* 189/72 (youth and man visiting two women); 226/10 bis
   (woman seated with distaff and man); 229/35 (A. youth seated with
   purse, two girls, flute-case in background, therefore the girl's house,
   B. youth with stick, two girls, basket in the background: perhaps
   arrangements to hire girls for a symposion); 246/12; 250/17, 46 bis;
   262/31, Oxford 1966.460 (man leaning on stick, wash-bowl, woman
   holding alabastron), 49 (woman walking with mirror between two

men, one of whom holds purse; the scheme is D but the mirror seems to put the woman in her house, cf. 279/2), 54 (the woman is seated with a wreath and a bird on her knee), 83; 272/55, 58; 331/11 (the woman is standing, spinning), so also 362/15, 363/29 bis; 365/59; 376/85 (the woman is seated with distaff); 394/48 (woman standing, with wool basket); 394/1–2, 3 (the woman spins, the youth is seated); 408/62 (the man has a purse); 421/82 (man holding out purse, woman refusing, man leaning on stick); 428/11 (the woman is seated spinning), 115 (the woman is standing with distaff), 178, 184; 468/144 (youths with purses, girl with flower, girl with wreath), 152, Oxford 1966.498 (the boy and the girl offer flowers, flute-case in background), 153, 154 (perhaps refusal of old man by women); 481/5 (man with purse, woman spinning).

C. Men making love to women: *ARV*² 224/7; 231/80; 315/2; 316/3; 319/2, 83, 87; 339/51–5; 367/93–4; 372/31; 376/101; 406/5; 408/36–8; 438/138, 144 (? mythical); 468/144 (I.), 146–8.

D. Men watching women: *ARV*² 250/24 (the woman has a hydria); 284/2 (A. the woman has a basket on her head, B. the girl looks back as she walks); 284 (the woman has a hydria on her head).

E. Sometimes the man or the woman pours a libation or has phiale or oinochoe for a libation: *ARV*² 184/27; 227/10; 257/17. This solemnizes departure or arrival. Once a boy with a lyre is seated among women; perhaps he is to compose for them or to play while they dance and sing; this scene becomes more common later: *ARV*² 441/186.

Early classical

B. *ARV*² 500/33; 506/28; 508/6 (the seated woman is called Nikarete); 520/37 (bald old man seated on chair holding out a flower, woman behind raising hand in surprise, woman in front seated on square seat, holding out wreath); 526/65 (man visiting gynaikeion), 74; 534/6 (woman holding out lyre and flute, youth with stick; could she be a Muse?, cf. 539/1); 544/65; 551/27 (man leaning on stick in gynaikeion; this is a nuptial lebes and should be included in the wedding vases), 89 (woman doing washing, man with purse; Beazley, *Panmaler*, 23, interprets as husband and wife), 123 (woman spinning, youth with purse, maid with mirror and wool basket), 124 (girl

with ointment vase and flower, boy with purse: Beazley, *Panmaler*,
24–5, interprets these two alabastra as showing married pairs); 565/
34 (one man holds a purse), 38 (on A. the woman holds a fruit, on
B. a skein); 566/6; 570/63, 81 (the woman spins), 82 (the women
work with wool); 573/13 (the woman is seated with mirror and
distaff); 581/3 (on A. the man holds a cock, the woman a box, on
B. the woman has a perfume vase); 582/1 (nuptial lebes); 586/53,
56; 623/63 (woman holding wool basket, woman running looking
round); 624/88 (woman standing with mirror, youth seated with
stick), 107 (the woman is playing ball; cf. also 648/27); 629/29;
652/33 bis (woman seated with fruit and flower, youth brings
francolin); 655/13 (woman with mirror at wool basket); 663/3
(woman seated spinning); 668/29 and 29 bis (woman offering lyre
to youth; cf. above, 534/6), 33, 45 (youth with pomegranate,
woman with sceptre and wrap; is she perhaps a goddess?); 669/2 bis,
3; 696/1 (woman seated with wreath); 714/172, 173, 176, 227, 238,
CV Norway, pl. 40/1–2 (A. woman seated, B. youth leaning on
stick), 243 (A. and B. youth leans on stick, woman runs up with
sash, presumably to decorate him with it); 723/2, 8 (woman with
bird, white dog between her and youth with stick); 735/108
(woman with distaff), 119, 149; 770 (on both sides, man talking to
woman seated on rock: is she perhaps a Muse?); 777/2; 785/8 (one
woman holds kothornoi, the other a distaff); 785/12 (the woman
lifts her chiton at the shoulder); 795/100 (woman seated spinning),
102, 103 (woman spinning), 104; 810/21 (A. and B., on B. the
woman has a mirror and the man is seated with a stick, but he is the
visitor); 810/22 (on both A. and B. the scheme is D but on A. the
woman has an alabastron, and on B. a mirror, so that she is presumably at home; cf. 262/49); 819/40 bis (A. the man has a purse,
B. the woman holds out a skyphos to the youth, a man is seated);
838/31 (woman running with sash between two youths, cf. 714/
243), 36, 37, 151–2; 876/6 (youth with purse); 876/1–2; 883/61 (the
woman holds a fruit in each hand; wool basket and spindle), 80 (on
B. one of the girls is playing ball); 892/19 (on B. woman running
with sash; cf. 838/31); 900/4 (the scheme is D, but the woman on A.
has a basket, on B. an alabastron, cf. 810/22); 906/109–10; 908/23–5,
27 (cf. 838/31); 925/20; 940/9–17, 29, 32; 969/75; 978/7.

C. Making love. 551/11; 570/88; 884/80 (I.); 908/8 (Eros and youth, Eros and woman).

D. Men watching women. 523/6, 10–11, 35 (on the last three the woman is a maenad; cf. above, p. 118), 36 (woman with torch and sprig), 546/18 (woman with torch), 34; 555/98 (woman with sacrificial basket on her head); 629/23 (girl moving away and looking back; the obverse is the mythical paradigm, Polyneikes and Eriphyle); 778/2; 785/8 (two women approaching temple); 876/5; 880/145 (on A. one of the boys offers a piece of meat; Beazley in Caskey-Beazley, ii, 66, says the women on both sides are *kosmiai hetairai*); 892/19; 908/21, 73 (the sandals hanging in the background perhaps imply that the women are walking past a palaistra).

E. The libation scene is common: 485/23 (probable, because of the wreath on the completely preserved male figure); 499/15; 523/8, 69 (?); 541/15–18; 603/55; 610/21 (probably a warrior's departure); 633/7 (possibly the departure of Achilles); 652/30; 655; 668/45 bis; 778/1 (?); 795/104 (B.). There are two scenes where a youth or man has a lyre among men and women: 541/40; 821/7 bis.

Classical

B. *ARV*² 1080/4, 21; 1082/1 (maid with coffer, woman seated spinning, man with stick and laurel wreath: probably husband returning home); 1083/2, 3 (with Eros); 1083/1 (woman seated with lyre, Eros, youth: visit to loved musician); 1099/49 (the woman has basket and sash), 51 (the woman has sash), 60; 1104/16 (visit to gynaikeion with Eros); 1109/45 (visit to musicians), 46 (woman seated spinning); 1116/38, 40 (woman seated with lyre), 45 (woman with lyre), 47 (with Eros); 1119/29 (visit to musician); 1121/14; 1122/3; 1123/9, 10 (woman working with wool, Eros); 1129/112 (woman taking sash out of box), 182 (with Eros), 183; 1138/39 (woman with sash); 1139/1 (woman holding out wreath); 1158/1, 6 (open air: woman holding sash, youth in chlamys and petasos with box, woman seated over kalathos, woman with mirror, woman; not Polyneikes and Eriphyle?); 1215/2 (youth with wreath, woman with alabastron); 1225/1, 2; 1, 2; 1259/51; 1268 (visit to musician); 1276/36, 52–4, 74 (visit to musician); 1282/10–13, 16–17, 19, 28, 34; 1294/1; 1296/3 (perhaps mythical).

C. 1206/41.

D. 1072/1 bis, *CV* Norway, pl. 35; 1138/48 (woman with torches); 1276/3.

E. Libation scenes: 1066/2; 1129/116, 186; 1176/31 (youth seated in petasos, and chlamys); 32, 33; 1193/2; 1206/6 (the youth standing in petasos, chlamys and holding spears), 43 (youth with lyre: perhaps a libation for his success in a musical or poetic contest); 1257 (youth seated with spears; woman with thurible).

The youths with spears may be young cavalrymen (cf. above, p. 185), and it is at least possible that some of these vases are meant for their graves: cf. also 1174/4, 9, where there is no libation.

The youth with lyre also occurs with women outside libation scenes: 1160 (with woman who has Eros in her arms and another woman: love-scene); 1224/1 (with women making music and Eros fluting at an altar; possibly they are Muses); 1259/1 (*Alkimachos kalos*, cf. above, p. 58), 2 (A. youth holding lyre among youths and women, B. women holding out lyre, youths and women, inscriptions *NAIA* and *KLEO*), 5 (inside: woman crowning boy; A. woman holding out lyre to youth, youth, B. youth with lyre, woman, youth), 6 (inside: Nike and youth; A. similar to A. on 5 but also woman pouring libation, B. youth seated fluting, woman with box, youth with lyre, woman with oinochoe and phiale), 7 (I. youth playing the flute, A. Apollo, Muse and youth, B. youth playing the flute, woman, woman with lyre). Possibly in all these the youths are poets or musicians and the women Muses.

Late fifth century

B. *ARV²* 1327/89 (visit to gynaikeion), 1353/7–9, 1392/27.

C. 1354/19.

E. Libation scenes, etc. 1349/8 bis (youth in chlamys with lagobolon: return from hunting); 1357/1; 1369/1–2 (girl advancing with basket and box, youth leaning on spear: probably a visit to his grave); 1370/2 (youth with one foot on rock, girl with wool basket and sash: again funerary?); 1392/28.

1402/1–9. Inside, youth with lyre and woman, A. B. youths with lyres and women.

The distribution of shapes is as follows:

	black-figure	red-figure: early	late archaic	early classical	classical	late fifth century
amphorai	2	1	1	1	0	0
neck-amphorai	7	0	4	25	4	0
cups	37	10	65	186	27	16
hydriai	2	0	1	17	24	
kraters (all kinds)	0	0	16	86	51	
pelikai	1	0	19	35	41	
stamnoi	1	0	4	5	1	
oinochoai	10	0	0	3	8	11
alabastra	8	11	1	10	1	
lekythoi (incl. squat)	30	1	3	17	8	5
pyxides	1	1	0	4	1	
lid	1	0	0	0		
onoi	5	0	0	0	5	
plates	1	1	0	0		
plastic vases	0	0	1	1		
loutrophoros	2	0	0	0		
nuptial lebes	0	0	0	2		
lekanis						1
amphoriskos						1
TOTAL	108	25	115	392	171	34

These figures compare strangely with the figures for athletes given in the last chapter. Overall they are distinctly lower with a surprising dip in early red-figure and ripe archaic red-figure and a surprising peak in early classical. A hint that these vases were primarily meant for women is perhaps given by the comparatively large number of onoi, and this hint is rather strengthened by the large number of hydriai in the early classical and classical period. Alabastra are certainly women's vases, and we have here a total of 31 compared with 3 alabastra with athletes. Lekythoi are not so easy to assess, but in the second half of the fifth century 7 of the 13 lekythoi are squat lekythoi, a shape which takes over from the painted alabastron as the women's perfume vase. Many of the neck-amphorai and pelikai are small and are probably perfume vases. The large number of cups may have been painted for women's parties as well as men's; so also some of the mixing-bowls, but on very many of them the scene of men and women is the subsidiary scene on the back of the vase and gives place to the three youths in himatia, who dominate in the second half of the fifth century.

Provenance figures are as follows:

	black-figure	early red-figure	late archaic	early classical	classical	late fifth century
Attica	11	5	1	13	6	
Greece and Greek islands	21	4	1	25	10	1
Sicily	1	0	1	11	8	
South Italy	5	0	1	10	5	1
Campania	2	0	1	10	11	1
Etruria	8	4	31	102	26	4
France					1	1
Spain	4	0	0	2	1	
Africa				3		
Syria	2	0	0	1		
Cyprus	3	0	0	1	2	
Asia Minor				1		
South Russia	1	0	0	1	1	
Bulgaria				1		
TOTAL	58	13	36	181	71	8

The figures here are small but suggest that the popularity of these vases in the Etrurian market did not really start until late-archaic red-figure.

17

Women

The numbers of vases with pictures of women alone increase greatly in the fifth century. The figures for shapes are:

	black-figure	early red-figure	late archaic	early classical	classical	late fifth century
amphorai		1	1			
neck-amphorai	4	1	2	24	3	
cups	14	29	80	68	32	35
hydriai	1		5	30	143	29
kraters			2	8	20	1
pelikai			7	26	43	20
stamnoi			2	7	5	
oinochoai	2		3	13	32	68
alabastra	7	5	12	56	1	
lekythoi	36	1	22	433	77	23
squat lekythoi			1	35	19	60
acorn lekythoi						2
pyxides	2	1	2	48	29	16
lid				1		
onoi	3				3	
plates	1	3	2			
plastic vases			2			4
lekanis					1	2
amphoriskos					2	
TOTAL	70	41	143	749	410	260

Provenances are:

	black-figure	early red-figure	late archaic	early classical	classical	late fifth century
Attica	6	9	13	107	38	36
Greece and Greek islands	8	1	9	126	43	15
Sicily	6		11	65	24	4
South Italy	1		7	25	6	17
Campania			5	38	42	12
Etruria	1	10	26	45	33	74
France					1	1
Spain			1	4	1	2
Africa	1		2	2	2	8
Syria	2			8	2	2
Cyprus		2			1	
Asia Minor		1				
South Russia					1	2
Bulgaria					1	1
TOTAL	25	23	74	421	195	173

The figures can be compared with the figures for athletes as the opposite pole, one of the most popular stock scenes of men alone. The total of attributed vases with athletes is 1,570, of vases with women alone 1,740. But the vases with women alone are well behind until the early classical period when there are nearly twice as many, twice as many also in the classical period and three times as many in the late fifth century. This surely signifies something about the Athenian attitude towards women, as has already been seen from the figures for vases with men and women. Again the vases which are meant for women's use show very high figures: hydriai, alabastra, squat lekythoi, pyxides, and there can be no doubt here about lekythoi being women's vases. Many of the neck-amphorai and pelikai are small, and therefore perfume vases rather than vases for wine or oil. Against these very high figures for vases intended for women's use, we have to set a comparatively low figure for cups and a very low figure for kraters – low not only in comparison with the figures for athlete-cups and kraters but (when the total numbers are remembered) in comparison with the figures for cups and kraters with men and women; this suggests that the large number of kraters and cups with pictures of men and women were painted not only for women but for men, who now wanted to be reminded of women while they drank.

The figures for provenance of the vases with women alone are also worth comparing with those for athletes. Attica accounts for a far higher proportion and Etruria for a far lower proportion all the way through. Even in the late fifth century Etruria only accounts for 43 per cent as against 66 per cent of athletes, and most of the high number of 74 vases with women is accounted for by Spina which probably had some Greek population. Attica, Greece, the Greek islands, the Greek cities of Sicily, South Italy and, interestingly enough, Campania account for the major proportion. The new interest in women spreads out from Attica and reaches Etruria last.

The pictures of women's activities become more and more detailed as time goes on.

Black-figure

In black-figure (and of course it must be remembered that black-figure vases with women alone do not begin much earlier than the beginning of red-figure and extend at least to the end of the late archaic period) the following types can be distinguished:

G (general, usually standing, but little more can be said about them, usually because of lack of description): *ABL* 200/29–31, 203/4 (2 women between eyes); *ABV* 483/5, 497/189, 189 bis (2 women between eyes); *ABL* 228/51–2 (4 women); 235/107 (3 women and youth), 112 (4 women with dogs and bird); *ABV* 554/439 bis, 519, 530–1, 546, 577, 589–90; 578/66; 585/1.

S (seated, at least one woman is seated): *ABV* 445 (2 women confronted: impossible to say whether they are women or goddesses); 469/69 (3 seated women with vine-sprays: probably maenads or women dressed as maenads); *ABL* 219/69 (2 confronted); *ABV* 482/10 (one seated, one standing), 497/185 bis (seated and standing), 186 (three seated, the middle one with a mirror); 498/2–3 (three seated); 502/108 (three: probably maenads), 109; *ABL* 227/39 (three, with swans between them); 237/111 (one seated); *ABV* 533/11 (one standing between two seated); *ABL* 244/63 (three seated);[1] *ABV* 554/405–6, 411 (seated and standing), 477, 477 bis

[1] From a child's grave in Athens.

(two with a fawn between); 578/53 (two seated to right holding wreaths: perhaps goddesses), 65.

R (running, included here because it is common in red-figure): *ABV* 578/61 (with wreath).

A (carrying alabastron or mirror: again these are very common in red-figure and the attribute normally means that the woman is at home): *ABV* 560/525, woman with mirror.

W (spinning or working wool): *ABV* 480/2 and γ; *ABL* 235/118.

M (music): *ABV* 482/4 (two, with lyres); *ABL* 227/50 bis (woman playing kithara and two cocks); 235/74 (woman with lyre, running); *ABV* 554/407–10 bis (woman seated with lyre between two seated women); 578/54 (two women with lyres seated); 661/8–9 (woman seated with lyre).

D (dressing): *ABV* 660/16 (woman holding a garment).

V (various): *ABV* 502/106–7 (woman reclining on the ground); 586/6–7 (women and girls at palm-tree: probably this should be taken as a dance of women and girls at Delos in honour of Artemis or Apollo).

Red-figure: early

G (general): *ARV²* 22/3; 55/36–7 (between eyes); 99/7.

S (seated): 9/1 (three women); 22/1, 2; 99/16 (one seated with mirror, one pouring from oinochoe on ground, one with flower).

R (running): 95/116–19, 133–4, 172/2. Several of these have wreaths. Possibly what we call running a Greek would often call dancing and these women are excerpted from a dance. Cf. 80/13 (woman dressed as maenad or maenad?).

A (alabastron or mirror): 99/22 (before two columns, temple or house, girl with egg and mirror, girl with fruit: this might be an excerpt from a watching scene (cf. chapter 16, pp. 217 ff., D)).

N (naked): 32/4, 53/2 (doing up her sandals, cf. 86), 87, 102; 75/60 (using olisbos; cf. 77), 80; 1624/4 (binding her leg); 85/1 (one dancing, one with skyphos on the back of her hand); 99/29; 110/8; 125/15 (using olisbos), 17; 134/7 (running, with basket and alabastron); 144/4–5; 163/10 (with phallus-bird); 176/2; 177/1, 2 (holding vessel of phalli).

V (various): 4/13 (women bathing, perhaps Amazons); 80/13 (woman lifting a hydria?).

Late archaic

G (general): 231/77; 264/61 (walking with flower: palm-tree; perhaps leaving home to worship Artemis); 264/62; 266/86; 276/74 (mistress and maid), 87; 296 (mistress and maids); 309/2; 310/10; 377/ 127-8, 136, 139, 213, Oxford 1966.486; 390/42; 393/26, 28, 31 (wool basket), 32, 44-5, 47 (two), 49 (two), 52; 395/4; 395/2 (wool basket); 396/16 (in doorway), 17-18, 21 (chair and wool basket), 22 bis, 25-6; 408/33 (women); 410/63 (women), 66 (holding basket); 423/129; 438/139 (women); 449/4 (woman smelling a flower); 450/ 26 (with basket); 470/175-9, 283 (with flower). Here the type, woman at home, is clearly settled. 'Mistress and maid' leads ultimately to the classical white lekythoi and the late fifth-century Hegeso stele.

S (seated): 262/48; 265/79; 303/12; 310/7 (with mirror); 331/11; 376/84; 377/104 (wool basket); 396/23; 410/67 (with mirror); 462/ 49 (with wreath).

R (running): 377/124, 126; 390/41; 393/29; 394/8; 395/1; 396/24; 423/124.

A (with alabastron or mirror; cf. also above, S): 264/60, 78; 289/14; 302/19; 305/2; 306/7 (with pomegranate also); 307/13 (with flower also); 309/10-11; 310/5-6 (running with mirror); 361/6; 363/29 (B. woman with box); 378/140 (woman standing with mirror and headband between stool and wool basket); 394/11; 396/19-20; 409/62 bis; 415/8; 428/60 (with mirror and alabastron between laver and wool basket on a chair); 451/34.

W (spinning and working wool): 211/207; 231/87; 258/18 (with other women); 311/1; 367; 370/11; 378/158, 160, 214; 394/51 (also woman seated); 395/3; 403/38; 435/95 (seated woman working wool on her shin, standing woman lifting chiton sleeve); 451/3 (three women spinning).

M (musicians): 211/196 (playing lyre); 264/55 (seated with lyre); 303/8 (with lyre); 384/216, 221 (playing the flute); 390/43 (with flute); 393/30 (singing); 407/10 (with kithariskos, before kalathos); 428/10 (playing the lyre); 452/4 (with lyre).

D (dressing, washing, etc.): 231/85; 238/9; 250/17, 17 ter; 257/17 (folding clothes to put in a box); 262/30; 294/61; 304/1, 2 (dressing); 361/6 bis; 377/103 (washing clothes); 378/123 (dressing); 389/ 21 bis; 396/12; 444/248, 250.

N (naked): 189/77 (washing); 236/4 (washing); 238/5 (with olisboi); 242/76 (with olisboi); 250/17 (laver); 279/2 (with phallus-bird); 329/130 (about to wash); 331/20 (about to singe herself); 377/122 (folding chiton); 390/44 (putting down clothes); 409/42 (laver); 441/186 (two, putting down clothes); 479/330 (laying down boots).

V (various): at well, 377/102, 109, 142, 145; perfuming a vessel, 444/ 249; playing ball, 302/2; 393/27, 395/4; at altar, 264/58-9, 377/125; libation, 276/77; 409/53, 423/130, 131.

Early classical

G (general): 493/2 (mistress and maids); 505/18 (three women), 22, 36-7; 515/16-17; 524/13 bis, 30-1; 527/66 (women and little girl); 531/31 (two), 61 (women); 537/8 (three); 540/5 (women); 603/36 (three); 617/14 (three); 622/47 (two); 64 (woman greeting, hydria, woman with sceptre, woman leaving: perhaps prayer and offering to a goddess), 90, 94; 626/1 (two), 5; 627 (with wreath); 629/12 (women), 15 (three), 17 (three), 21-2, 25 (two), 35-6 (three); 640/87 (putting lid on basket), 133; 645/5, 7 bis; 652/3 (mistress and maid: this is a standard white lekythos and should strictly be excluded); 656/26 (mistress and maid); 658/20 (two), 55, 90; 663/3; 666/5 (three); 667/40, 50; 670/8; 674/24-6; 674/2; 676/17 bis; 681/87 bis (wool basket), 94-7, 232 (wool basket); 690/7 (with flowers at a wool basket); 693/4; 696/5; 697/40-4, 78-9; 704/44 bis (wool basket), 74; 708/2; 708/1-4; 708; 708; 711/52 (with sceptre: goddess or priestess?), 69, 71-3, 128-31, 177 (two), 179 (two), 182-5 (two), 196, 244-6; 719/10 bis, ter (with distaff or mirror), 12 (at wool basket); 721; 722/2; 723/1 (two); 723/1 (woman with hen, woman with wreath, both walking from home to sacrifice?); 724/6 (two); 725 (with a tendril); 726/5, 7, 9-14, 17 (three), 18; 727/1-2; 727; 729/4; 734/96-102 (99-102 are white lekythoi but of BEL shape: all three show woman at tomb, so that they were meant for funeral offerings like normal white lekythoi), 109, 110 (two), 111 (mistress and maid), 113 (with sceptre), 114-15, 116 (woman and girl), 133, 147; 741/2, 4; 747/1-2, 747 (two women: probably all three should be omitted as standard lekythoi, the first two white); 758/96; 768/34 (two); 777/2; 778/3–5 (two); 805/88–91 (on 89 the women have names of Argive heroines, on 90 the names of nymphs); 811/36 bis; 815/1; 815/2 (women); 819/42 (women); 827/1 (women), 7–8 (women), 15 (women); 829/6 (three); 838/17 (mistress and maid), 18–19, 21, 25 (women), 26, 27 (three); 843/153 (mistress and maid); 852/4 (mistress and maid); 853/5 (two); 857/2 (mistress and maid); 860/15, 31 (women); 864/14 (mistress and maid); 890/171 (women); 899/145 (women); 906/111 (women), 113–14 (women), 116 (women); 907/1–3 (two); 908/13 (women), 198–204 (women); 921/38 (women), 39; 939/31 (women); 943/78–83 (women), 85 (mistress and maids); 947/19 (women); 948/7 (women and Erotes); 955/1–3 (women); 955/1 (two); 958/66 (mistress and maids), 67 (women), 72–3 (women); 963/87–96, 98–9, 94 ter (women); 970/91 (women).

S (seated): 489/101–3; 501 (seated making wreath, standing with alabastron, seated with mirror, walking with box, standing over chair); 503/18, 22–3 (feeding crane), 24 (woman standing spinning between woman seated with box and sash, and woman seated with box); 507/37 (seated with mirror, standing with kalathos); 520/36 (seated winding fillet between woman running up with spindle and wool basket, and woman with phiale); 529/56 bis (mistress seated with basket and maid with mirror and wool basket); 548/54–6 (woman seated between two women); 557/116 (seated with skyphos, and maid with ladle); 581/2 (seated with mirror, woman with thurible); 609/20 (seated between two); 624/86–7, 89 (seated at wool basket, and woman), 109; 626/3; 642/109, 122–3 (at wool basket); 645/3 (twining a wreath), 3 bis, 4; 652/34–6 (mistress seated with mirror and flower, maid with box: these are red-figure lekythoi of standard shape but may well be funerary); 660/56–8, 60, 80; 662/2; 663/4; 667/11, 28 (seated with mirror; muffled woman), 39 (seated; woman), 47, 48 (mistress and maid), 49 (seated; woman); 670/16; 674/27 bis (woman seated with wreath; from same sarcophagos as 16 bis, lekythos, Nike running to altar with basket); 681/102 (also Eros)–9, 210–13, 252, 259; 698/46 bis, ter; 705/4, 6; 1667 (seated with mirror); 705/1–3; 705; 708/12 (with torch? – if so, goddess), 13 (with mirror); 716/209, 224; 718/1, 21; 722; 726/3, 19; 729/7, 8 (with mirror), 23; 730/9; 735/112 (mistress seated and maid), 129 (do.); 748/2 (holding a lekythos); 771/3–4; 778/6 (woman seated, and woman); 811/36 bis (woman seated and two women); 815/1 (two seated, and one with mirror); 844/156–7 (with mirror), 864/13 bis; 906/112 (woman seated and woman); 918/208–14; 939/30 bis; 939/32 (women seated on stone seats between standing women in house); 958/71; 963/97.

R (running): 502/130 520/40 (fleeing women, probably mythical); 525/32, 39; 640/94–6, 100, 108, 111–12, 126; 645/2; 652/29 bis (woman fleeing: on the left, a palm-tree; perhaps a dance in honour of Artemis); 656/16; 659/88; 667/21; 669/2 (holding tendrils); 670; 676/17 ter; 680/75 (with oinochoe and phiale), 76–7, 234; 695/1–2 (with mirror), 3; 695; 703/52–65; 704/75–6; 706/6 (to wool basket), 8; 708/14–15; 711/74–92 (with sprig or ivy branch), 93 (with flower), 99–127, 198 (with flower), 199–204 (with sprig), 205 (with sash), 207–8, 245; 719/2 (with sprig), 9–10, 22 (with sprig); 721/3–4; 727/23 (with an apple in each hand); 728 (with wreath); 729/3; 731/ 26 (with sceptre), 40–1, 106; 739/1–4; 740 (with tendril); 741 (with tendrils); 778/6 (with basket); 958/68 (with sash), 69.

A (with mirror or alabastron): 501/39 (woman with mirror, woman with alabastron); 522/2 (alabastron and dish of loaves); 556/110 (holding wool basket and mirror); 624/85, 93; 640/88; 656/17, 23, 27 (also woman with wool at wool basket); 658/19 (also woman feeding goose); 27 (also woman tying her girdle), 32; 667/21 (with lekythos), 27 (woman with alabastron lifting her skirt, woman with sash: it looks as if the first is going out), 41 bis; 671/6 (also woman with box), 7 (also woman with torch: perhaps she has been made ready for a torchlight dance); 673/15, 21–3, 681/91–3, 233, 251, 254, 233 bis; 691/29; 696/3; 698/32; 700/82 (woman with alabastron and sash; girl with perfume vase and alabastron, a basket on her head: perhaps a visit to a tomb); 701/2; 703/43–5, 73; 1667; 711/54–67, 70, CV Norway, pl. 40, 3, 98 (running with alabastron), 178 (one standing with mirror, one moving with mirror); 190–5, 197, 206 (running with alabastron and basket), 224, 226, 239–40, 244 bis; 719/5 (running with alabastron), 6–7 (running with mirror), 7 bis (running with alabastron); 720/3; 721/2 (running with mirror); 721/1; 722/3, 5 (running with mirror), 10; 723/3 (woman with perfume vase, woman with alabastron); 725/4, 6; 726/2, 6, 16 (with woman with flower and girl with krotala), 19, 21, 22 (woman with wreath and mirror, woman with sceptre); 728/1 (two women with mirrors); 729/5, 6, 21 (also woman with fillet and wreath), 22 (also woman with sceptre); 730/4; 731/27–34 bis (running); 90 (woman with lekythos and basket), 132 (with perfume vase); 740/1 (with maenad); 741/1–2; 758/9 ; 804/63; 838/18, 37; 843/133, 161 bis; 852/2 bis; 981 (running).

W (spinning and working wool): 485/29 (woman seated spinning with three other women), 118; 503/24 (between two seated women); 557/122 (woman with yarn); 624/81, 82 (with wool basket), 93; 626/4 (taking wool from basket); 645/10 (at wool basket); 649/41 (with wool basket); 655/2 (at wool basket), so also 8, 10–12, 27; 671/10 (laying spindles on a table); 680/79–90, 209 (at wool basket); 696/2; 698/30 (at wool basket); 1702; 707/6 (at wool basket); 711/68; 724/5 (one spinning, one with wool basket); 725/2–3 (at wool basket); 726/1, 3 (at wool basket), 4, 24; 732/50 (at wool basket), 51–7, 61, 67–9 (at wool basket), 92; 739/1 (woman with perfume vase at wool basket); 810/35; 827/7 (seated preparing wool, and woman with mirror); 918/207 (seated spinning, and two women); 982/3 (A. seated spinning, B. standing with sash and alabastron).

M (musicians): 499/15 (three women, one playing flute, one with krotala); 507/32 (with flute-case); 557/115 (playing lyre); 608/99 (?do.); 610/23 (seated with lyre, fawn, standing with box and flutes); 618/2 (playing the flute, and women); 624/88 bis (woman seated with lyre, girl with flute, woman with lyre); 662/3 (woman with lyre at wool basket); 681/110 (seated with lyre), 111 (seated playing the flute), 222–3 (head of woman with lyre between columns: unexplained); 249–50 (woman playing flute); 700/7 (with lyre, walking with dog); 726/16 (woman with mirror, woman with flower, woman with krotala); 731/25 bis (seated with lyre by pillar of building), 39 (running with lyre); 777/1 (women with musical instruments); 777/2 (one playing kottabos, one testing the flute); 777 (seated with lyre); 815/1 (three women seated with flute, wreath and krotala); 825/19 (women with lyres and flutes), 30 (?Muses); 857/1 (?Muses, playing small kithara and playing flute), 7 (similar); 948/8 (seated playing lyre, and woman); 963/95 (women with lyres); 981 (woman with lyre).

D (washing, dressing, etc.): 497/14 (holding a garment); 500/31; 511/3 (dressing); 517/1; 552/86 (washing clothes), 89 (do.); 640/72 (woman binding her hair, and maid), 86 (laying himation on chair), 93 (do.); 645/7 (running in after bathing); 662/96; 670/13 (dressing); 674/3 (do.); 680/209 bis; 699/72 (picking up himation); 717/221 (tying girdle); 734/91; 747/29 (woman holding sash and flower, woman holding girdle); 821/2-5; 928/69-70.

N (naked): 505/19 bis (at laver); 524/29 (washing); 535/2 (laying clothes on chair); 551/10 (carrying phallos); 565/39 (washing); 681/113 (at laver); 729/23 (naked woman and woman); 821/2 (at laver), 3 (putting boot on), 24 (at laver); 823/1 (holding phallos).

V (various): holding sash, 642/106; 668/41 (also woman with sceptre: worshipper and goddess?); 699/71 (with baskets of sashes); 716/205 (running), 241 (with sash and basket); 720/24 (running); 732/38 (running); 917/201-2 (running, included in scenes with other women). At thurible, 631/43. With a child or children, 624/88; 644/134 (nurse); 727; 777/1; 864/13. Feeding dog, 642/107. Feeding pig, 658/54. With gosling, 658/19; 667/10. With piece of meat, 778. Playing ball, 656/19; 670/11; 688/231; 698/45-6; 700/10; 733/62-6; 819/42; 875/8 bis; 876/1; 961/94 bis. Spinning top, 643/119; 777/2; 845/163; 941/33. Playing yoyo, 748/1. Playing knucklebones, 671/12. See-saw, 569/49. With arms or armour, 658/29, 44; 659/54 bis; 690/6. At plant, 707/9 (squatting); 721/1 (standing). Libation, 489/107 (oinochoe), 116 (phiale); 1658 (oinochoe); 631/41 (both); 642/115 (both); 650/9 (A. Demeter, B. women with phiale), 15 (A. Athena and Nike, B. woman with phiale); 653/3 (both); 658/26 (phiale), 42 (oinochoe and two phialai); 669/46 (phiale); 674/1 (oinochoe and basket); 703/49 (running with phiale); 706/9 (phiale); 711/53 (phiale), 97 (running with phialai); 719/8 (running with phiale and basket); 722/4 (running with phiale); 732/45-7 (with phiale and staff: ?goddess), 48-9 (phiale). Reading, 611/36, 838/27, 852/5. With torches, 706/2 (seated), 727/1.

Classical

G (general): 1013/13 (three women); 1021/123 (two, one with basket), 125 (mistress and maid), 127 (two, one with wreath, one with box),

130 (two, one with box), 131, 143 (women); 1025/1 (three), 3 (women); 1033/5 (woman with wool basket, woman on either side with fillet); 1049/46 (women), 51 (women and youth), 55; 1061/156 (woman by chair, woman with sash); 1066 (three women); 1067/6 (A. Apollo and Muses, B. three women); 1068/20; 1074/18 (three); 1076/5 (three); 1078; 1085/34; 1093/96 (eight), 97 (three and Eros), 98–9 (three); 1095/2; 1129/109 (Eros and woman), 126–32 (two), 170–1 (two), 174 (Eros pursuing), 188 (two), 190, 191 (Eros flying to woman), 194 (with sash); 1137/25 (tending phalli), 32 (Eros pursuing), 33 (two), 44 (two); 1140/12–21 (two; on 13, one holds a sash, the other extends a hand over a rock to take it), 23; 1141/1; 1149/19 (three), 20–2 (two), 24 (three); 1150 (two); 1166/102 (mistress and maid), 109 (two), 117; 1175/8 (mistress and maid), 15, 20 (two, Eros), 21 (mistress and maids), 46–7 (two); 1178/1–3 (two); 1187/3–4; 1197/2 (with wool basket); 1198/13–14 (with wreath); 1202/10 (with wreath), 14–16; 1204/1–2; 9 (girl with wryneck perched on her hand); 1206/28, 33 (mistress and maid), 64–5 (with Eros), 66 (with box), 68 (Eros pursuing), 73; 1211/1 (mistress and maid); 1212/2; 1217/1–6 (two); 1220/2 (two); 1221/3–4; 1221/1, 3–5 (women); 1222/2–5; 1223/1–3 (with Eros or Erotes), 5 (women), 6 (with Erotes); 1223 (do.); 1223 (do.); 1250/27 (women), 28 (two), 33 (mistresses and maids), 101 (women); 1257/2 (mistress and maid); 1259/3, 12 (women), 13–14 (women), 61 (two), 83 (mistress and maid), 84; 1265/12 (two); 1267/11 (two); 1277/25 (women); 1303/1, 3; 1304/1–2.

S (seated): 992/71 (mistress and maid); 1011/19 (do.); 1020/91 (with two others), 96 (mistress with alabastron, maid with box and mirror), 124 (mistress and maid); 1048/42 (seated twining wreath, four women), 43 (do.), 44–5, 47 (as 42–3), 48 (with six women and youth), 50 (two women); 1060/148 (do.), 149 (with maid and youth); 1068/19 (women with box, woman with alabastron, woman seated with wreath, women with sash); 1071/2 (Eros flying to woman seated at wool basket); 1071/2 (mistress and two maids); 1074/17 (do.); 1077/1 (woman seated with phiale and stick, woman with wool basket, woman with ball of wool), 2 (woman seated with wool basket, woman with ball of wool, woman with sash), 3 (as 2); 1081/17 (woman seated and two women), 18 (woman seated and woman); 1085/23 (as 1048/42), 24 (the same but with six women) 28 (with woman and man), 32 (with Eros and woman); 1094/100 (at wool basket, and maid), 101 (with two women), 104 (door, bed, woman seated with mirror, woman with braiding frame, woman seated playing knucklebones, woman folding peplos, woman with box); 1100/58 (with three women), 59 (with youth and woman); 1103/7 (woman with box, woman seated with wreath, woman with mirror, woman with sash), 8; 1128/105 (with Eros), 151 (with Eros and two women), 165–9 (mistress and maid), 189, 200 (with Eros); 1135/2 (with women and Eros); 1137/34 (mistress with box, maid with alabastron); 1146/42 (with women), 58 (with women and a youth), 63 (with women), 64 (with two women), 66; 1148/14–15 (with four women), 16 (with five women), 17–18 (with two women), 23 (Eros with box and sprig, woman with basket); 1150 (with Eros and woman); 1158/4 (woman with sash, woman seated with box, woman with alabastron and box, woman with necklace, woman with mirror); 1166/104 (woman with mirror, seated woman with box, woman); 1175/12 (mistress and two maids); 1178 (also woman); 1179/6 (with Eros and woman), 7 (with women), 8 (as 6); 1187/34–5 (with Eros and four women, 34 also girl); 1199/32 (with basket), 33–4 (with alabastron and box), 41 (do.); 1201; 1202/ 6–8; 1686/1 (with sprig), 2 (with egg?), 3 (with mirror); 1206/10 (with Eros), 26 (with Eros and maid), 60–3 (mistress and maid), 71 (with Eros on her knee), 74–5; 1211/1–3 (mistress and maid), 6 (with woman in peplos), 7 (mistress and maid); 1222/2 (woman seated, three women running, woman taking wreath out of basket); 1223/7 (between two women running towards a door); 1224/3 (with Erotes and maids); 1248/10 (A. seated with mirror, B. Theano with alabastron and box, mythical therefore?), 11, 46; 1279/53; 1289/21 (with woman); 1296/25 (woman seated, five women, two Erotes with lyre); 1297/1 (also woman with sceptre, ?two goddesses), 2 (also woman with wool basket), 3–5 (also woman), 7 (inside, seated woman with sceptre, and woman holding box, offering to god- dess?; A. and B. woman seated and woman), 10 (as 1), 11–13 (also woman); 1298 (as 1297/1); 1302/4 (A. mistress seated on rock-seat at door of her house, B. maid running with basket).

R (running): 1135/2 (A. with basket, B. with sash); 1177/49 (with perfume vase); 1197/4; 1200/1 (with box, alabastron and sash); 1202/9, 9 bis, 30; 1203/1; 1220/3; 1220/6–7; 1249/23.

A (with mirror or alabastron): 1013/16 (also woman), 18 (do.); 1020/97 (also woman with sash), 128 (also one with basket), 129 (one with alabastron, one with mirror), 124 bis (do.); 1068/21 (also two women, one with basket); 1085/29 (seated with mirror, with youth and woman); 1196/1, 3, 4; 1199/26–8; 1207/26 bis (with woman and Eros), 46 (also one with basket); 1250/28 (also one with perfume vase); 1257/1; 1263/82 (also one with box); 1304/3.

W (spinning or working wool): 1023/144 (with youth and woman, woman holding child, woman, maid); 1082/21 (with three other women); 1083/1 (with two other women); 1085/25 (with woman and youth); 30 (do.), 31 (with two women); 1100/62 (with another woman); 1177/2 (with women with alabastron, mirror, braiding-frame, sash, top); 1267/20 (at wool basket); 1304/4 (do.).

M (musicians): 1022/126 (with lyre, and woman); 1033/3 (flautist and two women), 4 (lyrist and two women); 1040/19 (lyrist, six women and youth), 20 (lyrist and women), 21 (flautist and three women); 1046/13 (lyrist, women, Erotes); 1046/7 (lyrist, Eros, woman with flute and small kithara), 8 (lyrist, three women, one with box), 49 (lyrist and two women), 52 (lyrist, flautist, lyrist: perhaps Muses?); 1059/131 (lyrist and two women), 138 (Eros, three women with lyres, three women), 146 (lyrist, between two women), 147 (lyrist, Eros, women); 1075/10 (lyrist, two women entwined); 1077/4 (A. lyrist, woman with small kithara, woman with box, B. three women, one with a flute-case, one with a lyre; ?Muses); 1078 (A. two lyrists, woman with box, B. three women, one with lyre: ?Muses); 1083/4 (flautist, woman seated, woman running with box to door); 1084/10 (lyrist, Eros, women), 11 (the same, but also youth), 14 (lyrist, Eros, women), 26 (lyrist, Eros, woman), 27 (do.); 1090/47 (lyrist and two women), 48, CV Norway, pl. 34, 3 (flautist, woman with box, woman welcoming); 1118/25 (lyrist, flautist, woman with flute-case), 27 (flautist, women with box and flute-case); 1144/18 (lyrist and women), 62 (lyrist and two women); 1167/116 (lyrist, women playing a game); 1199/21–4 (lyrist); 1199/29 (lyrist), 30 (small kithara), 31 (woman seated beating tympanon:

maenad?), 31 bis (harp); 1207/9 (lyrist, woman with small kithara, woman with box), 27 (lyrist, woman with small kithara).

D (washing, dressing, etc.): 1040/23 (doing up her sandal; woman with lekythos and box; woman with perfume vase and basket); 1063/3; 1085/33 (with Eros); 1109/35 (washing); 1147/60; 1200/40 (tying girdle, at a hydria); 1200/2 (mistress holding up her cloak, maid holding out a basket); 1203/2 (at laver); 1204/6 (folding garment); 1248/16 (washing); 1256/9; 1263/81.

N (naked): 1016/38 (at laver), 122 (with Eros); 1034 (at laver); 1051/18–19 (do.); 1089/28–9 (do.); 1111/1 (washing); 1128/106–7 (with Eros), 108 (at laver, and Eros), 108 bis (naked woman, and naked girl bringing her a box), 155–6 (at laver), 157–8 (at laver, with Eros), 159 (with Eros), 160 (naked woman with himation, draped woman), 161 (naked woman with spindle, seated draped woman), 193 (holding rolled-up garment); 1141/22 (naked woman with box, draped woman); 1156/15 (at laver); 1166/98–100 (at laver); 1248/4 (putting on chiton), Noble, *Techniques*, fig. 158.

V (various): with sash, 1196/2; 1197/1–3 (running), 15; 1201/4 (running). Holding child, 1023/144; 1258/3. Playing ball, 1138/53; 1147/61 (with Aphrodite); 1202/17; 1687; 1204/7. Spinning top, 1177/2. Playing a game against Eros, 1132/175. Playing morra, 1257/2. Juggling, 1209/57; 1250/35. See-saw, 1011/17; 1179/5; 1271/38 bis. Swing, 1131/172–3 (Eros).[1] At plant, 1202/11–13, 12 bis; 1203/2–3. Libation, 1022/132; 1132/179 (two women, one with phiale); 1133/2 (phiale); 1197/5 (running with phiale); 1304/2 (A. woman with phiale, sacrificial basket in front of her, B. woman with incense in her hand). Reading, 1199/25, woman with volume (Muse?); 1212/4 (woman seated with roll, woman with alabastron).[2] Torch, 1197/1 (running).

Late fifth century

G (general): 1313/4 (women); 1320/2; 1321/4–5; 1327/81 (woman and maid, twice), 84, 90 (women and Erotes), 91, 97 (Eros, maid), 100–1, 103–9, 114–15; 1331/1–4 (mistress and maids), 5; 1 (three women); 1341/1 (three women), 2 (women with one foot up, talk-

[1] Cf. *ABV* 306/41, 308/74, which have been connected with the Aiora.
[2] Cf. above, pp. 60, 174.

ing or playing), 3, 4 (two), 5; 1349/2–2 bis, 12–12 bis (three), 13
(mistress and maid), 14–15 (with basket and sash), 18, 19 (three),
22–4 (three), 26 (two); 1691 (three); 1351/3; 1352/6 (Eros and two
women), 11–12 (do.), 14–16 (female head, and two women), 17–18
(female head, with Eros and woman), 19 (female head, and two
women); 1353 (Eros and woman, one with a strigil); 1353/4 (three),
5 (two); 1354 (woman with one foot on rock: Muse?); 1354 (two
women); 1355/12–17, 30; 1358/1–2 (two women); 1–3 (two); 1–2
(two); 1–6; 1359/1–2 (two women); 1 (woman with tendril); 1–5
(two women); 1361/25, 27; 1–2; 1362/3–9 (basket); 1; 1363/9 (with
wreath); 1; 1364/1 (two women), 3–12, 15; 1365/4; 1 (with
wreath); 1–6, 9 (with basket and sash); 1368/1–3 (two women);
1370/6; 1391/1–3 (two women), 26 (do.), 41 (do.), 48 (do.), 49, 57
(mistress and maid), 61 (women), 68; 1396/1 (two women), 12
(mistress and maids); 1549/3 (three women); 1551/21 (mistress and
maid).

S (seated): 1313/6 (woman nursing child, women: ?mythical), 16 bis
(two women seated on rock, Eros with necklace, woman with
mirror and basket); 1321/2 (woman seated, with Eros and women),
6 (do.), 7 (with women), 8 (two seated, two standing, Eros); 1325/
52 (with Eros, woman, seated woman, Hermes), 52 bis (with Erotes
and women), 58 (with two standing and one seated), 59–60 (with
Eros and woman), 61 (with woman), 69 (with Eros and three
women), 72–3 (mistress and maid), 78 (seated, with women and
Eros), 80 (do.), 82 (with women), 83, Oxford 1966.716 (with
woman with box, woman with sash, seated woman, woman with
box), 88, 93 (with Eros and woman), 94 (do.), 98 (women seated
and standing, with Erotes; one woman dresses, one ties her sandal),
102, 110 (with Eros and women), 111–13, 118; 1331/1–2 (mistress
and maids); 2–3 (mistress and maids); 1348/2–4 (mistress and
maids: on 3 and 4, mistress sits on rock); 1351/2 (with woman tying
her sandal), 3–5 (mistress and maid); 1353/18 (women with Eros);
1354/2 (mistress and maids), 9 (do.), 18–20, 25 (with two women),
27–9; 1356/2 (with Eros and maid); 1357/2 (with Eros); 1358/3
(with woman); 1360/1 (mistresses and maids), 2–5 (mistress and
maids: 2, 4–5 with Eros; 3 with Nike); 1363/1–6; 1–2; 1370/2
(mistress and maid); 1 (with two women), 9 (with Eros); 1393/32

(with woman), 79 (with four women); 1549/4 (with two women).
R (running): 1326/66 bis (with alabastron and sash, on her left arm a
goose: between two Erotes), 75 (with necklace and basket); 1349/
10–11 (with sash, basket and sash), 17 (with sash and basket); 1361/
24, 26; 1362/2–3; 1366/7, 8 (with ball); 1368/1–2 (with sprig and
box); 1370/7 (with box); 1405/7 (Eros between two women running); 1551/15 (with Eros).
A (with alabastron or mirror): 1349/3 (with two other women, one
with basket and sash); 1350/16; 1359/1–2; 1360/20, 22; 1361/1–6, 11
(woman with mirror and woman with alabastron), 12–13; 1363/2;
1–2; 1365/2; 1395/68; 1397/10 (with two women, one with box
and sakkos).
W (spinning or working wool): 1363/7–8 (at wool basket); 1397/11
(mistress and maids, one spinning).
D (dressing, etc.): 1313/11 (perfuming clothes); 1325/62 (woman
tying her sandal, and two women).
N (naked): 1319/1 (at laver; with women and Erotes); 1321/66 ter
(bathing, Erotes, Aphrodite and two goddesses: probably mythical);
1325/63 (with Erotes and women), 70 (two bathing, with Erotes
and woman); 1334/20 (at laver, with Eros and satyrs, mythical);
1354/21 (Eros and naked woman seated).
V (various): with sash, 1362/7, 1370/8; cf. also above. Holding child,
1313/6; 1326/65 (mother and child, with two women), 66 (women
and child). Playing ball, 1690 (with two women, goddesses?);
1359/2; 1365/13–14; 1365/2–3; 1366/8 (running with ball). Juggling, 1326/74; 1360/5 (mistresses and maids with Erotes; Eros and
woman balancing sticks on her hands). At plant, 1364/2 (picking
fruit?). Libation, 1362/10 (A. woman with phiale at altar, B.
woman running with phiale); 1394/60 (phiale).

The general picture is clear enough: an immensely increased interest
in women from the time of the Persian Wars. To be more precise is
difficult. Certainly a large number and probably the majority of these
vases were painted for women. Whatever vases women had bought
or been given for their own purposes before, they had not found on
vases pictures of their own occupations in such quantity before. The
vase-painters were meeting a new demand. When one thinks of the

restrictions on women's life in Athens, it seems probable that the demand came from men rather than from the women themselves. The vases were more often presents from men to women (or offerings at women's tombs) than purchases by women. And their attraction for men is made explicit by the presence of Eros, who appears more and more frequently in these women's scenes from the classical period onwards.

The general picture is clear even if our lack of knowledge makes a lot of reservations desirable. The most common subject is women at home. Home is indicated by alabastra or mirrors hanging on the wall and by tame birds or animals among the figures. The common occupations are spinning and working at wool, washing, dressing.

It is when we try to go further that precision becomes difficult. Where for instance can we draw a line between free women and hetairai? It is perhaps reasonable to suppose that naked women are hetairai. The young Athenian did not want his sisters painted in the nude even if they were only washing themselves; certainly the early pictures of women with olisboi or phalloi are hetairai. But even here the line is not quite clear: on a small pelike by the painter of London E 395 (1141/22) a naked woman brings a box to a draped woman. It seems to be an ordinary mistress and maid scene, but why is the maid naked?

The musical scenes also are difficult to interpret. Professional musicians in Athens were usually slaves. And the majority of the musicians on vases are the flautists and lyrists, who later played havoc with Menander's young men. But we cannot exclude the possibility that they were sometimes hired to play to the women in a respectable house while they did their work or that a slave or daughter of a respectable house could learn enough herself to entertain the women. Closely allied with music is reading from a roll, which we have already discussed as a mark of the professional musician (see above, p. 60). But there is another confusion which we may make: there is no good evidence for concerts of mixed instruments, and where we see these the women concerned are probably Muses.

Muses may be confused with musicians, and ordinary women may be confused with goddesses. In black-figure it is difficult to be certain whether the seated women may not be goddesses; in red-figure it is difficult to believe that the women with sceptres are ordinary mortals.

The boundary may have been clearer to the purchasers than it was to us. We have to admit that a woman with a sceptre may be a goddess or a mythical queen and that she is more likely to be one of these than an ordinary mortal. But this leads to another difficulty: can we separate mythological from everyday? The answer must be 'Not always'. We should never have thought of naming the women in an ordinary gynaikeion scene on a pyxis Iphigeneia, Danae, Helen, Klytaimnestra, Kassandra (805/89), but evidently the names of these famous ladies were an encouragement to the recipient of the pyxis, and the scene can be included under the general heading 'mythological paradigm'.

Probably more of the scenes than we can detect are concerned with religious celebrations. This is clear where an altar is shown or where a woman has oinochoe and phiale, or carries one of the sprigs with which one visited the gods. We have noticed also the presence of a palm-tree as indicating a dance in honour of Artemis or Apollo, and that an ivy-branch or tympanon may show that a woman is performing as a maenad. The baskets (as distinct from the wool basket (*kalathos*) and the basket-bag) which the women frequently have is the kind of basket with which women appear on white lekythoi bringing offerings to tombs, and the offerings include alabastra, lekythoi and tainiai which also appear in the women's scenes. I suspect that many of these scenes show preparations for taking offerings to shrines, as well as for walking in religious processions.

Some of the scenes are so like the scenes on funerary white lekythoi that the vases must have been used for the same purpose. The most obvious are the scenes of mistress and maid, e.g. red-figure lekythoi, 652/35-6, and the actual visits to a tomb: the white lekythoi of the Beldam painter's shape with women visiting a tomb (751/1; 751) are a precursor of the classical white lekythoi of the Achilles painter and his companions. (A parallel is given by early classical and classical red-figure lekythoi with men at a tomb (e.g. 730/5, 993/96).) In the classical period a red-figure hydria in the manner of the Washing painter has women at a tomb (1134/17) and a hydria is also a suitable shape for a funeral offering. But of these too we may say that they show the new fifth-century interest in women.

18

Various

(1) *School scenes*

Special school vases like the Douris cup,[1] the vases with inscribed rolls
and the vases with successful musical performances have been discussed
already. A number of other vases of the fifth century have scenes some
of which certainly took place in school, whereas others are most easily
included here although it is not quite clear where or at what stage the
writing-case was carried or the musical instrument played. There are
three objects which suggest a school scene: writing apparatus, lyres,
flutes. The following lists are classified under these and notes are only
added where desirable:

(a) *Writing-case, tablets or roll:* ARV² 104/4; 184/21; 231/82–3; 349/1;
407/26; 411/8; 428/6, 14; 431/220; 455/11; 784/25; 788/2; 866/1;
893/25; 959/2; 1208/67; 1262/62.

(b) *Lyre:* ABV 475/15; 576/10; ARV² 72/21 (exceptionally, youth
seated playing the kithara, *Hipparchos kalos*); 201/64; 231/75 (music
lesson); 263/50; 272/5, 52, 53, 69; 287/31; 349/1 (also writing);
362/23 (music lesson), 26; 383/197 (singing); 407/19; 411/1; 412/22
bis (youth with flute gives note to two with lyre); 437/120 (boy
sings to seated lyrist); 471/198, 207, 213, 260, 261, 270; 1655; 502/14;
504/3; 557/119 bis; 565/41–2 (music lesson); 579/87 (instructor with
lyre gives note to boy with flute); 627; 671/9; 778/9; 781/1; 788/1;
874/5; 880/4 (outside, boys with horses), 107–8, 120; 891/2; 893/25
(also writing), 32, 37, 73; 920/10, 12 (outside, athletes), 16, 25–6, 30;
949/6–7 (outside, athletes); 950/1 (outside, athletes); 959/2 (also
writing), 23–4, 62; 964; 965/2; 990/41–4, 52; 1006/5; 1031/41, 46;

---

[1] *ARV²* 431/48, Berlin 2285; cf. the fragmentary 49–51.

1053/32, 60; 1060/137 bis; 1084/36 (boy singing, no musical instrument); 1097/23, 61; 1102/6; 1104/14; 1108/12 (youth singing, no musical instrument); 1171/5; 1186/31 bis (music lesson); 1208/37 (music lesson); 1211/1; 1257/2; 1259/8; 1278/28–30, 68 (youth about to sing to seated lyrist); 1288/2 (inside, athletes).

(c) *Flute:* ARV^2 376/89 (boy singing to flautist); 404/1; 407/19 (also lyrist), 20 (youth singing to flautist); 411/1 (boy singing to flautist); 471/207 (also lyrist), 266; 565/41–2 (music lesson, also lyrists); 579/87 (music lesson, also lyrists); 638/48 (boy singing to flautist); 648/28 (do.); 866/1 (also lyrist); 893/37 (also lyrist); 959/23 (also lyrist); 1053/61; 1116/39 (boy singing to flautist), 39 bis (do.); 1150/30 (do. with judge); 1278/31, 69 (also boy about to sing).

In one 'writing' scene, 784/25, one lyre scene, 1031/46, and one flute scene, 893/37, one of the boys holds a sprig: this may mean, as normally, that religion is involved – he is going to pray for himself or his comrades, but in this context, where recitation and music are so obviously preparation for the symposion, it is legitimate to wonder whether the sprig is the myrtle branch held by singer or reciter in the symposion.

The shapes represented are 48 cups, 11 pelikai, 9 neck-amphorai, 7 kraters, 5 hydriai, 2 lekythoi, 2 squat lekythoi, 2 oinochoai.

(2) *Country occupations*

(a) *Hunting.*[1] Hunting was partly an aristocratic sport, partly a useful way of filling the larder. The vases show traditional pictures of lion hunts, boar hunts, deer hunts, hare hunts, but also huntsmen returning home with their game and youths armed with clubs or stones who are probably engaged in the hunt. The whole series runs from the middle of the sixth century to the end of the fifth.

Lion hunt: ABV 343/3, small hydria, shoulder, hunter running away from lion; 609/4, kyathos, lion hunt. ARV^2 92, 65–8, cups, panther attacking fawn, and youth, also have nothing to do with Athenian life.

Boar hunt: ABV 135/44, lid of amphora; 140/5, lekanis; 159/1, 227/13, cups; 266/4, 276/4, predella of hydria; 306/39, amphora; ARV^2 413/16, 33, cups; 577/52, dinos; 1294, cup.

[1] Cf. K. Schauenburg, *Jagddarstellungen*, 1969.

Youth attacking boar: ABL 216/66, neck-amphora; *ABV* 530/69, oinochoe; *ARV²* 179/3, hydria; 411/3, 770/5, 882/39, cups.

Deer hunt: ABV 135/44, lid (cf. above); 140/4, predella of hydria; 189/5, 18, 227/13 (cf. above), 252/1, 252, cups; 256/18, 266/1, 2, 5, 20, 30, 276/4, 6, 282/2, predella of hydriai; 267/23, shoulder of hydria; *ABL* 243/50, lekythos, 84, plate; 266/4, lekythos; *ARV²* 151/52, 174/15, cups; 182/4, b.f. scene on amphora mouth; 351/8, 413/16 (cf. above), cups; 600/17, volute-krater, neck; 828/34, cup.

Youth attacking deer: ABV 457/16, lekythos; *ARV²* 555/90, pelike.

Hare hunt: ABV 189/18 bis, 20, cup; 349, dish; 593/3, neck-amphora.

Return of hunter: ABV 111/42, lekythos; 153/31, olpe, 44, chous; 168/1, 181/1, cups; 302/4, small amphora; 473/16 bis, 476/1, lekythoi; *ARV²* 92/129, 111, cups; 302/21, lekythos; 1134/18, squat lekythos.

Youth engaged in hunt or going out to hunt: ABV 210/1, (?) cup; 218/16, Nicosthenic amphora; 319/6, neck of neck-amphora; 562/557, 579, 579/8–9, 630/2, 633/12, 42, 53, 118, cups; *ARV²* 99/11, 12, alabastra; 114/2, 169/4, 224/9, 324/61 (with spear and panther-skin, perhaps rather light-armed warrior), 341/87, 413/18, cups; 557/113, 118, lekythoi, very high quality, hunter going out; 641/98 bis, 690/9, 721/1, lekythoi; 779/3, oinochoe; 1002/13, lekythos.

Various: ABV 476/8 ter, lekythos, 635/78 bis, cup, man reclining and hunter approaching him; *ABL* 243/49, hunters on horseback, lekythos; *ARV²* 126/26, skyphoid, hunt; 1154/37, hunters, 1156/13, hunt, both bell-kraters.

It is clear that the traditional boar hunt and deer hunt often occur in subsidiary scenes. The returns are usually good, as are some of the lekythoi with hunters setting out; these may be dedications before or after a successful hunt.

(b) *Women in the orchard.* This is a fairly common subject in late black-figure but there are only six in red-figure. A fine black-figure hydria by the A.D. painter has already been mentioned because the women have names (*ABV* 334/6, Munich 1712, above, p. 62). Sometimes the women actually pick fruit, sometimes they are simply seated at a tree, but as when they are seated they sometimes have baskets they are probably all fruit-pickers. The rest are: *ABL* 220/75, neck-amphora; *ABV* 488/3, 489/188 bis, 503/1–2 bis, 504/1, lekythoi;

504/2, skyphos; 504, neck-amphora; 505/1, *ABL* 244/62, lekythoi; *ABL* 246/95, 246/3, mugs; *ABV* 553/400-4 bis, lekythoi, 473-6, mastoids; 561/531, 620-2, 580/8, cups; 586/10, lekythos; 604/67-8, doubleens; *ARV*² 503/21, hydria; 523/1, column-krater; 922/1, cup; 1317/2, bell-krater, women, youths and Erotes; 1364/2, squat lekythos. These may all have been painted for women; they certainly contain a considerable number of women's vases, and two of these belong to the late fifth century.

(*c*) *Flocks and herds: ABV* 189/9, cup, man chasing a ram; 349, kyathoid, goatherd; 363/42, hydria, shoulder, man catching goat; 385/27, hydria, shoulder, bull-taming; 518/27 ter, skyphos, A. man with bull, men carrying amphora, B. man catching boar, man and youth with shallow bowls (*skaphai*) and sprigs (this is probably a dedication of farm produce and should rather have been included under cult); 646/205, cup, I. herdsman, A. and B. copulation of cattle; *ARV*² 114/2, herdsman and bull, 454/4, youths mastering bull, cups; 275/62, column-krater, youth driving calf; 412/9, A. copulation of donkeys, B. calves and heifer coming home from grazing, cup.

(*d*) *Olives: ABV* 270/50, 116, neck-amphorai, olive-picking; *ABL* 251/41, skyphos, oil-press. (Sale of oil, sale of perfume, cf. above, pp. 61, 100.)

(*e*) *Wine* (for vintage, sale of wine, cf. above, p. 101): *ARV*² 178, cup, boy with grapes.

(*f*) *Fish: ARV*² 105/7, 110/6, fish-boy; 134, fish-porters; 173/9, boy fishing; 329/131, fish-boy; 464/72, man with cuttle-fish. All these are cups; a small pelike by the Pan painter, 555/88, Vienna 3727, *CV* pl. 76, has A. boy fishing and boy collecting catch in basket, B. fish-boy running to town past a herm. He has two baskets on a pole across his shoulder, and this identifies the other fish-boys.

(*g*) *Various:* Youth lifting stones, *ABV* 553/390, lekythos. Donkey-man, *ARV*² 45/99, 71/4, cups. Carrying baskets on a pole, *ARV*² 109/30, plate.

(3) *Preparing food*[1]

Women pounding corn, *ABV* 309/95, neck-amphora. Woman at oven, baking bread, *ARV*² 782, with a loaf on a plate, 812/59 bis, both

[1] Cf. B. A. Sparkes, *JHS* 82 (1962), 121; 85 (1965), 162.

cups. *ARV*² 360/1647, men making fire, cup. Man cutting up carcase, *ABV* 430/25, oinochoe. Man chopping meat, *ARV*² 250/21, pelike, 56 fragment; 266/85, head-kantharos; 366/89, 412/9, 467/130, cups; 691/19 lekythos. Man carrying meat, *ARV*² 57/44; 521/49, cups; 553/39, pelike, 660/68, lekythos. Man running with spits, *ARV*² 327/104, 467/ 130, cups. Man moulding dough to contain strips of meat, *ARV*² 467/ 130, cups. Man dragging skin of ox, *ARV*² 553/40, pelike. All these pictures of men dealing with meat are preparations for or aftermath of a sacrifice (cf. above, pp. 126 ff,). Cooks cutting up a tunny, *ABV* 377/ 247, olpe.

(4) *Craftsmen*
(*a*) *Potters:* Boy with lumps of clay, *ARV*² 178/2, cup. Building a kiln, *ABV* 520/26, skyphos. Potters and painters (cf. above, p. 8), *ABV* 147/7 (?amphora fragment); 362/36, shoulder of hydria; *ARV*² 342/19, cup; 676/17, lekythos; 803/60, cup; 1064/3, Oxford 526, *CV* pl. 24–5, here pl. 1, bell-krater. Sale of pots, *ARV*² 23/14, Baltimore, *CV* Robinson, 2, pl. 3, cup, *Chairias kalos*; 256/1, amphora B; 540/4, amphora B.
(*b*) *Metal-workers:* Smithy, *ABV* 378/264, lekythos. Cutler, *ARV*² 595/ 72, oinochoe. Armourer, *ARV*² 23/13, cup. Helmet-maker, *ARV*² 81/1, pyxis; 336/22, cup. Metal vessels, *ARV*² 92/64, cup; 571/73, hydria. Foundry, *ABV* 426/9, London B 507, oinochoe (cf. above, p. 66); *ARV*² 327/106, 400/1 (with sculptors and sculpture) *Dio-genes kalos*, cups. On a chous, 776/1, Athena is modelling a horse in clay, probably for casting.
(*c*) *Stone-carvers: ARV*² 75/59, 341/19 bis, 400/2, cups; 1139/1, pelike.
(*d*) *Carpenter: ARV*² 179/1, cup.
(*e*) *Shoemaker: ABV* 396/21, pelike; *ARV*² 786/4, cup.
(*f*) *Clinic: ARV*² 813/96, cup.

If we leave on one side the larger groups of school, hunters and women in an orchard and look at these vases, of which many have unique scenes, together, it is first obvious that their time range is restricted: the majority fall in the last quarter of the sixth century and the first quarter of the fifth with a certain extension into the second quarter of the fifth. Earlier certainly are the near Exekian pottery frag-ment, and perhaps the Centaur painter's cup with the man chasing a ram, the Antimenes' painter's olive-pickers, the Swing painter's women pounding corn and later, in the classic period, the Komaris painter's pottery and the pelike of a sculptor setting up a herm which recalls the Hasselmann painter. How many of these vases were special commissions it is impossible to say: we have noticed above (p. 67) the expanded *kalos* inscription on the Mys foundry oinochoe; ordinary *kalos* names occur on the foundry cup with bronze statues and on the Phintias cup with sale of pots. The fragment with Exekias pottery was dedicated on the Acropolis, but the potter by a follower of Douris (*ARV*² 803/60) was found in Etruria. Cups heavily outnumber other shapes, 52 against 29, of which the highest number is 6 pelikai.

(5) *Minor sports*

(a) *Cock-fight:* *ABV* 202/2–3, cups; 448/4, olpe; 477/9, hydria, shoulder; *ABL* 257/70–1, *ABV* 574/11 bis, *ARV*² 53/66 bis, cups; 274/30, 570/65, pelikai; 866/1, cup; 1077/4 bis, bell-krater. (Cf. P. Bruneau, *BCH* 89, 1965, 90.)

(b) *Coursing hare:* *ARV*² 63/90, 144/2, 153/3, 174/15, cups; 183/7, Panathenaic amphora; 213/242, *Krates kalos*; 315/1, *Leagros kalos*; 322/37, *Panaitios kalos*, 122, *Lykos kalos*; 333/2, *Panaitios kalos*, 344/52, 84, *Lysis kalos*, 353/15, 38, 56, 73 (victor), all cups; 414/34, stamnos; 430/32, 78, *Hippodamas kalos*, 475/266, all cups.

(c) *Toy chariots:* *ARV*² 480/337 (cf. above, p. 59); 810/20, cup.

(d) *Boy with hoop:* *ARV*² 215/13 ter, 276/76, oinochoai; 288/7, pelike, perhaps mythical; 293/55, pelike; 356/56 (also hare), 69 (carrying food), cups; 403/37 (do.), skyphos; 479/326 (do.), cup; 564/30, pelike; 871/90, pelike.

19

Mythological Scenes

Many vases have mythological scenes and these scenes reflect the changing tastes of the purchasers.[1] Here I am only concerned to ask what factors may have influenced the choice of scenes. It is, for instance, obvious that any scene connected with Dionysos is suitable on any symposion vase and this needs no illustration, but even within Dionysos scenes it may sometimes be possible to detect and account for a particular nuance. The story of Dionysos and Ariadne is suitable for vases because Dionysos is the god of wine, but the union of Dionysos and Ariadne is also a kind of immortal bliss which mortals hoped to share after death, and I suspect that from the time of the Heidelberg painter drinkers liked to be reminded of this. The commonest version of the story involved the desertion of Ariadne on Naxos by Theseus, and when Theseus became a prominent Athenian hero his conduct became a matter of concern to Athenians, and in answer the vase-painters make it clear that the Athenian goddess Athena was responsible because she wished Theseus to continue his Athenian career. In these fifth-century versions we can see the influence on the vase-painters either directly or through their patrons first of the original *Theseid* and later, probably, of Euripides' *Theseus*.[2] Here is a clear case where a story which is a natural one to put on symposion vases takes on a new turn because of a new literary version and the vases reflect the change. I suggested above that the Alkmaionids were responsible, if not for the conception, at any rate for the popularity of the new *Theseid* and used the vases to spread it: as

[1] These are indexed in the mythological indexes of *ABV* and *ARV²*. I have only given precise references where it seemed necessary. Cf. also for some myths F. Brommer, *Griechische Vasenlisten* (Marburg, 1956), and for late fifth century H. Metzger, *Les Représentations* (Paris, 1951).

[2] Cf. my article, *GR* 13 (1966), 22, and on the *Theseid*, above, p. 82.

a secondary result the vase-painters also reflected new interpretations of the desertion of Ariadne.

In looking at specially commissioned vases we saw two special factors which might lead to the choice of a particular myth, one that it was relevant either to an ordinary human scene on another part of the vase or to the present situation of the owner of the vase, what I called 'mythological paradigm',[1] and the other that the myth had been used in a recent dramatic, lyric or epic performance, and the vase was made for a symposion in celebration of the occasion, and we noticed that after that the story might become a stock scene.[2]

In the mythological paradigm the contemporary parallel may be expressed: we noticed that two vases of the Pioneer group which had athletes on one side had the wrestling of Theseus and Klytos and the struggle of Peleus and Thetis on the other. The successful athletes who use these two wine-jars are compared to the heroic Theseus and Peleus. There must be many examples of this kind of comparison, and I quote a few obvious ones: in black-figure, amphora B (*ABL* 220/87, London B 170, *CV* pl. 34), warriors setting out on one side, and the Dioskouroi on the other; small neck-amphora (*ABV* 597/14, London B 286, *CV* pl. 70), boy with lyre and boy dancing on one side, and satyr and maenad dancing on the other; in red-figure, pelike (*ARV²* 629/23, Lecce 570, *CV* pls. 1–4), man with purse looking at woman on one side, Polyneikes tempting Eriphyle on the other; skyphos (*ARV²* 785/1),[3] man with a purse facing a boy with the words, 'Hey, what a boy', on one side and on the other Herakles greeted by Zeus. A quite different example is a skyphos of the classical period by the Penelope painter (*ARV²* 1300/4), which has on one side an overseer (Philyas) and an architect and on the other a giant hauling stones for Athena. This must have been specially commissioned for a symposion celebrating the building of the Acropolis wall, and it then found its way by the second-hand market to Campania.

Often, however, only the mythological comparison is shown and the contemporary reference is left to the observer. So we interpreted Akamas and Demophon with their horses and Kastor and Polydeukes

---

[1] Cf. above, pp. 56, 153 f., etc.
[2] Cf. above, pp. 91 f., 94 f.
[3] Boston 01.8076. Cf. H. R. Immerwahr, *James Sprunt Studies*, 46 (1964), 20.

with their horse on one side of two vases by Exekias (*ABV* 143/1, 13)[1] with *Onetorides kalos* as probably indicating that Onetorides was an Athenian knight, and two black-figure hydriai (*ABV* 260/30, 37)[2] with weddings of Peleus and Thetis and Herakles and Hebe as paradigms of the actual weddings at which the vases were to be used. Two more examples, which are even clearer because of the shape of the vase, are a black-figure nuptial lebes (*ABV* 40/20) with the wedding of Menelaos and Helen and a red-figure onos (*ARV*² 1250/34) with allusions to three mythical marriages, Peleus and Thetis, Kadmos and Harmonia, Admetos and Alkestis.[3]

The second main class of specially commissioned vases with mythological scenes, which we may call vases of special occasion, owe their existence to some special outside stimulus which we can detect or assume. The vases which celebrate lyric or dramatic victories may have a tripod like the Marsyas vase (*ARV*² 1185/1) or chorus and actors in costume like the Pronomos vase (*ARV*² 1336/1) or the earliest of the *Prometheus Pyrkaeus* vases (*ARV*² 1046/10). The story also is new in each case. The Marsyas[4] story does not appear before the classical period and is then painted on 15 classical vases and 3 vases of the late fifth century; the *Prometheus Pyrkaeus* story first appears on 9 classical vases and then on 4 vases of the late fifth century.[5] The sudden popularity of these stories of itself demands an explanation in terms of some recent public event, and the additional evidence of the tripod and the stage-costume point the way to an explanation by the Marsyas song of Melanippides and a revival of Aeschylus' *Prometheus Pyrkaeus*. Once established, the Marsyas scenes and the *Prometheus Pyrkaeus* scenes continue to be popular and become stock scenes for the vase-painter.

The most impressive of these sudden bursts of popularity is that to which we have already alluded, the Theseus scenes in the late sixth century. The old popular scenes were Theseus and the Minotaur, Theseus and Helen, and Theseus in the Centauromachy (it is often difficult to detect which Centauromachy the vase-painter means but sometimes the presence of Kaineus fixes the reference to Theseus' Centauromachy). Much the most popular of these is Theseus and the

---

[1] Berlin 1720, Vatican 344. Cf. above, p. 66.   [2] Cf. above, p. 106.
[3] Athens 1629, *SB* (Heidelberg, 1961), 6. Cf. above, p. 107.
[4] In general, see K. Schauenburg, *MDAI(R)* 65 (1958), 42.
[5] In early black-figure Prometheus is represented six times but not afterwards.

Minotaur which occurs 10 times in early black-figure and 48 times in middle black-figure; the new scenes which are introduced in the late sixth century do not destroy its popularity since it goes on with 37 in late black-figure, 11 in early red-figure, 16 in late archaic, 31 in early classical and 8 in classical. But the new scenes come up strongly alongside it, chiefly the contests round the Saronic gulf on the way to Athens, the Bull of Marathon, the Amazonomachies with the rape of Antiope, and Theseus and Ariadne. Here we can distinguish an initial impulse and two subsequent impulses. The initial impulse in the late sixth century was the new *Theseid* and, as has been suggested, the Alkmaionid interest in setting up Theseus as a democratic hero; the vases, especially the vases showing a cycle of Theseus' labours, were a means of spreading the new idea.

The second impulse, as we have said,[1] was given half a century later by the bringing back of Theseus' bones from Skyros, and the building of the Theseion and the Stoa Poikile; its results are the great early classical Amazonomachies and the Centauromachies in the wedding chamber. Whether these vases were painted for public banquets in the Theseion or for the symposia of Peisianax and Kimon we cannot say. But they are certainly a new reaction to a new impulse and they set a type for later stock vases.

The third impulse is less important: suddenly soon after 450 a new version of Theseus and the bull appears.[2] The story itself seems to antedate the *Theseid*, as we have seen, and then has 5 examples in late black-figure, 9 in early red-figure, 22 in late archaic and 9 in early classical. In the new version Aigeus often looks on and Medeia runs away with jug and phiale. This version is plausibly connected with the production of Euripides' *Aigeus* in which Medeia first persuaded Aigeus to send Theseus to capture the bull and then when he succeeded attempted to poison him. The references are *ARV*[2] 1023/148, 1057/104, 1093/90, 1115/16, 1163/45, all in the classical period, and 1346/2 and 1347 in the late fifth century. It looks as if the new version was invented for a symposion celebrating Euripides' play (and there is no reason to suppose that one of the original set of symposion vases has been preserved) and then became popular.

[1] Cf. above, p. 85.
[2] Cf. B. B. Shefton, *AJA* 60 (1956), 159 f.; my *Tragedies of Euripides* (London, 1967), 77 ff., 297.

Besides the mythological paradigms and the special occasions we must recognize also the individual taste of the purchaser who without any political reason and with no need to celebrate a dramatic or lyric victory demands a new mythological scene on a vase. The Onetorides vases of Exekias[1] have what is probably the first battle over Patroklos' body, the first Achilles and Penthesileia and the first Ajax and Achilles dicing. These are superb vases and are likely to have been the first which started the fashion. The battle over Patroklos' body is copied on another kalyx-krater in the manner of Exekias and then occurs once in early red-figure. The death of Penthesileia was painted again by Exekias and then recurs once in late black-figure, and four times in red-figure. Ajax and Achilles dicing is much more popular: 4 in middle black-figure, 36 in late black-figure, 4 in early red-figure, 8 in late archaic, 3 in early classical, 1 in classical. The first scene comes from the *Iliad*, the second from the *Aithiopis*, the third presumably from the *Cypria*. If there was a special occasion which prompted Onetorides to order these vases (assuming that he was the purchaser), it is lost to us, and we can only attribute the orders to his taste and note that the dicing scene set a fashion.

We cannot hope to account for all the choices of myth, but we can note briefly what myths were popular at different times and where an explanation is needed. Attic myths are obviously relevant on Attic vases but some particular stimulus may account for their popularity at different times. We have already dealt with the Theseus story. Two figures may be connected with the Persian Wars. Pan helped the Athenians in 490 at Marathon (Herodotus, VI, 105), and appears on an oinochoe by the Geras painter a little later (*ARV*[2] 287/32);[2] then in the early classical period we have the lovely Pan pursuing a goatherd, possibly Daphnis, by the Pan painter (*ARV*[2] 550/1, Boston 10.185, Caskey–Beazley, II, pls. 47–9), and very interestingly the chorus of Pans, probably substitutes for satyrs in a satyr-play, on a kalyx-krater by the Niobid painter (*ARV*[2] 601/23). Boreas was summoned to damage the Persian fleet in 480 before the battle of Artemision, and the two earliest

---

[1] *ABV* 143/19, 7, 13; above, pp. 65 f. Cf. however on the first, K. Friis-Johansen, *Iliad in Early Greek Art*, 191 f. I do not feel clear that the earlier uninscribed fights over the body of a hero are battles over Patroklos, and the lost band-cup need not be earlier than Exekias. On Ajax and Achilles dicing, Caskey–Beazley III, 114.

[2] Cf. F. Brommer, *Marburger Jb.* 15 (1949/50), 14 ff.

pictures of Boreas and Oreithyia come soon after this: the Syriskos painter's column-krater (*ARV*² 260/9) was found on the Acropolis and may therefore be a dedication, the Berlin painter's column-krater (*ARV*² 208/150, Berlin 2186) was found in Etruria; after that there are no less than 35 Boreas scenes by early classical painters and 6 by classical painters. Once adopted, the theme becomes symbolic either of marriage or of death.[1]

The birth of Athena and the Gigantomachy with Athena taking a major part are obvious subjects for vases used in any assembly of patriotic Athenians. It is perhaps surprising that, whereas the Gigantomachy is popular through the whole period with a high peak in the late black-figure, the birth of Athena decreases steadily from the time of middle black-figure: the numbers are early black-figure 9, middle black-figure 9, late black-figure 5, early red-figure 2, late archaic 2, early classical 1, classical 1, late fifth century 0.[2]

The Gigantomachy[3] may have been popular partly because the Gigantomachy was woven into the peplos which was given to Athena at the Panathenaia. The Panathenaia must have been an occasion for many private celebrations, and one might suppose that the recitations of the *Iliad* and the *Odyssey* at the Greater Panathenaia suggested subjects to the potters. Unfortunately we cannot be certain when the recitations were introduced, but it is certainly tempting to connect them with Peisistratos' purification of Delos.[4] Pictures from the *Iliad* are not very common:[5] the chief scenes which recur are the duel of Ajax and Hektor (VII) in late black-figure and red-figure down to early classical; the embassy to Achilles (IX) with the same time-span; the battle for Patroklos' body (XVII), middle black-figure and early red-figure; Thetis and the arms of Achilles (XVIII), 6 in early black-figure, 6 in middle black-figure, 7 in early classical red-figure and 6 in classical; Achilles and Hektor (XXII), late black-figure and red-figure down to early classical; the funeral games of Patroklos (XXIII), twice in early black-figure; Priam and Achilles (XXIV), twice in early black-figure, 1 in early red-figure, 5 in late archaic, 1 in early classical, 1 in classical.

---

[1] Cf. pp. 107, 290.
[2] Cf. F. Brommer, *J.R.–G.Z. Mainz* 8 (1961), 66.
[3] Cf. F. Vian, *Répertoire des Gigantomachies* (Paris, 1951).
[4] Thuc. III, 104, probably before 550 B.C.?
[5] Cf. K. Friis-Johansen, op. cit., 250 ff., for full list.

The figures are too small to allow any large conclusions. It certainly looks as if Thetis and the arms of Achilles, the funeral games of Patroklos and the ransoming of Hektor's body were known before the Panathenaic recitations.

In the fifth century we have the near certainty that the pictures of Nereids bringing Achilles' arms on sea-monsters were inspired by Aeschylus' *Nereids*, and on Polygnotos' kalyx-krater (*ARV*² 1030/33 Vienna University 505) they are linked with Achilles' mourning for Patroklos and the ransom of Hektor, the third play of Aeschylus' trilogy. The vase is classical and possibly belongs among commissions given by Sophocles' association of actors (cf. above, p. 48). The early classical Nereids on dolphins or sea-monsters can certainly be associated with Aeschylus; it is not quite clear how far the late archaic embassies to Achilles and Ransoms of Hektor should be associated with Aeschylus rather than Homer.[1] In the absence of any indication of stage-performance[2] it is safer to take them as indicating an interest in the story on which Aeschylus could count.

Incidents of the *Odyssey* were illustrated before black-figure, and the Athenians certainly did not wait for the Panathenaic recitations for pictures of the shipwreck of Odysseus or Odysseus and Polyphemos. In our period there are extraordinarily few *Odyssey* illustrations, in black-figure only Kirke and Polyphemos, two exciting traditional stories for which no reason is needed. The Polyphemos episode in late black-figure has much the biggest number (20) of any Homeric scene. The Kirke episode goes on into the classical period of red-figure; it is just possible that Aeschylus' satyr-play *Kirke* should be considered as a stimulus. Otherwise we find a single Odysseus and the Sirens in late archaic red-figure, a Penelope and the suitors and a very doubtful Odysseus and Eumaios (*ARV*² 564/27, Cambridge 9.17, *CV* pls. 33–4) in early classical, but in classical red-figure three Nausikaa scenes, an Elpenor, a foot-washing paired with Telemachos' return to Penelope, and Odysseus slaying the suitors.

Here again, however, as with the late *Iliad* scenes, other influences than the *Odyssey* may be at work. Sophocles produced his *Nausikaa*

---

[1] Cf. Döhle, *Wiss. Ztschr. Rostock* 16 (1967), 431; M. Schmidt in *Opus Nobile* (1969), 141, on *ARV*² 361/7; K. Friis-Johansen, op. cit., 156, on *ARV*² 406/1.

[2] The elaborate tent in *ARV*² 406/1 may be suggested by the stage and more particularly by Aeschylus' *Myrmidons*, which could then be dated 480.

before 450 B.C., and one of the Nausikaa scenes has a reminiscence of stage-costume (ARV^2 1177/48, Boston 04.18); the Penelope painter's foot-washing (ARV^2 1300/2, Chiusi 1831) scene takes place in the presence of Eumaios, and Odysseus is washed by Antiphate instead of Eurykleia; possibly these variations come from Sophocles' *Niptra*. The great painter Polygnotos[1] painted Nausikaa, included Elpenor in his painting of the Underworld,[2] and he or one of his colleagues painted Odysseus slaying the suitors in the same scheme as the Penelope painter (ARV^2 1300/1, Berlin 2588). Tragedy and big painting rather than the *Odyssey* may have provided the occasion for these late *Odyssey* pictures.

On the whole the recitations of the *Iliad* and *Odyssey* at the Panathenaia, on our evidence, do not seem to have influenced vase-painters and their patrons very much. Other Attic myths which are represented include the mission of Triptolemos, Eos and Kephalos, and the early Attic kings. The mission of Triptolemos to acquaint the world with agriculture and the Eleusinian mysteries was one of the great glories of Athens, and so was a natural subject for any Athenian, not only the initiated, and for any foreigner visiting Athens, to choose on a vase.[3] In black-figure the painters show his arrival to give his instructions, 3 from the third quarter of the sixth century and 5 from the fourth; in red-figure the painters show his departure and his briefing by Demeter and Persephone, 3 early, 23 late archaic, 30 early classical, 24 classical and 1 late fifth century. Sophocles produced his *Triptolemos* in 468; in it Triptolemos was certainly briefed for his journey and his snake-drawn winged chariot was at least described, if not shown on the stage. But there is no obvious change within the early classical vases that we can ascribe to his influence.

The story of the winged Eos carrying off Kephalos appears first in ripe-archaic red-figure at the same time as the parallel myth of Eos and Tithonos: they both run through to the classical period. But they are distinct stories, and the representations are on the whole kept distinct.[4] Kephalos was an Attic hunter, and is often represented as a hunter

---

[1] E. Simon, *AJA* 67 (1963), 59.
[2] On Nekyia, cf. P. Jacobsthal, *Metr. Stud.* (1934), 117.
[3] Cf. C. Dugas, *Mélanges* (1950), 9; K. Friis-Johansen, *Meddelelser Ny Carlsberg* 26 (1969), 15, on ARV^2 362/19, A. Triptolemos between Demeter and Persephone, B. Theseus between Poseidon and Amphitrite. Two Attic heroes and their divine sponsors.
[4] Caskey-Beazley II, 37.

(Hesiod already has his rape in the *Theogony*, 986, and Euripides quotes it in the *Hippolytus*, 454, as an old story parallel to the love of Zeus and Semele). Tithonos was a young son of Laomedon, and was known very early as the father of Memnon (in Hesiod, *Theogony*, 984, and presumably in the *Aithiopis*). It is curious that four rather similar rapes, Boreas and Oreithyia, Eos and Kephalos, Eos and Tithonos, Zeus and Ganymede,[1] appear first on Attic vases in the late archaic period and last through the classical period. It is worth putting the figures side by side.

	late archaic	early classical	classical
Boreas and Oreithyia	2	35	6
Eos and Kephalos	4	35	39
Eos and Tithonos	4	57	20
Zeus and Ganymede	20	20	4

As we have a historical reason for the Boreas group, it is tempting to suppose that it was the first and suggested the two Eos groups, and that Zeus' pursuit of the Trojan Ganymede came in by analogy with Eos and the Trojan Tithonos; this is, of course, speculation, but we do not, as far as I know, have any obvious new literary source to account for the popularity of the other three. As to meaning, the nurse in the *Hippolytus* uses Eos' love for Kephalos as an argument against Phaidra: the gods yield to love and survive, why cannot you? It is a mythological paradigm. Later, Boreas' rape of Oreithyia appears on bronze funeral hydriai and has been explained as offering a hope of immortality.[2] In our period already Pindar (*Ol.* 10, 104, probably 474 B.C.) says that Ganymede's youthful beauty 'defeated shameless Death with the help of Aphrodite'. But the painter of a slightly earlier kantharos, who put Zeus pursuing Ganymede on one side and a man pursuing a boy on the other, clearly used the story as a mythological paradigm in the same sense as the nurse uses Eos and Kephalos in the *Hippolytus*. The purchaser could interpret these scenes either way, an encouragement to love if he bought the vase for the symposion, a consolation in death if he bought the vase for a grave.

The old Attic kings, Kekrops, Erichthonios, Erechtheus and Aigeus, with the possible exception of Erichthonios, do not appear at all in black-figure and are rare in red-figure, only occurring in the early classi-

---

[1] On Ganymede, see Sichtermann, *Ganymed* (Berlin, 1953).

[2] Cf. Picard, *Mon. Piot* 37 (1940), 90; G. M. A. Richter, *AJA* 50 (1946), 366; Verdelis, *AE* (1950/1), 80 (hydria containing 'Orphic' tablet and ashes).

cal and classical periods and the late fifth century. They and the Attic heroes have been studied by Beazley[1] and Brommer.[2] Their appearances are not very frequent – Kekrops 5 times, Erichthonios 10 times, Erechtheus 2, Aegeus 2 – outside the Theseus scenes discussed above. There is no doubt that the stories and cults of Erichthonios and Erechtheus were old, but it needed the new Athenian consciousness of the Persian War period to bring them into prominence. It is therefore interesting that the earliest Kekrops (inscribed, but not ending in snakes as later) occurs on a Boreas and Oreithyia scene (ARV^2 496/1, cf. 2):[3] Oreithyia's sisters fly to a king who is called Kekrops (instead of their usual father Erechtheus). Erichthonios was said to have invented the chariot and the Panathenaia, and so he has been recognized as a charioteer driving in the presence of Athena on a late black-figure cup (ABV 390) and on a classical red-figure hydria (ARV^2 1110/43 bis), but he is not inscribed.

This rise of Attic legends to a certain extent displaced other older legends; Theseus in particular comes up beside Herakles. Herakles was, of course, no native Attic hero, although he had his cults in Attica, particularly at Marathon.[4] The general pattern of Herakles scenes is a steady increase through black-figure and a decrease through red-figure, but there are some interesting variants, and a few new stories are introduced in red-figure. The two most popular scenes are Herakles and the Amazons and Herakles and the Nemean lion: I give both the totals for each period and in brackets the total as a percentage of the total number of vases with mythological scenes in each period:

	early b.f.	middle b.f.	late b.f.	r.f. early	late archaic	early classical	classical	late fifth century
Amazons	27 (14)	20 (5)	130 (10)	10 (5)	9‡(2)	4 (0·6)	0 (0)	0 (0)
Lion	13 (6·5)	79 (20)	202‡(17)	25 (13)	17 (4)	2 (0·3)	2 (0·4)	0 (0)

Other Herakles scenes which follow the same general pattern but with smaller total numbers are the struggle with Acheloos, with Apollo for the Tripod,[5] with the boar, with Kerberos, with Geryon (but this does

---

[1] *AJA* 39 (1935), 487.   [2] *Charites Langlotz* (Bonn), 152 ff.

[3] Pointed amphorai from Vulci by the Oreithyia painter, Berlin 2165, Munich 2345 (*CV* pls. 205–8).

[4] Wilamowitz, *Euripides Herakles* (Berlin, 1895), 36: 'Fast jedes Dorf hat in Attika sein Heiligtum des gottes Herakles.'

[5] Cf. Parke and Boardman, *JHS* 77 (1957), 276 ff.

not go on after the end of the sixth century), with the Hydra, with Kyknos, with Triton.

Reasons can be suggested for this popularity in the sixth and early fifth century. First, one probably felt a mythological paradigm: Herakles was the strong man who overcame monsters and marauders; so to have him on a cup or amphora might give the drinker something of his prowess. Only in the early fifth century was Herakles' violence questioned, and the questioning gave rise to a new conception of Herakles; all that we can see of the seventh- to sixth-century Herakles in Stesichoros' *Geryoneis* is quite uncomplicated joy in battle.[1] It has long been thought that Stesichoros was well known in Athens and that his choral poetry influenced the vase-painters. Professor Robertson[2] has studied the vase-paintings in detail and sees Stesichoros' influence already in the earliest Attic scenes and more completely in the red-figure cups of Euphronios and Oltos about 515 B.C. It is possible also that this late sixth-century interest accounts for the 23 black-figure vases with Herakles and Pholos, which start with the Antimenes painter (the scene occurs once in early red-figure, five times in late archaic red-figure, three times in early classical and then no more); Herakles' drinking with Pholos is quoted from Stesichoros' *Geryoneis*. We know that Stesichoros was sung in the symposion at Athens, and it is at least possible that parts of his long choral poems were performed by soloists in Athenian musical competitions. He also wrote a *Kerberos* and a *Kyknos*, which the vase-painters may have known.

I suggested above (p. 49) that Euphronios' picture of Herakles and Antaios (*ARV²* 14/2, Louvre G 103) was painted to celebrate the singing of an Antaios ode by the young flautist who on the other side of the kalyx-krater mounts the platform in the presence of Leagros and his friends, and we can imagine that Stesichoros was sung in Athens in the same way. We do not know who wrote the Antaios poem. The black-figure vases with Herakles and Antaios are all contemporary with Euphronios' kalyx-krater, and thereafter the scene occurs nine times in late archaic red-figure and then no more. It may be a new story; Pindar uses it in *Isthmian* III (70) probably in 474 B.C., and emphasizes

---

[1] Most conveniently in D. L. Page, *Lyra Graeca Selecta* (Oxford, 1968), pp. 31 f., 263 ff.
[2] *CQ* 19 (1969), 207; cf. also my article in *Agon* (1968), 1; Webster, *The Greek Chorus*, 76 ff., 112.

that Herakles was small but undaunted in spirit; the contrast between the small kempt Greek and the enormous unkempt giant is very clear in Euphronios and is something new, a new conception of Herakles which foreshadows Pindar.

Similarly two of the new red-figure Herakles scenes, the struggle with Alkyoneus, which runs from the earliest period into early classical, and the more popular struggle with Bousiris, which continues into the classical period, are not struggles with wild animals or monsters, like many of the early labours, but struggles with violent men, like the outlaws whom Theseus killed round the Saronic gulf. The earliest Alkyoneus is by Phintias, who is a colleague of Euphronios, and the earliest Bousiris is by Epiktetos and has the *kalos* name Hipparchos, who belongs to the same circle as Leagros.[1]

In one poem at least Pindar[2] was disturbed by the violence of Herakles and saw that Geryon and the Thracian Diomedes had a right to defend their property and appears to have put the justification of Herakles' action in his translation to Olympos. One story which can only be interpreted as showing the violence of Herakles is his murder of the music-teacher Linos, and this appears four times in late archaic red-figure and three times in early classical red-figure. The Pistoxenos painter's skyphos (*ARV*[2] 862/30) superbly catches the spirit of the proud boy walking with his spear while the old slave-woman carries his lyre behind him.

Herakles' translation to Olympos had a double interest for Athenians; it offered a hope of immortality, and he was introduced to Zeus by Athena. Athena's protection, which Stesichoros emphasized but which can be traced back before Stesichoros in Attic art, almost made Herakles an Athenian hero, and the story of his initiation into the Mysteries before he went to fetch Kerberos, which seems to have been known to Pindar[3] in the early fifth century, is implied by a fragment of an amphora[4] close to Exekias found in Locri with Herakles and Kerberos on the neck and Demeter arriving at Eleusis in the presence of Triptolemos, Athena and Herakles. The entry to Olympos appears on vases before 560 (e.g. *ABV* 60/20, London B 379, *CV* pl. 8, 2); there

[1] He appears as an athlete with Leagros on *ARV*[2] 13/1, Berlin 2180 (cf. above, p. 56).
[2] fr. 169.   [3] Cf. H. Lloyd-Jones, *Maia* 19 (1967), 206 ff.
[4] *ABV*, 147/6, Reggio 4001; Metzger, *Imagerie* 8 f., pls. 1–2. From the votive-deposit of a Persephone sanctuary.

are ten in middle black-figure, then a few in every period except the classical. The scheme varies: sometimes Zeus sits, sometimes he stands, Athena always accompanies Herakles, Hermes very often. Sometimes there are other gods present in Olympos. Occasionally Zeus is omitted; once Poseidon takes his place. On a late fifth-century bell-krater Herakles is young and Hebe stands behind him (ARV^2 1339/4, Villa Giulia 2382, CV pl. 1); eternal youth is his reward.

It is not always possible to be certain whether the scenes of Herakles and Athena, which are common from middle black-figure to the end of the fifth century, represent Herakles arriving in Olympos or going to Olympos, or setting out on a labour, or returning from a labour to Athena; in red-figure quiet scenes of Athena pouring a libation for Herakles are common, e.g. ARV^2 196, 1 bis, and this is presumably after or before a labour.[1] The mythological paradigm is clear: Athena blesses the man who fights for civilization.

A quite different scheme, which starts with Exekias and is very common in late black-figure, gives Athena and Herakles riding in a chariot often accompanied by other gods and goddesses. This also is probably the journey to Olympos but Herakles rides instead of walking. In classical red-figure (cf. particularly ARV^2 1186/30, Munich 2360, CV pls. 80–2) it takes on a new form: the chariot is driving up to heaven, Herakles is generally young and sometimes the burning pyre is represented.

In at least one of the walking scenes (ARV^2 639/56, Leningrad 640) it is made entirely clear that Herakles went to Olympos with the apples of the Hesperides; he is shown with the apple in his hand, and the other side of the stamnos gives the apple tree with perhaps Atlas, a Hesperid and Iris. This may be the common early version. At any rate we have no illustration of Herakles on the pyre until about 460 B.C. (ARV^2 498);[2] as this appears to bring in Philoktetes (who received the bow in return for lighting the pyre) it presumably implies the story of the poisoned shirt: it is at least possible that Aeschylus' *Philoktetes* is responsible. The story of the poisoned shirt seems itself to be old, as it is the sequel of Herakles shooting Nessos with an arrow, and this occurs on a fragmentary Attic stand of about 650 B.C.[3] But in the normal Nessos scenes

[1] Cf. J. D. Beazley, *AK* 4 (1961), 55.
[2] Villa Giulia 11688, *AJA* 57 (1953), pls. 45–8. *Etruscan Vase-Painting* (Oxford, 1947), 103 ff.
[3] J. M. Cook, *BSA* 35 (1935), 191, pls. 52 f.

(there are twelve in early black-figure and then they decrease;[1] the three in the late fifth century may be inspired by, but do not illustrate, Sophocles' *Trachiniae*), Herakles kills the Centaur with sword or club. The new conception of Herakles driving to heaven after burning on the pyre seems to go with a new conception of a spiritualized Herakles, and he is represented in art as a slim youth (e.g. among the Hesperides on *ARV*[2] 1313/5). This is the Herakles who in Prodikos' myth about 424 B.C. chose Virtue and rejected Vice – immortality for Excellence instead of immortality for Strength.

Another hero who was not Athenian and (unlike Herakles) had no cult in Athens but was extremely popular is Perseus.[2] Perseus slaying the Gorgon occurs on Attic vases already in the mid-seventh century, then thirteen times in early black-figure and from then on with decreasing popularity to the end of the fifth century. From the earliest times he is under Athena's protection, and this, apart from his attraction as a monster-slayer, may account for his popularity on Attic vases. In the ripe-archaic period the interest shifts to the beginning of his life when he was cast adrift with Danae, and these scenes continue into the classical period. Here we have to suppose a new impulse and it may be that Simonides' lovely poem (*PMG* 543) supplied it; in two cases, however, we can invoke drama: the Wedding painter's early classical pyxis (*ARV*[2] 922/35) with the chest being pulled ashore on Seriphos may be due to Aeschylus' satyr-play, *Diktyoulkoi*, although it omits the satyrs, and the five mid-fifth-century vases with Andromeda in Oriental dress being tied to posts while Perseus comes to rescue her, a subject only known earlier on one mid-sixth-century Corinthian vase, must have been painted to celebrate Sophocles' *Andromeda* (cf. above, p. 47).

Bellerophon also had Athena's help but on vases he usually appears alone on Pegasos, fighting the Chimaira. Bellerophon vases occur in very early black-figure and continue with the C painter and the Heidelberg painter, ending in the third quarter of the century with the Affecter and the BMN painter.[3] Here the essential interest is surely a brave young man who fought a monster.

---

[1] The form Doianeira on *ARV*[2] 174/20 implies a lyric source (cf. Kretschmer 77). A selection in K. Firtschen, *Gymnasium* 77 (1970), 3.

[2] Cf. K. Schauenburg, *Perseus* (1960).

[3] On attributed red-figure he appears only twice: *ARV*[2] 1067 and 1439, the latter fourth century.

Other stories can be treated very briefly. Clearly Athenians had a great and wide interest in mythology, and we cannot hope to account for all their choices. Particularly in the sixth century a love of heroic action seems to be enough, but it may be worth noting in view of his evident popularity where Stesichoros had also treated the theme. The three great actions of the generation before the Trojan War, the hunt of the Calydonian boar, the Argonauts, and the Seven against Thebes are all represented, and Stesichoros wrote a *Boarhunt*, a *Funeral games of Pelias* and an *Eriphyle* (but we do not know how much of the Argonaut story or of the Theban story he included in the last two). The Calydonian boar is frequently painted, particularly on large vases, in early black-figure, and twice in middle black-figure, but then died out, except for a classical cup by the Codrus painter, until a fourth-century revival of Meleager and Atalante pictures, which was probably due to Euripides' *Meleager*.

The Argonaut story is represented by the Boreads chasing the Harpies and by the funeral games of Pelias very early and by Medeia boiling the ram in middle to late black-figure. The Phineus story re-appears on four early classical vases and one classical vase, which may fairly be attributed to the interest caused by Aeschylus' *Phineus* in 472 B.C. It is not clear whether Medeia's magic was originally intended to kill Pelias; my belief is rather that three stages can be distinguished in the development of the story: in the earliest version, to which the pictures of the funeral games belong and the black-figure pictures of Medeia and the ram, Medeia youthened Pelias and he later died a natural death. Pindar (*P.* IV, 250) in 462 is our first evidence that Medeia killed, or caused his daughters to kill, Pelias; this version, who-ever first popularized it, is represented on late archaic red-figure vases.[1] The third version, which refines this by introducing a dissension be-tween Alkestis and the other daughters, is the version of Euripides' *Peliades* in 455 B.C. and is reflected in later vases, starting with the Villa Giulia painter's hydria.[2]

The Theban story starts in early black-figure with the departure of Amphiaraos and the death of Eriphyle, nothing in middle black-figure, then two late black-figure deaths of Eriphyle and one Oidipous and

[1] Cf. E. Simon, *Gymnasium* 61 (1954), 207.
[2] Cf. my *Tragedies of Euripides*, 34, 300; add *ARV*[2] 499/16, Philippaki, pl. 40.

sphinx (this continues through red-figure). Then from the early classical period the story reappears with Euphorbos and the child Oidipous,
Oidipous' murder of Laios, the temptation of Eriphyle, the departure of
Amphiaraos, the Seven against Thebes, the supplication of the Epigonoi, and here again tragedy is probably responsible as also for earlier
portions of the Theban legend, the Ino story, the Aktaion story, the
Pentheus story, the Niobe story.[1]

The Trojan War story begins with the marriage of Peleus and Thetis.
This is a common subject all through, and in its primitive form of a
wrestling match can be, as we have seen, a mythological paradigm both
of wrestling and of marriage. The most splendid representation is the
main scene of the François vase by Kleitias (Florence 4209, *ABV* 76/1)
which must almost have been a very magnificent wedding present, sent
nevertheless after use to Etruria. The young Achilles was given to the
centaur Cheiron to educate: the subject possibly occurs in Attic geometric, certainly in the seventh century, all through black-figure, but
not after late archaic red-figure. The birth of Helen from the egg, however, only occurs in classical and late fifth-century red-figure; its
popularity then may be due to the new Nemesis temple at Rhamnous.[2]
The judgement of Paris[3] runs through the whole period, though the
style changes: the bearded Paris of early black-figure gives place to the
shepherd boy among his flocks in early red-figure, and then to the
young Oriental, who is probably inspired by Euripides' trilogy of 415.
Paris' rape of Helen does not appear until late archaic red-figure but
then continues.[4] The next common scene is the healing of Telephos,
which occurs three times in the early classical period: but here perhaps
the source is Aeschylus.[5] The dicing of Ajax and Achilles is discussed
above. Achilles and Troilos are represented from early black-figure (including the François vase) to late classical red-figure.

After the period treated by the *Iliad*, which has already been

---

[1] For some of the vases inspired by tragedy, cf. above, pp. 91 ff. For a full list, see *BICS*
Supplt. 20, appendix. Note, for instance, the Io story, the Danaos story, the Amymone
story.
[2] Cf. Caskey–Beazley III, 163; *EVP* 40.
[3] Cf. T. C. W. Stinton, *Hell. Soc.*, Supplt. Paper, no. 11; C. Clairmont, *Parisurteil* (Zürich,
1951).
[4] Cf. Caskey–Beazley III, 140; L. B. Ghali-Kahil, *Les Enlèvements et le retour d'Hélène*
(Paris, 1955).
[5] Cf. Caskey–Beazley III, 154.

discussed, we have a string of scenes from the latter part of the Trojan War: Achilles and Penthesileia from Exekias to classical red-figure, Achilles and Memnon[1] with various different schemes (including the weighing of the souls of the heroes) from Exekias to early classical red-figure, Ajax carrying Achilles' body from early black-figure to late archaic red-figure, the quarrel over the arms of Achilles and the trial in late black-figure and in red-figure to early classical, the summoning of Neoptolemos only in late archaic and early classical red-figure, Philoktetes in early classical red-figure (Aeschylus' influence is possible here), then the actual sack of Troy[2] (and we have to remember that Stesichoros wrote a *Sack of Troy*), the death of Priam, the rape of Kassandra, Helen and Menelaos[3] from early black-figure, Aineas and Anchises from middle black-figure to early classical red-figure and beyond but the stealing of the Palladion and the rescue of Aithra only in red-figure. Finally the death of Agamemnon and the death of Aigisthos on a ripe-archaic kalyx-krater seems best explained by a special performance, perhaps of Stesichoros' *Oresteia* (cf. above, p. 96); Aeschylus' *Oresteia* shows a fairly swift reaction in *Choephoroi* and *Eumenides* pictures.

It is fairly clear that in the fifth century presentation of scenes on the stage gave a new reason for representing them on vases. Actual allusion to stage production by representation of masks or costume is comparatively rare, but the clue for us is either that a new incident in a story suddenly becomes popular or that an old incident is reinterpreted, sometimes after it has fallen out of the repertoire. Sometimes certainly we can say that these vases were special commissions (cf. above on the Euaion vases), but many of them were probably painted for stock. There is also the special set of stories, sometimes connected with the stage, which I have termed Release stories and Resistance stories. I think that, like the Dionysos and Ariadne story, they never quite lost their religious significance; the Ariadne story always conveyed the possibility of immortality, and the Release and Resistance stories always recalled the solemn need of new fertility in crops, herds and men every year. The Resistance stories are in each case a resistance to Dionysos. Pentheus scenes[4] start in early red-figure with Euphronios, followed by

---

[1] Cf. Caskey–Beazley II, 14. On the psychostasia, III, 147.
[2] Cf. M. Wiencke, *AJA* 58 (1954), 285.
[3] Cf. L. B. Ghali-Kahil, op. cit.
[4] Cf. Caskey–Beazley II, 1 ff.

one by the Berlin painter, and later one by the Meidias painter (Thespis may have given the initial impulse, and other Pentheus plays are known before Euripides' *Bacchae*). Lykourgos scenes only occur in the classical and free period, and Aeschylus can certainly be invoked. The slaying of Orpheus by Thracian maenads is first painted about 480 and remains very popular until the end of the classical period:[1] Aeschylus' *Bassarai* may be responsible. These scenes are not only directly relevant to Dionysos as god of the symposion but also we can point to a possible source in drama.

Of the Release stories the earliest represented in Attic is the return of Hephaistos[2] with 6 in early black-figure, then 7 in middle black-figure, 23 in late black-figure, 1 in early red-figure, 10 in late archaic red-figure, 12 in early classical, 22 in classical, 1 in the late fifth century. Two of the early classical pictures (*ARV*[2] 591/20, 763/4, Pickard-Cambridge, *Festivals*,[3] figs. 41, 44) and one of the classical pictures (*ARV*[2] 1053/39) show satyrs in stage-costume and must therefore be inspired by a satyr-play; Achaios' *Hephaistos* may be responsible for the third, but not for the other two. In Corinth it is extremely likely that the story was sung by padded dancers and so in some sense performed:[2] the same may have been true in Athens in the sixth century, and some indication of this may be seen in the fact that on an early neck-amphora (*ABV* 89/2) one of the satyrs in the scene has a frontal face which suggests a mask, on an early dinos (*ABV* 90/1) Attic komasts appear next to the return of Hephaistos in the same frieze, and on a Tyrrhenian ovoid amphora (*ABV* 103/111) dancing *men* appear with the satyrs in the scene.

The other Release stories only appear in the fifth century. It is probable that a dithyramb inspired the hammering satyrs of the Eucharides painter (cf. above, p. 94) and that a satyr-play by Sophocles inspired the hammering satyrs releasing Pandora on two early classical volute-kraters (cf. above, pp. 89, 92) and a classical bell-krater (*ARV*[2] 1053/40). (What the relation of this Pandora rising from the ground is to Hesiodic story, represented on two early classical vases (*ARV*[2] 601/23, 869/55, Anesidora), is unclear, but Sophocles seems somehow to have combined them.) Aphrodite rises with dancing Pans (*ARV*[2] 888/155,

[1] Cf. Caskey–Beazley II, 73.
[2] F. Brommer, *JDAI* (1938), 198.
[3] Cf. A. Seeberg, *JHS* 85 (1965), 103 ff.

1041/ 11, on which see below, 1218/2) but also with hammering satyrs, since the rising head with hammering satyrs on a black-figure lekythos by the Athena painter (*ABV* 522/87, Cab. Med. 298, Metzger, *Imagerie* 12, pl. 3) must be Aphrodite and the tradition continues into the fourth century.[1] Persephone (inscribed Pherephatta) also rises in the presence of Hermes and Pans (*ARV²* 1056/95) on a classical kalyx-krater. The Niobid painter's chorus of Pans in costume (on his Pandora kalyx-krater) shows that they could be an alternative chorus for a satyr-play, and we have seen that Pans were new in fifth-century Attic art; the figure rising from the ground may have originated as a stage device (cf. later Eirene in Aristophanes' *Peace*). It is therefore possible that Aphrodite and Persephone as well as Pandora were so represented in satyr-plays, or the inspiration may be more directly religious, nature represented by Pans or satyrs helping and celebrating the revival of the earth-goddess in spring. In either case this is a joyous presentation suitable for wine-vases, and contrasts with more solemn scenes where the emphasis is different: when Persephone rises in the presence of Demeter and Hermes (*ARV²* 1012/1), this is a holy mystery rather than a scene of rejoicing, and when Aphrodite is clothed by Charis and Eros as she comes out of the sea on a pyxis (*ARV²* 899/144), it is a solemn occasion, probably a mythological paradigm for a human wedding and the pyxis a wedding present. Rumpf[2] suggested that a similar scene on a hydria (*ARV²* 1041/11, Syracuse 23912, *CV* pl. 24) alludes to Attic cults – the sanctuary of Aphrodite and Eros and the cave of Pan under the north slope of the Acropolis and Ares and the Eumenides on the Areiopagos, and this is another possible explanation of Pan in the other Aphrodite scenes. Perhaps one should also remember that the shrine of the Nymph, where loutrophoroi were dedicated,[3] is also under the north slope of the Acropolis on the way to the Areiopagos, so that the local references of the hydria make it also a suitable wedding present.

The history of vase-painting is the history of style, but the style of the painter evidently corresponds with the taste of the purchaser. The vigorous clear style of early and middle black-figure expresses the manly, uncomplicated stories of the great heroes: the stories were

---

[1] *ARV²* 1472/4, 1512/12; Buschor, *SBA* (1937), figs. 11–12, which explains the whole series with reference to the stage. Cf. also pp. 142, 145, rising heads.
[2] *JDAI* 65/5, 166.   [3] Cf. above, p. 106.

known, but, as far as we can see, Stesichoros was a superb narrator, and his poems were sung in Athens, so that it may be right to think of him as in some sense responsible. A new need to interpret is found already in the late sixth century, by when the vigorous style had become softer and much more elaborate, and finds its expression in late archaic vases and still more in the strong style of early classical painting: the generation of Pindar and Aeschylus re-evaluated the stories, and we have seen signs of this also in the vases. This was an assessment in terms of hybris and sophrosyne. The next generation preached more quietly and was perhaps more interested in particular characters than general rules: this is the generation of the Achilles painter, whose patrons were prepared to accept a simple nobility, to us extremely moving. The fifth century ends with the luxury style of the Meidias painter (the other pole of the free style, emotionalism, only shows itself in late white lekythoi): this is a world which Aphrodite dominates, and the new myths such as Phaon, Adonis and the rape of the Leukippids honour her.[1] This see-saw of artistic style is also a see-saw of taste, the patron's taste: to some extent both are determined by the similar development of poetic style and thought, Stesichoros, Simonides, Aeschylus and Pindar, Sophocles, and Euripides. Sometimes, particularly in the vases of special occasion, their influence can actually be documented in the vases, but more generally they provide the ambience which decides how the patron chooses his mythological paradigms and determines his personal choice.

[1] See on these and other late fifth-century mythological pictures particularly, H. Metzger, *Les Représentations* (Paris, 1951).

20

Purchasers and Patrons

GRAFFITI

The letters painted or incised on vases, usually under the feet, ought to throw some light on the pottery trade, but in fact they are very difficult to interpret. Some are painted in glaze paint, and they must have been put on before the vase was fired; some are painted in red paint and they, like the incised letters, may have been put on either before firing or after firing. The glaze-paint 'dipinti' must have been put on in the potter's shop before the vase was fired; the other 'dipinti' and the 'graffiti' may have been put on at any moment until the vase left Attic hands.[1] It is perhaps in general more likely that dipinti are put on before firing and graffiti after firing but this is clearly not a safe rule.

All the dipinti in glaze paint that I know of have the letters SO. Most of the vases are unattributed.[2] One of these is the Panathenaic amphora with 'Hiketes *kalos*' discussed above.[3] The two attributed vases are neck-amphorai in the manner of the Antimenes painter (*ABV* 278/27) and by the Michigan painter (*ABV* 344/11); the second is important because the same letters appear in red on other vases by the Michigan painter (*ABV* 344/10, neck-amphora; 343/1, 2, 3, stamnoi) and by his colleague in the Perizoma group, the Beaune painter (*ABV* 344/1, 4). It may be possible to distinguish between SO on the other vases and OS

[1] We have at least one instance of a list of shapes, numbers and perhaps prices inscribed in Sicilian Doric on an Attic r.f. pelike: *Arch Reports* (1957), 30, fig. 7. Some vases were given Etruscan graffiti on arrival in Etruria, e.g. the Nikosthenic amphora, *ABV* 221/42. *ARV²* 1297/4; cf. *JHS* 88 (1968), 139, pl. 7a, has an Etruscan owner inscription; 1639, two verses by the Syleus painter with the same Etruscan graffito.

[2] The basic work on the whole subject is Hackl, *Münchener Archaeologische Studien* (Munich, 1909). I have been very much helped by a Manchester dissertation of 1940 by D. M. Edwards. On stamnoi B. Philippaki, *The Attic Stamnos*, is invaluable. What follows is based on a small selection of the material.

[3] Louvre F 283, cf. above, p. 64.

on the vases by the Michigan and Beaune painters,[1] but it is not possible
to distinguish between the glaze-paint dipinto and the red dipinti on the
Michigan painter's vases. They must refer to the same man. A stamnos
by the Beaune painter (*ABV* 344/1)[2] takes us a stage further because it
has the same two letters in dipinto on the foot and in graffito on the
mouth. Here then we can say that SO or OS put his mark on neck-
amphorai and stamnoi by the Michigan and Beaune painters in their
workshop, sometimes in glaze paint, sometimes in red paint, sometimes
in incision. He cannot have been the painter because two painters are
involved.

The glaze-paint dipinto of the Michigan painter looks very like the
glaze-paint dipinto on the Hiketes Panathenaic (Louvre F 283), which
is unlikely to have been made in the same workshop. It looks therefore
as if SO were a purchaser who marked the pots he intended to have
before they were fired, and the Hiketes Panathenaic shows every sign
of being a bespoke vase: the inscription says 'Hiketes appears *kalos* to
me', and SO put his mark on it, so that presumably he ordered the inscription and is the person to whom Hiketes appeared *kalos*. It finally
reached Etruria but there is no reason here for connecting SO with that.
One other vase (*ARV*[2] 248/2, London E 261, *CV* pl. 4) with a *kalos*
name has an SO dipinto, an amphora by the Diogenes painter of the
early fifth century, found in Vulci, with Dionysos and satyrs on one
side, and three young men and a boy on the other; two other young
men are named Antimenon and Thrasykleides and the boy is Diogenes
kalos, again one would be inclined to say a present from SO, but it need
not be the same SO.[3]

Miss Edwards compared as far as possible the handwriting of the SO
inscriptions and suggested that thirteen vases go together. They are
hydriai by the Antimenes painter, *ABV* 267/18, Circle of Antimenes
painter, *ABV* 276/4, 5; neck-amphorai, 287/5, 344/10, Michigan
painter; hydria, Madrid painter, *ABV* 329/3; stamnoi, Beaune painter,
344/1, and Michigan painter, 343/2; the Hiketes Panathenaic amphora,

---

[1] Cf. Philippaki 22 f., and fig. 10.

[2] Note that the lid with a common graffito, perhaps a price, according to the *Corpus* (*CV*
Cab. Med. pl. 77) does *not* belong. (This distinction is not clear in Dr Philippaki's
drawing.)

[3] Dipinto and graffito are given in the *Catalogue of Vases*, E 261, but not in the *Corpus*. On
the graffito lambda with an iota under it, see below.

Louvre F 283; three unattributed neck-amphorai in Bonn, inv. 38, of about 520; an unattributed hydria of about the same date in Würzburg, 304, *ABV* 678; a very early red-figure hydria, *ARV²* 12/7. I suspect that at least the other vases by the Michigan and Beaune painters with the same two letters should be included. But whether they are included or not, we seem to have the purchases of an Athenian of rather ordinary taste over a number of years from about 530 onwards, of which seven certainly, and probably more in fact, ultimately reached Etruria. If the association of the stamnoi by the Michigan painter and Beaune painter with the rest is justified, they do raise the question whether this SO was in fact at the Athenian end of the Etrurian trade-route because it is tempting to regard these curious vases on which athletes and revellers wear white loincloths as designed for the Etruscan market.[1] The other SO graffiti and dipinti extend the range backwards to the Affecter and forwards to the Diogenes painter's amphora discussed above. SO is the beginning of so many Greek names that several people may be involved, and the amphora by the Diogenes painter is the only special commission outside the Hiketes amphora.

It is the inscriptions in glazed paint that make it possible to fix SO as a purchaser in Athens. We can next look at the few vases found in Athens with 'trade' inscriptions. A black-figure fragment from the Acropolis has the graffito SMI.[2] This graffito occurs on nearly fifty other vases. Again there is the problem of identification, and names such as Smikros and Smikythos, both known from early red-figure vases, are possible. The attributed vases are not far apart in time: they are Antimenes painter and his circle, *ABV* 269/44, 270/59, 272/90, 274/119, 277/14, 278/30, 37, 282/2, 283/9, 286/5, 288/19; Psiax, *ABV* 293/6; Euphiletos painter, *ABV* 324/38, 39, 327/2; Pasikles painter, *ABV* 328/1; Painter of Würzburg 173, *ABV* 327/1; Manner of Lysippides painter and related to him, *ABV* 261/40, 263/2; painter of Cambridge 51, *ABV* 340/1; Daybreak painter, *ABL* 59; Leagros group, *ABV* 361/18; class of Vatican 433, *ABV* 424/2. Again this is a very normal group of good-quality black-figure, neck-amphorai, amphorai,

---

[1] The Etruscan inscription on *ARV²* 969/66, found in Populonia, is said to have been painted on before firing: perhaps ordered by an Etruscan in Athens? It is by an undetermined Penthesileian so that nothing can be said about findspots of other vases by the same painter.

[2] Graef–Langlotz 127, 1517, no. 414.

hydriai, one stamnos and an oinochoe, shape I, covering at most the last three decades of the sixth century. They come from several different shops, and only one of them is likely to have been a special commission: the Pasikles vase has 'Pasikles *kalos*'. At least 15 of these vases have Italian provenance, mostly Vulci but one Nola, but there is nothing like the white loincloths of the Perizoma group to suggest that any of them were designed for the Western market. If the group is a unity, the very large number of large vases and the complete absence of cups perhaps suggest a dealer rather than a private purchaser; the vases with 'Leagros *kalos*', on the other hand, consist of 15 large vases, 39 cups, 1 lekythos, 1 alabastron, 1 moulded aryballos. Both are, of course, chance selections, but the Leagros group is much more what one would expect the private purchaser to buy for his symposia. SMI therefore probably was a trader and the Acropolis fragment proves that he was based in Athens.

The other 'trade' inscriptions found in Athens come from the Agora. Only two vases and three glazed lamps, which were probably made in the potteries, concern us. A small black-glaze single-handled jug has on the bottom the price 60 for 1 drachma (=6 obols) and a black-glaze skyphos has the price 10 for 13 obols.[1] These are important as giving prices in Athens. The three lamps[2] all have a number inscribed on the bottom, and this is presumably either a stock or an order: the large numbers 180 on no. 219 and 695 on no. 300 are perhaps best explained as stock-in-trade, but no. 93 is inscribed 19 DE and this may rather be an order for the state (*demosion*), lamps for the council house or the like.

These two classes of inscription, prices and numbers, occur frequently on other pots. The Agora evidence shows that such inscriptions were put on in Athens. The evidence from Vassallagi[3] shows that Sicilians who dealt in Attic pots put prices and numbers in Sicilian dialect. It seems therefore reasonable to suppose that Attic inscriptions were put on in Athens, but this cannot be proved because there is always the possibility of an Attic dealer travelling or an Attic dealer resident abroad.

The price inscriptions have been dealt with so fully by Professor

---

[1] M. Lang, *Hesperia* 25 (1956), 16, nos. 68 and 69. The first seems remarkably low and compares with the export prices for *lekythides* inscribed on two vases by the Syracuse painter: 111 and 120 for 10 obols (*ARV*² 520/32 and 35; *Hesperia* 33 (1964), 83).
[2] Howland, *Athenian Agora* IV, *Greek Lamps*.   [3] *Arch. Reports* (1963–4), 42.

Amyx that I can confine myself to certain general topics and problems.[1] First, it seems to me that he has shown conclusively that the prices are given in obols unless drachmai are indicated either by word or symbol. But a glance at his very useful table of recorded prices shows a strange range. I quote those that seem capable of interpretation: (1) amphora, 2 obols, (2) larger lydia, $\frac{1}{2}$ obol, (3) hydria, 12 obols, 18 obols, (4) krater, 4 obols, (5) bathea, $\frac{1}{3}$ obol, (6) oxides, $\frac{1}{7}$ obol, (7) kados, 18 obols, (8) lekythos, 1 obol. The last two are prices given by Aristophanes, and in general prices in comedy were magnified: in any case the 'kados for the farm' is sold in a time of scarcity (*Pax* 1202), and we do not know how big it was. The lekythos comes in the *Frogs* (1236): 'You will get a very noble one for an obol'. The reference here, as is shown by the whole scene ('lost his lekythion'), is to what archaeologists call an aryballos, and an Attic aryballos by Douris[2] is in fact inscribed 'lekythos of Asopodoros'. The 'noble' aryballos might have been either black-glaze or decorated. Allowing for comic exaggeration this does not seem out of line with the Agora price of 10 black-glaze skyphoi for 13 obols. Against these the prices for amphora, krater, bathea and oxides seem low, and the prices for hydriai extremely high. The one direct comparison is perhaps between the bathea and the Agora skyphos, since the natural interpretation of bathea is deep skyphoi as distinct from shallow skyphos or cup-skyphos. The Agora skyphoi cost perhaps $1\frac{1}{2}$ obols each with a discount; the 20 bathea listed on the bottom of two red-figure bell-kraters by the Kadmos painter cost 7 obols, or one-third of an obol each with a discount; the same lists give the bell-kraters at 4 obols.[3]

Assuming that inscriptions giving the prices of hydriai and kraters include the actual hydriai and kraters on which they are written, I find it very difficult to reconcile 4 obols for good bell-kraters decorated by the Kadmos painter and the Pothos painter with 12 obols and 18 obols for hydriai from the group of Polygnotos,[4] particularly when the later vases should be *more* expensive than the earlier. The difference between the prices of the hydriai, as Amyx says, may be explained by their size; the height of one is 0·41 m and of the other 0·47 m. The amphora again

[1] *U.C. publications in Classical Archaeology* 1 (1941), 179; *Hesperia* 27 (1958), 275 ff., 287 ff.
[2] Cf. above, p. 45.
[3] *ARV*² 1185/10, 18; cf. 1190/24, 25, and 1154/37, all quoted by Amyx.
[4] *ARV*² 1060/138, 141.

is much smaller, 0·288 m, and a hundred years earlier when prices were much lower; moreover, as I said above,[1] I believe that Beazley's interpretation of the inscription painted on the reverse is correct; it is a joke, 'two obols, and you do not get me'. The corresponding price of such an amphora at the time of the hydria might well have been 6 obols or more.

The prices of the amphora and the hydriai are high and those of the kraters and the rest are low. The amphora is a special case because the joke price is painted in the picture. The form of graffito under the foot of the hydriai is quite different from the form under the foot of the kraters. The hydriai inscriptions read (*h*)*ydtridrachpoi*, (*h*)*ydidrachpoi*, an abbreviation for 'Three-drachma painted hydria' and 'Two-drachma painted hydria'. The form of the krater inscriptions is 'krateres 6, price, 4 drachmai; bathea 20, price, 1 drachma 1 obol, oxides 10'. I take this to be a note of a transaction put on the bottom of a krater to remind the dealer that the other vases are to be included when the order is packed, and in this order the dealer throws in 10 little vinegar saucers (oxides). The hydria inscription is a price, and I take it to be a price advertised as distinct from a price received.[2] If this is right, the high prices and the low prices represent two different stages in the marketing of pots. The high prices are what the potter asks, the low prices are what the dealer gets. The potter hopes that someone will come in and buy the hydria for a symposion at the high price. If this happens, the buyer may sell the hydria at a lower price to the dealer after the symposion. If it does not happen, the potter may himself sell off the hydria at a lower price to the dealer. (Unfortunately we do not know where either of these two hydriai was found.) The kraters and the other small vases sold with them reached the dealer by either or both of these routes, and he made what he could from his purchaser, and this is the price actually recorded. Again unfortunately, we do not know where they were found, but the orders for several big vases and a larger number of small vases which would pack inside them sound very like an export order.

A number of other vases with price graffiti were found in Etruria and it is worth looking at some of these. A stamnos by the Hephaisteion painter and a stamnos by the Dokimasia painter come from the same late archaic workshop, probably the Kleophrades painter's, and have

[1] Cf. p. 78. Here, pl. 10.
[2] The price was inscribed before fixing (Dr Ann Birchall).

under the foot a monogram, AR in ligature, and similar price inscriptions:[1] Hephaisteion painter, 'larger lydia 10, 5 (obols); lepastides
20, 7 (obols)'; Dokimasia painter, 'myrtotai 20, 7 (obols)'. These evidently belong to the low price-range, although we cannot say for
certain what the shapes are. The inscriptions seem to be written by the
same hand. The AR ligature occurs on four other stamnoi, three by the
Copenhagen painter and of his class, one by the Aegisthus painter and
of the transitional Berlin painter's class.[2] It does not stand for either
painter or potter but may stand for dealer. The Aegisthus painter's
stamnos and the Hephaisteion painter's stamnos were found in Vulci.
The Hephaisteion painter's stamnos has the not particularly common
subject of Medeia and a daughter of Pelias with the ram and a *kalos*
name Nikostratos. It therefore was second hand when the dealer
sold it with 10 lydia and 20 lepastides perhaps direct to the merchant
who took it to Etruria.[3]

Some black-figure hydriai of the Leagros group found in Etruria
introduce new symbols. They all have a ligature of LE and another sign
in addition to the price inscriptions which are: *ABV* 361/12, 'Leky 34,
38 (obols)'; 362/36 'Leky 29, 39 (obols)'; 364/49 'Chytri, 23, 7 (obols)';
364/50, 'Ly 38, 30 (obols)'.[4] It is clear that although these are late sixth-
century vases and the red-figure vases discussed above are fifth-century,
the comparable prices are higher instead of lower. 'Ly' should be
'lydion' and 38 'larger lydia' at the early fifth-century price would cost
17 obols instead of 30. The 'Leky' is more expensive than the 'noble
lekythos' of the *Frogs* more than a century later, but here it could be
argued that these may be decorated lekythoi instead of a plain aryballos; Aristophanes himself uses the word for a funeral lekythos in the
Ecclesiazusae (1111). The same may be the explanation of the lydia; if,
as seems possible, the Lydian vases are what we call alabastra, large un-
decorated alabastra might well be cheaper than normal-sized painted
alabastra, which were not uncommon in the late sixth century. It may
be, however, that Attic vases fetched a comparatively higher price
abroad in the late sixth century than later.

[1] *ARV²* 297/1; 414/34; Amyx, pl. 53 f and g; Philippaki 49 f.

[2] *ARV²* 258/21, 22; 259; Philippaki 63; *ARV²* 505/16, Philippaki 36.

[3] For three other red-figure exported vases with price inscriptions see Beazley, *AJA* 45
(1941), 597–8, and Amyx, loc. cit. The interpretation is unclear.

[4] Add *ABV* 360/11, published *Münzen und Medaillen*, Auktion 40, no. 71. 'Leky 30, 38
obols).'

The extra sign on these vases and a number of other vases of the late sixth century looks like a delta with an iota crossed by two short strokes underneath it. It occurs very frequently on vases which also have the LE graffito, but they sometimes do not have it (e.g. *ABV* 366/84, 85 Leagros group);[1] it also occurs without the LE graffito, e.g. on two hydriai of the Leagros group, *ABV* 361/18, 363/42. Two variant forms are found, one a lambda with an iota under it on the Diogenes painter's amphora bought by 'SO' (*ARV*[2] 248/2, see above, p. 271) and the other a delta with the iota under it uncrossed on two early classical stamnoi, *ARV*[2] 620/30, 593/43, by the Villa Giulia painter and the Altamura painter. Amyx[2] made the attractive suggestion that these signs were prices, 12 obols (crossed) or 11 obols uncrossed. They would then presumably be the price of the vase on which they occurred. The question is whether the prices are plausible and it seems worth listing all our high prices in chronological order with the heights of the pots:

1	540 B.C.	amphora	*ABV* 136/50[3]	Ht 0·288 m 'Much more than 2 obols'
2	515 B.C.	neck-amphora	*ABV* 370/126	Ht 0·416 m 12 obols
3	515 B.C.	hydria	*ABV* 364/49	Ht 0·518 m 12 obols
4	480 B.C.	amphora	*ARV*[2] 248/2	Ht 0·52 m 11 obols
5	460 B.C.	stamnos	*ARV*[2] 593/43	Ht 0·375 m 11 obols
6	460 B.C.	stamnos	*ARV*[2] 620/30	Ht 0·345 m 11 obols
7	440 B.C.	hydria	*ARV*[2] 1060/138	Ht 0·41 m 12 obols
8	440 B.C.	hydria	*ARV*[2] 1060/141	Ht 0·47 m 18 obols

Considering that prices were generally rising during this period I do not think that the rise from the small amphora to the large hydria of 515 B.C., or the price of the two stamnoi, or the price of the large hydria of 440 are unlikely. The surprising prices are the equation of the two large and small vases of 515 and the fall to the equally large Diogenes amphora in 480 and the large discrepancy between the two hydriai of 440. But the discrepancy between the late hydriai is attested by the inscriptions, and therefore perhaps we should accept the equation in 515 and the fall in 480 and accept also the delta–iota signs as prices. But they are high prices, and this corresponds with the high prices for lydia and lekythia on three of these vases.[4] It certainly looks as if the inscriptions

[1] On *ABV* 360/11, the 'delta' serves also as the lambda of 'Leky'.
[2] *UC publications in Classical Archaeology* 1 (1941).
[3] New York 56.171.13. Cf. above, p. 78. Here, pl. 10.
[4] Cf. above, p. 276.

for lydia and lekythia were put on at the same time as the sign interpreted as 12 obols, so that there is a case for interpreting all these prices
as original workshop prices rather than reduced export prices. One possible argument against this is the nature of the order; would anyone
have purchased one hydria and 34 lekythoi or one hydria and 30 lydia
except for export? If this is accepted, then export prices were much
nearer workshop prices in the late sixth century than they were in the
second half of the fifth century. We have to admit that many special
circumstances operated of which we know nothing.

One question remains here. What is the significance of the incised
LE ligature which appears on the majority of the vases with the delta-
iota combination. It occurs on over forty vases with some minor variations. The great majority were found in Etruria, and no other provenance is recorded. All but ten have been attributed: 5 are Pioneer
group, the rest are all Leagros group except for one olpe of the dot-ivy
group (*ABV* 447/21), one neck-amphora by the Lysippides painter
(*ABV* 256/16), which has *Mnesiphila kale*, and one hydria painted by
the A.D. painter and made by the potter of the Heavy Hydriai (*ABV*
334/1) which has named women at a fountain. The five Pioneer group
vases are the very fine Euthymides amphora with Theseus carrying off
Helen (*ARV²* 27/4, Munich 2309), and four hydriai, *ARV²* 23/7,
Munich 2421, Phintias' music lesson for Tlempolemos in the presence
of Euthymides (see above, p. 42), 24/8, Munich 2422, Phintias' komos,
30/1, Hypsis' Amazons, Munich 2423, and 33/8, Louvre G 41, Pioneer
group sundry, Dionysos with Ariadne, Poseidon with Amphitrite,
Hermes and on the shoulder chariot and warriors making ready; this
has greetings to Sostratos and Euthymides (cf. above, p. 43). All of
these, except the Phintias komos and Hypsis' Amazons, are special
commissions. They all also have graffiti on the bottom; the amphora
'12 kylikes', the hydriai '11 chytriai', '18 chytriai', 'leky' (?1 lekythos)
and '1 chytria' respectively; these are simply numbers; no price is
indicated either for them or for the vases on which they occur. Except
for the absence of price these sound like the same kind of orders as on
the vases with price inscriptions, particularly *ABV* 364/49, Leagros
group hydria, inscribed under the foot '12 obols; 23 chytriai, 7 obols'.
I am inclined therefore to take LE as the sign of a dealer who exported,
and to suppose that, as suggested above, export prices were nearer

workshop prices in the late sixth century than in the second half of the fifth.[1]

The number inscriptions are parallel to the '19 DE' on the Agora lamp, and there are other examples: for instance, NY appears with 3, 5, 35, 35 and 4 on one amphora and four stamnoi of the late sixth and fifth centuries, *ABV* 367/86, dipinto, Leagros group, and the rest graffiti, *ARV*² 292/29, 499/14, 628/7, 305/3. The only name that suggests itself for NY is something like *Nymphion*, and as it occurs so commonly on stamnoi it may be the trade-name for a stamnos; this interpretation is slightly supported by the 'N' with delta over iota on the stamnos by the Villa Giulia painter noted above. Similarly *Milesiorge* 13 on a bell-krater from Etruria[2] gives the trade-name for bell-krater, and *Korinthierge* or *Korinthioi* for column-kraters.[3]

A number of other inscriptions may denote painter, potter or workshop. The difficulty here is that they do not occur sufficiently commonly to make the deduction safe. The following are worth consideration.[4]

(1) Lydos, the painter of Louvre F 6 and the painter of Vatican 309, who worked in the same shop, seem sometimes to put a distinct mark on their pots. Lydos paints lambda upsilon on *ABV* 110/30. The painter of Louvre F 6 paints a double lambda on *ABV* 125/39, 51, 67. The painter of Vatican 309 has a variant on *ABV* 121/14.

(2) The graffito 'SA' appears on five stamnoi from the Berlin painter's workshop painted by the Berlin painter, Providence painter and the group of London E 445: *ARV*² 207/137, 140, 141; 217/3; 639/58. This may be a workshop mark rather than a dealer's mark.

(3) The graffito psi appears on two stamnoi by the Siren painter and one by the Syleus painter, which all belong to the class of the Siren painter: *ARV* 289/1, 2; 251/31. This may be a potter's mark.

(4) A stamnos (*ABV* 388/3) with a graffito possibly sigma mu, which might belong to the SMI group discussed above, has a further

---

[1] It has also been explained as a technical term: Miss Edwards suggested *lepsis*, 'receipt', H. R. W. Smith, *lekythos*, which seems to me unlikely.

[2] Mingazzini, *MDAI(R)* 46, 150.

[3] Beazley, *AJA* 45 (1941), 497.

[4] The material is drawn from Miss Edward's thesis, no. 1, and the rest, nos. 2–4, from Dr Philippaki's *Attic Stamnos*.

graffito which is a ligature of kappa lambda. Dr Philippaki[1] notes that the KL graffito occurs on a pelike and a psykter painted by the Kleophrades painter (*ARV*[2] 184/27, 66) and that the stamnos is similar to one of the classes of stamnoi painted by the Kleophrades painter. It is tempting to suggest that KL is the beginning of the name of the potter Kleophrades.

FINDSPOTS

The graffiti and dipinti tell us a little about traders, Attic and foreign, prices and workshops. We can sense something but all too little of the network linking the potter to the ultimate destination of the pot. If we now look at provenances, it is in the hope of learning by this means something of the demand, something of what the potter could expect to be able to sell. For our purpose three main kinds of findspots, sanctuaries, private houses and tombs,[2] can be distinguished, and three main areas in which vases are found, Athens and Attica, other Greek cities (including the western Greek colonies) and thirdly Campania and Etruria. To examine the material in *ABV* and *ARV*[2], let alone the whole material, would be impracticable, but it is possible to take a few samples, and ask first what the Athenian bought for dedication in a sanctuary, for use in a house, or as a grave-offering; for other Greek cities there were two obvious possibilities, visitors to Athens might take pots home and traders might buy in Athens what they knew had a market at home (or where they traded). The demands of the third area, Campania and Etruria, can only have been conveyed to the potter through traders[3] and possibly through a chain of traders (the same obviously holds true for areas further away like Spain and perhaps also for the more distant Greek cities).

(a) Attica

(1) *Sanctuaries*

Many of the dedications are of the highest quality, as a glance through the publications of the Acropolis fragments shows.[4] Many dedications

---

[1] Philippaki 18, n. 2.

[2] Langlotz, *Wiss. Ztschr. Rostock* 16 (1967), 474, has interesting interpretations of vases found in tombs including the pursuit scenes and Dionysiac scenes discussed below. He overemphasizes the funerary use of vases; the fact that 80 per cent were found in graves does not mean that 80 per cent were designed for graves.

[3] For a possible Etruscan trader in Athens, cf. above, p. 272.

[4] Cf. Graef–Langlotz, *Die Acropolis-Vasen*; *Hesperia* 4, 216 ff.; 5, 254 ff.; 7, 172 ff.; 9, 149 ff.

of potters and of others have already been discussed; many have been claimed as special commissions, including the magnificent kalyx-krater of Exekias with 'Onetorides *kalos*' and the fight for the body of Patroklos.[1] We have also noticed at least one case of a special kind of vase made for a special ceremony, the late red-figure oinochoai with a Panathenaic Athena.[2] Many votives are of the highest quality, but there are plenty of ordinary oinochoai, lekythoi and cups too,[3] and in any case a Greek god was expected to like what his worshipper liked and so the vase need not be specially painted or illustrate his own mythology.

One particular site in Attica which has recently been published is the sanctuary of Artemis at Brauron.[4] Here there is one special shape: a small krater on a stand (which is made with it) with the figure scene, generally girls dancing or racing with torches to an altar, painted directly on the clay without underpainting for the white as is normal in black-figure. One can only guess that these are miniature survivals of what was essentially a vessel for heating water, not unlike the louteria, which are supposed to have been used in the worship of the heroized dead.[5] A special shape and a special technique one would expect to be the work of local potters, but then how does one account for the few parallel examples in the sanctuary of Artemis Aristoboule and the Cave of Pan at Eleusis?[6] Were they after all a product of the Kerameikos, but at the same time destined for a limited number of cults?

Besides ordinary worshippers, the sanctuary at Brauron was frequented by the Attic girls, called 'bears', who lived in the precincts until they were married. Wedding-vases like loutrophoroi and nuptial lebetes (here miniature) are expected, and onoi (used for working wool) are a natural dedication. It is surprising to find an onos of about 500 B.C. with a boy's horse-race and a *kalos* name, '[?Peisand] rides': perhaps it was a present from boyfriend or brother that the girl dedicated.[7]

[1] *ABV* 145/19. Here, pl. 7.
[2] Cf. above, p. 132.
[3] e.g. examples from the articles quoted above will be found in *ABV* 442, 444, 461, 468, 582–3, 621–2, 630, 647.
[4] L. Kahil, *AK* Beiheft 1, 6; *AK* 8 (1965), 20; Kontis, *AD* 22A (1967), 221 ff.
[5] Cf. B. B. Shefton, *Hesperia* 31 (1962), 330. Cf. also Van Hoorn, *Choes* (Leyden, 1951), fig. 10.
[6] R. S. Stroud, *Hesperia* 35 (1966), 83.
[7] Perhaps a white-ground cup with Nike and *Epidromos kalos*, *ARV²* 1577, should be similarly explained.

Similarly alabastra and pyxides are expected; but why is a very fine alabastron by the Diosphos painter decorated with two boys between whom Eros is flying? It is certainly a beautiful object, but why this scene on a girl's vase and on a girl's vase dedicated to Artemis? Was the girl possibly asking that two young friends, who were perhaps hunters, should have the blessing of Artemis? A pyxis lid has an unknown mythical scene with two warriors moving towards an altar (*ARV*² 1651, Foundry painter), another pyxis has Perseus and Medousa, but against these we can set several with scenes of women, one with Menelaos and Helen (*ARV*² 631/42) and one with the rending of Aktaion, a myth in which Artemis was directly concerned. The cups also show a similar mixture of scenes: wonderful white-ground cups, one with Artemis and three with women (*ARV*² 827/1; 1701), a red-figure cup with a Scythian archer and another with a naked archer (these may have been dedicated to Artemis by male archers), but also red-figure cups with Persephone and Demeter (*ARV*² 1689), with a maenad running with torch and snake, and with purely male scenes like the symposion (*ARV*² 1649). At least we can say that a number of the vases are relevant to Artemis, and that although a number of them, particularly the white-ground cups, are of extremely high quality and may have been special orders, the stock cup or pyxis with a picture of women was also acceptable to Artemis, and clearly one could also assume that she was prepared to accept any vase without considering the relevance of its picture.

(2) *Houses*

We seldom have much in the way of pottery from the ruins of actual houses but two are worth quoting. The ruins of the early houses to the west of the Areiopagos contained a kalyx-krater by the Eucharides painter with athletes and a bell-krater by the Leningrad painter with a symposion or komos.[1] These were both stock vases. The second house rather suggests that it may have been common practice to have painted mixing-bowls (or other large vases) but all or a majority of the cups and smaller vases of plain black-glaze. This was the Dema house, a large country house on the north slope of Mount Aigaleos occupied roughly from 422 to 413 B.C.[2] It contained a bell-krater with a symposion on

[1] *Hesperia* 18 (1949), 224; *ARV*² 227/17; 567/5.   [2] *BSA* 57 (1962), 88.

one side and a Dionysiac scene on the other, a fragmentary column-krater and a nuptial lebes, which was earlier than the other vases and may therefore have been a wedding present; in addition to these there were black-glaze skyphoi, cups, bowls, jugs, pyxides, salt-cellars and a quantity of cooking pots.

More often our knowledge of houses is derived from the excavation of their wells, and I select four rather different examples. The first[1] is dated about 460 B.C. It contained a very fine white-ground bobbin with Helios on his chariot (this might well have been a special commission) and a red-figure cup decorated on the inside only, with a woman; a number of black-glaze skyphoi had *kalos* names scratched on the bottom, presumably by the drinkers; thirteen black-glaze kylikes had the letters 'DE' incised inside the bowl.[2] Miss Talcott explains this as 'state' and suggests that this was a dining room for state officials. Like the lamps already quoted, the cups are evidence for the state as a patron of potters.

The second well[3] seems to have belonged to a private house, and the pottery is mid-fifth century. The red-figure was four amphorai (including one by the Boreas painter with a man pursuing a woman), four bell-kraters (including one in the manner of the Niobid painter with Menelaos and Helen), a skyphos with men and women by the Akridion painter, two oinochoai, a kantharos, a stemless cup, a lekythos, a squat lekythos, a pattern lekythos and two late black-figure cups. Against this must be set more than 62 black-glaze vases. A number of loom-weights suggests that it was a private house.

The third well[4] had red-figure of about 440–430 including a Polyg-notan kalyx-krater with Dionysos, satyr and maenad, a pyxis by the Drouot painter with women, a squat lekythos by the Well painter with a maenad at altar, a skyphos with an owl on the handle, and a skyphos with a woman carrying a basket on one side and a man on the other; then a great deal of black-glaze and unglazed ware, including six Chiote wine amphorai. The last suggested to Miss Talcott that these might be the throwouts of a rich taverna rather than of a private house.

[1] *Hesperia* 5 (1936), 333; *ARV*² 396/18, 1561, 1611.
[2] Cf. also the skyphos *Hesperia* 18 (1949), 341, no. 138, from a cistern north of the Hephaisteion. See now *Agora* XII, nos. 436, 578, 764.
[3] *Hesperia* 22 (1953), 59; *ARV*² 539/41, 609/12; 980/1.
[4] *Hesperia* 4 (1935), 476; *ARV*² 1057/101; 1223/5; 1220/1; 984/3; 1304/2.

But in any case the proportion of red-figure to black-glaze is much the same as in the houses, and the red-figure is in no way remarkable.

The fourth well[1] has the special red-figure Panathenaic amphora with the officials carrying the prize oil and the stamnoid vase with the Panathenaic torch-race. The pottery includes 22 red-figure vases and a large amount of good black-glaze and coarse ware, possibly too much for a single house. The red-figure vases are the Panathenaic amphora, a bell-krater with Herakles Kallinikos and Athena, another with Apollo and Hermes and a fourth with Triptolemos, the torch-racer stamnos, a small lebes gamikos of 440–430 and two others of the late fifth century (it looks as if they survived from weddings in two generations), three squat lekythoi (one with a crawling child), four cups, all with athletes, one of them certainly and one possibly with Nike, a fine chous with a torch-racer (this seems to be rather later than the stamnoid vase; did the torch-racer carry on or was this a younger member of the family?), a small chous with two babies, a ring vase (probably for ritual), an askos, a skyphos with an athlete. Here we seem to see something of a family both patriotic and athletic. They lived on the southern slopes of the Kolonos Agoraios. The well also contained an unfinished bit of marble-relief and a mould for terracotta. It seems likely therefore that the father was a sculptor.[2]

These Attic houses show something of the ordinary household demand, a great deal of coarse pottery, a large amount of black-glaze, particularly cups, bowls and salt-cellars, and a small amount of red-figure, sometimes evidently treasured for some time but rarely specially commissioned.

(3) *Tombs*

There is no need to document further the use of white lekythoi or funeral loutrophoroi as grave-offerings. I note instead two rather special cases of red-figure offerings and a number of black-figure offerings. A Mycenaean tomb on the Areiopagos[3] was evidently reopened, presumably accidentally, in the early fifth century, and the dead were propitiated by five cheap lekythoi, one red-figure with a Nike by the

---

[1] Cf. above, pp. 51, 131; *Hesperia* 18 (1949), 290; *ARV²* 1221/10; 1190; 1277/14; 1404/2; 1405/11.

[2] The marble-worker's house reported in *Hesperia* 38 (1969), 382, had apparently all black-glaze pottery except for one red-figure nuptial lebes.

[3] *Hesperia* 24 (1955), pl. 77; *ARV²* 729/9.

Beth Pelet painter, three white lekythoi and one pattern lekythos. Similarly a fine volute-krater[1] by the Eucharides painter with a fight and a chariot is explained as a votive-deposit in a Hero's tomb.

The earliest Panathenaic amphora, called the Burgon amphora after its finder, was used as a funeral amphora and buried outside the Acharnian Gates on the road leading to Thebes.[2] The vases found with it (and, according to the excavator, inside it) were a black-figure lekythos with a running youth between two draped youths, a black-glazed olpe, a hand-made unglazed aryballos and three black-glazed skyphoi. The Panathenaic amphora can probably be dated very near to 566 B.C.; the lekythos is unlikely to be earlier than 500. It seems perfectly reasonable that a Panathenaic victor should keep one of his prize amphorai and that it should be used to bury him in. The other vases are humble, three perfume vases and three drinking cups. In the same way the lovely aryballos made specially by Douris for Asopodoros was found in a grave with a considerable number of cheap lekythoi datable ten to fifteen years later.[3]

The interest of the burials within the city walls described by Rodney Young[4] is again that they were graves of humble people dating from the second half of the fifth century. They were adults of both sexes ranging from fifty years old to sixteen, and children. The painted vases are all black-figure lekythoi of the Hermione group, Dolphin group, Fat Runner group, group of Vatican G 52, Phanyllis group and Cock group. The subjects are three with warriors leaving home, five with athletes, one with youth courting boy, one with a siren between panthers and one with a lion between sirens. The last two, which are among the earliest, preserve the tradition of the great black-figure funeral vases with sirens; the rest are decorated with normal male pursuits like the lekythos with the runner in the Burgon tomb. All are cheap vases turned out by the hundred to hold a little perfume as an offering to the dead.[5]

[1] *Hesperia* 27 (1959), 152.
[2] P. E. Corbett, *JHS* 80 (1960), 52 ff.; *ABV* 89/1.
[3] Athens 15375, *ARV*² 447/274; *ABL* 133.
[4] *Hesperia* 20 (1951), 67, pls. 40–8; *ABV* 456–8; 460–1; 464–5; 467–9.
[5] Cf. *ABL* 128–9. A similar series in the late fifth century is given by S. Charitonidis, *AE* (1958), 1 ff.

(*b*) Greek Cities

We have already noted a number of examples where visitors to Athens seem to have taken home Attic vases which for one reason or another particularly appealed to them: a striking example is the two red-figure pictures of the Tyrannicides found in Sicily, one of which was found in the shrine of the Hero-founder of Gela.[1] The very fine amphora[2] by Exekias with Demeter arriving at Eleusis in the presence of Triptolemos and Herakles was found in the shrine of Persephone at Locri Epizephyrii and was an appropriate dedication to her by someone, local or Athenian, who had bought it, and perhaps ordered it, in Athens for that specific purpose. A column-krater with women by the Orchard painter, which was dedicated in the hall of votive gifts at Samothrace, is a much more ordinary vase,[3] but a krater of the late fifth century with Dionysos apparently in the company of actors is a very fine piece indeed and one wonders whether a visiting actor dedicated it.[4] The small lekythos which gives the name to the Phanyllis class (*ABL* 199/1) was dedicated by Phanyllis to Hera in her shrine at Delos, but the picture is Dionysos between eyes: the goddess was expected to accept it for the perfume, not the picture.

Two wells in Corinth give some idea of imported Attic household ware. The black-figure[5] includes a hydria by the painter of Louvre F 6, not the best of Lydos' companions, lekythoi of the group of Vatican G 52 and the Phanyllis group, skyphoi of the CHC group, the sort of vases found in contemporary Attic graves. The red-figure[6] includes an early cup, a pelike by the Villa Giulia painter, a column-krater by the Nausikaa painter, a kalyx-krater by the Phiale painter, bell-kraters near the Phiale painter, from the group of Polygnotos, by the Barclay painter, and by the painter of London E 497. These are more imposing than the black-figure, but none of them is more than second class, and none of them is other than a stock vase.

For examples of Attic vases which found their way into tombs in Greek cities, let us look first at Delos and then at Lipari in the Aeolian islands. Delos was cleansed in 424 and the contents of its graves trans-

[1] Cf. above, p. 77.   [2] *ABV* 147/6, Reggio 4001.
[3] *Hesperia* 22 (1953), pl. 2d; *ARV*² 524/30.
[4] J. R. McCredie, *Hesperia* 37 (1968), 204, pl. 59c.
[5] *Hesperia* 7 (1938), 569; *ABV* 124, 461, 464, 619, 622.
[6] *Hesperia* 6 (1937), 257; *ARV*² 177, 622, 1017, 1025, 1055, 1067, 1682.

ferred to Rheneia.[1] I consider here only the material from Rheneia which is included in *ABV* and *ARV*. (There was also a considerable quantity of black-glaze.) The black-figure vases are not imposing, three hydriai, two amphorai, a lekanis and a plate of the bad early sixth-century Polos painter (*ABV* 44, 45, 47), a hydria and an amphora by followers of Lydos (*ABV* 121, 126) – the hydria has a fight with women watching (perhaps Achilles and Memnon) and the amphora a warrior leaving home – a lekythos by the Amasis painter (*ABV* 154) with a winged horse between youths (a symbol of victory in a horse-race), a black skyphos signed by Priapos (*ABV* 170), a pelike by the Eucharides painter (*ABV* 396) – this has the rare scene of a sale of oil on one side and on the other a man reclining and a man playing the flute: one would suppose that it was originally specially made for a perfume-seller, and then came to Delos by the second-hand market – finally a lekythos of the Haimon group with a chariot.

The figures for the red-figure shapes are interesting: 21 hydriai, 15 pelikai, 13 neck-amphorai, 6 nuptial lebetes, 4 cups, 1 bell-krater, 2 lekythoi, 2 squat lekythoi, 1 alabastron. Pelikai were found with ashes in them,[2] hydriai are known as funerary vases, and we have suspected this before for nuptial lebetes. This may also account for the consider-able number of neck-amphorai. Dugas makes the interesting point that there is less early red-figure than one would expect. He suggests that the Delians went on importing black-figure for some fifty years.

The scenes are mostly stock scenes with no special relevance so that it was the gift of a vase that mattered, not the subject on the vase. Some-times, however, one may suspect relevance. Dionysos, satyrs or maenads carry a hope of immortal happiness (*ARV*[2] 133, cup; 185, pelike; 215, neck-amphora; 526, pelike). A youth leaving home may obviously be relevant (1136, pelike). A number of quiet scenes of the type 'mistress and maids' recall Attic grave-reliefs or white lekythoi: 514, nuptial lebes; 545, 1025, hydria; 1025, pelike; 1049, hydria; 1135, nuptial lebes; 1149–50, hydriai; 1178, squat lekythos. A surprising number of vases are decorated with gods or men pursuing women: 247,

[1] See Rhomaios, *AD* 12 (1929), 181; Dugas, *Délos* (Paris, 1952), 21. See Mykonos in the museum index of *ABV*, *ARV*[2].

[2] Cf. also Charitonidis, *AE* (1958), 116, pl. 26, from the Syntagma graves in Athens; Karuzu, *BCH* (1947–8), 389, fig. 4, from near the Royal Stables in Athens, in the tomb of Hephaistes of Chios (?Thetis bringing Achilles the arms from Hephaistos); my article in *Klearchos* 37 (1968), 65; cf. also Karouzou, *BCH* 95 (1971), 107, Tanagra.

hydria, Achilles and Polyxene; 587, hydria, Poseidon; 648, neck-amphora, youth; 1025, hydria, Hermes; 1137, hydria, Theseus (?); 1138, hydria, youth; 1139, two pelikai, Eos and Kephalos, and youth pursuing woman; 1209, neck-amphora, Theseus (?). The youths may be heroes rather than ordinary mortals, and probably these pursuits by gods and heroes were felt as a symbol of immortality.[1]

Only two vases may be special commissions.[2] A fine nuptial lebes by the Syriskos painter (261/19) has a complicated dance of women to Apollo's music: the women may be Muses or the Delian maidens. The vase might well be a wedding present specially painted in Athens for a Delian bride. The other vase is a small neck-amphora (534/7) in the manner of the Alkimachos painter with a youth setting out on one side and on the other side a youth by a pillar with a painted inscription 'Timokrates *kalos*'. Two other vases,[3] both from Gela, have 'Timokrates *kalos*', one a red-figure lekythos with Nike and the other a white lekythos with a youth leaving home. Possibly all three were commissioned for Timokrates' grave in Athens and then were cleared off his tomb and came to Delos and Sicily by the second-hand market;[4] an alternative, I suppose, is that the vases were ordered but not taken, and then the potter sold them off to a trader.

The Aeolian island, Lipari, has a long series of graves: in three of them we can see attributed Attic red-figure vases in their context.[5] In tomb 233 a lekythos related to the Ikaros painter was found with a black-glaze phiale. The lekythos was decorated with a woman with mirror and distaff.[6] In tomb 135 a very small and late lekythos by the Providence painter with a woman running was found with a stamnos of grey clay which had small vases inside it. These two lekythoi are of the kind one finds in humble Attic graves. The third tomb, 207 bis, had a bell krater of the Polygnotos group with Prometheus and the satyrs, and a skyphos of black-glaze. Probably the bell-krater was used for the ashes. Again one wonders whether the satyrs receiving fire from Prometheus carried any hopeful meaning.

[1] Cf. above, p. 278.

[2] Dugas (*Délos* 21, 4) thinks that the nuptial lebetes are all special cases in the sense that a wedding present was buried with the dead woman. This may well be true.

[3] *ARV*[2] 1610.   [4] Cf. above, p. 46.

[5] L. Bernabo Brea, *Meligunìs-Lipara* (Palermo, 1965), II, 47, 68, 81, pls. 10, 49, 62: *ARV*[2] 642, 1053, 1702.

[6] Graffito: *Phi* 20, perhaps a number and a trader's (?) name. Cf. *ABL* 216/1.

Purchasers and Patrons

At Vassallaggi near Caltanissetta in Sicily[1] the tombs for men usually contained an Attic red-figure krater and either a pelike or an oinochoe, and the tombs for women either a red-figure krater or a pelike. They do sometimes include neck-amphorai but not, apparently, hydriai. As in Delos, satyrs and maenads, including Marsyas, may have been thought relevant; they occur on four kalyx-kraters (ARV^2 1046, 1120, 1162 and one from tomb 10). One bell-krater (ARV^2 1054) has Achilles and Polyxene, which we have noted already at Delos. Otherwise the subjects have no relevance, and at least the bell-krater with Andromeda in Oriental dress tied to a stake was probably a special order for a symposion in Athens after the production of Sophocles' *Andromeda*.[2]

What this small selection of vases found in Greek cities shows is that they provided a market for the whole range of Attic pottery from the best to the worst. Certain shapes and certain kinds of pictures were felt appropriate for tombs, but evidently to include an Attic vase was in itself an honour to the dead. The trader was not a trader in funeral vases but in vases for all purposes, and the potter had contact only with the trader. Presumably it was through a trader that Thrasyboulos of Akragas got the Attic cups, which Pindar thinks of him using in the symposion (fr. 124 Snell), and Thrasyboulos' taste would have been exacting. But in addition to the trader we have to remember the visitor to Athens and the traveller from Athens; they were probably responsible for commissioning or buying from stock some of the best Attic vases found in other Greek cities.

(c) Campania and Etruria

In quality the Attic vases in two tombs in Campania are higher than anything in the tombs at Vassallaggi or indeed Delos. The tomb at Capua which is known as the Brygos tomb[3] contained (1) the signed cup by the Brygos painter with, inside, Chrysippos served with wine by Zeuxo and, outside, Hera and Iris attacked by satyrs; (2) the skyphos signed by Hieron and painted by Makron with the departure of Triptolemos; (3) the sphinx rhyton decorated by the Sotades painter with Kekrops and Nike; (4) a ram's head rhyton in the manner of the

[1] A. D. Trendall, *Arch. Reports* (1963-4), 43; cf. (1957), 30.
[2] Cf. above, p. 47.
[3] J. D. Beazley, *AJA* 49 (1945), 153; ARV^2 370/13 (Cambitoglou, *Brygos painter*, 20); 459/3; 764/8 (Brommer, *Charites Langlotz*, pl. 21/4); 766/12; 498/2; 498/5.

Sotades painter; (5) a stamnos by the Deepdene painter with A. Eos and Kephalos, B. youth with spear, and women; (6) a stamnos by the Deepdene painter with A. Boreas and Oreithyia, B. Eos and Kephalos. The first two can be dated on style about 490–480 and the last four about 460, so that it seems likely that the first two were treasured possessions and the last four offerings put in the tomb at death. In view of the frequency of the pursuit themes at Delos, the two stock stamnoi by the Deepdene painter may have been felt relevant. The sphinx is well known as a guardian of tombs, but the Sotades painter's Kekrops must have been painted for the Attic market but perhaps did not find its purchaser there. The same is probably true of the two superb early vases.

The other tomb, the Blacas tomb[1] at Nola, I mention because again there is a difference of date in the vases it contains. They are (1) an Attic red-figure stemless cup of about 400 by the Meleager painter with Dionysos and Ariadne inside and outside Dionysos with satyr and maenads; (2) an Attic red-figure hydria of 400–375 in a 'petty style, imitating the Meleager painter' with a chariot drawn by Erotes in the presence of satyrs, maenads, seated women and other Erotes – one of the rather common interminglings of the circles of Dionysos and Aphrodite, which start in the late fifth century; (3) Campanian hydria by the Revel painter, 375–350, satyrs and maenads; (4) Campanian skyphos with maenads; (5) Campanian skyphos with satyrs and maenads (nos. 4 and 5 belong to the same group as 3). The last three belong to the time when the tomb was made; possibly, granting a long period for travel, the Attic hydria could have been bought at the same time, but the cup is thirty years earlier. Professor Corbett suggests that 'it is just possible that these vases were selected as funeral furniture because the figures on them were felt to be appropriate to the grave.' This is an attractive suggestion. But the cup at least must have been a treasured possession of the dead man; he may have bought it because the scenes carried this hope of immortality or he may have bought it simply because Dionysos was suitable for a wine-cup, and then his executors gave it the special interpretation when they added the other vases.

Capua and Nola were not far from Greek colonies and had them-

[1] P. E. Corbett, *JHS* 80 (1960), 58; *ARV²* 1414/89, 1417/1; Trendall, *BSR* 20 (1952), nos. 27, 29, 30; *LCS* 211/61; 206/49–50.

selves a considerable Greek population. The biggest market of all would seem to have been Etruria. Before looking at one peripheral but extremely productive Etruscan site, the one question to which one would like to have an answer is how much the Greek potter knew about his market in Etruria. The answer does not in any way affect our view of the second-hand market: this route must have existed to account for the François vase, the Exekias Ajax and Achilles dicing, the Euphronios Herakles and Antaios, the Penthesilea painter's name cup, the Codrus painter's name cup, to choose obvious examples over the whole period of vases painted for Athenian occasions which were found in western Etruria. And that these imports were highly prized is proved by the rare cases of actual copying of Attic vases in Etruria [1] (as well as by the much more common bad imitations). The positive evidence of Attic potters catering for the Etruscan market is first of all the Nikosthenic amphorai, a special shape, which has parallels in Etruscan bucchero: as far as provenances are known, the Attic examples are only found in Etruria. More recently [2] it has been suggested that the dipping-cup known as kyathos, which also originated in Nikosthenes' shop and again has bronze parallels in Etruria, was made for the Etruscan market; this seems very likely but here it must be admitted that the shape did win a certain popularity in Athens in the early fifth century since kyathoi are found dedicated on the Acropolis, more than one has a *kalos* name, and one has an inscribed roll: [3] these, at least, must have been made originally for Attic consumption. Still it seems probable that in the sixth century Nikosthenes was inspired by Etruscan models, probably bronze, to make Nikosthenic amphorai and kyathoi for the Etruscan market.

In the case of shapes a trader must have shown the potter an Etruscan example and encouraged him to copy it but with his own decoration. Mr Boardman [4] has revived the old suggestion that the so-called Tyrrhenian amphorai of early black-figure were made for the Etruscan market; again the finds suggest this. These are ovoid amphorai with usually more than one picture band and a wide range of mythological pictures. Technically they are more than competent but the drawing is

[1] Cf. B. B. Shefton, *Wiss. Ztschr. Rostock* 16 (1967), 529 ff.
[2] M. M. Eisman, *AJA* 74 (1970), 193.   [3] *ARV*² 329, 333, 383.
[4] *The Greeks Overseas*, 212. Note, however, *ABV* 100/67 from Sicily, 122 from Athens, 105/2 from Athens, 106/1 from Rhodes.

not of high quality. I believe they were succeeded by the black-figure mannerists, the Affecter and his colleagues,[1] whose amphorai again are distinctive in shape, brilliant in technique, but extremely dull in subjects and drawing: they run beside the early Amasis painter as an export product. At this point, roughly, Nikosthenes takes on, and towards the end of the sixth century, as I said above, I should like to consider the athletes with loincloths of the Perizoma group as also painted for the Etruscan market. If that is right, the trader who signs 'SO' might be the latest in a line of traders going back to about 570 who encouraged potters to make for export.

In the fifth century the western Etruscan market seems to have been content with stock vases and second-hand vases, and it is at least possible that the direct link was broken, although plenty of Attic vases still reached, for instance, Vulci, Cervetri and Orvieto.

Two fifth-century shapes might perhaps be considered: the obviously metallic beak-mouthed oinochoai VI include a single early example from Athens, six from Etruria, one from Campania and two unknown.[2] Stemmed plates[3] come almost exclusively from Spina; three are recorded from Ruvo in Apulia and two from 'Italy'. Whether these were designed for the Western market or not, they show clearly the shift of emphasis, the three late archaic beaked jugs found in Etruria come from the west, Chiusi, Orvieto, Cervetri, the three classical beaked jugs and all the classical stemmed plates with Etruscan provenance come from Spina. Spina[4] is on the Adriatic and was a mixed settlement of Enetians, Etruscans and Greeks, although later Greek geographers and historians claimed it as a Greek city. Whether the thousands of graves that have been excavated are Greek or non-Greek or both is not clear. The Greek graffiti which have been quoted could certainly have been put on before the vases were exported.[5] The arguments for a specifically Athenian settlement do not seem to me sound: Professor Robertson says that a nuptial lebes in tomb 1166 and white lekythoi in tombs 405 and 136C perhaps imply Attic expatriates. We

[1] The Affecter himself was found in Naukratis 245/58, 96–7, 248/1–2, and Attica 245/58: otherwise purely Etruscan. Elbows Out had a wider circulation.

[2] *ARV²* 276, 363, 385, 424, 1176, 1217, 1263.   [3] *ARV²* 1273, 1281, 1305 ff.

[4] J. Boardman, *Greeks Overseas* (London, 1964), 235; Aurigemma, *Il R. Museo di Spina²* (Ferrara, 1936); *La Necropoli di Spina* (1960), (1965); rev. M. Robertson, *Gnomon* 39 (1967), 819.

[5] I find it hard to believe that there was a Xanthippos (T. 709) in Spina.

have met exported white lekythoi before, and although many nuptial lebetes have been found in Attica, they are also recorded from Delos (five in *ARV²*), Boeotia, the Peloponnese, Ialysos in Rhodes, and South Russia, besides a good many from Greece (unspecified), and ten in *ARV²* have no provenance. The point is not important because these are only three tombs out of more than 3,000 at Spina.

What the potter in Athens knew was what the trader at the end of the chain which linked him with Spina wanted. It looks as if he knew from about 450 that stemmed plates and beaked jugs were in demand. The large vases are of such high quality that many of them were probably special commissions and the trader got them second hand: we have suspected this[1] for the very large cup by the Penthesilea painter with the two young knights, which was found in tomb 18C, and for the volute-krater with the Seven against Thebes on one side, the supplication of the Epigonoi on the other and a satyr-play on the neck, which was found in tomb 579, a woman's tomb. Personal names or *kalos* names are also signs of a vase specially commissioned in Athens; a not particularly interesting cup by the Bonn painter (*ARV²* 351) with Hipparchos as an archer was found in tomb 475, a very good kalyx-krater by the Achilles painter with 'Axiopeithes *kalos*' (*ARV²* 991) was found in tomb 1052. The kalyx-krater which gave the Peleus painter his name was found in tomb 617; it has '*kalos* Alkimachos'. These are sufficient instances to show that Spina got second-hand vases as well as new vases.

Some of the vases, and particularly the large vases, were not originally purchased in Spina as grave vases because they are earlier than other vases in the tomb. (We have seen this before in Athens and in Campania.) They were treasured possessions, and several of them, like the Achilles painter's kalyx-krater, were mended in antiquity, presumably after arrival in Spina. There are many examples of the time-lag between vases in a single burial. The Penthesilea painter's cup (pl. 11), which is the large vase of tomb 18C, was found with a volute-krater by the Boreas painter, ordinary cups by the Aischines painter and the painter of Bologna 417 and a rhyton with a maenad by the Sotades painter which may be contemporary, but a rhyton by the Persephone painter should be later, and an oinochoe with an Amazonomachy akin

[1] Cf. above, pp 79, 88.

to the Eretria painter is surely some twenty years later.[1] In tomb 308[2] the big vase is an early classical column-krater by the painter of Bologna 228 with Artemis in a chariot on one side and satyrs and maenads on the other; cups by the Alkimachos painter with Eos and Kephalos, by the Penthesilea painter with satyr and maenad, and by the Nikon painter are contemporary, but two skyphoi were made in the late fifth century. In tomb 313[3] the large vase is a double-row kalyx-krater by the Niobid painter of about 450 with Gigantomachy, Triptolemos, and Dionysos with satyrs and maenads, but the other vases, an oinochoe by the Shuvalov painter, a cup with Amazonomachy, stemmed plates and an askos with satyrs all belong to the last quarter of the century. Finally two tombs with a minor gap, the large vases of the classical period and some of the small vases from the last quarter of the century: the large vase of tomb 271[4] is a hydria by Polygnotos with an unusual picture of Peleus and Thetis; two small lekythoi, one with palmettes, one black, should be twenty years earlier; the late vases are two oinochoai with Dionysiac scenes, a cup, two stemmed plates and an askos. Tomb 512[5] has two smallish classical bell-kraters instead of a single large vase, oinochoai by the Eretria painter and the Shuvalov painter and two cups, all of which look later, and two of the late stemmed plates. Usually the large vase is the earliest, but in three tombs at least it comes in the middle: I have already noted the two small, early lekythoi of tomb 271; in tomb 503 the lovely Danae cup by the Eucharides painter (ARV^2 231) must be at least ten years earlier than the column-krater by the Pig painter (ARV^2 563), and in tomb 128 two head vases of about 480 (ARV^2 1536) are associated with a volute-krater of 440–430 (ARV^2 1052).

What this time-lag shows is that treasured possessions were included in the tomb as well as recently imported vases. It shows that the vases were imported not as funeral gifts but for use. The selection made for the tomb was made by the executors in Spina; the traders who linked back to Athens had nothing to do with it. The subjects on the vases may have influenced the executors' choice: in the tombs described many vases have Dionysiac scenes, and there are many more in other tombs,

[1] ARV^2 536, 882, 718, 910, 766, 1013, 1213.

[2] *ARV* 511, 533, 889, 1664; 1401, 1403.

[3] ARV^2 602, 1207, 1310; Robertson, op. cit., 821.

[4] ARV^2 1032, 1281, 1309, 1356, 1403; Robertson, op. cit., 822.

[5] ARV^2 1086, 1206, 1249, 1292, 1306; Robertson, loc. cit.

including the very fine volute-krater in tomb 128[1] with Dionysiac votaries and a seated god and goddess, perhaps Sabazios and Kybele; the same tomb contained a strange vase decorated with plastic phalli and a kalyx-krater with an Amazonomachy. Eos and Tithonos, Peleus and Thetis, youth pursuing woman may have carried a hope of immortality as suggested above. In the fourth century this seems also to be true of Amazonomachies, and if this were already so in Spina, it would account for the large number: in Athens the Amazonomachies had their relevance as a piece of Attic history, and the big mid-fifth-century vases like the Achilles painter's krater had, as we have seen, a recent inspiration in the paintings of the Stoa Poikile and Theseion, but in Spina they may have meant something different.

The collection of vases in a single Spina tomb with one treasured large vase, four or five smaller red-figure vases and a good deal of black-glaze is not unlike the collections that we have seen from Athenian houses and Athenian tombs, and in fact of course a tomb does reflect the final state of the china cupboard. The trader in Athens who bought for the Spina market bought much as an Athenian would buy for his own house, except that he knew that stemmed plates would sell well.

PURCHASERS AND PATRONS

The potter produced fine painted pottery, black-glaze ware and probably lamps, and coarse household ware. His patrons were Athenians of all grades of society, foreign visitors, traders and, if he won a competition, the state. What the state wanted, as far as we know, was Panathenaic amphorai, perhaps the special Panathenaic jugs, and, on the evidence of DE graffiti, black-glaze ware. This is supported for the fourth century by the Bakchios inscription from Ephesos where Kittos and Bakchios contract to make black ware for the city and a hydria for the goddess (*JDAI* 35 (1920), 70). From the point of view of demand, most other purchasers were alike, and the only signs of special demands (other than special commissions) that we can see are the Etruscan demand for Nikosthenic amphorai and kyathoi, probably earlier for Tyrrhenian amphorai and the pots of the Mannerists, then again later the stemmed plates and the beaked jugs: it is certainly possible that a

[1] *ARV*² 1052. On the same tomb, see also 1041, 1252, 1536.

single workshop from 570 to 500 produced Tyrrhenian amphorai, Mannerist pots, Nicosthenic amphorai and kyathoi: the stemmed plates also probably came from a single shop. But these are the exceptions. The other potters do not seem to have developed special lines for the export market presumably because they did not need to do so. The trader who exported knew that he could sell Attic vases of all ranges and sizes abroad, and whether he was selling to Greek cities or to Etruscans or Campanians he knew that they liked mythological pictures but were prepared to buy all sorts of pictures. So he took what he could get from the market, new or second hand. Convenience of packing must have had some influence on his choice, and he would take small lekythoi and black-glaze bowls and salt-cellars because they could be packed in column-kraters and bell-kraters; but the number of Attic cups found abroad shows that this was not a very important consideration.

There was a market at home or abroad for the full range of Attic painted pottery, large and small, good or bad. If we look over the product of the Kerameikos from 570 to 400 B.C., surely one of the startling things is the speed with which the product changes, not only in style but also in shape and to some extent in the subject-matter of the pictures and in the conception of the subject-matter. Because of this speedy change any painted pot can be dated within ten years, and the dating, which is based on fixed points, is confirmed again and again by new finds. And the small, roughly made lekythos with a minimum of figures dashed in shows these changes as well as the elaborate krater with a superbly drawn picture.

This speed of change in the potters and painters implies both a speedy change in the appreciation of the purchaser and also someone to set the pace. Tragedy provides a kind of parallel – a rapidly changing poetic drama performed to mass audiences but written by men who moved in the highest circles: Aeschylus' *Persae* was produced by the young Pericles, and Kimon and his board of strategoi awarded Sophocles his first victory. The readiness of a mass audience to accept the *Oresteia* probably means two things, both that the minimum education necessary to understand the story, music and dance of tragedy was practically universal and that the difference between wealth and poverty, and therefore the isolation of rich art, was much less than it is today.

These factors would cause a similar universal appreciation of the changing styles and the treatment of subject in Greek pottery.

But who were the pace-makers? We can argue that Aeschylus, Sophocles and Euripides moved in the same circles as Kimon, Pericles, Protagoras, Polygnotos and Pheidias. But would one find Exekias or Euphronios or the Niobid painter in these circles? At least in an inter-knit society with a common minimum education and a comparatively small range of wealth it is not unthinkable, and it is a possible interpretation of Raubitschek's conclusion from the size and number of potter dedications on the Acropolis that the potters 'played an important part as individuals in the life of the city'.[1]

Let us approach this suggestion gradually. First, the mythological scenes on vases (except in so far as they are tied to Athenian cult or to belief in an after life) seem largely to reflect the poetry sung, recited or discussed by different generations in the symposia of the rich – Stesichoros, the new *Theseid*, tragedy. It is, of course, true that this literature was known through public performances to a much wider section of the Athenian populace. But where we can point to a beginning we find someone in high society. Unfortunately we do not know who Exekias' patron, Onetorides, was, but the case that the new Theseus scenes were inspired by the Alkmaionids and then revived in a new artistic form by Peisianax and Kimon is good, and Euaion, son of Aeschylus, is the name associated with some of the best early tragic vases.

Then the scenes from ordinary life. Chariot-races, cavalry, horse-races, hunting, athletics, symposia, komoi and musical competitions are all aristocratic pursuits, and again where we have names the names belong to high society – Leagros and Glaukon, Phayllos, Xanthippos, Lakedaimonios son of Kimon, Kallias. But again the ordinary man enjoyed seeing cavalry and athletic and musical events, and the difference between the aristocratic symposion and the ordinary man's symposion was a difference of degree and frequency rather than a difference in kind. The ordinary man owned his painted mixing-bowl and drank out of black-glaze cups; but Leagros commissioned a whole set of painted mixing-bowls and cups for a single party.

This difference of degree in the symposion ware used by the rich and

---

[1] Cf. above, p. 8. On their patrons see J. K. Davies, *Athenian Propertied Families* (Oxford, 1971).

not so rich points straight to the aristocrats as the pace-makers for the potters and painters. The whole argument of the earliest chapters of this book, which need not be repeated here, is that a number of the best Athenian vases illustrated unique Athenian occasions (or stock occasions which were made unique by the addition of names) and that a considerable proportion of them were found overseas in places which could have had no interest in these occasions. The easiest explanation of this is that they were special commissions for special symposia and then after being used once were sold on the second-hand market.

The people who gave the special commissions and their friends were the pace-makers, and we know them partly from the names written by the figures and partly by the names with *kalos* attached, whether the *kalos* name means purchaser or recipient or both. Many of these names cannot be identified; the name may occur in this casualty list or in that decree of the assembly, but whether it is the same man we cannot now say. But a number of the identifications are safe: Leagros, who was strategos in 465, and his son Glaukon, who was strategos in 433, the Crotonian athlete Phayllos, Xanthippos the father of Perikles, the Alkmaionids Megakles, Alkmeon and a younger Megakles, the poet Anakreon, Euryptolemos, Kimon's father-in-law, Lakedaimonios son of Kimon, Euaion son of Aeschylus, Aresias one of the thirty, the late fifth-century poet Phrynichos, the Theban flautist Pronomos. There can be no doubt that pictures of them are pictures of high society made for high society.

The patrons were the aristocrats and their commissions set the pace. Sometimes we can see how stock vases derive from specially commissioned vases, and probably there were far more instances than we can now know. Athenian society was sufficiently integrated for this to be practicable. But to say that the patrons were aristocrats is not to say that potters and patrons moved in the same circles. The evidence for that is first the potter dedications which Raubitschek has emphasized.[1] The expensive dedications of Andokides and Nearchos put them for that moment at any rate in the same class as the victorious athlete or the commander of cavalry. Beazley[2] has noted that in their pictures vase-painters look no different from other young men, the athletes or symposiasts named in the preceding paragraph. We know nothing of the potters and vase-painters beyond their names and occasionally the names

[1] Cf. above, p. 5.   [2] *PP* 11, 19 f.

of their fathers; the only name which leads outside the trade is the name of Euthymides' father Pollias, who has been convincingly identified with a good sixth-century sculptor.[1] Euthymides was not therefore low in the social scale. And it is precisely from the Pioneer group to which Euthymides belonged that we find a link to the aristocratic world of Leagros.

The evidence has been quoted already. On a fragmentary kalyx-krater[2] by Euphronios the vase-painter Smikros takes part in a symposion with Theodemos, Melas, Suko and Ekphantides, and 'Leagros *kalos*' is written on the other side above the mixing-bowl from which two boys are fetching wine; it looks as if Leagros ordered the vase for this party. On another kalyx-krater[3] by Euphronios he sits in the audience with Melas and Kephisodoros while Polykles sings. Melas therefore links a party with the vase-painter Smikros, in which Leagros was in some way concerned, to a concert at which Leagros was present. Given this link, we can give full value to the inscriptions on an un-attributed Pioneer hydria:[4] *Sostratos chaire, chaireto Euthymides* – the double greeting surely implies that the two were friends. Sostratos appears on Phintias' psykter[5] with the international athlete Phayllos, and himself probably won a chariot-race at the Panathenaia in the early fifth century. Euthymides, the vase-painter, was welcome at a symposion at which one of the guests was the kind of athlete for whom Pindar sang slightly later. Melesias, the great Athenian trainer of the earliest fifth century, was the father of the Thucydides who led the opposition to Perikles.

The evidence is slight, but suggests that at any rate in the late sixth century the vase-painters who were the leaders in style were on terms of familiarity with the highest society in Athens. I should suppose that the same sort of familiarity existed between Exekias and Onetorides. I do not know whether we can trace it any further back; it is certainly attractive to think that whoever commissioned the François vase was also a friend of Kleitias. How long did it last? Special commissions certainly went on; after the Kleophon painter's bell-krater with the dithyramb[6] we have the Pronomos vase at the end of the century.[7] But

[1] Raubitschek, *Dedications* 522.   [2] *ARV*² 14/3 bis. Now Munich 8935. Cf. above, p. 42.
[3] *ARV*² 14/2, Louvre G 103. Cf. above, p. 49.
[4] *ARV*² 33/8, Louvre G 41. Cf. above, p. 43.
[5] *ARV*² 24/11, Boston 01.8019, here, pl. 5(*a*). Cf. above, p. 55.
[6] *ARV*² 1145/35, Copenhagen 13817.   [7] *ARV*² 1336/1, Naples 3240.

a special commission does not necessarily imply any close connection between patron and painter. I think we may perhaps guess that at any rate in some cases a *kalos* name does imply a personal relationship between patron and potter or painter. It is interesting to see how the numbers of names with *kalos* attached to them decline through the red-figure period: 530–500 B.C., 66; 500–475 B.C., 51; 475–450 B.C., 33; 450–425 B.C., 22; 425–400 B.C., I. I am inclined to think that this may be significant. The Pioneer group are friends with the Leagros circle, and this goes on into the time of the Euphronios cups; it goes on into the Glaukon generation with the Pistoxenos painter and others, and I would suppose that Euaion son of Aeschylus was well known to the Phiale painter and Axiopeithes to the Achilles painter. But after that time, although many good vases were still made and some special commissions were still given, the general quality declined and stock vases increased in proportion to unique vases. It is generally said that the advance in the technique of painting, particularly the invention of perspective and shading, put the vase-painter at a disadvantage in the second half of the fifth century and there is undoubtedly something in this, but the best late fifth-century painters, like the Meidias painter, the Pronomos painter and the painters of group R, found a perfectly satisfactory compromise. We noticed before the decline in pictures of cavalrymen and pictures of chariots from the end of the early classical period. Leagros and his son Glaukon were both cavalrymen, and one of the later chariot pictures has the *kalos* name Megakles. It is conceivable that the next generation, Alkibiades and his circle, did not celebrate their successes with specially commissioned pottery, and that so the link between artist and patron was weakened. The vase-painter and to some extent also the potter may have lost his high standing, and Plato's scorn of the craftsman may have been foreshadowed in the young aristocrats of the late fifth century.

But in the wonderful hundred years from 550 to 450, with precursors from about 570 and successors till about 430, painter and patron knew each other and shared their ideas so that the best of black-figure and red-figure pottery is as true and efficient an expression of Athenian ideals and ideas as a tragedy of Aeschylus or Sophocles, and so has a unique value not only to the art historian but to all who want to know what Athens stood for and how its civilization worked.

Index

Index

Index

Index

Index

Index

Index

Yale Lekythos, painter of the,
23 f., 31 f., 35 f., 168
Yale Oinochoe, painter of the, 145
Zannoni painter, 15, 35
prices, 9, 78, 273 ff.

rough pottery, 8, 283

shapes
export, 291 f., 295
perfume, 98, 99, 101 ff., 108, 110, 173
symposion, 99, 126
wedding, 100, 105 ff.
chous, 101, 164, 166, 167 ff., 201,
209, 211 ff., 284
hydria, 61, 98, 104, 106, 108, 134,
137, 172 f., 176, 201, 224, 227,
231, 243, 268, 287
louterion, 281
loutrophoros, 51, 100, 105 ff., 128,
157, 175 f., 185, 187, 193, 216 f.,
268, 281
nuptial lebes, 100, 105, 107, 124,
128, 175 f., 208, 220 f., 252, 281 f.,
284, 287 f., 292

oinochoe, 100, 101, 132
Panathenaic amphorai, 3, 8, 11, 13,
51, 63, 70, 78 f., 100, 102, 122,
129 f., 145, 153 f., 157 ff., 172, 181,
189, 192, 194 ff., 197 ff., 201 ff.,
204 ff., 207 ff., 213, 249, 271,
284 f.
pelike, 99, 100, 101, 128, 137, 140,
224, 287, 289
size of workshops, 3, 8
special commissions, 42–97, 116, 197,
199, 251 f., 278, 288 f., 288 f., 291,
293, 298, 300

vases
funerary, 46, 99 f., 106 ff., 185 ff.,
193, 217, 223, 230–3, 243, 280,
284 f., 287 ff., 292 ff.
perfume, 98, 99, 101 ff., 108, 151,
157 f., 177, 214, 224, 227
symposion, 99, 115, 120, 134, 140,
157 f., 173, 177 f., 180, 214, 227,
268
wedding, 100, 105 ff., 268, 281

2 SUBJECTS

aphlaston, 75 f., 156
apobatai, 156 f., 173, 182, 185, 190 f.,
195
athletes, 55 f., 58, 77 f., 139, 143,
146 f., 161, 163, 165, 173, 185,
201 ff., 203, 205 ff., 208 ff., 213,
244 f., 282, 285
acontists, 130, 156, 171, 197 ff.,
200 ff., 203 ff., 206 f.
ball-players, 177, 203, 213
boxers, 153, 156, 184, 197 ff., 200 ff.,
203 ff.
discoboloi, 157, 171, 173, 197 ff.,
201 ff., 203 ff., 206
foot-races, 147, 156, 167, 196 ff., 199
jumpers, 58, 130, 145, 157, 163 f.,
171, 197 ff., 201 ff., 212
hoplitodromoi, 147, 153, 157, 173,
198 ff.
palaistra, 57, 197 f., 208

pankration, 199, 204, 206, 213
pentathlon, 63, 213
torch-races, 44, 99, 131 f., 149, 151,
157, 200 f., 284
victories, 78, 152 ff., 202, 210, 213,
287
wrestlers, 154 f., 182, 197, 199 ff.,
203 ff., 206

book-rolls, 58 f., 174, 235, 239, 242,
291

carpenters, 248
chariots, 43, 57, 63 f., 150, 153, 156 f.,
173, 184, 189 ff., 285
wheeling, 153, 183, 195
choral lyric (including dithyramb), 48,
69, 72, 93 ff., 117 f., 122, 130, 132 f.,
150, 165, 168 ff., 174, 252, 267
clinic, 248

307

Index

Index

Index

Marsyas, 69, 72, 94, 252, 289
Memnon, 45, 79, 102, 266, 287
Menelaos, 107, 252, 266
Mousaios, 58
Neoptolemos, 266
Niobids, 88 f., 265
Odysseus, 79, 136, 256
Oidipous, 264 f.
Oreithyia, 107, 255, 258 f., 290
Orestes, 92, 266
Orpheus, 44, 96
Paris, 59, 96, 265
Patroklos, 66, 92, 192, 254 f.
Peleus, 56, 106 f., 251 f., 265, 294 f.
Pentheus, 266 f.
Penthesileia, 87, 254, 266
Perseus, 47, 263, 282
Philoktetes, 262, 266
Priam, 192, 255, 266
Prometheus, 44, 92, 288
Telephos, 265
Tereus, 177
Thamyras, 47, 86, 201
Theano, 237
Theseus, 56, 65, 67, 74, 79, 82 ff., 92, 95, 117, 147, 162, 167, 177, 184, 250 ff., 257 ff., 288
Tithonos, 44, 67, 107, 167, 257, 295
Triptolemos, 161, 257, 261, 284, 286, 289, 294
Troilos, 265
mythological paradigm, 56, 58, 62, 66, 81, 106, 107, 153 f., 181, 184, 189, 192, 195, 222, 232, 243, 251 f., 255, 258, 260, 262, 265, 269, 287 f., 290

olive harvest, 247
olive-oil merchant, 61, 67, 100, 287

perfumes, 101, 103
poet, 133, 169 f., 223
preparing food, 247 f.
potters, 4, 8 f., 128 f., 248

rhapsode, 61, 171

school, 42, 58, 164 ff., 168, 171, 174, 185, 244 f.
shoemaker, 248
statues, 66, 68, 141, 199, 200, 248
stone-carver, 248
symposion scenes, 42 f., 53, 55, 77, 109 ff., 114, 141, 143 ff., 147, 150, 164, 173, 176, 177, 219, 234, 245, 282, 287

tribes and tribal heroes, 44, 48 f., 70, 76, 133, 165

verses, 42, 55, 58 ff., 61
vintage, 101, 247

warriors, 61, 65, 143 ff., 147, 149 f., 154, 163, 173, 181, 183 ff., 190, 195, 222, 285, 287
weddings, 105 ff., 123, 149, 175, 220, 251, 282
wine-merchant, 101
women, 145 f., 148, 166, 168, 171, 216 ff., 226, ff., 241 ff., 286
  dressing, washing, etc., 229 f., 235, 239 ff., 241 f.
  music, 60, 71, 148, 149 f., 171, 217, 220 ff., 229 f., 234, 238, 242
  naked, 98 f., 114, 134, 148, 229, 231, 235, 239, 241 f.
  orchard or vineyard, 62, 216 f., 228, 241, 246
  playing ball, etc., 221, 231, 235, 239, 241
  spinning and working wool, 146, 151, 175, 217, 219 ff., 222, 229 ff., 232 ff., 236 ff., 239, 241
  with torches, 118, 122, 126 f., 136, 144, 146, 149 ff., 222 f., 232 f., 235, 239, 281
writing cases, 58, 75, 142, 174, 244 f.

310

Index

Index